Africa and the Global System of Capital Accumulation

Africa and the Global System of Capital Accumulation offers a groundbreaking analysis of the strategic role Africa plays in the global capitalist economy.

The exploitation of Africa's rich resources, as well as its labor, make it possible for major world powers to sustain their authority over their own middle-class populations while rewarding African collaborators in leadership positions for subjecting their populations into poverty and desperation. Middle-class obsessions such as computers, mobile phones, cars and the petroleum that fuels them, diamonds, chocolate – all of these products require African resources that are typically obtained by child or slave labor that helps to generate billionaires out of foreign investors while impoverishing most Africans. Oritsejafor and Cooper demonstrate that "primitive accumulation," believed by both Adam Smith and Karl Marx to be a process that precedes capitalism, is actually an integral part of capitalism. They also validate the thesis that capitalism incorporates racism as an organizing tool for the exploitation of labor in Africa and on a global scale. Case studies are presented on Nigeria, Côte d'Ivoire, Ghana, Liberia, Congo, Tanzania, Somalia, Angola, Namibia, Sao Tome and Principe, and South Sudan. There are also chapters analyzing the interests of Russia and China in Africa.

This book will be of interest to students and scholars of African politics, development, and economics.

Emmanuel O. Oritsejafor is Chair of the Political Science Program at North Carolina Central University, USA.

Allan D. Cooper is Professor of Political Science at North Carolina Central University, USA.

Routledge Contemporary Africa Series

Gendered Violence and Human Rights in Black World Literature and Film
Edited by Naomi Nkealah & Obioma Nnaemeka

Justice and Human Rights in the African Imagination
We, Too, Are Humans
Chielozona Eze

The Literature and Arts of the Niger Delta
Edited by Tanure Ojaide and Enajite Eseoghene Ojaruega

Identification and Citizenship in Africa
Biometrics, the Documentary State and Bureaucratic Writings of the Self
Edited by Séverine Awenengo Dalberto and Richard Banégas

Africa and the Global System of Capital Accumulation
Edited by Emmanuel O. Oritsejafor and Allan D. Cooper

The East African Community
Intraregional Integration and Relations with the EU
Edited by Jean-Marc Trouille, Helen Trouille and Penine Uwimbabazi

Regionalism, Security and Development in Africa
Edited by Ernest Aniche, Ikenna Alumona and Inocent Moyo

The Fourth Industrial Revolution and the Recolonisation of Africa
The Coloniality of Data
Everisto Benyera

For more information about this series, please visit: www.routledge.com/Routledge-Contemporary-Africa/book-series/RCAFR

Africa and the Global System of Capital Accumulation

Edited by
Emmanuel O. Oritsejafor
and Allan D. Cooper

Routledge
Taylor & Francis Group
LONDON AND NEW YORK

First published 2021
by Routledge
2 Park Square, Milton Park, Abingdon, Oxon OX14 4RN

and by Routledge
52 Vanderbilt Avenue, New York, NY 10017

Routledge is an imprint of the Taylor & Francis Group, an informa business

British Library Cataloguing-in-Publication Data
A catalogue record for this book is available from the British Library

Library of Congress Cataloging-in-Publication Data
Names: Oritsejafor, Emannuel O., editor. | Cooper, Allan D., editor.
Title: Africa and the global system of capital accumulation /
edited by Emmanuel O. Oritsejafor and Allan Cooper.
Description: Abingdon, Oxon ; New York, NY : Routledge, 2021. |
Series: Routledge contemporary africa | Includes bibliographical references and index. |
Summary: "Africa and the Global System of Capital Accumulation
offers a groundbreaking analysis of the strategic role Africa plays in the global
capitalist economy. This book will be of interest to students and scholars of
African Politics, development, and economics"– Provided by publisher.
Identifiers: LCCN 2020052414 (print) | LCCN 2020052415 (ebook) |
ISBN 9780367430900 (hardback) | ISBN 9781003017486 (ebook)
Subjects: LCSH: Saving and investment–Africa. |
Capitalism–Africa. | Africa–Foreign economic relations.
Classification: LCC HC800.Z9 S325 2021 (print) |
LCC HC800.Z9 (ebook) | DDC 332/.042096–dc23
LC record available at https://lccn.loc.gov/2020052414
LC ebook record available at https://lccn.loc.gov/2020052415

ISBN: 978-0-367-43090-0 (hbk)
ISBN: 978-0-367-77419-6 (pbk)
ISBN: 978-1-003-01748-6 (ebk)

Typeset in Bembo
by Newgen Publishing UK

Contents

Africa: A political map

Map 0.1 Political map of Africa.

This book analyzes some key political issues related to Africa. The map illustrated here also reflects political aspects of Africa that adversely affect global perceptions of the continent. The process of converting a round earth onto a flat surface necessitates distortions of the shape and size of all land masses on the planet. The Mercator projection is the distortion of choice commonly used in the Northern Hemisphere which enlarges the size of countries in that hemisphere, making Greenland appear to be the same size as Africa. In reality, Africa is fourteen times larger than Greenland. For populations residing in the Northern Hemisphere, Africa seems a much smaller (and therefore less significant?) place than it really is.

The map provided in this book is a compromise between the Mercator projection and the Peters projection, the latter being a more accurate reflection of land masses on earth since the equator is placed in the middle of the globe as it should be. The Peters projection was developed in 1973 by Arno Peters who based his cartographic work on the research of Scottish clergyman James Gall (1808–1895). In 2010, Kai Krause developed a computer manipulation of the Gall-Peters projection that more clearly reveals that Africa is larger than the USA, Europe, India, China and Japan combined. Readers of this book should keep this in mind when they consider that the wealth reflected in these global powers is produced by primitive accumulation activities employed in Africa, a landmass equal in size to all the major economic powers in the Northern Hemisphere.

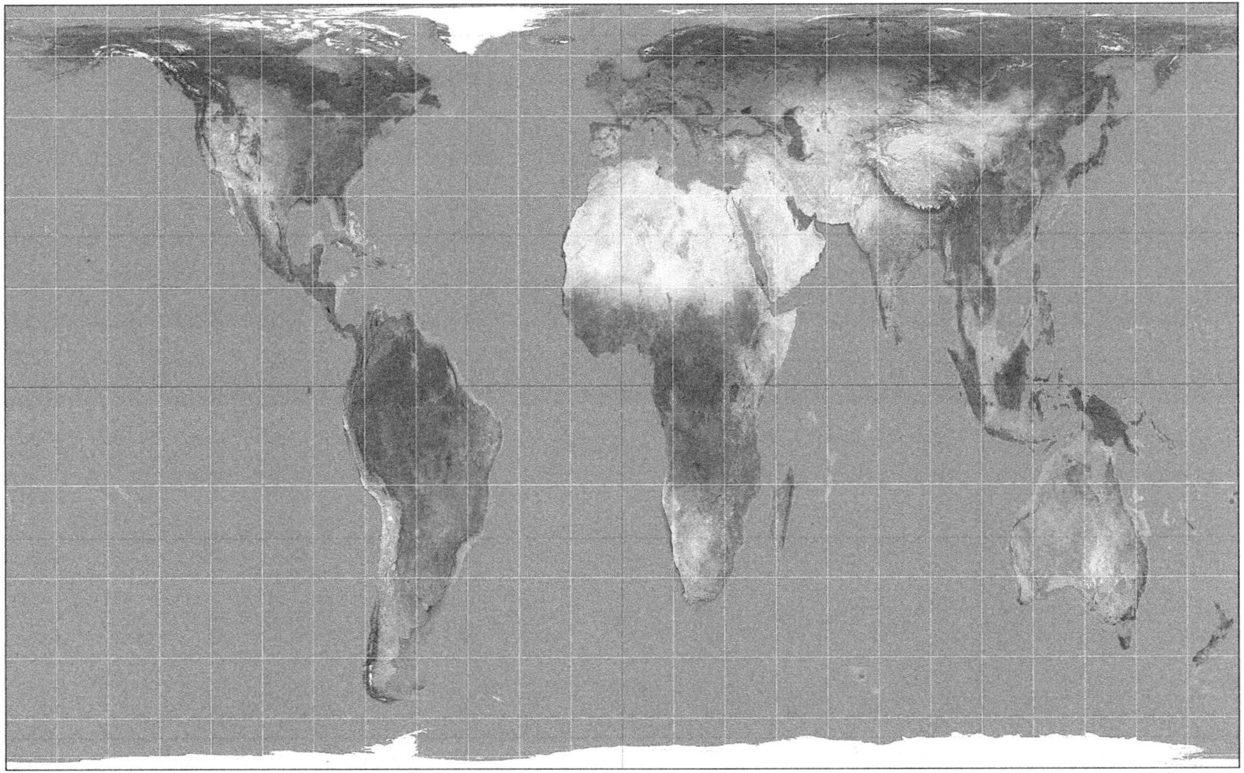

Map 0.2 Gall-Peters projection of the world.
Source: Daniel R. Strebe, available on Wikimedia Commons, the free media repository.

Figures

Tables

Contributors

Brian Adeba is completing his doctorate at the Royal Military College of Canada. He has published extensively on the conflict in South Sudan, and is Deputy Director of Policy at the Enough Project, where he is responsible for governance issues in East Africa.

Allan D. Cooper is a professor of political science at North Carolina Central University. He is the author of six previous books related to Africa and the international law of human rights.

Andrew Ikeh Emmanuel Ewoh is a professor of political science at Texas Southern University. He has published dozens of articles related to public policy and the political economy of African states. He currently serves as the editor of the *African Social Science Review.*

Mohamed Haji Ingiriis is a Ph.D. candidate in Modern African History at Oxford University. He serves as Associate Editor for the *Journal of Somali Studies*. This chapter was assisted by a grant from the Conflict Research Programme managed by the Department of International Development, London School of Economics and Political Science, in cooperation with funds provided by the UK Department for International Development.

George Klay Kieh Jr. serves as the Dean of the School of Public Affairs at Texas Southern University. He is the author of several books on Liberia and West African politics. In 2005 he was a candidate for President of Liberia.

Musifiky Mwanasali holds a Ph.D. degree in Political Science from Northwestern University. His professional experience spans over three decades in academic teaching and research in Africa and the United States, and in the policy world working for the Organization of African Unity, the African Union and the United Nations. He has collaborated with reputed think tanks in Africa and the United States. He has published extensively on issues ranging from political economy to human rights and peace and security.

Victor Ojakorotu graduated from the Obafemi Awolowo University, Ile-Ife, Nigeria, with undergraduate and graduate degrees in International Relations.

He received his Ph.D. from the University of Witswatersrand, Johannesburg, South Africa. Dr. Ojakorotu is currently with the Department of Politics and International Relations, North-West University, Mafikeng, South Africa.

T. Y. Okosun is associate professor of justice studies and African and African American studies at Northeastern Illinois University.

Emmanuel O. Oritsejafor is a professor of political science at North Carolina Central University. He has published extensively on questions related to economic development and food security in Africa. He is currently the Managing Editor of the *African Social Science Review*, an editorial board member of the *African Journal of Technical Education & Management*, an Advisory Board member of the *Journal of Pan African Studies*, the Executive Secretary of the *African Studies Research Forum*, and co-editor of *The Liberian Studies Journal*.

Ian Taylor is Professor in International Relations and African Political Economy at the University of St Andrews, and also Chair Professor in the School of International Studies at Renmin University of China. He is also Professor Extraordinary in Political Science at the University of Stellenbosch, South Africa, and a Visiting Professor at the Institute for Peace and Security Studies, University of Addis Ababa, Ethiopia.

Kitojo Kagome Wetengere is a Professor of Economics at the University of Arusha, Tanzania. He also serves as the Deputy Vice-Chancellor - Academic at the University of Arusha. Wetengere has over 40 scholarly contributions. He also participated as a Scientific Advisor in Tanzania's team in a worldwide research project titled "Determining the Dimensions of Poverty and How to Measure Them."

Radoslav A. Yordanov is a Center Associate at the Davis Center for Russian and Eurasian Studies at Harvard University.

Tim Zajontz is a Postdoctoral Research Fellow in the Centre of African Studies at the University of Edinburgh, where he works in the African Governance and Space (AFRIGOS) project that examines transport corridors, border towns and port cities in four African regions and is funded by the European Research Council. Tim is also a Research Fellow in the Centre for International and Comparative Politics at Stellenbosch University, South Africa. His current research is concerned with the political economy of Chinese infrastructure projects in Africa, with specific focus on Tanzania and Zambia.

Preface

Outside observers of Africa were once comfortable calling it the Dark Continent. This perspective reflects the racist lens that blinded these observers from understanding the inhabitants as anything more than people of color who have been targeted for exploitation in primitive accumulation activities. To the extent that the darkness over Africa denotes a certain mystery about the humans that populate the vast continent, it is argued in this book that it is the outsider that typically has been left in the dark about the savage exploitation of Africans and their rich and abundant resources envied by global powers.

There is a well-known African saying that when the elephants fight it is the grass that suffers. This book attempts to explain Africa within the context of understanding the global forces that have competed to gain control over African labor and resources to shape the capitalist world economy. Most textbooks on African politics offer a sample of major countries, treating each as distinct units with their own unique history and individual personalities. This book starts from the point of view that Africa is the product of extensive relations with its neighbors both on the continent and, especially in recent centuries, beyond the continent. The analytical paradigm used by outsiders to describe Africa has cast a darkness over the ability to fully understand the integral role Africa has played in the making of global powers as well as the enrichment of major corporations and their billionaire owners. This darkness has contributed to an ignorance among outsiders about the genocidal practices that continue to be applied by major powers to African people.

The stories told in this book shine light on the relations African states possess with the world around them. Rather than focus on the cold quantitative statistics of GDPs and debt ratios of individual African states, each chapter offers a qualitative analysis of the systemic ways global capitalism functions to produce poverty and corruption throughout Africa. The book aims to explain how the privileges of the wealthy throughout the world depend upon the impoverishment of the poor who are disproportionately black among the human population. While most chapters highlight the interests of individual states on the continent, they also emphasize the commodities and products that are the foundation of economic exploitation that sustain global capitalism.

The editors have been blessed with the array of scholars that have contributed to this study. We invited researchers who have demonstrated in their previous scholarship a commitment to explore the global economic and political linkages that connect Africa to the larger world capitalist system. Each offers a valuable vantage point for analyzing the strategic role Africa plays in generating global wealth and, more directly, in establishing the power relations that dominate world politics. The contributors include scholars that are affiliated with some of the leading research universities in the world such as Oxford, Harvard, and Edinburgh, in addition to a number of researchers from some of the most reputable Historically Black Colleges and Universities in the United States, as well as experts from African academic institutions. Some of the contributors are up-and-coming scholars who are in the process of completing their doctoral studies, while others have been engaged in African studies for several decades. Some of the researchers hail from the African continent, while others are Africanists from Europe, Russia, and the USA. This manuscript is a dream come true for the editors, both of whom received their Ph.D.s from Atlanta University and who have become brothers from different mothers over the last few decades.

The chapters that follow are organized in a manner that reveals the different global structures of power that have shaped African history. Following the first chapter that provides a theoretical analysis of development and capitalism, the next four chapters explore African states and markets that have been wedded to Western commercial interests for centuries up to the present day. T.Y. Okosun, situates Cote d'Ivoire and Ghana in the historical context of being near ground zero in the primitive accumulation of European colonial powers. He shows how the colonial maldevelopment of West African societies fit into global schemes that arose elsewhere in places like Haiti where African labor was put to work to provide products of luxury for the rising middle classes of Europe. George Klay Kieh Jr. moves this history over to Liberia, where Western commercial interests were able to use national leaders to forcibly displace indigenous Liberians to make way for the development of rubber plantations and iron ore mines, both of which exploited the displaced populations to serve as underpaid laborers to extract significant profits for foreign interests as well as Liberian leaders. Musifiky Mwanasali extends this argument to the Congo, a major resource-rich territory that attracted fierce competition from Western economic interests beginning in the mid-19th century. While most of the world's population is slowly beginning to recognize that the competition for Congo resources continues today in the deadliest conflict since World War Two, especially for coltan ore that makes possible computers and mobile phones, Mwanasali analyzes the political history of Congo to show how the people of that country have been sidelined by leaders collaborating with foreign actors, thus turning these leaders into billionaires while the Congolese suffer from poverty. Andrew Ikeh Emmanuel Ewoh follows with a case study from one of Africa's smallest countries, showing how Sao Tome and Principe has played a significant role in primitive accumulation within the global capitalist economy for several centuries up to the present.

Beginning with the chapter from Radoslav A. Yordanov, the next three chapters analyze areas of Africa that have been the subject of Russian interests, showing how African states have played the competition between Russia and the USA to their advantage (or detriment). Yordanov examines how the fall of the Soviet Union led to a retreat of Russian interests in Africa, and how President Putin has recently begun to appreciate the strategic military and economic value that Africa offers to Russia's global objectives. Allan D. Cooper provides a case study of Namibia, where Russian economic interests have challenged American dominance over an important commodity that generates billions of dollars to the world economy – diamonds. Cooper explains how this competition for diamonds has contributed to the creation of a ruling class in Namibia, and how neighboring countries have been affected by the competition between DeBeers and its major rival tied to President Putin in Russia. This section of the book then explores the effects of a similar Cold War competition for control over the Horn of Africa; Mohamed Haji Ingiriis offers an analysis of Somalia that explains how a strategically located state, especially in the context of the Cold War between the USSR and the United States, came to be regarded as a "failed state" even when some of its citizens (as well as neighbors) found a way to prosper from Somalia's instability. Ingiriis analyzes how even "failed states" can make millionaires out of some capitalists.

The following three chapters review how China is advancing into strategic markets in Africa. Brian Adeba looks at the critical role China played in the disintegration of Sudan and the emergence of South Sudan. Victor Ojakorotu follows with an examination of how China stepped into the vacuum of Cold War relations governing Angola and helped to establish that country as one of the most successful economies in Africa. Tim Zajontz and Ian Taylor demonstrate how Chinese trade with Africa serves to more intimately connect Africa into the global system of accumulation, especially by focusing on the development of infrastructure projects that facilitate the export of Africa's resources to the major countries dominating the global economy. While Africans may see Chinese involvement in the continent as an alternative to Western commercial ambitions, Zajontz and Taylor demonstrate how China's interaction with Africa actually serves the interests of global capitalism by maintaining primitive accumulation.

Finally, the next two chapters reveal how African states are attempting to position themselves to advance economic agendas that are of their own making; the success and failure of these ventures are analyzed to help us understand whether such efforts make African states more independent of global forces that exploit Africa, or whether such strategies increase African dependence upon the systemic capitalist structures of power that continue to dominant world politics. Emmanuel O. Oritsejafor takes an in-depth look at the billionaires that have emerged in Nigeria, and especially the rise of Aliko Dangote who exercises unprecedented influence in Nigerian politics. He questions whether

Dangote, Africa's richest citizen, is an independent investor offering Africa an alternative method for creating economic development, or whether he is an appendage of the global elite seeking to strengthen the global capitalist linkages that have forced Africa into poverty. If creating African billionaires to compete with foreign commercial elites is not the answer, perhaps the solution to impoverishment in Africa is a use of the state to organize economic production in a manner that results in a more just distribution of food and the decrease in income inequalities among African citizens. Kitojo Kagome Wetengere analyzes the remarkable transformation of Tanzania as a country once considered one of the poorest on the planet, to an economic superstar capable of feeding a large area of Africa. Are there lessons in this case study that the rest of Africa can learn from?

The concluding chapter by the editors provides an overview of the challenges facing Africa as it struggles to improve the life circumstances of its people, and to remind readers that Africa must be an integral part of any movement that proclaims that black lives matter.

1 The role of primitive accumulation and racism in capitalist systems

Allan D. Cooper and Emmanuel O. Oritsejafor

Throughout recorded history, humanity has been organized into patriarchal elites that have access to surplus and privilege, and then the vast majority of people that offer their labor and services in exchange for the substances that extend life. For most of history, workers have been compelled to provide their labor through practices that both Adam Smith and Karl Marx characterized as previous, or primitive, accumulation. In recent centuries, "free labor" has been promoted by economic elites, allowing people to sell their labor to the most accommodating bidder. The invitation to engage in "free" labor has not been universally distributed and, as a result, a disproportionate percentage of black laborers remains trapped in relations characterized as primitive accumulation that typically generates the highest surplus value (profit) within the global economy due to its extreme level of exploitation. Clearly, the transition to free labor has yet to eliminate poverty in even the most prosperous of countries, simply because most humans continue to be compelled into forms of production that are "unfree" or compensated at rates that fail to meet a livable wage.

Africa has been a major focus of academic discussions of poverty and underdevelopment. Most professional audiences embrace a paradigm that there is something endemic to Africa that accounts for the vastness of poverty to be found there. Likewise, countries with significant populations deriving from Africa have often rationalized the maldistribution of wealth in their societies by blaming the "poverty of culture" possessed by their African communities. The recent rise of African and African-American billionaires constitutes an anomaly that is often explained by attributing such successes to the Western and modern values possessed by these fortunate few that have recently acquired enormous wealth. What remains unexplained is why most individuals, regardless of color, continue to live paycheck-to-paycheck and in various states of psychological depression and anxiety over their circumstances of powerlessness, fostering a mental illness industry that grows more fertile year after year.

The emergence of the nation-state in the 18th century spawned various paradigms that needed to rationalize why some people experience privilege while most do not. Adam Smith conceptualized a system of capitalism that incorporated private property as an engine for the production of surplus value.

He devoted little attention to the question of how property owners derived their surplus capital in the first place. Karl Marx and Friedrich Engels would later critique the accumulation of capital that derives from capitalist economies for their inherent exploitation and alienation of labor required to produce surplus value. Marx and Engels attributed the accumulation of surplus capital in the pre-capitalist era as resulting primarily from violence and expropriation, but otherwise ignored this phase of capital accumulation as something separate and distinct from capitalism.

Following the ascendancy of the United States as a world power in the mid-20th century, the debates engendered by Smith, Marx and Engels became manifested in the ideologies of modernization and development. It was assumed that capital accumulates in those societies that are most productive, while poverty remains stagnant in communities that are less productive. Nils Gilman (2007) offers an exhaustive analysis of how modernization theory partnered with American foreign policy during the early years of the Cold War to persuade African states to embrace capitalism in the aftermath of colonialism. Modernization was reified as an acceptable construct once people accepted what Stanziani (2014) calls "the invention of backwardness" (23).

The vocabulary and values of modernization continue to dominate the contemporary literature of "development studies" to this day. Moss (2011), like most academics who study development, measures economic status in terms of gross national product (GNP). Utilizing such standards, he can accurately claim with regard to African nations that "South Africa may be a regional giant, but its economy is about the same as the state of Indiana. The other forty-seven economies' total are about the same size as metropolitan Chicago" (Moss 2011, 14). The problem with this perspective is that it ignores how Africa's wealth is stripped from the continent before calculations of a GNP are ever assembled in the first place. Furthermore, minerals and agricultural crops are extracted from Africa at rates far below market value, and then assembled in places like Indiana and Chicago for final distribution into capitalist markets. In short, because the values of African resources are not gained until they reach their final destination, the GDP of Indiana ends up reflecting the surplus value of African resources rather the balance sheets of an African state's gross domestic product (GDP).

The scholarly literature on African development also tends to focus on Africa's poverty, and to assign blame for this on any number of factors: weak states (meaning the government has little control over the country outside of the capital), ethnic rivalries and the continuing influence of traditional authorities, bad governance or institutions, excessive regulation by the central state, lack of democratic institutions and values, budget deficits, etc. The problem is that the countries with the highest GNPs such as the United States possess many, if not all, of these characteristics as well, but no one regards the USA as a poor developing state. What contemporary scholars tend to overlook is that, in the early days of capitalism, blame for poverty in Europe was also directed at the source of labor as well. Adam Smith avoided any analysis of how

Britain subjected the Irish and Scots to slave-like conditions, and he attributed their poverty to their stubbornness to hold on to their traditional ways (see Perelman 2000, 262). Jonathan Swift saw the situation for what it was: "Poor Ireland maketh many rich" (quoted in Perelman 2000, 307). Classical political economists characterized Irish civilization as barbaric in recognition of the wretched poverty. Perhaps if Swift observed the world today, he would accept that Africa is the new Ireland.

Scholars that study African development note that billions of dollars of aid flow from rich countries to Africa each year, and yet Africans remain in extreme poverty. Generally ignored in such analyses is how such aid is provided with conditions that it go towards supporting economic activities that are export oriented to facilitate access to Africa's wealth for global consumer markets, or is actually designed as a kick-back to national elites for collaborating with major global interests and helping to make millionaires out of these foreign entrepreneurs. Another factor in accounting for African poverty is the manipulation of international trade rules by major economic powers to destroy subsistence farming and community economic initiatives in Africa and elsewhere. For instance, local coffee growers in Africa face restrictions on setting the value of their production since global coffee prices are influenced by the terms of the Coffee, Sugar and Cocoa Exchange in New York City, which has been establishing coffee prices since the 1880s. Since 1995, the World Trade Organization has been supporting these global standards with devastating consequences to coffee growers in Ethiopia, Kenya, Burundi, Tanzania, Uganda and other states.

While modernization theory developed in earnest after World War Two, so did dependency theory. The first serious application of dependency theory relevant to Africa came in 1972 with the publication of *How Europe Underdeveloped Africa* by Walter Rodney (1974). Rodney drew a direct correlation between the enrichment of European economies and the growing poverty of Africa. Immanuel Wallerstein (1974, 2004) expanded this theory to argue that there is a "world-system" in which periphery nations such as those in Africa contribute to the power of core nations. Each nation plays a specific role in the maintenance of the global economy by providing cheap labor, resources, etc. or by providing finance capital, insurance, consumer markets, etc. Tom Brass (2013) aptly notes that Wallerstein was correct to acknowledge that the world economy requires both free and unfree labor, but he overlooked the reality that the combination of free and unfree labor can operate not only in the periphery but also within the capitalist core itself (145). This anomaly might also explain why dependency theorists struggled to explain the radical transformation of the economy of India in the early 21st century, or why it was that socialist economies failed to achieve economic growth. Andre Gunder Frank (1977) took Rodney's thesis and applied it to Latin America, and he too posited that primitive accumulation was a "companion" to capital accumulation within global capitalism (89). Capital accumulation depends on primitive accumulation, argued Frank (1977, 101).

Primitive accumulation

Adam Smith conceptualized that "the accumulation of stock must, in the nature of things, be previous to the division of labour" (Smith 1976, 277). As Michael Perelman has pointed out, Marx translated Smith's word "previous" as "ursprunglich" which became translated into English as "primitive" (Perelman 2000, 25). Perelman supports Marx's position that Smith's assertion about primitive accumulation is ahistorical, and criticizes the notion that the division of labor has always been present in human societies. Perelman claims that the division of labor is independent of the accumulation of capital (Perelman 2000, 25). Both Smith and Marx fail to adequately address primitive accumulation; for Smith, it diverted attention away from his central argument that capitalism enhanced the human rights of wage workers and was therefore a major advancement in the development of humanity. For Marx, primitive accumulation diminished the exploitative and violent capacity of capitalism by taking such economic relations as just one of the historical processes that oppress the masses that have included slavery and other forms of forced labor. Marx preferred to see primitive accumulation as something that happened in the transition from feudalism to capitalism, and he reserved most of his critique for the exploitative qualities of capitalism itself.

When Soviet economists analyzed African development during the Cold War, they also acknowledged that African economies had failed to develop due to insufficiencies in primitive accumulation. Polshikov (1981, 105) argued that

> An increase in the volume of capital investment is an important factor in accelerating economic growth rates; its stability and dynamics, however, depend not only on the magnitude of the financial resources mobilised but also on the conditions for realizing them productively, because money capital is only the starting point in the process of accumulation and is followed by the stage of its conversion into productive capital. The conditions of transforming surplus value into productive capital are thus decisive for accumulation; it is through this conversion that the self-expansion of capital takes place and the structure of capital investment itself is altered.

Soviet analysts were just as quick to blame Africa's poverty on considerations intrinsic to Africa as were Western scholars. Explains Polshikov (1981),

> Because of their great economic backwardness, the complexity of the demographic situation, the predominance of extensive growth factors over intensive ones, the present-day economic development of new African countries is extremely unstable, and scientific and technical advances are employed on a limited scale and in specific forms.
>
> (200)

At the end of the day, Polshikov argues, "The difficulties being experienced by African countries in increasing accumulation and using it effectively are largely due to the low social productivity of labour" (206). Marxist scholars have been left with two rationales for why socialism has failed to take hold in Africa: either the conditions necessary for a socialist transition have yet to be realized, or for a variety of reasons it is no longer possible to transcend capitalism as a system of production (Brass 2013, 138).

The methods used historically to overcome poverty and to generate development begin with "primitive accumulation." In his limited explanation of primitive accumulation, Marx describes it as a pre-capitalist phase of capital accumulation in which laborers are compelled to produce wealth with little or no compensation:

> The discovery of gold and silver in America, the extirpation, enslavement and entombment in mines of the indigenous population of that continent, the beginnings of the conquest and plunder of India, and the conversion of Africa into a preserve for the commercial hunting of blackskins, are all things which characterize the dawn of the era of capitalist production. These idyllic proceedings are the chief moments of primitive accumulation.
> (Marx 1977, 915)

For our purposes, there are several concepts contained in this description that shape our contemporary understanding of primitive accumulation and the place Africa serves in the 21st-century global economy: extirpation, enslavement, conquest and plunder. Primitive accumulation, based on Marx's own words, results from removing people and their resources from a territory, subjecting free humans to a state of unfree labor, the theft of land and the destruction of self-determining communities. Today, we know of these processes by such names as piracy, slavery, organized crime, bureaucratic corruption, kleptocracy, eminent domain and nationalization/privatization. Tom Brass (2013) offers other examples of primitive accumulation: debt bondage, peonage, sweatshops, convict labor, contract migrant labor and the gangmaster system (2). Each represents activities that fall outside the normal functioning of a capitalist system, for example, where the state engages in violence and domination to secure possession of resources, and where employers and employees fail to respect certain rules of engagement such as the negotiation of wages and labor practices. A mature capitalist system allows the state to enforce rules and procedures that advance the production of surplus capital in ways that reinforce the privileges and influence of the bourgeois class that dominates the respective state. Primitive accumulation tends to operate outside this legal framework. As David Roediger (2017) notes, when we speak of primitive accumulation we are addressing "relations of terror" (27).

Perelman (2000) provides ample evidence that "primitive accumulation" is not a phase of capital accumulation that precedes capitalism but, rather, is an integral feature of capitalism itself. This perspective is shared by Luxemburg (1951); Miles (1987); Patnaik and Moyo (2011); Bales (2012); Beckert and

Rockman (2018); Stanziani (2014); Sanyal (2013); Mies (1999); Ayelazuno (2011); Harvey (2003); Amin (1974); Shirji (2009); and Brass (2013). David Ricardo (2004) and Sir James Steuart (2019) gave much scholarly attention to primitive accumulation in the late 18th century and early 19th century. Since Smith and Marx relegated primitive accumulation to a residual category in their respective theories, we do not have a common language in which to conceptualize the components of primitive accumulation. What we do have is increasing evidence of the role such activities play in creating the surplus value needed to finance industrialization and to subsidize the cost of developing a "middle class" to ensure a level of political stability that would sustain capitalist practices into the future. Surplus profit lies at the heart of capitalism, and it thrives on activities that embrace primitive accumulation. Thus, "development" is not only a development of wealth but a development of poverty. Leon Trotsky insisted that accumulation occurred in advanced and in backward societies simultaneously, as part of the same systemic unity (see Brass 2013, 99).

Antonio Giustozzi (2001) counters that primitive accumulation may be a prerequisite to state formation, but not necessarily capitalism. He cites the work of the Arab writer Ibn Khaldun who provides examples where, once the power of a ruler is consolidated, others are excluded from possessing property and the leader subsequently appropriates whatever possessions subjects may have for his own use (see Giustozzi 2011: 24). Giustozzi explains how "Bedouins" conquered various communities and forced them to adopt more hierarchical structures that eventually led to state formations (25). This assertion is shortsighted, however. As the chapter on Somalia in this book demonstrates, primitive accumulation in the form of piracy and other extraconstitutional activities are still utilized to generate local and regional elites independent of efforts to reify state formation. In either case, the development of capitalist economic structures, and its creation of profit or surplus value, seems to be a product of violent processes.

Regardless of one's ideological orientation, the main question remains: how can African states accumulate the capital necessary to invest in development in the first place? African scholars have struggled to identify the role of the state in creating wealth. Many analysts agree with Mahmood Mamdani (2018) that "the nature of political power becomes intelligible when put in the context of concrete accumulation processes and the struggles shaped by these. From this point of view, the starting point of analysis had to be the labor question" (23). The implicit question was whether it is possible to separate the labor question from the state question: that is, can the State service democratic objectives or only capitalist ones? Ellen Meiksins Wood (2017) has argued that "capitalism developed in tandem with the process of state formation" (169). She claims that "the economic powers of the feudal lord could never extend beyond the reach of his personal ties or alliances and extra-economic powers, his military force, political rule, or judicial authority" (177). The state offered capitalism a political environment within which to regulate and coerce contracts, and to sustain the conditions of accumulation promised by the system of capitalist property (178). Robert Miles argues that

> the state is not simply a political institution which "intervenes in" the economy. Rather … it is an ensemble of structures and practices which directly constitutes the relations of production. Its very existence is essential to the formation and maintenance of the relations of production that it constitutes, and therefore it is a relation of production in its own right.
>
> (Miles 1987, 181)

Miles (1987) provides numerous examples of how states enforced policies of primitive accumulation in order to develop functional capitalist systems, such as helping "settlers" confiscate land from indigenous peoples (107), creating criminal sanctions for breach of contract by servants (122), creating migrant labor systems to maximize surplus value of labor (126) and organizing the violence necessary to suppress resistance by laborers and their families (184). The imposition of taxes and tariffs forced many people into wage labor and defined which industries would be targeted for growth and therefore a demand for labor. Analyzing the state separate from the economic system (or vice versa) prevents a full understanding of the structure of power that governs in the modern epoch.

Antonio Gramsci (1973) analyzed how the bourgeoisie seizes and retains state power. He examined how the ruling class propagates the ideological values that govern the capitalist system and ensure the legitimacy of the state itself. Kalyan Sanyal (2013) recounts how, in the case of India, neo-Gramscians argue that a general theoretical framework for conceptualizing post-colonial capital and its relation to the state is built on the following claims:

1) The post-colonial bourgeoisie has to form alliances with dominant pre-capitalist groups to enter into state power;
2) The state, representing the national populace, has to legitimize capitalist accumulation on the level of the people-nation;
3) The need for legitimization rules out the process of primitive accumulation;
4) The state therefore has to protect, preserve, and promote the pre-capitalist modes of production. The strength of the post-colonial capital thus lies in its ability to use the ideological construct of passive revolution to carry on expanded reproduction in the modern sector and, at the same time, ensure reproduction of the pre-capitalist, traditional sectors of the economy.

The case studies examined in this book provide a different perspective on the role of the state in capital accumulation. The lessons offered by African states would amend the above theoretical framework as follows:

1) The post-colonial bourgeoisie has to form alliances with global capitalist groups to enter into state power, and with dominant traditional groups to maintain power;
2) The state, seeking approval from the national populace, has to legitimize capitalist accumulation on the level of the people-nation;

3) The need for legitimization requires assertions that primitive accumulation is unacceptable and being investigated;
4) The state therefore has to protect, preserve and promote primitive accumulation even when its public statements contradict such policies.

Sanyal (2013) seems sympathetic to the above framework and joins other contemporary scholars in claiming that the post-colonial state employs primitive accumulation as an integral process in creating surplus value. That is, primitive accumulation is not a stage in the development of capitalism but, rather, an important feature of capitalism itself. Throughout the global economy, aspiring capitalists engage in primitive accumulation to obtain money, and then convert this money into capital (means of production) and invest in free (wage) labor (see Sanval 2013, Chapter 3). Andre Gunder Frank (1969, 9) noted a similar process at work in Latin America, arguing that

> development and underdevelopment are the same in that they are the product of a single, but dialectically contradictory, economic structure and process of capitalism. Thus, they cannot be viewed as the product of supposedly different economic structure or systems. One and the same historical process of the expansion and development of capitalism throughout the world has simultaneously generated … both economic development and structural underdevelopment.

At the root of capitalist relations is the question of why people would suspend activities that achieve subsistence in order to succumb to wage labor? Perelman (2000) provides an extensive review of how humans were historically separated from their property and forced into becoming laborers, both free and unfree. In many cases, capitalists imposed conditions of poverty upon people, providing them with little choice but to seek employment. Perelman (2000, 23) quotes a London police magistrate who observed in 1815 that

> Poverty is that state and condition in society where the individual has no surplus labour in store, or, in other words, no property or means of subsistence but what is derived from the constant exercise of industry in the various occupations of life. Poverty is therefore a most necessary and indispensable ingredient in society, without which nations and communities could not exist in a state of civilization. It is the lot of man. It is the source of wealth, since without poverty, there could be no labour …

The bourgeoisie relies upon the state to implement the conditions necessary for primitive accumulation, and to regulate the terms of employment that bind employers and employees. Rosa Luxemburg (1951) opined that the primitive accumulation of capital involves the use of force, fraud, oppression and looting; "political power is nothing but a vehicle for the economic process" (452). The state also is recruited to criminalize activities that promote self-sufficiency, such as hunting and fishing, that can be pursued only with a license from the appropriate government jurisdiction. Such regulations were necessary in 18th-century Europe to create wage labor and were equally relevant to European colonialization of Africa beginning in the 19th century. Walter Rodney (1974) identifies how the Mandja people in French Equatorial Africa were banned from hunting by the French, and once the Mandja were denied a source of meat from their own hands they became more willing to work on French cotton plantations to earn wages with which they could now buy such meat (166). Dumett (1999) describes how Ghanaians were forced off their land during the Gold Rush beginning in 1877, with the collaboration of local chiefs. When the Ovambo in Namibia trained their dogs to retrieve game, white South African authorities imposed a tax on dogs beginning in 1921. The Administrator of the Mandated Territory reported to his superiors in Pretoria that

> The law has already fulfilled its immediate object in the prevention of the pernicious evil perpetrated by certain whites and blacks in keeping large numbers of dogs to forage for them, ruthlessly destroying quantities of game, and affording these vagrants and loafers any easy means of livelihood, which relieves them of any need to work.
>
> (see Cooper 2001, 78)

The production of poverty becomes a strategic prerequisite for capital accumulation and the creation of surplus value. The main difference between unfree labor and free labor (slaves versus wage laborers that possess a right to contract with the employer of their choice) was not the nature of the work that was required. Rather, workers were differentiated upon the basis of the kind of relationship they possessed with their employer. As Perelman (2000) explains, "Some slave owners felt an obligation to care for their sick and aged chattel. Employers of wage labor were generally unburdened by such thoughts" (78). Unfree labor is created under conditions where poverty is less severe or non-existent; wage labor derives from environments where poverty has been successfully imposed, and it is the degree of poverty that ultimately determines the price of wages. Johann Karl Rodbertus, a German member of the Prussian national assembly, acknowledged in the mid-19th century that "Hunger makes almost a perfect substitute for the whip" (see Perelman 2000, 103).

Adam Smith believed that the relations between capitalists and wage earners would generate high levels of surplus value, and lead to economic advances that would lead to the progress of civilization. Such relations were objective and driven by market factors. Argued Smith, "Society may subsist among different men as among different merchants, from a sense of its utility, without any mutual love or affection" (quoted in Perelman 2000, 200). Smith acknowledged that the accumulation of surplus wealth would require a substantial number of workers to live in poverty: "for one very rich man there must be at least five hundred poor, and the affluence of the few supposes the indigence of the many" (Smith 1978, 670). As Perelman observes, Smith conceptualized a capitalist system where personal relations counted for little relative to market relations (200). Yet right in front of his eyes, Smith witnessed a world where Africans and women were forced into relations of production that were deprived of any opportunity to become free labor. Personal and ideological biases played an integral part to the development of capitalism.

Mies (1999) argues that patriarchal structures of power are at the foundation of capital accumulation during the modern era. In short, men demonstrate their individual influence and wealth by diverting their discretionary income to the women they favor; these women adorn themselves with symbols of surplus value obtained by their husbands, fathers and partners, "turning them into showpieces of their accumulated wealth" (Mies 1999, 101). Werner Sombart (1967), writing in 1913, argues that the modern epoch established women as objects of beauty who served as the measure of male success, and these women were motivated by "a desire for wealth, glitter, conspicuous consumption, grand entertainment, and the like" (see Sombart 1967, xx). Sombart claims that it was the desire to meet the consumer demands of women that compelled men to purchase sugar to accommodate the widespread use of stimulants such as cocoa, coffee and tea (Sombart 1967, 99). Other luxury products in demand by women included medicaments, spices, perfumes, dyestuffs, raw materials for textiles, ornamental objects and dress materials (Sombart 1967, 120–121). The production of these commodities, made profitable by the use of unfree labor, played a significant role in the development of capitalism. Cooper (2019) argues that patriarchal structures have been essential to the ability of states to recruit soldiers and to provide support for the military aims of the capitalist state. In short, the development of capitalism has always been accompanied by primitive accumulation and patriarchal structures of power.

The association between capitalism and slavery is also related to drugs. It is not clear whether it is the exploitative elements of capitalism that generate a demand for drugs to help motivate workers to engage in economic production, or whether there is a need for drugs to sedate workers to lessen the alienation and trauma of performing labor within an exploitative relationship (or both). In any case, the market in psychoactive drugs has always served as the largest industry within capitalist markets since the establishment of nation-states; the global trade in drugs surpasses that of petroleum.[1] The market for psychoactive drugs is made affordable (and profitable) by the use of unfree labor, and in fact the slave trade was organized specifically for the harvesting and production of drugs, both legal and illegal, to meet the demand of consumers/workers resident in industrial states.

Psychoactive drugs include such stimulants as caffeine, nicotine and cocaine. Caffeine can be found in coffee, tea, and soft drinks. Empathogens such as Ecstasy serve to produce experiences of emotional communion and empathy. Anxiolytic medications such as barbiturates act to inhibit anxiety. Depressants include alcohol and opioids including heroin. Hallucinogens inspire perceptual anomalies and subjective changes in thoughts, emotion and consciousness, and include such substances as LSD, psilocybin, peyote and mescaline. Sugar produces psychoactive effects but is generally not classified as a drug since it fails to modify chemical physiology. Recent research suggests that the psychoactive effects resulting from the consumption of chocolate is directly correlated to higher amounts of sugar contained in commercially available chocolate products, and not to the amounts of cocoa (Casperson et al. 2019).

Most of these luxury goods are labor intensive and, therefore, only profitable if labor costs are severely reduced or curtailed. Unfree labor, including child labor, has constituted a much-utilized scheme for achieving surplus value in the market for these drugs and other items of conspicuous consumption. The enforcement of such methods of primitive accumulation tends to depend upon the monopoly of force possessed by the state; James Steuart, a contemporary of Adam Smith whose work was widely read by America's founding fathers, argued that trade begins with government support of luxury exports (see Perelman 2000, 219). Female labor represents the lowest level of free labor available to capitalists that operate within patriarchal structure of power across the globe. As we see in the Congo, the mining of coltan in central Africa is characterized by unfree labor of children, and the use of this coltan in the production of computers, laptops and iPhones also relies on the exploitation of female labor in China so that Apple (and other makers of smart phones) can obtain surplus profits, allowing corporate owners to emerge as some of the richest billionaires on the planet. Meanwhile, laborers find themselves alienated from the product of their labor. The children harvesting cocoa beans have usually not tasted chocolate and have no idea why these beans are so highly valued; the Chinese women working to assemble iPhones cannot afford to purchase these mobile devices. Likewise, Mies (1999) acknowledges that the women in India producing lace for consumer markets in North America, Europe and Australia "had absolutely no use in their huts for the lace goods they made. They were not even aware of the use that was made of these goods" (134). According to Mies (1999), the girls and women working in the electronics industry in Asia are severely underpaid and lose their jobs if they get married since the responsibilities of being a parent conflict with the requirements of producing labor (136).

Slavery, and other forms of unfree labor, has been at the heart of capital accumulation for over 2,000 years. The manner in which slavery was implemented varied from place to place and, in general, was employed to compensate for debts of one kind or another. It was not until the institutionalization of slavery in the United States, and in applications of colonialism in Africa, that the denial of freedom was forced upon humans for who they were as opposed to debts they may have incurred. Slavery outside the United States did not constitute a form of property, even if the organization of labor otherwise seemed comparable. Inasmuch as slavery took various forms at various times in various places, the same can be said for other forms of unfree labor such as serfs, servants, indentured immigrants and rural laborers. What differentiated these categories of unfree labor is not the work they performed, but the legal rights each possessed. Stanziani (2014) maintains that "the gap between Russian serfdom and European wage labor is narrower than is usually held" (10), and in France the terms *serf* and *slave* were used interchangeably (27).

Slavery produced surplus capital necessary to build new technologies of warfare. It is also clear that slavery created the surplus capital necessary to invest in industrial modes of production that gave political and economic advantage to Europe and the United States from the 15th century through the 19th century. Eric Williams (1994) was among the first scholars to document how the profits from slave-grown sugar subsidized the Industrial Revolution in Britain. Once this mode of production had become established, the British organized the abolitionist movement to curtail capital accumulation among its chief economic competitors. Sven Beckert and Seth Rockman (2018) have offered substantial evidence of how the American slave trade had ramifications for the rise of global capitalism from the 19th century. Wakefield, writing in the decades preceding the American War for Slavery, acknowledged that "Slavery appears to have been the step by which nations have emerged from poverty and moved toward wealth and civilization" (cited in Robbins 1939, 160), and he predicted that if slavery were abolished in America then the prosperous cities of the North "would sink into insignificance" (cited in Winch 2017, 97). Wakefield essentially argued that wage labor developed out of slavery (see Perelman 2000, 332). Wakefield did not envision the ability of capitalists to create new racial forms of unfree labor, especially in processes tied to colonialism, or racialized social structures as found in countries established by European settlers.

The contemporary literature on modernization, development and dependency theory all accept this general notion that the capitalist bourgeoisie typically derive their initial surplus capital from primitive, or previous, accumulation. What the contributors to this volume demonstrate in their respective chapters is that primitive accumulation is not a prior stage in the development of capitalism but, instead, is an inherent process in sustaining capitalist accumulation. The enslavement and plunder described by Marx remains part of the accumulation process of capitalist states as well as the global economic system as described by Immanuel Wallerstein (2004). Slavery provided the unfree labor that was essential to creating the surplus value necessary for industrialization as well as for the reification of a middle class in advanced capitalist states. The global economy remains structured to ensure that some areas of the world are available for primitive accumulation in order to generate surplus value. As Mahmood Mamdani (2018) explains, "The end of slavery in the Western hemisphere underlined the practical need for organizing a new regime of compulsions, except this time within newly acquired African possessions" (37). In short, the end of slavery in the United States helped to motivate European states to "scramble for Africa" to establish colonial possessions in the decades following that conflict that facilitated primitive accumulation among a larger population of Africans to provide cotton and sugar previously supplied by Southern states in the USA.

Colonialism in Africa was an expression of primitive accumulation designed to transform "chiefs" into labor recruiters to provide unfree labor for European commercial interests. As one French official noted in reference to the colony of Guinea, "The chief will attend to the tax and furnish manpower, or he will be smashed like a glass" (Suret-Canale 1988, 155). Colonialism in Africa reduced subsistence farmers to unfree and free labor available to European settlers as well as economic interests based in Europe. Each colony achieved this objective in unique ways; for instance, British settlers in Kenya benefitted from the Native Authority Ordinance that required all African adult men to perform six days of unpaid labor every three months (see Mamdani 2018, 157). Non-settler colonies employed different strategies for primitive accumulation and the creation of surplus value, usually involving compulsory cultivation of maize, cotton, cocoa or other commodities desired by European consumers. Other colonies were oriented towards the mining of diamonds and minerals, and traditional authorities were used to serve as recruiters for labor to such enterprises. The Swazi Royal House levied a tax on each migrant recruited for the mines of South Africa that amounted to approximately one-fourth of the wages collected (see Mamdani 2018, 171). Pass laws were enforced in South Africa to prohibit African labor from moving about the colony to get the best wage possible; free labor was not free to seek the most favorable terms of employment under these circumstances. Both free labor and unfree labor took the form of forced labor. The Masters and Servants Act made it a criminal offense to break a labor contract, and other laws criminalized efforts to protect the rights of children to remain with their parents (see Mamdani 2018, 227–228).

In general, there is a correlation between the most extreme and oppressive forms of primitive accumulation and higher rates of surplus value. The imposition of slavery in the United States resulted in exports of cotton at a price that undercut all other sources of the commodity prior to the War for Slavery. The apartheid policies of the white minority regime in South Africa generated the highest rates of return on investment during the 1960s and 1970s, attracting thousands of foreign companies to take advantage of this opportunity to accelerate profits to their shareholders. Anti-apartheid divestment campaigns required corporate leaders and shareholders to address ethical concerns in being complicit with this form of primitive accumulation, leading to capital withdrawals from the apartheid economy and ultimately the collapse of the white-minority regime in 1994. At the time of independence, South Africa's unemployment stood at 15 percent; 20 years later it had grown to 25 percent as capitalist investors replaced free labor with migrant labor from neighboring African states that promised greater surplus value in the name of primitive accumulation (Chengu 2015).

Racism as a function of capitalism

What is ignored by most of the major theorists of capitalism, modernization, development, as well as communism and dependency, is why the enslavement of labor and plunder of resources integral to primitive accumulation are directed primarily at blacks and women. Mack H. Jones (2014) has argued for decades that there is a "relationship between capital accumulation and social deprivation and depravity, between the affluence of Euro-America and the poverty of Africa and African Americans" (Jones 2014, 37). A growing literature has developed claiming the inherent and integrated nature of "racial capitalism" (Roediger 2007; Roediger 2017; Engerman 1999; Tomich 2003), and much of this argument can be traced to the writings of W. E. B. Du Bois (2014) and Cedric J. Robinson (1983). As we have already noted, Maria Mies has made a similar argument for the relationship between patriarchy and capitalism (1999). In short, why does the primitive accumulation of capital disproportionately affect non-Caucasians and women more adversely?

Throughout history, slavery functioned most effectively when it was not employed within one's community; the slave always involved members of "other" groups that were distinguishable from the society that was doing the enslaving. Avenues for escape were more limited when the slave was a recognizable "other," and the ideology supporting slavery was more tenable when the slave could be reified as an inferior human, or perhaps lacking in humanity altogether.

Ancient Egypt, as one of the earliest state empires, already had institutionalized a slave network that reached southward into Africa and the rise of other Mediterranean powers merely assumed control over this network once Egypt lost its power over the region. When Muslim empires assumed power over the Mediterranean and beyond, they used ships to acquire new slaves from East Africa that vastly increased the number of black slaves available to the growing elites of "white" Arab/Muslim powers in the Indian Ocean as well as the Mediterranean Sea. Beginning in the 16th century, European states copied these technologies to secure slaves from the west coast of Africa for markets in the New World. US economic power continued to rely on the enslavement and discriminatory practices against people of African descent within that state following its independence from England.

African authorities prospered from the slave trade as well. Slavery was profitable to African leaders who accumulated wealth from European slave traders, especially when slaves were bartered for weapons that could be used for military objectives within Africa itself. African leaders obviously underestimated the ability of Europeans to eventually gain control over the continent, since the technologies and wealth they received were substantially inferior to those acquired by their European benefactors.

Robinson and Gallagher (1961) offer a "collaboration thesis" for explaining how colonial officials were able to secure domination over larger populations of subjected peoples. In essence, foreign rulers dominate larger populations through collaborators from the targeted groups. Again, Mack H. Jones (2014) describes how this process works within multi-ethnic states such as the United States where urban voters elect African American leaders who are dependent upon white business interests to organize the resources that will make it possible to achieve political aims:

> The elected black political leadership that emerges from these circumstances will be one that, even though propelled into office by black votes, has no organizationally based support. There are no regular structures for political debate and deliberations between black officials and black rank and file. Political discussion of consequence continues to be monopolized by the white commercial and business elite and the elected officials. Under these circumstances, the political empowerment of the black community remains a goal to be attained rather than an already realized milestone.
>
> (Jones 2014, 128–129)

Jones goes on to argue that political leaders generally serve the interests of the economic elite and, thus, the rise of black elected officials should not be confused with any promise of advancement for the black voters that secured this electoral outcome:

> Institutionally black officeholding in many instances serves as a conduit for cultural and political domination of the black community, and it becomes part of the apparatus that manages the oppressed masses in the interest of the dominant economic elite.
>
> (Jones 2014, 135)

The evidence provided in the chapters that follow validates that the same manner of institutional power relations exists between African political elites and various global powers. As with the black officeholders being referenced by Jones, most African leaders have no visible means of support other than the positions they hold in their respective government. Their capability to pursue any nationalist agenda requires an ability to secure the financial resources necessary to implement any such agenda. This forces African political leaders to defer to the interest of global business elites and, in the process, "they become functionally integrated into the process and apparatus that create and sustain the problems" of the populations they serve (Jones 2014, 139). For the global capitalist elite, the recruitment of collaborators constitutes an investment for securing the political stability that sustains a capitalist environment conducive to generating surplus value.

Proponents of racial capitalism, including Jones (2014), argue that when capitalism is operating routinely, it creates the conditions that force large numbers of workers to live in poverty. Thus, poverty is not an anomaly but a direct outcome of the capitalist economy (see Jones 2014, 172–173). According to Miles, "racism also has the potential to legitimate a particular ensemble of relations of production and a signified group to justify the assignation of particular people to a particular position in the productive process" (Miles 1987, 188). As such, "racism, therefore, became an ideological relation of production. Racism was not an ideology which 'reacted back upon' economic relations but was itself an economic relation" (Miles 1987, 191).

The argument that capitalism and racism go hand in hand was articulated by Cedric J. Robinson as far back as 1983. Robinson details how slavery served as the principal basis for the creation of surplus value from Antiquity, through feudalism, to the contemporary modern era. At each historical juncture, slavery targeted different groups and was justified on separate philosophical and political rationales. But at each point the most "ideal" slaves were Africans who were less able to "pass" for membership in the competing nations seeking to dominate capitalist expansion. Robinson (1983) speaks to "The extension of slavery and the application of racism to non-European peoples as an organizing structure by first the ruling feudal strata and then the bourgeoisie of the fourteenth, fifteenth, and sixteenth centuries" (67), and then followed from the seventeenth century on by English merchant capital incorporating African labor in precisely these terms (67). For European capitalists, "it was the African's colour of skin that became his defining characteristic" (cited in Robinson 1983, 75–76). African slave labor became the foundation for the settlement and economic development of the Americas and validated the thesis that the source of all economic value is labor (see Robinson 1983, 113).

The end of slavery in the United States did not liberate Africans from the exploitation of their labor, it merely transformed the nature of that exploitation. Structural racism intensified the income inequality and political subordination of those freed from slavery, and this social order became a model for Europe's colonial project of the African continent. The black petit bourgeoisie being nurtured by the white nationalist elite within the United States eventually became a model for the 50 or so African nation-states developed by European powers during the last century. W. E. B. DuBois came to realize that this Black elite within American society served a reactionary ideological status in the capitalist structure that required the extreme exploitation of black labor to sustain the privileges of its white elite (see Robinson 1983, 197). Countless African intellectuals have argued that the same model applies to the post-colonial leadership of African states. Robinson (1983) purports that the petit bourgeoisie of black leaders, both in the USA and in Africa, is "a class whose members recognize their dependence on the bourgeoisie for social privileges. Their political loyalties were to the bourgeoisie and as such they were understood to be reactionary by their class-nature" (233). This only amplifies the observations of Mack H. Jones (2014).

Since the operation of the state requires managers (known as political leaders), global businesspeople compete to develop collaborators among the nationalist leadership class to exercise control over the territory and its material and human resources. Some states collaborate with one global power, while other states attempt to balance one global power off another. Still, there are some states that struggle to organize governments with command over the nation, and they experience a level of instability that will persist until one global power finally gets recognized by the others as having this state as an ally or subsidiary. Typically, these states possess resources or a piece of strategic real estate that make the global competition to control this state much more intense. When such competition reaches a point that no government can exercise control over the state, it is often referred to as a "failed state." To the point, a failed state is a country that lacks a unified government with a monopoly of force over the territory as a whole. Yet, even within failed states there are individuals and interests that continue to amass wealth through various "back channels" available in the global economy. In recent decades, Africa has witnessed failed states in Sierra Leone, Liberia, Angola, Libya and Somalia. In other words, these states possess resources so strategic that the competition by outside global powers rendered each incapable of establishing a unified government able to monopolize the distribution of basic services to its population. This failure to govern has more to do with the outside competitive politics of world powers than any deficiency in the management abilities of the nationalist leaders themselves. After all, the vast majority of African states are relatively stable entities, including some of these so-called "failed" states.

The flip side of this argument is that the definition of a successful and stable state in Africa is one that has joined forces with outside commercial interests, where the national leaders are being handsomely rewarded for collaborating with global powers in their manipulation of the world economy that enriches a small number of billionaires that command influence over world politics. In recent decades, Africa has started to generate its own billionaires, but it remains unclear whether these billionaires are members or clients of a global capitalist elite. It also is not clear whether these billionaires are creatures created by their respective states or whether they are being rewarded by global powers to oversee the public administration of their home countries. This book, in part, seeks to answer these questions.

In short, this book offers a unique analysis of African development that deviates from the traditional approach of studying African governments and their ability to increase their domestic national product. Instead, it focuses on the people and workers of Africa and their capacity to earn a livable wage and to enjoy a sense of freedom about how they live their lives. The fact is that income inequality in Namibia is comparable to the United States, yet there is a tendency to regard one of these states as "developed" and the other as "underdeveloped." In reality, each plays a role in the global economy that benefits a small elite that can enjoy privileges within the global marketplace to the detriment of the masses in both countries. It is important to keep in mind that, at the time of this writing, there are about 7.5 billion humans inhabiting the planet, but only 135 of them possess more wealth than Aliko Dangote of Nigeria. A list of the richest Africans shows a disproportionate number from countries identified as "undeveloped" according to theorists of development and modernity (Table 1.1).

Other Africans whose names appear on various rankings as billionaires, or reaching levels close to it, include Strive Masiyiwa (Zimbabwe), Stephen Saad (South Africa), Anas Sefrioui (Morocco), Jannie Mouton (South Africa), Desmond Sacco (South Africa), Michiel Le Roux (South Africa), Charles Ampofo (Ghana), Ernest Taricone (Ghana), Sam Esson Jonah (Ghana),

Table 1.1 List of African billionaires

Billionaire	*Net Worth*	*Country of Origin*
1) Aliko Dangote	$16.4 billion	Nigeria
2) Mike Adenuga	$10.3 billion	Nigeria
3) Nicky Oppenheimer	$ 6.6 billion	South Africa
4) Christoffel Wiese	$ 6.2 billion	South Africa
5) Johann Rupert	$ 5.4 billion	South Africa
6) Nassef Sawiris	$ 4.4 billion	Egypt
7) Nathan Kirsh	$ 4.0 billion	South Africa/Swaziland
8) Isabel dos Santos	$ 3.1 billion	Angola
9) Issad Rebrab	$ 3.1 billion	Algeria
10) Naguib Sawiris	$ 3.0 billion	Egypt
11) Mohamed Mansour	$ 2.5 billion	Egypt
12) Othman Benjelloun	$ 1.9 billion	Morocco
13) Mohamed Al Fayed	$ 1.9 billion	Egypt
14) Femi Otedola	$ 1.8 billion	Nigeria
15) Youssef Mansour	$ 1.7 billion	Egypt
16) Folorunsho Alakija	$ 1.5 billion	Nigeria
17) Allan Gray	$ 1.4 billion	South Africa
18) Koos Bekker	$ 1.4 billion	South Africa
19) Yassen Mansour	$ 1.3 billion	Egypt
20) Aziz Akhannouch	$ 1.2 billion	Morocco
21) Patrice Motsepe	$ 1.1 billion	South Africa
22) Abdulsamad Rabiu	$ 1.1 billion	Nigeria
23) Onsi Sawiris	$ 1.0 billion	Egypt
24) Mohammed Dewji	$ 1.0 billion	Tanzania
25) Rostam Azizi	$ 1.0 billion	Tanzania

Source: Mfonobong Nsehe, "The African Billionaires 2016," *Forbes* (March 1, 2016).

Abdirashid Duale (Somalia), Mohammed Al Amoudi (Ethiopia), Azeb Mesfin (Ethiopia), Berhane Gebrekiristos (Ethiopia), Seyoum Mesfin (Ethiopia), Abay Teshay (Ethiopia), Mama Ngina Kenyatta (Kenya), Daniel Moi (Kenya) and Manu Chandaria (Kenya). The number of global billionaires that owe some part of their wealth to investing in Africa is presumably a much larger number than that of African billionaires.

Strategies of primitive accumulation

Primitive accumulation constitutes those strategies and tactics that use unfree labor to acquire surplus value. It involves economic activities that fall outside the framework of a contract between an employer and an employee. In most cases, the activities that are associated with primitive accumulation are criminalized by states and/or the "international community" to prevent the accumulation of capital necessary to challenge political and financial authorities who themselves may have utilized primitive accumulation to achieve their status of power. It is implied that primitive accumulation employs far more cruel and inhumane measures than would be tolerated by the proletariat encompassing free workers and consumers. Both political philosophers and leaders have argued over time that inhumane conditions are more tolerated by people who are perceived as inferior, and for more than a thousand years people of African descent have been targeted for the practices of primitive accumulation. These racist ideologies have been propagated with great success, especially among white populations, to sustain capitalist systems both at the state level and the global arena. These practices result in general public acceptance of discriminatory and unethical work conditions for people of African descent. Disparate incomes among free labor based on race, or the use of unfree labor in Africa, continue to generate higher standards of living for both the billionaires and millionaires of the world, as well as for the middle-class bureaucrats and workers who serve them. Unfree workers continue to be found in capitalist economies in the form of chattel slaves, foreign migrants and convict labor – all of which constitute a disproportionate percentage of non-white laborers.

In large measure, primitive accumulation is a form of violent theft. It can be achieved by direct force, or through policies of the state that include debt resolution or claims of eminent domain or by the sanctioning of a hostile takeover between corporate entities. Forcing people off the land that provides them subsistence converts these individuals into workers with only labor to exchange for currency with which to purchase the subsistence they once produced on their own. A shift from unfree to free production relations is undertaken by capitalists to purchase political stability among exploited workers and to reify an expectation that laborers have an investment in a system that provides accumulating wealth, comfort and security. Likewise, a shift can occur from free to unfree production in order to lower costs and increase profitability in the labor process that is already owned or controlled by the capitalists (see Brass 2013, 149). This can be achieved by state authorities collaborating with global capitalists, or through the establishment of state-supported "terrorist" groups whose existence provides political cover for the state actors utilizing such methods of primitive accumulation. Some groups, like Boko Haram in Nigeria, use violence to accumulate capital from ransoms for kidnapped civilians and to extort money from state and local authorities. Terrorist groups like UNITA in Angola were supported by the United States in exchange for sharing the harvesting of diamonds in territory under their control. Al-Shabaab in Somalia supported piracy to extort ransoms from ship owners to rescue personnel and property being transported.

States operate as authorities and referees to sanction primitive accumulation methods utilized to accumulate capital. For instance, in the transition of socialist USSR to capitalist Russia, the state intervened to transfer state property into the hands of private individuals who would become "oligarchs." Brass (2013) recounts how the Russian Government issued shares in companies to individual workers of these corporate entities. But when companies began to withhold wages, workers were forced into poverty. Some companies set up shops to provide necessities to workers with the proviso that workers surrender their shares in exchange for supplies. Workers were also permitted to surrender their company shares in exchange for currency that could be used to rescue their families from deprivation. In short, the Russian state created a legal mechanism for oligarchs to force their workers into debt, and to compel these workers to surrender any control or partial ownership in order to survive (see Brass 2013, 161). This book explores the extent to which African states have acted similarly to create their own oligarchs that exercise power throughout Africa.

Whereas most capitalist philosophers and economists argue that primitive accumulation creates the conditions for capitalist accumulation, this book demonstrates that economic activities in Africa support the perspective that primitive accumulation acts as a form of capital accumulation that continues to make billionaires both in Africa and among major global states. Capitalism, including primitive accumulation, is ultimately a form of control used by the state.

A brief overview of major strategies of primitive accumulation follows.

Piracy

Piracy has been a feature of global politics from the beginning of recorded history. It flourishes when there is a lack of central control, especially in regions beyond the reach of major powers (Konstam 2008, 10). The first known pirates were the Lukkans who raided the south-eastern cost of modern Turkey beginning in the 14th century BC (Konstam 2008, 10). Many of the most influential states in world history began with piracy as a source of primitive accumulation. Even the Ancient Greeks pursued piracy throughout the Mediterranean Sea, an endeavor that ended once Athens became the dominant naval power during the 5th century BC (Konstam 2008, 13). When Rome emerged as a global power, they legislated an anti-piracy law in 101 BC to mark their territory along Mediterranean shores (Konstam 2008, 19). By the 16th century, it was French pirates attacking Spanish shipping (Miles 1987, 74). In the 17th century the English were attacking Spanish and Portuguese ships (Miles 1987, 74).

Pirates sometimes act autonomously, and sometimes are sponsored by states. On some occasions they engage in theft, while other times they kidnap in pursuit of ransoms or operate as terrorists on the open seas. One person's pirate can be another person's privateer. Sir Francis Drake was considered a national hero in England for enriching Queen Elizabeth I, while the Spanish labelled him a pirate (Konstam 2008, 39, 81). Piracy has manifested itself in every region of the world, among populations embracing every major religion. In the early 17th century, Barbary pirates operated an extensive slave trade against Christians, with some 20,000 Christian slaves within the walls of Algiers at any given time. Some of these slaves could gain freedom by converting to Islam – a process described as "turning Turk" (Konstam 2008, 90). Christian slaves captured in Ireland were taken away family by family, and separated individually to a lifetime of slavery to the highest bidder (Konstam 2008, 91).

Piracy tends to arise in areas where there is an absence of sovereign control by a state, or where there are competing claims by various states, or where the governing state is itself controlled by a corrupt or criminal element that prospers from criminal activities (see Palmer 2014, 8–9). It was perhaps inevitable that piracy would arise in Somalia, given the weak character of its government and the fact that it possesses the longest coastline of any African country. Piracy became one of the few avenues for capital accumulation with which to finance national development. In Somalia, a percentage of ransoms from ships held hostage by pirates went to public infrastructure, including hospitals and schools (Palmer 2014, 11). The lack of a strong central government in Somalia opens up other possibilities for primitive accumulation by neighbors such as Ethiopia, Eritrea, Djibouti, Kenya and Yemen. The Red Sea is also a major site of competition among Egypt, Iran and Saudi Arabia. In short, the opportunities for primitive accumulation in and around Somalia are relatively endless.

Pirates organized social structures that reflected democratic principles, in part to recruit the best manpower in the available labor pool. Historically, the captain and quartermaster on pirate ships were both elected, and decisions tended to be reached by consensus. There essentially was no such thing as a mutiny on a pirate ship (Konstam 2008, 161). While the popular image of pirates may be that they were anti-authoritarian rebels who exercised freedom from social responsibilities, the overwhelming evidence is that most were simply sailors who engaged in a form of labor that lacked the oppressiveness of the capitalist wage system (Konstam 2008, 318). Oftentimes, men became pirates because other economic opportunities were not available. Once wars ended, many sailors found themselves unemployed, and piracy became a way to utilize their naval skills in a way that put food on the table (see Konstam 2008, 152). Despite the popular image of pirates as savages bent on criminal behavior, Leeson (2009) argues that "a pirate ship more closely resembled a fortune 500 company" pursuing business to achieve profit, just like any other capitalist enterprise (6). The main difference is that piracy, as a form of primitive accumulation, was capable of rewarding pirates with a much higher income than could be gained by free labor as a merchant sailor; "At a time when Anglo-American seamen on a trading voyage to Madagascar were collecting less than twelve pounds sterling a year … the deep-water pirates could realize a hundred or even a thousand times more" (see Leeson 2009, 13). Free labor as a seaman provided a regular, if low, income, while a single successful pirating venture could earn enough for a pirate to allow him to retire from future employment altogether (Leeson 2009, 14).

Working conditions carried their risks, but overall pirates worked in environments with democratic checks and balances against abusive leaders, while free laborers faced much more humiliating and oppressive work conditions. Pirates could almost always guarantee their fair share of any bounty obtained, whereas citizens of nation-states today, most specifically African states, are confronted with dysfunctional capitalist economies that facilitate rulers and entrepreneurs transferring wealth from laborers to their personal tax shelters located in remote islands outside the regulatory reach of any government. In short, pirates were more likely to be better compensated and function within more democratic systems than any free laborer could. This may help to explain Leeson's (2009) claim that "pirate ships were more orderly, peaceful and well organized than many merchant ships, vessels of the Royal Navy, or indeed, even the British colonies" (81). Given the racist nature of the free labor system, it should not be surprising that, during the heyday of piracy, a disproportionate percentage of pirates were of African origin, seeking to avoid the violence of the capitalist system; Leeson (2009) estimates that up to 30 percent of its crewmen of the average pirate crew had African origins (159). Unlike "legitimate" capitalist enterprises, pirate ships prospered from having the most productive workers/thieves, and racial identity was of secondary importance.

Andrew Palmer argues that piracy is not the behavior of those inclined toward criminality but, rather, a lesson for all of us about what can happen when inequality becomes extreme. Asserts Palmer (2014):

> Somalia is a warning of what happens when nations fragment and the basest elements take control; we need to learn from this sad experience. Piracy is not about Somalia itself, it is really about human beings trying to exist in a world where they have nothing, where greed is the only guide, and there are no restraints.
>
> (316)

Slavery

Slave labor has been the standard method for wealth creation for thousands of years. The characteristics and protocols for engineering this labor practice vary from place to place, and from one time to another. In general, slaves tend to be "others" who lack kinship with their masters; that is, they speak another language, have a different religious worldview and manifest a different culture than that possessed by their owner. Historically, most slaves were taken into custody through warfare to be used as reparations for the cost of the war. Enslavement has also occurred as a form of legal punishment for serious wrongdoing. Slavery has been instituted as a method for paying off debts. And on rare occasions, slavery was imposed on a target group to render them as property in perpetuity, allowing the slaveowner to be accorded legal authority to control not just an individual slave but everyone born of that slave. In such a situation, the slaveowner possessed complete control over the slave; the slave had no rights including the right to control their sexual access and reproduction. Compared to free labor, "the slave has a very limited incentive not only to work but also to improve the contribution of his or her labour power to the production process" (Miles 1987, 29). Violence, and the threat of violence, proved an effective incentive to induce the slave to produce surplus value from his or her labor.

Every empire has utilized some form of slavery to accumulate and display wealth. Egypt used slaves as bonded laborers, while others were captives of war. Italian city-states during Antiquity maintained slave markets of Circassian and Abkhazian slaves. During feudal days, Mongols sold Greeks, Bulgarians and Romanians to merchants from Mediterranean ports (Stanziani 2014, 76). In 1459 the Venetian Senate lamented the scarcity of slaves since most of the Slavic and Tatar slaves were being diverted to Egypt and Turkey (Stanziani 2014, 77). In the 14th century, Indians became the slave of choice among world powers. Africans dominated world slave markets from that point on, with about 11 million Africans traded along Indian Ocean routes between the 7th and the 20th century and another 11 million African slaves traded on trans-atlantic routes from the 15th to the 19th century (see Stanziani 2014, 90). Islamic powers grew in power and wealth with the use of the trade in slaves through the Indian Ocean, while Western markets expanded with the trans-atlantic trade in slaves. Russia was geographically situated on the periphery of the African slave trade and its ability to compete with Western economies stagnated as a result. Instead, Russia obtained slaves from war captives, facilitating the colonial expansion into Central Asia that later resulted in the establishment of the USSR. Whereas cities became the engines for Western capitalist growth, Russian cities were not locations of industrial activity or free labor but, rather, centers of administrative and military outposts (Stanziani 2014, 113). Even today, Russia's interest in places like Africa focuses on potential locations of military bases rather than economic trade. Still, it is important to note that, even if Russia failed to employ slaves from Africa, it engaged in other forms of primitive accumulation that exacted surplus profits on a scale that made it competitive with European powers during the early days of the modern era. By 1788, the average Russian was as rich as their English equivalent and only 15 percent poorer than the average French citizen. During the Napoleonic Wars, Russia surpassed the French in average household incomes and remained competitive with the British (Stanziani 2014, 138–139). In the 19th century, as European powers were integrating Africa into the global economy, Russia pursued primitive accumulation by placing nearly half of its male population into serfdom; more than half of these serfs were controlled by the top 4 percent of serf owners (Hoch 1989, 2–3).

Marx (1976) argued that

> Without slavery you have no cotton; without cotton you have no modern industry. It is slavery that gave the colonies their value; it is the colonies that created world trade, and it is world trade that is the precondition of large-scale industry. Thus slavery is an economic category of the greatest importance.
>
> (167)

The United States transformed slavery from a strategy for paying off debts to an institutional form of permanent enslavement of people of African descent. Having said this, most Americans associate slavery with an economic system in the South that came to an end with the War for Slavery. In reality, the Northern economy was just as dependent upon slavery as the South. New England and the Mid-Atlantic states prospered from the sale of food to feed millions of slaves both in the South and in the Caribbean. Hundreds of textile mills in New England required cotton grown on slave plantations in the South. New York City emerged as America's largest city due to its status as the leader in exports of slave-produced cotton. In fact, enslaved African Americans made up about one-fifth of New York City's population in the 18th century (Farrow et al. 2005, xxvi-xxvii).

America's slave-produced cotton contributed to the global economy as well. In 1850 there were over 75,000 cotton plantations in the US South, and most of the cotton produced by these slaves was shipped to Liverpool for global markets (Farrow et al. 2005, 10).

Decades after the American War for Slavery ended, US capitalists prospered from global sources of unfree labor, in particular among African colonies. For instance, American chocolate producers obtained cocoa from plantations in Sao Tome and Principe, controlled by Portugal, that utilized unfree labor from Angola. British cocoa manufacturers protested the advantage gained by their American competitors and justified their criticism on the fact that the surplus value obtained from the purchase of chocolate products by American companies included the costs of slavery. This argument did not dissuade customers from purchasing American chocolate. To this very day, as Ewoh demonstrates in his chapter in this book, Sao Tome and Principe (and other West African states) use primitive accumulation strategies to provide cocoa beans to global chocolate consumer markets. Chocolate producers continue to enjoy a very profitable enterprise that engages a high level of child labor. Two different chapters in this book detail some of the economic and political factors involved in this industry and how it affects Africa's role in the global accumulation of capital.

Organized crime

Organized crime is distinguished from piracy or kleptocracies by nature of the fact that the primitive accumulation process is not tied to political motives. Organized crime may often require relationships with political leaders or bureaucrats, but the goal is not to convert capital into power over the general population but, rather, to lubricate the capitalist system by performing functions that states cannot pursue without putting at risk the "legitimacy" of the state as a representation of the popular will. What organized crime may have in common with piracy is a Robin Hood mission statement that the surplus value obtained by primitive accumulation will be shared, however sparingly, with the poor. Mafias, drug cartels and the like often gain public support through the willingness of such criminal organizations to provide financial support to members of the community who otherwise shield them from official scrutiny.

Organized crime also functions as "terrorists-for-hire" against domestic opponents or unfaithful actors. While these activities serve the interests of the state, they constitute contract relations that are superimposed upon the syndicate that otherwise is primarily engaged in primitive accumulation for its own sake. It is only when such criminal actors actively participate in the political process that we differentiate organized crime from kleptocracy.

Bureaucratic corruption/kleptocracy

Katherine Hirschfeld (2015) has written extensively on the relationship between organized crime and the establishment of "gangster states" that practice "kleptocracy."

It can be argued that all state bureaucracies function with some degree of "corruption," with the proviso that more developed administrative systems are better at obfuscating such transgressions of the rule of law. For instance, in the United States where "campaign contributions" are permissible to incumbents throughout their term of office, it can be exceedingly difficult to prove whether official actions taken by a legislator result from a bribe or are incidental to a legal financial contribution. In a fragile state, such as Somalia, obfuscation of political decision-making is less refined. Andrew Palmer (2014, 49) asserts how the Transitional National Government (TNG) of Somalia used "businessmen" to print currency to be used in funding government efforts to protect the financial interests of their political allies from violent activities from militias:

> The currency import business was the system whereby some Somali businessmen had Somali currency printed abroad, imported it and used it as the local medium of exchange. The printing and issue of currency was therefore a private venture and no Somali "government" was involved in the process. Banknotes are not always produced by government banks; in Hong Kong three banks issue banknotes, as do eight banks in the United Kingdom. This group of businessmen in fact provided the main financial support to the TNG because it was more cost-effective to pay the TNG to provide protection from the militias than to pay the militias. Another reason for supporting the TNG was that it regarded at least part of their payments as loans, rather than as revenue. The businessmen could therefore expect to be repaid from foreign aid; when the TNG received $15 million from Saudi Arabia, this gift was used to repay local business supports.

Somalia's blatant use of primitive accumulation contributes to its labeling as a failed state, but what is important here is not the use of corrupt practices in building state authority but only its lack of sophistication in disguising such kleptocratic policies from the public. Successful states, such as the United States, engage in similar business practices but are "successful" in shielding them from any public disclosure (Hirschfeld 2015; Bunker and Bunker 2019; Vaughn and Finch 2017; Mattli 2019; Kolhatkar 2017; Bullough 2019; Shelley 2018). A good example of such corruption is the distribution of military contracts in the aftermath of the September 11, 2001 attacks on the United States by the

George W. Bush administration to the Carlyle Group that was directed by the President's father as well as members of the Bin Laden family (Briody 2003).

Debt bondage

The "IOU" has been a mechanism for control throughout recorded history. Gifts and loans are used for securing favors, including unfree labor. Whether on farms or ships, laborers are encouraged to obtain necessities from a company store that trades goods at an excessive surplus value. When pay day arrives, such purchases are subtracted from wages earned so that the workers receive little if anything for services provided. In fact, the laborer might even owe their employer, requiring them to submit to additional unfree labor to satisfy the debt. If the tactic works correctly, the worker that labors to pay off a debt ends up increasing their debt, thus extending the duration of time of unfree labor. Colonialists established conditions of debt through policies requiring hut taxes, head taxes, dog taxes, income taxes, labor recruitment fees, etc. Even today, one of the largest categories of the national debt in the United States is student debt, derived from requiring that desired jobs be obtained with a college transcript whose cost exceeds most family available assets, thus subjecting individuals to acquire debt prior to employment. The debt does not force an individual into unfree labor but, rather, it is a situation where free labor compels one to enter the marketplace of labor to surrender one's time to the advantage of the employer, or a class of employers. Should the debtor be unable to exercise their status as free labor to find employment to pay off their debts, they face the prospect of engaging in primitive accumulation to obtain the financial resources necessary to satisfy their debt to the creditor. Under US law, individuals can declare bankruptcy on nearly all forms of debt, but not student debt.

In either case, the laborer's productivity is independent of whether they are regarded as free labor, unfree labor or the subject of primitive accumulation. Rather, they are a collaborator in a capitalist system that demands the provision of labor to avoid punishment based ultimately on violence or coercion. All ranks of labor compel workers to produce surplus value within a relationship that encompasses some degree of coercion or threat thereof. Hilaire Belloc (1924) argues that "There is no reason why a free man working for another's profit should do his best. On the contrary, he has every reason to work as little as possible, while the slave can be compelled to work hard" (99–100). But capitalism as an economic system is not designed to produce a perfect product, just a profitable one. Whether a worker is giving their all is not the question; obtaining maximum value out of another's body is what generates surplus value independent of the quality of the product itself. Surplus value can be created with any system of labor. The advantage of employing free labor is that compensation is limited only to the time for which labor is employed, whereas unfree labor (including machinery) requires a cost from the capitalist even for the time when a commodity is not being produced (see Brass 2013, 36–37). Another disadvantage of unfree labor is that it results in no wage accumulation from which to purchase commodities that include surplus value within its retail price, thus the capitalist is denied an additional source of profit.

Finally, debt is a method for separating individuals from the property they own. For rural workers, the establishment of debt forces peasants and self-sufficient farmers to surrender their property to satisfy the imposed debt. Among urban residents, debt serves a similar function of forcing homeowners to surrender their property to resolve their financial burdens.

Eminent domain and nationalization/privatization

In 1625, the Dutch scholar Hugo Grotius used the term *dominium eminens* to argue that all land is under the sovereignty of a state, and this state possesses responsibility to ensure that land serves the public interest:

> The property of subjects is under the eminent domain of the state, so that the state or those who act for it may use and even alienate and destroy such property, not only in the case of extreme necessity, in which even private persons have a right over the property of others, but for ends of public utility, to which ends whose who founded civil society must be supposed to have intended that private ends should give way. But, when this is done, the state is bound to make good the loss to those who lose their property.
>
> (Edited by Neff 2012, 226)

In the 18th century, John Locke joined a growing chorus of philosophers who claimed that improving the land (i.e., making it more productive) should be the basis of property rights and that the failure to improve land could lead to the forfeiture of the right to property. For Locke, productivity for profit became a measure for determining whether property was being improved. Locke took the position that, since Native Americans added no value to their land, they had therefore failed to establish a right to it. Unimproved land was "waste." Mere occupancy was insufficient for establishing property rights (see Wood 2017, 156–165). Implicitly, colonialism did not rob people of their land, but added value to it on behalf of the common good (Wood 2017, 165).

States therefore possess the agency to take property as needed to advance the public good. Such actions have been common for the building of government buildings, roads, or to develop public utilities. But courts have also permitted states to confiscate intangible property such as patents, contract rights, trade secrets and even professional football teams in the United States. In essence, claims of eminent domain constitute strategies of primitive accumulation in which states determine who becomes enriched at the expense of another.

Tariffs and taxation

The state serves the capitalist system by requiring free labor to part with a share of their labor in the form of taxes, as well as tariffs imposed on certain products that are popularly consumed. The justification for such taxes is that the state serves the society as a whole by creating public infrastructure such as roads and schools that benefit everyone and, therefore, are deserving of everyone's financial contribution. The other side of the coin is that it keeps free labor from enjoying the direct benefits of their employment, and encourages workers to continue working in order to satisfy the desire to accumulate enough surplus value that will, at a minimum, eliminate the anxiety they face in making ends meet (or at least to possess enough surplus to purchase drugs that will temporarily reduce this anxiety).

Taxes can be secured on economic activities that encourage subsistence, such as hunting and fishing. Taxes can be organized by the state to demonstrate the authority of the state, especially in its mission to recruit wage labor. For instance, in 1720, Peter the Great replaced the household tax in Russia with a soul tax imposed on all males of all ages, regardless of household, to finance a national army. In various places under British colonial rule in Africa, the household tax was referred to as a "hut" tax that forced Africans into the colonial economy as wage earners. In Natal, African men that lived in British-style houses with only one wife were exempt from the tax.

Migrant labor

The use of migrant labor offers capitalists a form of labor that maximizes surplus value, in that migrant workers cannot afford to demand the conditions of free labor. As Brass (2013) explains,

> If migrant workers asked for higher wages, better working conditions or a shorter working day, and began to organize so as to withdraw their labour in furtherance of these objectives, a landowner possessed the political capacity quickly to arrange for their deportation.
>
> (179)

Brass offered this observation in relation to farm workers in Germany during World War One, but it applies just as much to the use of migrant labor in the mines of South Africa today, or to Latino migrant workers in the United States, or Turk migrants in Germany, or Algerian migrants in France, or Palestinians in Saudi Arabia, or Bangladeshis in India, or Malaysians in Indonesia, or Filipinos in Singapore, or Vietnamese in South Korea, or Bulgarians in Finland, or Armenians in Russia, and so on.

Primitive accumulation remains at the center of the capitalist system today, and nowhere is this more clear than in African economies. South Africa may have placed the apartheid legal system into the dustbin of history, but the same primitive accumulation activities that made billionaires out of white settlers in that country continue to function unabated, even if much of the unfree labor today in that country is provided by migrant labor from neighboring states. Some of the enormous wealth resulting from primitive accumulation now finds itself in the hands of African leaders of the South African state who have demonstrated great willingness to collaborate with these white settlers and their foreign business partners. In the case studies that follow, there is not a chapter on South Africa since the story of apartheid is well-known, and very little has changed in the capital accumulation process of that country since it became a multi-racial democracy in 1994. Post-apartheid South Africa remains the leader among global economies in the inequality of incomes. Not only have the current leaders of South Africa failed to interrupt the primitive accumulation of wealth in their country, they have acted to guarantee that they profit from it.

The chapters that follow demonstrate that the philosophy of primitive accumulation that functioned under both apartheid and post-apartheid South Africa is being practiced in their own particular ways in every other African state as well.

Note

1 Workman (2019) estimates that global crude oil shipments totaled $1.133 trillion for 2018. Avinash Tharoor (2017) calculates the highest value of illegal drugs as follows: cannabis ($287 billion), cocaine ($143 billion), opiates ($132 billion) and amphetamine-type stimulants ($90 billion) for a total of $652 billion. Among caffeine producers, the global coffee trade is about $80 billion (PBS), tea production is valued at $50 billion (Statista: tea), and carbonated soft drinks is a $375 billion market although this includes both caffeinated and non-caffeinated products (Statista: soft drinks). Nicotene production generated $800 billion in 2019 (Statista: tobacco). Total global drug production adds up to nearly $2 trillion.

References

Amin, Samir. 1974. *Accumulation on a World Scale: A Critique of the Theory of Underdevelopment*, Vol. 1. New York: Monthly Review Press.

Ayelazuno, Jasper. 2011. "Continuous Primitive Accumulation in Ghana: The Real-Life Stories of Dispossessed Peasants in Three Mining Communities." *Review of African Political Economy*, 38(130) (December), 537–550.

Bales, Kevin. 2012. *Disposable People: New Slavery in the Global Economy.* Berkeley, CA: University of California Press.

Beckert, Sven and Rockman, Seth. Eds. 2018. *Slavery's Capitalism: A New History of American Economic Development.* Philadelphia, PA: University of Pennsylvania Press.

Belloc, Hilaire. 1924. *Economics for Helen.* New York: G. P. Putnam's Sons.

Brass, Tom. 2013. *Labor Regime Change in the Twenty-First Century: Unfreedom, Capitalism and Primitive Accumulation.* Chicago, IL: Haymarket Books.

Briody, Dan. 2003. *The Iron Triangle: Inside the Secret World of the Carlyle Group.* New York: John Wiley & Sons.

Bullough, Oliver. 2019. *The Inside Story of the Crooks and Kleptocrats Who Rule the World.* New York: St Martin's Press.

Bunker, Robert and Bunker, Pamela Ligouri. Eds. 2019. *Plutocratic Insurgency Reader.* Bloomington, IN: Xlibris.

Casperson, Shanon L., Lanza, Lisa, Albajri, Eram, and Nasser, Jenifer A. 2019. "Increasing Chocolate's Sugar Content Enhances its Psychoactive Effects and Intake." *Nutrients,* 11(3), 596; https://doi.org/10.3390/nu11030596.

Chengu, Garikai. 2015. "Xenophobia in South Africa; The Apartheid Legacy of Racism and 'White Corporate Capitalism.'" *Global Research.* Centre for Research on Globalization. www.globalresearch.ca/xenophobia-in-south-africa-the-apartheid-legacy-of-racism-and-white-corporate-capitalism/5443965. Accessed 14 November 2019.

Cooper, Allan D. 2001. *Ovambo Politics in the Twentieth Century.* Lanham, MD: University Press of America.

Cooper, Allan D. 2019. *Patriarchy and the Politics of Beauty.* Lanham, MD: Lexington Books.

Du Bois, W. E. B. 2014. *The World and Africa, and Color and Democracy.* Oxford: Oxford University Press.

Dumett, R. E. 1999. *El Dorado in West Africa: The Gold Mining Frontier, African Labour, and Colonial Capitalism.* Athens, OH: Ohio University Press.

Engerman, Stanley L. Ed. 1999. *Terms of Labor: Slavery, Serfdom, and Free Labor.* Stanford, CA: Stanford University Press.

Farrow, Anne, Lang, Joel, and Frank, Jenifer. 2005. *Complicity: How the North Promoted, Prolonged, and Profited from Slavery.* New York: Ballantine Books.

Frank, Andre Gunder. 1969. *Latin America: Underdevelopment and Revolution.* New York: Monthly Review Press.

Frank, Andre Gunder. 1977. "On So-Called Primitive Accumulation." *Dialectical Anthropology,* 2(2) (May), 87–106.

Gilman, Nils. 2007. *Mandarins of the Future: Modernization Theory in Cold War America.* Baltimore, MD: Johns Hopkins University Press.

Giustozzi, Antonio. 2001. *The Art of Coercion: The Primitive Accumulation and Management of Coercive Power.* New York: Columbia University Press.

Gramsci, Antonio. 1973. *The Prison Notebooks.* London: Lawrence & Wishart.

Harvey, David. 2003. *The New Imperialism.* Oxford: Oxford University Press.

Hirschfeld, Katherine. 2015. *Gangster States: Organized Crime, Kleptocracy and Political Collapse.* London: Palgrave Macmillan.

Hoch, Steven L. 1989. *Serfdom and Social Control in Russia: Petrovskoe, a Village in Tambov.* Chicago, IL: University of Chicago Press.

Jones, Mack H. 2014. *Knowledge, Power and Black Politics.* Albany, NY: State University of New York Press.

Kolhatkar, Sheelah. 2017. *Black Edge: Inside Information, Dirty Money, and the Quest to Bring Down the Most Wanted Man on Wall Street.* New York: Random House.

Konstam, Angus. 2008. *Piracy: The Complete History.* Oxford: Osprey Publishing.

Leeson, Peter T. 2009. *The Invisible Hook: The Hidden Economics of Pirates.* Princeton, NJ: Princeton University Press.

Luxemburg, Rosa. 1951. *The Accumulation of Capital.* New Haven, CT: Yale University Press.

Mamdani, Mahmood. 2018. *Citizen and Subject: Contemporary Africa and the Legacy of Late Colonialism.* Princeton, NJ: Princeton University Press.

Marx, Karl. 1976. "The Poverty of Philosophy." In Karl Marx and Frederick Engels. *Collected Works,* Vol. 6. London: Lawrence & Wishart.

Marx, Karl. 1977. *Capital.* Vol. 1. New York: Vintage.

Mattli, Walter. 2019. *Darkness by Design: The Hidden Power in Global Capital Markets.* Princeton, NJ: Princeton University Press.

Mies, Maria. 1999. *Patriarchy and Accumulation on a World Scale: Women in the International Division of Labour*. London: Zed Press.
Miles, Robert. 1987. *Capitalism and Unfree Labour: Anomaly or Necessity?* London: Tavistock Publications.
Moss, Todd J. 2011. *African Development: Making Sense of the Issues and Actors*. Boulder, CO: Lynne Rienner Publishers.
Neff, Stephen. C. Ed.. 2012. *Hugo Grotius on the Law of War and Peace*. Cambridge: Cambridge University Press.
Nsehe, Mfonobong. 2016. "The African Billionaires 2016." *Forbes,* March 1.
Palmer, Andrew. 2014. *The New Pirates: Modern Global Piracy from Somalia to the South China Sea*. London: I. B. Tauris.
Patnaik, Utsa, and Moyo, Sam. 2011. *The Agrarian Question in the Neoliberal Era: Primitive Accumulation and the Peasantry*. Cape Town: Pambazuka Press.
PBS. 2019. *Black Gold*. www.pbs.org/independentlens/blackgold/economics.html. Accessed December 31, 2019.
Perelman, Michael. 2000. *The Invention of Capitalism: Classical Political Economy and the Secret History of Primitive Accumulation*. Durham, NC: Duke University Press.
Polshikov, P. 1981. *Capital Accumulation and Economic Growth in Developing Africa*. Moscow: Progress Publishers.
Ricardo, David. 2004. *The Principles of Political Economy and Taxation*. London: Dover.
Robbins, Lionel Charles. 1939. *The Economic Basis of Class Conflict and Other Essays*. London: Macmillan.
Robinson, Cedric J. 1983. *Black Marxism: The Making of the Black Radical Tradition*. Chapel Hill, NC: University of North Carolina Press.
Robinson, Ronald, and Gallagher, John. 1961. *Africa and the Victorians: The Official Mind of Imperialism*. London: Palgrave Macmillan.
Rodney, Walter. 1974. *How Europe Underdeveloped Africa*. Washington, DC: Howard University Press.
Roediger, David. 2007. *The Wages of Whiteness: Race and the Making of the American Working Class*. London: Verso.
Roediger, David. 2017. *Class, Race, and Marxism*. London: Verso.
Sanyal, Kalyan. 2013. *Rethinking Capitalist Development: Primitive Accumulation, Governmentality and Post-Colonial Capitalism*. New Delhi: Routledge.
Shelley, Louise I. 2018. *Dark Commerce: How a New Illicit Economy is Threatening our Future*. Princeton, NJ: Princeton University Press.
Shivji, I. G. 2009. *Accumulation in an African Periphery: A Theoretical Framework*. Dar es Salam: Nkuki na Nyota Publishing.
Smith, Adam. 1976. *An Inquiry into the Nature and Causes of the Wealth of Nations*. Edited by R. H. Campbell and A. S. Skinner. 2 vols. New York: Oxford University Press.
Smith, Adam. 1978. *Lectures on Jurisprudence*. Edited by R. L. Meek, D. D. Raphael, and P. G. Stein. Oxford: Clarendon Press.
Sombart, Werner. 1967. *Luxury and Capitalism.*. Ann Arbor, MI: University of Michigan Press.
Stanziani, Alessandro. 2014. *Bondage: Labor and Rights in Eurasia from the Sixteenth to the Early Twentieth Centuries*. Oxford: Berghahn Books.
Statista: Soft Drinks. 2019. www.statista.com/outlook/20020100/100/carbonated-soft-drinks/worldwide. Accessed December 31, 2019.
Statista: Tea. 2019. www.statista.com/statistics/326384/global-tea-beverage-market-size/. Accessed December 31, 2019.

Statista: Tobacco. 2019. www.statista.com/outlook/50000000/100/tobacco-products/worldwide. Accessed December 31, 2019.

Steuart, James. 2019. *An Inquiry into the Principles of Political Oeconomy: Being an Essay on the Science of Domestic Policy in Free Nations, in which are Particularly Considered Population, Agriculture, Trade, Industry, Money*. Miami, FL: HardPress.

Suret-Canale, Jean. 1988. "The End of Chieftaincy in Guinea." In *Essays on African History: From the Slave Trade to Neocolonialism*. Trenton, IL: African World Press.

Tharoor, Avinash. 2017. "Report: Global Drug Trafficking Market Worth Half a Trillion Dollars." *TalkingDrugs,* April 21. www.talkingdrugs.org/report-global-illegal-drug-trade-valued-at-around-half-a-trillion-dollars. Accessed December 31, 2019.

Tomich, Dale. 2003. *Through the Prism of Slavery: Labor, Capital, and World Economy*. Lanham, MD: Rowman & Littlefield.

Vaughn, Liam and Finch, Gavin. 2017. *The Fix: How Bankers Lied, Cheated and Colluded to Rig the World's Most Important Number*. London: Wiley/Bloomberg Press.

Wallerstein, Immanuel. 1974. *The Modern World System*. New York: Academic Press.

Wallerstein, Immanuel. 2004. *World-Systems Analysis: An Introduction*. Durham, NC: Duke University Press.

Williams, Eric. 1994. *Capitalism and Slavery*. Chapel Hill, NC: University of North Carolina Press.

Winch, Donald. Ed. 2017. *James Mill: Selected Economic Writings*. New York: Routledge.

Wood, Ellen Meiksins. 2017. *The Origins of Capitalism: A Longer View*. London: Verso.

Workman, Daniel. 2019. "Crude Oil Exports by Country." December 6. www.worldstopexports.com/worlds-top-oil-exports-country/. Accessed December 31, 2019.

2 Cocoa in Côte d'Ivoire and Ghana

Chocolate and neoliberal capitalism

T. Y. Okosun

Introduction

This chapter focuses on the unequal economic relationship between Western corporations and West African cocoa farmers, specifically in Côte d'Ivoire and Ghana. On the one hand, cocoa generates revenue for both African nations, but for the massive export of this high-quality product to Western corporations, revenue returns are non-proportionate with negligible economic benefit. On the other hand, Western corporations make massive profit and revenue by turning African cocoa beans into chocolate and other products.

African cocoa has become a global product with economic, social and cultural significance. To West Africans farmers, it is a treasured raw material that provides basic income. West African cocoa is nestled in complex colonial, post-colonial and contemporary economic, capitalist and political configurations that leave farmers in perpetually impoverished conditions. Within West Africa, a large part of the small cocoa revenue is used to service international loans; a very small part feeds into negligible internal development, and the rest disappears through the invisible cracks that wind through government leaders and their business friends. To Western corporations, cocoa beans are comparable in value to gold, diamonds and coltan, and hidden behind the scene are the heavy hands of neoliberal capitalism. This economic system drives unbridled and non-compassionate consumerist control of cocoa beans, from farming, market dynamics, and export, to revenue distribution.

To explore this unequal relationship between Western corporations and Côte d'Ivoire and Ghana, four elements regarding cocoa farming and global interaction are highlighted. The first consideration examines the history. This is a necessary background to help recollect the de-emphasized history of Western exploitation of African nations. The second focus of attention is the indirect (yet direct) control of cocoa beans by Western markets and interests. These interests are generally sustained by inflexible neoliberal capitalist rules that construct advantages only in one direction, namely massive profits to the West. The third consideration is the exploitation of African labor (women, men and children) who farm and produce cocoa beans for the ultimate benefit of Western corporations. This delineates the absence of collaborative benefits: a loss for African cocoa farmers but a win for Western corporations.

The fourth consideration examines future prospects in terms of whether Côte d'Ivoire and Ghana would be able to stand their ground and take complete control of their cocoa production, marketing and export. Such a move may help them substantively, bringing much needed revenue for internal development and improving their global economic standing. Within the fourth reflection, a discussion of global economic/market ethics adds to the global clamor for fair economic exchange. The chapter concludes with a brief discussion of several ideas on how West Africa and Western corporations may collaborate on developing socio-economic transformation options that are useful for sustaining better life chances for cocoa farmers.

European exploitation of Africa

The direct and coercive beginning of the exploitation of African human and raw materials began in the 1400s with Portugal (SAHO 2019). Prior to that, West Africa had been one of the academic, creative and trade nodes of Africa, connecting Northwest and West Africa to East Africa and beyond through the Saharan transit interaction (Davidson 1991, 77–128; Meredith 2016, 71; see also Diop 1974). West Africans even used their interactive globalization to connect and interact with the Americas before Europeans got there (see Van Sertima 1976).

The Portuguese began by roaming West and East African coasts for raw materials, and then (and soon followed by other Europeans) quickly expanded into exploitation of Africans for labor and other primitive accumulation activities, including forced slavery (SAHO 2019; Terreblanche 2014, 199; Ryan 2011). African subjugation into slavery spanned much of Europe's colonial empire, especially the Americas (Killingray 1987; UNESCO 1979). The exploitation of raw materials and the removal of Africans from their continent involved considerable violence (Terreblanche 2014, 349–355). By the middle of the 1600s, the shipping of Africans, condemned into slavery, to Europe and the Americas had become a massive capitalist venture, sustaining Europeans for the centuries of capitalist development that followed. Slavery deprived Africans of advantages and advances. They labored for hundreds of years to build economies for Europe, the United States and the rest of the Americas (Terreblanche 2014, 507).

During the exploitation of Africans and raw materials, European exploitative behaviors empowered several European organizations (European African and Geographic Societies) to penetrate into the interior of Africa, with the intention to occupy the entire continent. By 1650, the Dutch had a permanent camp in what is now South Africa, with English, Germans, French and others following on the rest of the continent. By the later years of the 1700s, Europe began funding expeditions to the interior of the African continent (for instance, Mungo Park and David Livingstone) (Meredith 2016, 190, 261). Colonization followed with the intention to completely own Africa. England, Belgium and Portugal used brutal coercion, and the French used inclusion subterfuge to bind its section of Africa to France (Meredith 2005). Australia, New Zealand and the Americas became overwhelmed with mass illegal migration of Europeans who violently took over these lands. In the European scramble for Africa, the Berlin Conference of 1884–1885 (SAHO 2019) divided Africa up, prompting the most destructive European colonial behavior on a continent (Terreblanche 2014, 309).

Africa's fate could have followed that of the Americas, Australia and New Zealand, but for African resistance and the impenetrability of Africa's interior. Still, European exploitation forced Africans into subservience and disadvantages. In addition, Africans became the content of negative narratives (Camara 2005) in Europe and the Americas, dehumanizing and casting them as low-life and irrational entities only fit for physical labor. In several instances, Africans were massacred for resisting, insubordination and/or for asserting their self-determination (Terreblanche 2014, 78–89). These exploitative behaviors subverted Africans' histories, philosophies, astronomy, religions, cultures, architectures, democracy and early scientific knowledge. Important commerce and learning centers (Timbuktu, Khartoum, Jenne and others) were de-emphasized. African leaders, such as Sunni Ali and Mansa Kankar Musa, and the well-organized empires of Mali, Songhai and Benin that were sources of gold and other raw materials were destroyed; meanwhile, human beings were forced into slavery (Meredith 2016, 77). Europeans funded expeditions and paid out rewards to many eager explorers – August René Caillié who got to Timbuktu, and Richard and John Lander who got to the end of the Niger River (Davidson 1991, 319) – all in attempts to reach the interior of Africa. Eurocentric narratives largely ignored or suppressed the innovative and leadership roles African women played within Africa. Three examples suffice here. Fatima al-Fihri founded the oldest university in the world, Al Qarawiyyin University, in Fez, Morocco in 859 (Arbaoui 2012). Queen Aminatu of Zazzau, the 16th-century powerful leader, secured trade routes and consolidated northwest areas of Nigeria (Khumalo 2020). And, Yaa Asantemwaa, the 19th-century Ghanaian powerful leader and warriorfought against the British in Ghana, preventing them from having access to the Golden Stool, and won (Hawkins 2018).

Hidden beneath Eurocentric narratives of colonial history are indelible facts. Africans, more so than Europeans, own a vast and diverse continent filled with abundant resources. Africans were never at any time irrational or low-life. They were the origin of humanity and the first explorers who populated the globe, thereby giving life to everyone (Stringer and McKie 1996). They set up early civilizations, complete with all kinds of early learning from which the West (once upon a time Africans) copied. African agricultural knowledge domesticated wildlife and plants (see Veen 1999). They understood seasons and conditions and how to manage their lives within them. Long before Europeans came along, Africans mined gold, silver and other natural ores. Africans understood the value of gold and adorned their world with its open display as jewelry, throne decoration (Golden Stool of Ghana), gifts and commercial exchange (Diop 1987, 105–106).

Europe's ultimate intention to take possession of the entire continent was spurred on by Africa's vast resources, favorable geographic and weather conditions, and imperial capitalism eager for primitive accumulation. Over the centuries, Western markets increasingly became bullish and inflexible, controlling raw materials, mineral mining and life chances on the African continent (see Seabrook 2001; Terreblanche 2014). Even the reconstruction of Africa's histories – to highlight its past resplendence and its current contributions to the globe (see UNESCO 2019 – *General History of Africa*, volumes 1 to 11) – are of no consequence to European markets. Cocoa, gold, diamonds, coltan, wildlife, are more important to global markets than the well-being of Africa's peoples. These cheaply sourced raw materials sustain corporate accumulation and capitalist economies at the expense of Africans and their human rights and dignity. Fair-trade rules are of no consequence because foreign capitalist activities regarding African resources are unidirectional and unilateral. This has been true since slavery and colonization, and continued during neo-colonization to the present time.

Cocoa revenue: Côte d'Ivoire, Ghana and beyond

Cocoa (or cacao) has an extensive history. It was in South America during the Maya and Aztec empires. Named Theobroma Cacao, the crop appeared in equatorial regions (including West Africa), and by the 1860s it was already popularly used as a beverage in Europe. The cocoa pods are harvested, cut open to extract cocoa seeds (cocoa beans), then fermented, cleaned and prepared (Cook 1982). By the 1950s in Africa, Ghana, Côte d'Ivoire, Cameroon and Nigeria emerged as large producers. In the 1960s, Ghana was the largest cocoa producer but was overtaken by Côte d'Ivoire in the 1970s. Côte d'Ivoire produces about 1.8 million metric tons of cocoa beans, about 40 percent of world production (Yock 2018), and Ghana produces about 900,000 metric tons of cocoa beans, about 20 percent, together comprising approximately 60 percent of the world's annual cocoa beans (GhanaWeb 2019). The revenue generated by the two nations exporting cocoa beans is only $6 billion ($4 billion for Côte d'Ivoire, and $2 billion for Ghana) compared to the $100 billion distributed among European corporations and privateers (GhanaWeb 2019).

In addition to poor revenue, West Africans contend with aging cocoa trees, global warming and European statements about cocoa surplus on the global market (GhanaWeb 2019). In 2017, Côte d'Ivoire was compelled to slash prices by 36 percent, and the country thus lost $1.1 billion in revenue (Yock 2018), further reducing West African cocoa revenue. Because West African cocoa farming accounts for millions of jobs, including about 1.3 million child laborers (Yock 2018), diminished revenue is economically and socially detrimental. Côte d'Ivoire cocoa farmers only make $0.97 per day, and Ghanaian farmers about

$0.40 to $0.45 per day, so much less than the global minimum wage of $1.90 per day (Yock 2018). In this scenario, global rules regarding human rights and fairness in revenue distribution proportionate to goods and services do not include West Africans.

West African cocoa farmers face other complications. For instance, when parts of their farms fail to yield, or when Western nations impose high tariffs on exports, there are no government bailouts. When ill-health or adverse conditions take them out of farming, they lose everything. Compensation for their labor is non-existent because buyers only focus on cocoa beans in bags. To successfully increase quality and high yield, farmers sacrifice personal and family well-being, often dragging their children into labor and disregarding health and quality of life issues.

Cocoa: West African social experience

Social and economic experiences in Côte d'Ivoire and Ghana are somewhat defined by and around cocoa. For instance, in the 1960s and early 1970s, Ghanaian citizens used income from cocoa to build homes and send their children to school, with many of them receiving Cocoa Marketing Board Farmers' scholarships (Ghana Cocoa Board 2020b). Cocoa was so important that the University of Ghana had a residence hall named Akuafo (Farmers) Hall (Ghana Cocoa Board 2020b). Tetteh Quarshie had an interchange named after him for bringing cocoa seeds from Equatorial Guinea into Ghana in 1876 to start his own farm (Essegbey and Ofori-Gyamfi 2012). By the 2000s, the vibrant relationship between Ghanaians and cocoa farming somewhat diminished due to urbanization and social decentering wrought by unidirectional globalization. Today, the streets and market stores of Accra and other cities bubble with all kinds of non-revenue-producing products dumped into Ghana by Europe and China.

Despite reductions in interest in cocoa production, Ghana, the world's second largest producer after Côte d'Ivoire, has approximately 800,000 farmers, who work on 1.9 million hectares of land in six of its ten regions to generate its yearly 900,000 metric tons of cocoa, about $2 billion annual revenue (Ghana Cocoa Board 2020a). A majority (67.6 percent) of Ghana's cocoa export ends up in Western Europe (Netherlands: 33.8 percent, United Kingdom: 12.1, Belgium: 8.9, Germany: 3.6). Japan and the United States receive 7.2 and 3.3 percent respectively. Unfortunately, despite Ghana's cocoa exports and revenue, most farmers live in poverty, with yearly incomes between $983.12 and $2,627.81 (ICI 2017).

To many citizens of Côte d'Ivoire, the world's largest cocoa producer, cocoa farming is usually an important channel of basic income. Cocoa revenue also sustains government, education, housing and some infrastructure (Adams 2019). Yet, when West Africans attempt to set cocoa prices to their own advantage, they often meet with backlash from Western corporations (CNBCAfrica, 2019) that seek cheap cocoa beans. To fight the interests of West Africans, Western corporations lobby and muster the powers of their governments for trade policy support, the consequence of which traps Africa farmers in perpetual low wages.

As recently as 2018, Côte d'Ivoire and Ghana set a floor price of $2,600 per ton of cocoa beans (CNBCAfrica 2019; Yock 2018). Even though the set price is not enough to correct the existing inequalities in revenue, it is West Africa's way of attempting to throw ethics and conscience into the cocoa market. Africans assume that Western corporations will not walk away from a region that produces a whopping 65 percent of global cocoa. While West Africans struggle to gain their footing in the global market, a World Bank economist concludes that Côte d'Ivoire only makes about 8 percent of total profit from the trade in cocoa/chocolate (Morisset 2019). Morisset's assessment appears to blame Côte d'Ivoire for not utilizing its cocoa resources to develop and sustain a national economic engine. Further, he points out that Côte d'Ivoire does not have two major components to complete the cycle of cocoa and chocolate control and ownership, namely internal processing and chocolate manufacturing. Morisset's assessment fails to recognize that decades of exploitation by the International Monetary Fund (IMF), World Bank, Western corporations and Western governments place various destructive obstacles to Africa's economies and development (see Terreblanche 2014, 507–510).

Morisset's report joins others (see John Ffooks & Co. n.d.) that paint Côte d'Ivoire as a nation simply caught up in internal and political turmoil, without ever accounting for massive external interference. These reports conclude that Côte d'Ivoire ought to get its act together and plant new cocoa trees to replace aging ones. This presumably will get West African cocoa production primed and ready for more years of Western exploitation. Nestlé, a Swiss corporation, uses similar tactics to subtly flex its imperialist and capitalist muscle. It offered $2.7 million (a pittance compared to the revenue they make in chocolate production) to Côte d'Ivoire to help fight deforestation (Peel 2020). The Swiss solution, similar to the behavior of other Western corporations, is to throw small crumbs to secure full and continued access to West African cocoa beans. These corporations are aware that whatever monies they throw at initiatives to protect raw materials for themselves, most often these funds never get to cocoa farmers. They are indirect ways to titillate West African government leaders to enact favorable policies, fight deforestation and preserve cocoa bean production for Westerners.

It is useful to point out that Nestlé does not concern itself with Morisset's assessment which urges that indigenous processing and chocolate production should be developed within West Africa. This means that many Western corporations are not interested in Africans acquiring or developing technologies and chains of production to challenge European control of chocolate, cocoa liquor, butter and other products for the global market. The few dollar crumbs here and there, and simulated interest in helping African cocoa farmers, endear them to African leaders, who quietly support the prolonging of poverty, underdevelopment and miserable farming conditions.

It is important to their national interests that Côte d'Ivoire and Ghana stand their ground by insisting on $2,600 per ton of cocoa beans. Already, several Western corporations, for instance Lindt & Spruengli AG (Gretler and de Sousa 2020), are stoking Western markets by projecting price hikes of chocolate products. This is a message to Western consumers to view West Africans as problematic players who indiscriminately jack up cocoa bean prices (part of the narrative of African irrationality). In this configuration, capitalist accumulation does not care to understand that the sources which make their accumulation possible are as important as the profit they make.

In other words, the needs and interests of Western consumers disregard the massive inequality and poverty that capitalist sourcing of cocoa imposes on cocoa farmers, their families and their nations. When Africans ask for fair play on the global marketplace, they are met with countering economic and market manipulative psychology and already entrenched negative narratives about Africa (see Bush 2006, 135–137). For Westerners, the set price of $2,600 per ton of cocoa beans, though a pittance compared to Western accumulation, is spun as the fault of West Africans jacking up cocoa prices, hence the increase in chocolate prices. Unfortunately, even with a set price, exploitative capitalism knows no boundary to the unbridled accumulation that harms African nations.

Another way to understand this behavior is to point to a concern raised by Nigeria's Aviation Minister, Hadi Sirika, who remarked on the difference in British Airways fares from Accra, Ghana, to Heathrow, London, and from Lagos, Nigeria, to Heathrow (the shorter distance). Sirika was informed by a British Airways representative that Nigerians were charged more because they could afford it (Akeredolu-Ale 2020). This is part of the incomprehensible logic of exploitative capitalism. British Airways charges less for Accra–Heathrow, possibly to groom Ghana as a future cash cow, but makes up for Ghana's lower fare by charging Nigerians more. In this scenario, both nations are exploited by British Airways, a function that sustains capitalist accumulation at the expense of Africans.

Cocoa farming and capitalist exploitation

Since the "end" of European colonization of Africa (Ghana in 1957, Côte d'Ivoire in 1960), Africa's raw materials have remained indispensable economic staples for Europe and beyond. It is rare that Western corporations ever slash the prices of their own manufactured goods and services to favor African nations. Transactions with Africa are designed to favor foreign capitalist markets, forcing Africans to pay exorbitant prices for European goods and bank services. Additionally, Africans are forced to settle for extremely low revenue from products exported to Westerners (or otherwise to suffer economically). Despite the massive export of cocoa beans, African cocoa farmers live in poverty and desperate conditions (see Von Dacre 2019). Richard Scobey (President, World Cocoa Foundation) recognizes that the exploitative conditions of child labor and poverty remain the central issue of inequality in cocoa production and revenue (Scobey 2020). But many Western corporations and systems, aware of these desperate conditions, insist on European superiority as the foundation of their wealth (see Landes 1998), and also maintain that Africa's plight is due to internal corruption and inept leadership. It is possible that many African leaders are corrupt (see Moyo 2009), but there is no doubt that such behaviors were constructed by past imperial, colonial and neo-colonial factors, and continue to be exacerbated by current powerful external interference such as accumulation, regime change, adverse policies and sanctions (see Terreblanche 2014).

For these reasons, much of West Africa remains mostly stagnant and heavily dependent on the IMF and the World Bank, two major anchors of neoliberal capitalism. This exploitative logic forces Africans into perpetual need, subservience and dependence on Western systems (Moyo 2009). Because revenue from cocoa and other natural resources exports are not enough to sustain these nations, many African leaders erratically tilt towards loans from the West and now also from China. In their desperation to survive, they neglect the implications loans may have for their future self-determination and sovereignty. Consequently, because social and economic conditions fail to improve, many West Africans – dissatisfied with menial or no jobs at all – take to the seas in rickety dinghies and migrate to Europe (Pew Research Center 2018; UN News 2019) where they are often unwelcome and face further humiliation.

Meanwhile, cocoa from Côte d'Ivoire and Ghana ranks next to gold and diamonds in generating profits for foreign capitalist markets. Cocoa beans are transformed into chocolate delights in Europe, the United States and beyond. The point here is not to disparage the ingenuity of transforming cocoa beans into delicacies and desired products, but to remark on the use of market violence to exploit Africans and their products. Though Japan, and more vehemently China, have successfully insulated themselves from Western control, they have also long sought access to African resources on their own terms (Sun 2014; also see Lee 2017). However, the most burdensome exploitation is marked by European trade and market rules which generally devalue African resources and standing on the global scene. This devaluation offers a clue as to why the massive export of cocoa, petroleum, bananas, palm oil and other products have not helped to significantly improve the lives of West African farmers and their nations.

Years ago, Rodney (1972) pointed to some of the ways Europe exploited and underdeveloped Africa (imperial manipulation and economic extraction). However, by the 1980s and 1990s, the exploitation had reached a fever pitch. Instead of helping, IMF and World Bank loans (with high interest rates) and initiatives complicated, and in some ways crippled, many African nations (see Moyo 2009). Africans still spend much of their hard-earned revenues on servicing billions of dollars of international loans (United World 2020), while Western and Chinese corporations quietly exploit African resources. They do so amid the underdevelopment, hoping that no substantive African advancement and development ever emerge to be an impediment to their unbridled control and accumulation.

For instance, in negotiations to end apartheid, Nelson Mandela acceded to White South Africans' control of their Western driven economic configuration. South Africa transitioned from apartheid to "economic apartheid" which still controls South Africa's gold, diamonds, wildlife and other resources for export to the Western world. Apartheid supposedly ended in 1994, but in 2020, most indigenous (Black) South Africans still suffer from its legacy and continue to experience fundamental disadvantages (Amnesty International 2020; Terreblanch, 2002).

Even in Zimbabwe, Robert Mugabe's African-led defeat of Ian Smith's apartheid government had continued destructive economic consequences for Zimbabwe. This would be similar to the Haitian revolution by African slaves who defeated the French (between 1789 and 1804) and gave Haiti its independence (Ott 1999). That independence eventually led to a Western imposed paralysis on Haiti, making it now the poorest nation in the Western Hemisphere (see Farmer 2005, 86).

The 5 percent of the population of Europeans in Zimbabwe, who owned approximately three-quarters of all farmland in that country (see Dzirutwe, 2019), focused on trade and exported raw materials directly to Europe, accumulating much of their capital in Europe rather than for Zimbabwe. Mugabe's decision in 2000 to seize some farms and place them in indigenous hands landed him and Zimbabwe a death blow (Dzirutwe 2019). Mugabe and Zimbabwe were thrown under the crushing bus of "global" market punishment.

It is useful to point out here that not even compassionate Europeans in Africa or elsewhere are allowed to change capitalist accumulation rules. Mugabe, supported by compassionate Europeans within and outside of Africa, pursued capitalism to improve the lives of Zimbabweans. But he failed to spur massive innovation and to empower indigenous self-determination and self-sustenance. Mugabe's dictatorial greed, inflexibility, corruption and stoking of ethnic divisions, common among African leaders (save for Thomas Sankara and later Jerry Rawlings), are conditions Westerners exploit against African nations. For asserting self-determination, Mugabe pulled the "suicide trigger" on himself and Zimbabwe. Most Zimbabweans focused their anger squarely on Mugabe, the erratic and corrupt dictator. Unfortunately, hidden from their sight were the invisible hands of Western power and markets. These invisible powers simultaneously gnawed at Mugabe as the culprit, cheered Zimbabweans on as innocent victims of a dictator, while tactically tearing down Zimbabwe's economy.

Here is a less plausible but possible angle to Western exploitation. Suppose that Côte d'Ivoire and Ghana decisively take control of their cocoa, shift exports to China, and produce their own chocolate. Western retribution would be instantaneous. This may come in the form of employing Monsanto, Cargil and other biogenetic groups, who may already possess genetically reconfigured African cocoa seeds. Monsanto and other biogenetic groups play god with seeds and can adversely control food production, a concern raised by Shiva in the documentary *Seed* (Betz and Siegel 2016). Shiva clarifies this danger and encourages indigenous seed collection and protection. In other words, biogenetic seed control can produce a denial of production, similar to the denial of service in the computing world. In this scenario, cocoa farms in Côte d'Ivoire and Ghana may be biogenetically attacked, while Westerners approach money-strapped and vulnerable African and Latin American nations on the same equatorial belt to grow and produce cocoa beans. Most of these nations would be unable to protest because of the legacies of animosity against each other sewn into their colonial and post-colonial psyches.

Exploitation, poverty and affluence

Generally, no matter what information on inequality is presented to readers, those inebriated with negation find ways to insist that such conditions are brought about by African indolence and incapability. This later position notwithstanding, inequalities between Western and African nations continue to soar because of deliberate global economic arrangements (see Moellendorf 2009; Osberg 2018).

Côte d'Ivoire and Ghana began significant exports of cocoa in the 1960s. The negotiations for independence depended on new African leaders agreeing to the economic conditions laid down by their European predecessors. At the time, new African leaders dealt with Europeans in terms of collaboration. In agreeing to European terms for independence, they may not have foreseen that such arrangements would create eventual economic and other deficiencies in Africa, maintaining African natural resources under European global market control. Part of the catch was endearing new African leaders and politicians to Western, upper-class and high-society lifestyles, which included dependence on European processed products. Many were rewarded with trips to Europe for European education or pleasure, with the hope of infusing them with Eurocentric ideas on economics, militarism and affinity to Europeans, who soon called in favors for different raw materials.

Within Africa, cocoa, diamonds, gold, copper and other mineral products are regimented into foreign capitalist corporate control. In South Africa, for instance, instead of collaboration, Europeans in South Africa hoarded everything and excluded indigenous South Africans from access to their diamond and gold wealth. Indigenous Africans were exploited as poorly paid miners and farmers, expelled from their own lands, and forced into unbelievable hardship and squalid camps, which were eventually patched together as townships. After apartheid, European South Africans still control the Diamond Trading Company (Terreblanche 2002).

Moreover, daily hard labor on cocoa farms that draws children away from school into cheap labor occurs in unbearable conditions. Here, West African adults and children, their labor and their cocoa beans are undervalued. Whereas Western corporations make tremendous profit from cocoa, West African cocoa farmers are at the mercy of poor infrastructure. There are no emergency medical intervention units in the state-of-the-art medical centers abundant across the nation to respond to their conditions. There are no expert doctors who train specifically to handle the kinds of problems and illnesses that cocoa farmers experience. There are no specializations in the regions of cocoa production either in Côte d'Ivoire or Ghana which focus on farming transformation. It is simply accepted that cocoa farming is a low-class and dirty job, done by low-class, "undeserving" West African farmers. In 2020, most farmers barely have basic necessities such as farming equipment and accessories. Adult and child cocoa workers rely on machetes and, to move their products, many roads in and out of small communities are unpaved and difficult to drive on.

Côte d'Ivoire and Ghana's entanglement with capitalist accumulation is fraught with difficulties. Exploitative capitalism is not interested in shared collective benefits. Rather, it focuses on subjective, non-negotiating action to drain resources from everywhere on the planet. This accounts for why there is no concerted global outrage or response to eliminate child labor on cocoa farms. In other parts of the globe, any opposition to capitalist exploitative behavior often meets with the abandonment of local laborers, mostly women and children (see Moyers 2003). Capitalist exploitation rejects any attempt to temper its behavior, and never thinks of its adverse impact on the human dignity and rights of exploited global citizens, or of the health of their environment.

Comparative labor and fair compensation

Consider the difference between African labor on cocoa farms and European labor in chocolate production. It may not occur to Europeans that cocoa farmers in Côte d'Ivoire and Ghana are natural agricultural engineers, whose hard labor, sweat and physical work with machetes produce cocoa beans. Consumers in European and other nations are mostly oblivious of hardworking and ill-equipped West African farmers and child laborers.

All European chocolate producers depend mostly on products (cocoa beans, sugar, salt, lecithin, vanilla, fruits, nuts, etc.) from the hard labor of poor farmers in poor nations. These imported materials and ingredients are combined to create exotic tastes that titillate, if not addict, consumers into chocolate consumption. Overall, Western European corporations generate billions of dollars of revenue from chocolate sales which end up in the hands of a few wealthy individuals. None of that revenue goes to fairly and adequately compensate West African cocoa farmers for their incredible hard labor and high-quality cocoa beans.

The question of fair and adequate compensation for cocoa beans and the labor involved to produce them still lingers. Exploitation of child labor remains the gravest concern (Balch 2018; Guilbert 2017; O'Keefe 2016). Even the expressed commitment (see Sethi 2018) to resolve child labor by Mars, Hershey, Ferrero, Nestlé and Kraft Foods by 2020 mostly yielded minimal results. What if cocoa was only grown in Europe and the United States? Would Western systems allow child labor, or even allow Africans to have access to the product, let alone buy the beans cheaply? Would Westerners allow African stock markets prospectors in Abidjan, Accra or Lagos to set fluctuating market prices for cocoa beans?

Were cocoa grown and farmed in Europe and North America, Africans probably would not have access to the product, save to buy the beans at prohibitive prices. Farm labor to produce the crop would overwhelmingly involve slave labor, much like the kind drawn from low-waged migrant and undocumented workers who work in vegetable, fruits, poultry, hog and other farms (see Gross and Honig 2020). After harvest, the products would be sold to generate billions of dollars, but much of that money would not reach poor low-waged workers. In this hypothetical scenario, poor low-waged workers in the West would not be treated any differently than cocoa farmers in West Africa – always exploited in primitive accumulation.

This brings us to concerns regarding global changing conditions. Development, advancement, technologies, standards of living, rules of law and economic opportunities appear to be useful for Western populations. However, Westerners prefer these developments for themselves, and are often not interested in collaborating with groups they have disadvantaged to create similar living and economic standards. This is clearly because the nature of under-development in terms of technology, infrastructure, healthcare and economic opportunities plays into the narratives that shape Western policies regarding Africa and its resources. African cheapened resources generally leave Africa with alacrity and without discrimination. But Africans seeking improvements and desire for inclusive interaction with Europeans are routinely excluded, with even subtle actions such as visa denial to enter Europe or North America. While their lives are devalued, their cheaply accessed natural resources seamlessly move to the West. Something appears to sustain this disconnection. It may be that Westerners are aware and afraid that full development in Africa may expose Western deficiencies and force the West to render reparations and to play by ethical global market rules.

One of the most difficult parts of delineating Western exploitation of Africa's raw materials is not having access to the secret meetings in many board rooms across Europe, the United States and China. Imaginably, wealthy capitalists most probably laugh at the sheer ease with which they push over so many African leaders to gain access to African raw materials. They revel in the shrewdness of their forefathers who planned things out in ways that are now beneficial to the current generation. In turn, they callously pledge to keep things that way for their own future generations. Africa, then, faces continued exploitation to enrich Europeans and others.

Then there is the concern about parity. Since millions of tons of cocoa beans leave Côte d'Ivoire and Ghana for Europe and the rest of the world, capitalist rules for equal exchange ought to apply so that Africans should receive equivalent or proportionate revenue. All things being equal, some of this revenue might then be used to improve the challenging conditions that still exist in African cocoa farming communities. For instance, some of the revenue might be used to build good roads, good housing, good and abundant healthcare systems, technologies, processing plants, chocolate producing systems and other essential infrastructure.

Unfortunately, in the case of African cocoa producers and European markets, parity is not a useful economic constant or even a variable. The revenue from cocoa beans export is unequivocally a pittance. The governments of Côte d'Ivoire and Ghana appear to spend much of the little revenue they receive on servicing international loans, inadvertently feeding the revenue back to Europe and the IMF, while neglecting major internal development. Western consumers with their individual struggles do not often consider poor farming conditions and child labor in Africa. Most consumers, disregarding these conditions, assume that humanitarian organizations such as fair-trade groups would help. But not even humanitarian groups are able to dent the massive problems of underdevelopment created by decades of exploitation.

Even with Europeans buying fair-trade cocoa and chocolate, African farmers must still produce millions of tons of cocoa beans every year, without much internal and external support. The minor monetary support from fair-trade organizations in Europe was never designed to create parity, but rather served as a sort of "band-aid" in the mist of massive capitalist exploitation. In fact, the crumbly support that fair-trade NGOs offer only appear to prop these farmers up, mostly leaving their difficult conditions largely intact. Even in these difficult conditions, farmers are expected to produce more cocoa beans, which are still cheaply accessed by Western markets. Since there is no parity in terms of export and revenue, even NGOs and their fair-trade activism have unwittingly sustained the logic of capitalist exploitation which largely leaves African cocoa farmers poor, and millions of children still exploited without the education necessary to obtain meaningful lives.

Capitalism and ethical consciousness

The considerations of capitalism and ethics are still important for global behavior. Unfortunately, capitalism and ethics have very different meanings depending on the part of the world where they are discussed. When Western capitalism is applied to Africa, Westerners tend to follow no ethical rules. African bodies had and still continue to only have value for Europeans capitalists only as exploited labor for primitive accumulation. This began when Europeans changed the rules of interaction with Africans centuries ago, opening the way for their enslavement. Until this capitalist logic that devalues African bodies is discontinued, Europeans may never see themselves as co-participants with Africans on a global scene where revenue from the earth's resources is used to take care of each other. Ethical capitalism provides equal opportunity and parity, but exploitative capitalism is hinged on manipulating labor to extract massive profits at the expense of laborers, their families and communities. At the ethical realm, there has never been any constructive African and European interaction, so that collaborative profit sharing is the standard modus operandi. Instead, the normalized standard remains the exploitative capitalist drive to access raw materials, bought at the lowest price possible, without concern whether African farmers or miners have good health, live or die. The focus is always on raw materials, cocoa, wildlife, safaris, gold, diamonds, coltan, petroleum and much more.

So, what ought Côte d'Ivoire and Ghana do to sustain their cocoa product and stand their ground in terms of demanding equity? They ought to set yearly cocoa beans prices based on chocolate sales and consumption in Europe and beyond, which they have done, and they need to set an agenda for collaborative development, something to which they have always been open. The simplest solution is always the best, as reasoned by William of Ockham (1285–1347), because in global market arrangements, complexity hides abuses. In the United States, for instance, there are so many laws in each state so that the aggregate of laws across the nation drowns the true nature and quest for justice.

The point here is that exploitative capitalism tries to control global resources with complex market laws. Complexity and mystification of the rules of engagement help with exploitation. In this configuration, many poor cocoa farmers may never find out who and what is destroying and ripping their world apart. It is useful to link the past to the present by pointing out that enslaving Africans and colonizing Africa helped provide an advantageous platform for Europeans to develop ways to manipulate global markets and economic conditions (Terreblanche 2014). This exploitative logic is also used to devalue Blacks living within Europe, the United States, Australia, New Zealand and Canada. It is also used to exclude Africans from entering and visiting European nations. Africans who stay in their respective nations are forced to endure global arrangements organized in Europe, North America and beyond. Within Africa, they are forced to endure neo-slave conditions on farms and mining pits to furnish raw materials to European corporations, while they live with poor health, poor roads, poor equipment and minimal compensation.

The only option Westerners have for Africa is the demand that Africans accept to survive under European global control, albeit as third- or fourth-class global citizens or entities. Unfortunately, when Africans raise objections to the exploitative nature of global capitalism, Westerners devise more punitive ways to increase exploitation, control or exclusion. African leaders who capitulate and endorse Western exploitation of their resources are given monetary compensations (bribery). Buying off African leaders is a decades-long tactic used to soften them up to accept Western market conditions.

Prospects for the future

In 2018, Côte d'Ivoire and Ghana set the cocoa beans price at $2,600 per ton. This is an attempt to change market rules to be slightly more useful to cocoa farmers and national revenue, but foreign buyers remain elusive because of their addiction to cheap access. There appears to be a way to broach the subject of parity in terms of revenue between Africans and Westerners. Aside from the competitive obstacle that China poses to Westerners, a starting point would be to accept that Europe and North America are tremendous global economic powers. From this perspective, perhaps a commonsense appeal for ethical behavior may help Westerners to see that African resources, which they cheaply acquire and monopolize, ought to provide equal or proportionate revenue to both Africans and Westerners. In this interactive globalization, true and sensible market ethics would require that African cocoa farmers receive similar or comparable wages ($10 per hour, a great starting point) that Europeans would expect to receive were they actual cocoa farmers and workers in Europe or the United States.

The first prospect to consider here is whether Côte d'Ivoire and Ghana, and the set cocoa price, can take complete control of their cocoa production, marketing and export to improve revenue. Setting a floor price of $2,600 per ton of cocoa aims to improve life chances for cocoa farmers, the value of cocoa produce and larger revenue. To stand their ground, both Côte d'Ivoire and Ghana have laid out a reduction of cocoa exports for 2020/2021 until an agreement is reached on their demand to accept the basic floor price of $2,600 for a ton of cocoa. Will they continue to hold their ground?

It is useful to remark that, for more than 50 years, both nations have suffered economic losses because Western capitalist market manipulations have always devalued Africans and their resources, forcing them, in most scenarios, to accept depreciation, low market values and consequently tragic economic consequences. Setting a floor price for cocoa is a painful outcry to the Western world that its exploitation needs to stop. From assessing the revenue made from cocoa by Ghana and Côte d'Ivoire, about 2 percent of that made by Western corporations on chocolate and other products from cocoa beans, a floor price of $2,600 is still pittance compared to years of exploitation or the sudden effort to recover current losses.

The second prospect considers the idea that Ghana and Côte d'Ivoire may be able to drive responsible economic and market ethics into Western corporations to encourage and sustain positive and fair-trade changes. This move may help to sustain global ethical (legal) regulations that encourage constructive and positive behaviors from individuals and corporations in nations that desire West African cocoa beans. To cause such a change would be to have economic resources to ameliorate many internal national conditions and increase revenue for responding to other national issues (agricultural infrastructure, healthcare and transportation).

The third prospect considers internal government and private sectors in West Africa, and why it is useful for them to collaborate in constructing a more stable market experience for farmers, West African cocoa processors and African prospectors. Responding to inequalities and quality of life issues depends on good governance and consistent public policies that use taxation, tariffs and revenues from export and other sales to develop national systems, bringing needed infrastructure (good roads, advanced freight train system and incentives to adult labor) to local processing so as to further increase the value of cocoa farming and the product. This prospect would also include doing whatever it takes to close the gap that Morisset (2019) spoke about in his assessment, namely, to develop cocoa bean processing and chocolate-making facilities across their nations. These products could be sold all over Africa to generate more revenue.

On the part of Western Europeans, it is now obvious that inconsistent and half-hearted ephemeral responses, for instance, Tony Chocolate in the Netherlands, and the now forgotten blood diamonds charade, have not done much to improve lives in Africa. Even Western governments, fair-trade activists, the IMF and World Bank activities still leave Africa largely exposed to inflexible capitalist exploitation. In the end, the solution may simply lie in Europeans everywhere choosing to adopt compassionate and ethical behaviors in their trade dealing with Africa. European governments and corporations can insist that all cocoa workers in Africa, Western buyers and chocolate producers have parity of exchange in terms of equally distributed proportionate revenue, an approach applicable to other natural resources.

This would reduce or eliminate the angst of activist fair-trade NGOs and conscience titillated chocolate makers who watch helplessly as conditions in Africa hardly improve. Following capitalist market rules, when chocolate consumption increases, so should the price per ton of cocoa beans. This, according to capitalist arrangements, ought to give access to shared equity in terms of revenues. Layers of exploitation include international loans that trap Africans in perpetual underdevelopment. For this reason, European governments, the IMF, the World Bank and powerful Western corporations ought to consider reparations to Africa for centuries of exploitation beginning with loan forgiveness. On their part, African leaders, mindful of the dire need for national development, would use cocoa and other revenues to advance their nations rather than use them to pay down international loans.

From a different angle, Africans can straddle both the Western and Asian worlds. While negotiating with Westerners on commonsense and ethical market rules, they can use China's model of self-determination and self-development to improve their internal conditions. The China model may work for African nations if they are willing to function as a unit (African Union) without the excesses of national and ethnic allegiances. For advancement, Africa has plenty of already developed technologies they can tap into and replicate for infrastructure. Such growth and expansion require massive revenue, as well as ethical commitment on the part of European and Asian corporations to offer proportionate revenue for products procured from Africa. The final part of the puzzle of internal development would be for Westerners to stop using high tariffs to stifle Africa's internal entrepreneurial activities, for instance, chocolate confectionary development in Côte d'Ivoire, Ghana and Nigeria. For these prospects to work, African leaders would need to eradicate their corruptive propensities, realign cocoa and other revenues for internal development and focus on negotiating with Westerners and China for loan forgiveness.

Conclusion

This chapter has focused on four considerations. Revisiting an essential historical background was useful for recollecting an easily forgotten history of Western exploitation of Africa. Consideration of cocoa exports from West Africa and chocolate production in Western contexts shows glaring revenue inequality. Poverty and poor conditions regarding cocoa farming also show that current global arrangements are dictated by massive corporations undergirded by inflexible neoliberal capitalism. The final consideration focused on several prospects for rethinking African resources, revenue, global ethical behavior and interaction with the Western world.

Ultimately, the prospects of cocoa revenue and socio-economic transformation in West Africa lie in the hands of West Africans and compassionate Westerners. There is tremendous human suffering and sacrifice in the production of cocoa (hard labor, low wages, child labor, harvesting, fermentation and preparation of raw cocoa for the market, and minimal opportunities for advancement). This suffering cannot be justified in the face of the massive inequality in cocoa and chocolate revenues between Africa and Westerners. Western corporations sourcing cheap cocoa beans from West Africa need to pause and take a hard and close look at the faces and lives of poor West African cocoa farmers. This request has been on the table for decades.

Arguably, Western corporations and systems do not openly exploit European farmers and chocolate-makers in Europe and North America as they do African farmers. The concern then becomes why Western corporations do not prefer equitable treatment for African farmers whose abundant raw material they rely on for their livelihood. Of course, this is an ethical and political juxtaposition. Ethical, because it asks Western corporations and systems to prick their conscience and think about how their behavior affects other people's lives. Political, because once they have an understanding of their own decades of exploitative behavior of vulnerable and poor populations, then they can, if so desired, affect systemic changes that would transform lives across Africa.

Moreover, the idea of interrogating ethics as a form of justice as compassion and fairness in economics and revenue accumulation is because it is the right thing to do, and probably the only appeal left for Africans. Justice as compassion calls for the continuous insistence on the collective responsibility of bringing about positive coexistential experiences for African farmers and Western buyers. Such ethical concern was touched upon in an episode of the Netflix documentary entitled *Rotten* (Harper 2019). This appeal is important because the Western world has proven impervious to litigations, sanctions or outcry, and certainly its exploitative behavior of Africans and their resources is the least of its worries. Yet, the justice of compassion and fairness links West Africans to the claim of dignity and human rights, and the notion that ethical global trade (just-trade, proportionate-trade, shared-equity trade and fair-trade) is an exchange that creates better conditions, not just for a few, but for everyone.

African nations and Western systems may need to think together on transformation options that are useful for constructing better life chances among cocoa farmers and citizens in Côte d'Ivoire and Ghana. Three simple and doable options already exist. The first option is fair value exchange for West African cocoa beans. The West simply needs to buy cocoa beans as they would any product it produces. Profit is useful, but it must be made on the conditions that revenue is generated fairly and not through exploiting poor farmers. The second option is working alongside ethical rules. Ethics is simply how an individual's or group's behavior affects others, either positively or adversely. The West ought not to be content that its behavior has for centuries adversely affected Africans, their lands and resources. Ethical rules make it possible for global interaction in the marketplace to be responsive to the dignity and rights of all workers.

The third option is engaged and genuine collaboration. Collectively, the Western world is certainly wealthier than most parts of the world, but that wealth and domination is directly linked to their disadvantaging of Africa (Drayton 2005). It is inconceivable that Western corporations, systems and governments are not capable of understanding that their assisting Africans (by being fair, ethical and supporting of equitable exchanges) to build sustainable lives is a win-win prospect. Westerners' contribution to Africa's transformation would need to be collaborative and mindful that IMF loans and World Bank initiatives have been linked to Africa's impoverishment and fragmentation.

For centuries, Westerners have controlled African experiences and resources to Africa's disadvantage, but now would need to support the same rules of engagement that exist in their own contexts in order to make equitable benefits possible for everyone. Clearly defined and implemented inclusive international policies, equitable rules of economics and trade and shared social engagement help to de-emphasize propensities towards exploitation, child labor, massive refugee crises, terrorism, corruption, ineptitude and a seemingly unending African impoverishment and poverty.

References

Adams, T. 2019. "From Bean to Bar in Ivory Coast, a Country Built on Cocoa." *The Guardian*, February 24. www.theguardian.com/global-development/2019/feb/24/ivory-coast-cocoa-farmers-fairtrade-fortnight-women-farmers-trade-justice

Akeredolu-Ale, L. 2020. "How Nigeria is Attracting the World of Aviation – Minister." ChannelsTv.com, February 3. www.youtube.com/watch?v=U4qYpxetrAQ

Amnesty International. 2020. "South Africa: Broken and Unequal Education Perpetuating Poverty and Inequality." February 11. www.amnesty.org/en/latest/news/2020/02/south-africa-broken-and-unequal-education-perpetuating-poverty-and-inequality/

Arbaoui, L. 2012. "Al Qarawiyyin of Fez: The Oldest University in the World." Moroccoworldnews.com, October 2. www.moroccoworldnews.com/2012/10/59056/al-karaouin-of-fez-the-oldest-university-in-the-world/

Balch, O. 2018. "Child Labour: The Dark Truth behind Chocolate Production." *Raconteur*, June 20. www.raconteur.net/business-innovation/child-labour-cocoa-production

Betz, J., and Siegel, T. Directors, Eds. 2016. Seed: The Untold Story [Film]. San Francisco, CA: Canopy Streaming.

Bush, B. 2006. *Imperialism and Postcolonialism*. London: Person Longman.

Camara, B. 2005. "The Falsity of Hegel's thesis on Africa." *Journal of Black Studies,* 36(1), 82–96. https://doi.org/10.1177%2F0021934704268296

Cook, L. R. 1982. *Chocolate Production and Use*. New York: Harcourt Brace Jovanovich.

CNBCAfrica. 2019. *The Future of West Africa's Cocoa Industry* [Video]. Youtube, June 27. https://www.youtube.com/watch?v=ws2LM-D2v7c

Davidson, B. 1991. *African Civilizations Revisited*. Trenton, NJ: Africa World Press, Inc.

Diop, C. A. 1974. *The African Origins of Civilization: Myth or Reality*. Chicago, IL: Lawrence Hill Books.

Diop, C. A. 1987. *Precolonial Black Africa*. New York: Lawrence Hill Books.

Drayton, R. 2005. "The Wealth of the West was Built on Africa's Exploitation." *The Guardian*. www.theguardian.com/politics/2005/aug/20/past.hearafrica05

Dzirutwe, M. 2019. "Mugabe's Farm Seizures: Racial Justice or Catastrophic Power Grab." Reuters, September 6. www.reuters.com/article/us-zimbabwe-mugabe-land/mugabes-farm-seizures-racial-justice-or-catastrophic-power-grab-idUSKCN1VR156

Essegbey, G. O., and Ofori-Gyamfi, E. 2012. "Ghana Cocoa Industry: An Analysis from the Innovative System Perspective." *Technology and Investment,* 3, 276–286. doi:10.4236/ti.2012.34038

Farmer, P. 2005. *Pathologies of Power: Health, Human Rights, and the New War on the Poor*. Berkeley, CA: University of California Press.

Ghana Cocoa Board. 2020a. "Cocoa." *Cocobod.gh*. https://www.cocobod.gh/home_section.php?sec=1

Ghana Cocoa Board. 2020b. "Cocoa Child Education Support." *Cocobod.gh*. https://www.cocobod.gh/social_esponsibility.php

GhanaWeb. 2019. "Ghana, la Cote d'Ivoire Combined US$6bn Yearly Cocoa Revenue Meagre – COCOBOD CEO." Ghanaweb.com, June 7. Retrieved from https://www.ghanaweb.com/GhanaHomePage/business/Ghana-La-Cote-d-Ivoire-s-combined-US-6bn-yearly-cocoa-revenue-meagre-Cocobod-CEO-752898

Gretler, C., and de Sousa, A. 2020. "Lindt CEO Issues Chocolate Price Warning on Africa Cocoa Premium." Bloomberg.com, March 3. www.bloomberg.com/news/articles/2020-03-03/lindt-ceo-issues-chocolate-price-warning-on-africa-cocoa-premium

Gross, L., and Honig, E. 2020. "Migrant Farm Workers Feed America – and they're at Risk for a Coronavirus Outbreak." Huffpost, March 26. www.huffpost.com/entry/farmworkers-coronavirus_n_5e7cd0b2c5b6cb08a9298f68

Guilbert, K. 2017. (June 12). "Falling Cocoa Prices Threaten Child Labor Spike in Ghana, Ivory Coast." Reuters. www.reuters.com/article/us-westafrica-cocoa-children-idUSKBN1931ZQ

Harper, A. (Director). 2019. "Bitter Chocolate" (Season 2, Episode 5, of *Rotten*). J. Andrukanis and K. Rozansky, Executive Producers), Rotten Production Company.

Hawkins, K. (Producer). 2018. "Yaa Asantemaa and the Fight for the Golden Stool." July 10. www.bbc.com/news/av/world-africa-44772345

International Cocoa Initiative (ICI). 2017. "Cocoa Farmers in Ghana Experience Poverty and Vulnerability." December 1. https://cocoainitiative.org/news-media-post/cocoa-farmers-in-ghana-experience-poverty-and-economic-vulnerability/

John W. Ffooks & Co. (n.d.). Ivory Coast. *John W. Ffooks & Co.* https://mail.jwflegal.com/countries/ivory-coast/

Khumalo, T. 2020. "Amina: The Warrior Queen of Zazzau." February 20. www.dw.com/en/amina-the-warrior-queen-of-zazzau/a-52448399
Killingray, D. 1987. *The Transatlantic Slave Trade.* London: Batsford.
Landes, D. 1998. *The Wealth and Poverty of Nations: Why Some are So Rich and Some So Poor.* London: W.W. Norton & Co.
Lee, C. K. 2017. *The Specter of Global China: Politics, Labor and Foreign Investment in Africa.* Chicago, IL: University of Chicago Press.
Meredith, M. 2005. *The Fate of Africa: From the Hopes of Freedom to the Heart of Despair: A History of 50 Years of Independence.* New York: PublicAffairs.
Meredith, M. 2016. *The Fortunes of Africa: A 5000-Year History of Wealth, Greed, and Endeavor.* New York: PublicAffairs.
Moellendorf, D. 2009. *Global Inequalities Matter.* Basingstoke: Palgrave Macmillan.
Morisset, J. 2019. "How can Côte d'Ivoire Escape the Curse of Cocoa?" World Bank Blogs, July 11. https://blogs.worldbank.org/nasikiliza/how-can-cote-divoire-escape-curse-cocoa
Moyers, B. 2003. "Rich World, Poor Women" (Season 2, Episode 33) [TV series episode transcript]. *Now with Bill Moyers,* September 5. www.pbs.org/now/transcript/transcript233_full.html
Moyo, D. F. 2009. *Dead Aid: Why Aid is Not Working and How there is a Better Way for Africa.* New York: Farrar, Straus & Giroux.
O'Keefe, B. 2016. "Bitter Sweets." *Fortune,* March 1. https://fortune.com/longform/big-chocolate-child-labor/
Osberg, L. 2018. *Economic Inequality and Poverty: International Perspective.* London: Routledge.
Ott, T. O. 1999. *The Haitian Revolution, 1789–1804.* Knoxville, TN: University of Tennessee Press.
Peel, A. G. 2020. "Nestlé Invests $2.7m to Protect and Restore Forest in Cote d'Ivoire. July 22. www.foodbev.com/news/nestle-invests-2-7m-to-protect-and-restore-forest-cover-in-cote-divoire/
Pew Research Center. 2018. "At least a Million Sub-Saharan Africans Moved to Europe since 2010." March 22. https://www.pewresearch.org/global/2018/03/22/at-least-a-million-sub-saharan-africans-moved-to-europe-since-2010/
Riobello, J. 2019. "The Dark Side of Globalization: Exploitation of Coltan in the Democratic Republic of Congo." August 13. https://sdwatch.eu/2019/08/the-dark-side-of-globalization-exploitation-and-trade-of-coltan-in-the-democratic-republic-of-congo/
Rodney, W. 1972. *How Europe Underdeveloped Africa.* London: Bogle-L'Ouverture Publications.
Ryan, Orla. 2011. *Chocolate Nations: Living and Dying for Cocoa in West Africa.* London: Zed Books.
SAHO. 2019. "Africa, Portugal." September 3. https://sahistory.org.za/article/africa-portugal
Scobey, R. 2020. "To Stop Child Labor First Address Poverty." World Cocoa Foundation, August 11. www.worldcocoafoundation.org/blog/to-stop-child-labor-first-address-poverty/
Seabrook, J. 2001. *Children of Other Worlds: Exploitation in the Global Market.* London: Pluto Press.
Sethi, S. 2018. "Cocoa has a Poverty Problem. You Can Help by Eating More Dark Chocolate." July 7. https://thecounter.org/chocolate-farmers-ivory-coast-ghana/

Stringer, C., and McKie, R. 1996. *African Exodus: The Origins of Modern Humanity.* New York: Henry Holt & Co.

Sun, Y. 2014. "China's Aid to Africa: Monster or Messiah?" February 7. www.brookings.edu/opinions/chinas-aid-to-africa-monster-or-messiah/

Terreblance, S. 2002. *A History of Inequality in South Africa, 1652–2002.* Pietermaritzburg, SA: University of Natal Press.

Terreblanche, S. 2014. *Western Empires, Christianity and the Inequalities between the West and the Rest: 1500 – 2010.* Johannesburg: Penguin Books.

UNESCO. 1979. *The African Slave Trade from the Fifteenth to the Nineteenth Century: Reports and Papers of the Meeting of Experts Organized by UNESCO at Port-au-Prince, Haiti, 31 January to 4 February, 1978.* UNESCO.

UNESCO. 2019. *General History of Africa,* Vols. 1–11. Paris: UNESCO. https://en.unesco.org/general-history-africa

UN News. 2019. "More than 90 Percent of Africa Migrants Would Make Perilous Europe Journey Again, Despite the Risks." *UN News,* October 21. https://news.un.org/en/story/2019/10/1049641

United World. 2020. "How Much does Africa Owe, and to Whom?" United World, August 29. https://uwidata.com/13450-how-much-does-africa-owe-and-to-whom/

Van Sertima, I. 1976. *They Came Before Columbus: The African Presence in Ancient America.* New York: Random House.

Veen, V. D. 1999. *The Exploitation of Plant Resources in Ancient Africa.* New York: Kluwar Academic/Plenum Publishers.

Von Dacre, J. S. 2019. "How your Chocolate Addiction Traps Cocoa Farmers in Poverty." November 7. www.insideover.com/society/how-your-chocolate-addiction-traps-cocoa-farmers-in-poverty.html

Yock, E. 2018. "Cocoa in the Côte d'Ivoire." ESRI. www.arcgis.com/apps/Cascade/index.html?appid=dd19d4b6444e492da5b069d62d2c3ecb

3 Capital accumulation in Liberia's rubber and iron ore sectors

George Klay Kieh, Jr.

Introduction

The finalization of Liberia's incorporation into the world capitalist system in 1926, and the resulting emergence of this peripheral capitalist state, heralded the commencement of private capital accumulation in the country's rubber and mining sectors (Kieh 2008, 97–99). In addition, the "Open Door Policy," which was enunciated by the Tubman regime about two decades later, provided the *terra firma* for the influx of metropolitan-based corporations into the Liberian economy (van der Kraaii 1983). This was because the "Open Door Policy" provided an enabling environment for unfettered capital accumulation. For example, corporations were offered generous concession agreements by the Liberian state that included tax holidays and the unrestricted repatriation of profits (van der Kraii 1983).

Importantly, the penetration of the Liberian economy by metropolitan-based corporations from the United States and various European states such as Germany and Sweden, especially in the rubber and mining sectors, spurred the rise of local entrepreneurs in these sectors, albeit in secondary roles (the metropolitan-based corporations were the "movers and shakers" in these two sectors). In the rubber sector, for example, local entrepreneurs established private rubber farms and plantations. In turn, these local rubber farms and plantations served, and continue to do so, as suppliers of latex and rubber to the major metropolitan-based corporations such as the Firestone Plantations Company, the hegemon in the sector. However, in the mining sector, the trajectory is different; private miners buy licenses from the state that give them *carte blanche* permission to prospect for, and sell, minerals such as gold and diamonds to various buyers.

Another major dimension of the emergent capital accumulation phenomenon is that state managers use the agency of their various offices for the private accumulation of capital. That is, state managers in the executive and legislative branches of the Liberian government use, and continue to use, their respective positions to accumulate capital through various illegal means in their parasitic relationships with both metropolitan-based corporations and local entrepreneurs in the rubber and mining sectors.

Against this background, the purpose of this chapter is to investigate the nature and dynamics of capital accumulation in the rubber and iron ore sectors of Liberia. In other words, how is capital accumulated in Liberia's rubber and iron ore sectors? In order to address this research question, the chapter is divided into four major parts. First is the examination of the peripheral capitalist Liberian state as the crucible for capital accumulation. Second, the capital accumulation processes in Liberia are deciphered for the purpose of locating the major actors that are involved in capital accumulation. Third, the chapter analyzes the sectoral accumulation of capital by examining the major actors in the rubber and iron ore sectors. Finally, the study draws several major conclusions.

The crucible of capital accumulation: The peripheral capitalist Liberian state

Background

The peripheral capitalist Liberian state is critical to capital accumulation in the country. This is because it serves as the crucible within which capital accumulation occurs. An examination of its pedigree is indispensable to understanding the state's service as the crucible of capital accumulation. This section of the chapter examines the nature and functions of the peripheral capitalist Liberian state.

Nature

The peripheral capitalist Liberian state is the by-product of the finalization of the country's incorporation into the world capitalist system in 1926. As an appendage of the global capitalist system, the peripheral capitalist Liberian state, as Magdalene David (1984) aptly observes, "straddles not one but two levels of articulation: between the world capitalist economic system and the peripheral social formation as a whole" (58). At the level of the world capitalist system, the peripheral capitalist Liberian state serves as an export enclave for rubber and minerals, among other materials, that are needed to feed the industrial-manufacturing multiplexes in the core states such as the United States and China. In other words, under the "international division of labor," the peripheral Liberian state contributes to the ongoing socio-economic development of the core states, while neglecting its internal development. Essentially, to use Andre Gunder Frank's (1966) formulation, the development of the core states and the simultaneous underdevelopment of Liberia are two sides of the same process.

At the domestic level, the peripheral capitalist Liberian state pretends to be "relatively autonomous." This strategy hides its class character as a handmaid for the general interests of the Liberian ruling class. Under its disguise of "relative autonomy," the peripheral capitalist Liberian state attempts to establish relationships with various social forces, including the cultural, economic and political. The overarching objective is to maintain propitious conditions for capital accumulation.

Functions

The peripheral capitalist Liberian state performs several functions in its efforts to ensure the accumulation of capital by metropolitan-based corporations and the members of the local ruling class. A major function is the reproduction of economic, political and social structures that ensure the hegemony of the ruling class (Fatton 1988). For example, the class structure has divided Liberian society into three major clusters: ruling, petit bourgeois and subaltern. The ruling class has two major wings: local and foreign. The local wing is composed of state managers that occupy high-level positions in the executive and legislative branches of the Liberian government, such as the President, Vice President, Speaker of the House of Representatives, President Pro-Tempore of the Senate, cabinet ministers, heads of autonomous agencies and heads of public corporations. Caio Prado (1966) refers to these individuals as the "bureaucratic bourgeoisie." The petit-bourgeois class comprises the intelligentsia, artists and other entertainers. Significantly, some of the members of this cluster have committed what Amilcar Cabral calls "class suicide" (see Meisenhelder 1993). That is, they have renounced their class positions, and have formed alliances with various segments of the subaltern classes. For example, from the 1970s to 1990s, some of the members of this class were active in two major national social movements – Movement for Justice in Africa, and the All People's Freedom Alliance (APFA) – and the student movement, including the University of Liberian Student Union that formed alliances with the labor movement, including those in the rubber and mining sectors. The third cluster consists of the subaltern classes, an amalgam of the working class, the peasantry, the unemployed and hoi polloi.

Another major function is to maintain what William Graff (1994) calls "law and order." The apparatchik of the peripheral capitalist Liberian state does not hesitate to employ the full battery of its instruments of coercion, including the military and police, to oppress the forces of resistance such as labor unions. That is, when the forces of resistance protest the vagaries of exploitation, which is the root of the capital accumulation process, the state deploys its coercive instruments to cow them into submission. This includes beating, arresting and imprisoning the leaders of labor unions and other forces of resistance such as the student movement.

The peripheral capitalist Liberian state superintends the processes of capital accumulation, in compliance with its mission. One way in which the peripheral capitalist Liberian state does this is through the use of public policies such as the investment code to create propitious conditions for metropolitan-based corporations, local entrepreneurs and state managers to accumulate capital.

Further, the peripheral capitalist Liberian state maintains relationships with the various class forces in Liberia. However, the nature of the relationship is shaped by the position of each class in the country's political economy. In the case of the ruling class, the state maintains a harmonious relationship with the class as a whole. This is because the central mission of the peripheral capitalist Liberian state is to serve the general interests of the ruling class. As W. Ziemann and M. Lanzenderfer (1977) argue, "The state is the business chief organizing the economy in the interests of the ruling class" (146). Central to this is the state's mediation of conflicts within the ruling class. That is, "it is the job of the state to mediate conflicting interests among the various factions of the bourgeoisie, to be able to administrate in the common interests of the whole class" (Miliband 1973, 85). In the case of the subaltern classes, especially, the working class, the peasantry, the unemployed and hoi polloi, the peripheral capitalist Liberian state has failed to cater to their material well-being as it (the state) as it has done for the ruling class (see Kieh 2017).

Problematizing the capital accumulation processes in Liberia

Background

Historically, the accumulation of capital has been, and continues to be, based on two major trajectories: predatory and primitive. Although these two processes share the common core of the centrality of exploitation, cheating and chicanery as the engines that power capital accumulation, the major actors concerned are different. In the predatory capital accumulation process, the key actors are the state, corporations, private entrepreneurs and labor. On the other hand, for the primitive accumulation process, the key players are state managers, corporations and private entrepreneurs.

The predatory accumulation of capital process

At the vortex of the process of the predatory accumulation of capital is what David Harvey (2007) aptly refers to as "accumulation by dispossession" (159). By this he means:

> the continuation and proliferation of accumulation practices … [that] include the the commodification and privatization of land and the forceful expulsion of peasant populations … conversion of various forms of property rights (common, collective, state, etc.) into exclusive private property rights … suppression of rights to the commons; commodification of labor power and the suppression of alternative (indigenous) forms of production and consumption; colonial, neocolonial and imperialist processes of appropriation of assess (including natural resources) …
>
> (Harvey 2007, 159)

Drawing from David Harvey's (2007) formulation, the predatory accumulation of capital process in Liberia has several major planks. A key one is dispossession. Businesses, especially metropolitan-based corporations which have invested in the various sectors of the country's economy, have dispossessed the citizens in many ways. A major one is depriving peasants of large swaths of land by converting their farms into arenas for production and other activities of the corporations. In so doing, private and communal lands have been converted to corporate enclaves. Similarly, dispossessed peasants are forced into the growing ranks of the unemployed. However, some of them are employed in low-level positions in some of the corporations.

Another plank of the predatory accumulation process is the role of the peripheral capitalist Liberian state. As Guillermo Flichman (1990) perceptively asserts,

> the state is always present when capitalist accumulation takes place ... In general terms, it can be said that the main role of the capitalist state is to create and guarantee the necessary conditions for the 'normal' development of capitalist accumulation and production.
>
> (1)

The peripheral capitalist Liberian state has performed its role in the interest of capital in various ways. One is that the Liberian state serves as the handmaid of corporations in taking away lands from peasants for the purpose of ensuring the production processes. Similarly, the peripheral capitalist Liberian state creates propitious conditions for the capital accumulation process by, inter alia, granting corporations various benefits, including tax holidays, duty-free privileges, the right to repatriate profits and the policing of the labor force.

Corporations exploit labor as the centerpiece of the predatory capital accumulation process. The linchpin of the exploitation is in the area of wages. That is, the various corporations do not pay workers wages that are proportional to their contributions to the production process. Hence, by underpaying workers, the capitalists, who own the various corporations, create what Karl Marx (1887) calls "surplus value." This is the central method that is used to accumulate capital through profit-making. In turn, the profits that are generated by these corporations are appropriated by the capitalists who own them.

Furthermore, the oppressed, including workers and community groups, resist the vagaries of dispossession to which they are subjected, especially by metropolitan-based corporations. The nodes of resistance include go-slows, strikes, sit-ins and armed struggles. In the specific case of the working class, for example, they resist the exploitation of multinational corporations that want to "bid down the wages of workers to the lowest possible level" (Cudd 2006, 1).

The primitive accumulation of capital process

In his treatise on primitive accumulation, Karl Marx (1887) provides a historiography of capitalism. Building on Marx's seminal work, I have developed a framework of the primitive accumulation process. The centerpiece of the framework is the postulate that primitive capital accumulation entails the generation of wealth by state managers through the use of sundry illegal means, including bribery and extortion. In essence, primitive capital accumulation is devoid of any investment by state managers in the production process. Claude Ake (1966, 29) paints a vivid picture of the process:

> [through] the use of political power for the accumulation of wealth … [the ruling classes] are generally people who have acquired wealth through state power by political corruption, by access to state contracting, agency rates or concessions such as import licenses – wealth which does not usually involve those in direct productive activity.

In this vein, the primitive capital accumulation process is powered by several major engines. One concerns the major actors. There are three major sets of actors: state managers, who hold positions in the executive, legislative and judicial branches of government; businesses in the various sectors of the economy; and local private entrepreneurs in the various sectors of the economy.

Another major engine is the capital accumulation dynamic. At the core is that state managers use the agency of their respective offices to establish and maintain parasitic relationships with the other two sets of actors. That is, state managers use the other two sets of actors as the principal conduits for capital accumulation. Ugumanium Bassey Obo et al. (2014, 63), describe the capital accumulation dynamic thus:

> those who occupy state offices … use their positions not for service delivery to the the people, but for the primary goal of self-enrichment … those at the helm of affairs of the … state … have used its institutions and apparatus to further their nests at the expense of delivering public goods and services.

Several major methods are used in the primitive capital accumulation process. One is the use of bribes. Corporations and local private entrepreneurs offer bribes to state managers at various levels as the quid pro quo for various favors, including concession agreements, contracts, licensing, tax breaks, duty-free privileges and document processing. Importantly, the size of the bribe is often contingent upon two major factors: the position of the government official and the nature of the transaction. For example, the president of a country would receive a bigger bribe than an average civil servant. In addition, a single transaction may require the payment of bribes at multiple levels of the state bureaucracy.

Similarly, state managers use extortion as another major vehicle for the private accumulation of wealth. Essentially, state managers occupying positions at various levels of the state require financial payments for dispensing favors to corporations and local entrepreneurs. Like bribery, the amount of the extortion is dependent upon the official position of the extortionist and the nature of the transaction. For example, the president of a peripheral capitalist state will demand a higher payment compared to a cabinet minister. Like bribery, acts of extortion may be performed at various levels of a peripheral capitalist state.

Sectoral capital accumulation: The cases of the rubber and iron ore sectors

Predatory capital accumulation

The rubber sector

THE FIRESTONE PLANTATIONS COMPANY

The Firestone Plantations Company was established in Liberia in 1926 by Harvey S. Firestone, an American industrial capitalist, whose business empire was headquartered in Akron, Ohio, United States.[1] As a member of the American ruling class, Harvey Firestone used his connections to influence the American government to use its leverage on the Liberian government as the latter's neo-colonial patron, to negotiate a lucrative concession agreement. Coincidentally, Harvey Firestone's economic interests were aligned with the United States' strategic interest of having a reliable source for the supply of rubber (see Ghoshal 1982, 96). Thus, the US Congress allocated $500,000 to assist Firestone in conducting a survey of Liberia (Ghoshal 1982, 96).

During the negotiation of the concession agreement, the United States took two major steps to ensure the expansion of its neo-colonial stranglehold on Liberia. First, the United States government made Firestone include a $5 million loan at a 7 percent interest rate that the Liberian government did not request as part of the concession agreement (Choshal 1982, 96). Second, the American government incorporated the Firestone loan into the framework of the United States' 1912 loan to Liberia. Under this framework, Liberia's customs revenues were placed under American receivership managed by General Receiver of Liberian Customs, "an American appointed by the President of the United States" (Ghoshal 1982, 97).

In addition, Firestone was given one million acres of land for an initial period of 99 years. In 2005, the life span of the concession agreement was extended by 37 more years (see Walters 2019). Significantly, the implementation of the concession agreement required the peripheral capitalist Liberian state's appropriation of the land owned by peasants for the establishment of Firestone's rubber plantation. Consequently, thousands of peasants were dispossessed of their lands. To make matters worse, the peripheral capitalist Liberian state conscripted most of these peasants into Firestone's army of cheap labor, including as rubber tappers.

At the core of Firestone's capital accumulation strategies was the exploitation of labor with the support of the Liberian peripheral capitalist state. A key strategy was paying the workers very low wages. For example, by 1980, the average rubber tapper earned less than $30.00 per month (see Kieh 2008, 97). Another was requiring one rubber tapper to provide labor that could have been shared by multiple tappers. A major case in point was that "a rubber tapper was required to tap 700 rubber trees within an eight-hour period, collect the latex, and physically transport it in aluminum buckets hoisted on a bar" to various receiving stations across the company's 45 divisions (Kieh 2008, 97). As well, Firestone failed to invest in the provision of humane living conditions for the workers in the lowest rung of its labor force, especially the rubber tappers. For example, rubber tappers lived in mud huts with thatched roofs, cramped space, no running water and electricity, and a lack of indoor plumbing (Kieh 2008, 97). Further, with the acquiescence of the peripheral capitalist Liberian state, the Firestone management prevented the workers from unionizing for almost six decades from the inception of the corporation's operations in Liberia (Kieh, 2008, 91). However, even after the workers unionized in 1980, in the aftermath of the April 12, 1980 coup, the new military junta, which had professed to be pro-labor, promulgated Decree No. 12 that criminalized labor strikes (Kieh 2008, 91). In 2005, the International Labor Rights Fund (ILRF) filed a lawsuit against Firestone in an American court for subjecting "thousands of workers, including minors, to toil in slavery" (Rizvi 2005, 1).

Historically, the workers have resisted Firestone's predatory accumulation of capital based on their labor power. For example, there were labor strikes in 1961, 1964 and 1975 that paralyzed the entire operations of Firestone (Kieh 2008, 91). Even the intervention of the peripheral capitalist Liberian state, on the side of Firestone through the deployment of its coercive instruments including the military and police, did not deter the workers from demanding higher wages and better living conditions. Similarly, in 2007, the workers engaged in strike action when both the management of Firestone and the Sirleaf regime refused to recognize the authority of the new leadership of the workers' union (see Butty 2007, 1). The reason was that both Firestone and the Sirleaf regime wanted a union leadership that would be compliant with Firestone's perennial predatory capital accumulation activities. Again, in 2018, the workers undertook another strike action demanding better wages (Wiakanly 2018, 1).

THE LIBERIAN AGRICULTURAL COMPANY (LAC)

LAC was established in 1959, initially as a by-product of the Liberian government's effort to pursue a strategy of quasi-state capitalism. Under this economic trajectory, the Liberian peripheral capitalist state was desirous of investing in the rubber sector for the purpose of capital accumulation. However, the strategy was short-lived, as evidenced by the Liberian government's decision to sell LAC to Uniroyal. Initially, LAC covered a land expanse of 7,000 hectares. To gain access to this land, the Liberian peripheral capitalist state had wrested the space away from scores of peasants and peasant-based communities.

In 2007, LAC was purchased by Socfin, a Luxemburg-based corporation, which owns various rubber and palm oil plantations in various African and southeastern Asian states (*Front Page Africa* 2019, 1; Cenpetel 2015, 1). Currently, LAC's concession area spans a rubber plantation and rubber processing plant that covers 122,500 hectares of land. This means that more peasant lands were appropriated by the peripheral capitalist Liberian state in the quest to satisfy the demand of LAC for the increased accumulation of capital.

Like other corporations, the exploitation of labor is the centerpiece of LAC's predatory accumulation of capital. For example, in 2020, a rubber tapper was paid less than a $1.00 per hour. However, a rubber tapper was required to do a yeoman's job that included "tapping over 600 rubber trees and clean[ing] over 300 rubber cups and pack[ing] them at the same time [per day]" (Tah 2020, 1).

Workers have engaged in various acts of resistance to protest the exploitation of their labor. For example, in late January 2020, aggrieved rubber tappers, who constitute the motor force of LAC's labor force, engaged in a "go-slow action." The workers argued that the rationale for their action was to protest the corporation's refusal to meet their demands for "their just entitlements – leave allowances and increased wages" (Tah 2020, 1).

THE SALALA RUBBER CORPORATION (SRC)

The SRC was established in 1959 under a concession agreement that awarded it 8,000 hectares of land. Characteristically, local peasants and peasant-based communities were robbed of their lands by the peripheral capitalist Liberian state so that SRC could establish its plantation. In 1998, Socfin, the emerging global rubber and palm oil mega-multinational corporation, bought SRC (David 2019, 1).

Significantly, from 2008 to 2014, SRC undertook a systematic campaign of dispossessing the local communities near the concession area of their land. As *Front Page Africa* (2019) laments, "[SRC engaged in] a violent expansion of the plantation, bulldozing some towns, took land forcefully, and in some cases destroyed the people's crops with no compensation" (1). Importantly, this was done with the acquiescence of the Sirleaf regime, which was a handmaid of metropolitan capital *par excellence.* The recent dispossession campaign was in furtherance of SRC's need to expand the ambit of its operations for the purpose of increasing the accumulation of capital.

Undaunted by SRC's predatory accumulation of capital activities, 22 dispossessed local communities resisted the corporation's "land grab crusade" via a battery of activities, including protests, advocacy and public education (see Advocates for Community Alternatives 2019, 1).

The Iron ore sector

THE LIBERIAN MINING COMPANY (LMC)

Interestingly, the concession agreement for LMC was signed in 1951 between the Liberian government and Landsdell Christie, an erstwhile officer in the US military (van der Kraaij 1983). This was a strange development because Christie neither had the capital nor knowledge about iron ore (van der Kraaij 1983). But his ties to the American government were pivotal in securing him the concession agreement, given Liberia's status as a neocolony of the United States. Under the terms, the agreement was for 80 years with the allocation of 3 million acres of land (van der Kraaij 1983). In addition, LMC paid the Liberian government an exploration tax of US $100.00 per month (van der Kraaij 1983). As always, various individuals and groups, including peasants, were dispossessed of their lands. Hence, without a source of livelihood, scores of these dispossessed peasants were constrained to work for LMC in various low-level positions.

With a lucrative concession agreement, Christie was able to mobilize capital to fund the investment in LMC. Initially, the Dutch Muller Company was the key financier, with additional responsibilities for administrative and technical matters. However, the Republic Steel Corporation subsequently became the principal funder of the investment.

Unhappy with their low wages, amid the accumulation of wealth by the capitalists who owned LMC, the workers went on strike in 1955. Their overarching demand was for better wages (Iskenderov 1964). Importantly, from its beginning in 1951 to its closure in 1977, LMC accrued $540 million, but paid the Liberian government $84 million in royalties (van der Kraaij 1983). This meant that LMC made a windfall. However, after exploiting Liberia's iron ore and workers, LMC folded its operations in 1977, leaving thousands of workers unemployed.

THE BONG MINING COMPANY (BMC)

The Bong Mining Company was established in 1958, under a concession agreement among the Liberian government and German and Italian capitalists. As usual, the establishment of the corporation's concession area involved the seizure of the lands of various groups and individuals, including peasants, by the peripheral capitalist Liberian state. In turn, having been dispossessed of their lands, these individuals were then constrained by the imperative of survival to join BMC's corps of low-wage earners.

Undaunted, the workers of BMC resisted capitalist exploitation recurrently. One of the major acts of resistance was the 1979 strike (Kieh 2008, 91). Importantly, the action paralyzed the operations of the corporation and sent shock waves through its owners and the compradorial mangers of the peripheral capitalist Liberian state. Fearful about the adverse effects on the capital accumulation process, the Liberian government intervened by deploying military and police personnel to brutalize the workers. In addition, several leaders of the workers' union were arrested and imprisoned by the Liberian government.

When the April 12, 1980 coup occurred, the workers at Bong Mines were hopeful that the new military junta would keep its promise of promoting social justice. However, once the members of the ruling People's Redemption Council (PRC) were incorporated into the local wing of the Liberian ruling class, they, among others, adopted an anti-labor orientation. As noted, the PRC promulgated Decree No. 12 that made labor strikes illegal (Kieh 2008, 91).

Having exploited both the iron ore resources and its workers for more than three decades, BMC folded its operations in 1988. The rationale was that

BMC's profits had declined, due to the decrease in the price of iron ore. The major consequence of this action by BMC was that thousands of workers lost their jobs and joined the growing ranks of the unemployed. In addition, the loss of jobs also contributed to the expansive pool of poverty-stricken Liberians.

THE LIBERIAN AMERICAN SWEDISH MINERAL COMPANY (LAMCO)

The idea of establishing LAMCO was conceived by a group of American capitalists. The motor force was to exploit Liberia's vast iron ore reserves in Mount Nimba, which is located in Nimba County, a region in the north-central region of the country. However, since the American capitalists did not have expertise in mining, they sought capitalists with mining know-how (Bruno 2018, 625). The result was the development of an investment partnership between the American capitalists and "the Wallenberg family, a Swedish family of bankers and industrialists that directly or indirectly controlled major parts of Swedish industry" (Bruno 2018, 625). Subsequently, other Swedish capitalists were incorporated into the partnership, including Grangesbergsbolaget (Granges), Skanaka Cementgjuteriet, Ifoverken and Sentab. In addition, US Bethlehem Steel, an American corporation, German capitalists and the peripheral Liberian state were incorporated into the partnership. The investment partnership was dubbed the LAMCO Joint Venture Operating Company. LAMCO began its operations in 1963. Like all concession-based capitalist ventures in Liberia, individuals and groups in the Yekepa area, where the corporate headquarters was established, and sections of Buchanan City, where the ore processing plant was set up, were dispossessed of their land by the Liberian government.

Characteristically, LAMCO, like all capitalist corporations, engaged in sundry exploitative activities. A key one was denying workers the right to unionize for almost a decade after the establishment of LAMCO (Kieh 2008, 91). LAMCO, along with the Liberian government, was determined to prevent the workers from organizing a vehicle through which to channel their resistance to capitalist exploitation, especially in terms of wages. By the mid-1970s, LAMCO made more than $485 million in profits from an initial investment of approximately $250 million (van der Kraaij 1983). Of this amount, the Liberian peripheral capitalist state received $100 million in royalties (van der Kraaij 1983). Undaunted by the exploitation, the LAMCO Workers Union organized a major strike in 1978 that brought the corporation's operations to a virtual halt (Kieh 2008, 91). Again, the peripheral capitalist Liberian state intervened on behalf of LAMCO, deploying the state's security apparatus to intimidate and harass the workers. In addition, the leaders of the union were arrested and detained.

When the April 12, 1980 military coup occurred, the workers, like their counterparts in various sectors of the Liberian economy, were hopeful that the People's Redemption Council (PRC), the ruling junta, would pursue a pro-workers' agenda, as per the PRC's pronouncements. However, those hopes were dashed by the promulgation of Decree No. 12.

Having exploited Liberia's vast iron ore reserves in the Nimba region, as well as its workers, LAMCO ended its operations in 1989. The central reason, as Karl Bruno asserts, was that "at first a profitable venture, LAMCO's future waxed and waned with global business cycle" (Bruno 2018, 624). The closure of LAMCO led to the unemployment of thousands of workers. This had profound adverse ramifications for their families, who were dependent upon them. In addition, various local Liberian businesses that were dependent upon LAMCO as a major source of revenue witnessed the collapse of their financial foundations.

ACELOR MITTAL

Acelor Mittal was established in 2005 as the successor to LAMCO. This meant that Acelor Mittal inherited some of LAMCO's major assets, including the facilities in both Yekepa and Buchanan. Acelor Mittal was given the concession agreement for 25 years. The corporation is a branch of a global multinational empire that has branches in more than 60 countries around the world (see All Africa 2020).

Like other capitalist ventures, Acelor Mittal has been engaged in the exploitation of Liberia in sundry ways. A key one is paying workers low wages as the linchpin of the capitalist accumulation strategy. In addition, the corporation has failed to pay workers vacation pay. This means that workers are denied paid leave.

Exasperated by Acelor Mittal's exploitative activities, the workers have undertaken various acts of resistance. For example, in August 2018, there was a strike over work security, low wages and vacation benefits (Menkor 2018, 1). The workers were able eventually to force the corporation to make concessions to their demands.

CHINA UNION MINING COMPANY

The China Union Mining Company was established in 2009 as the successor to the Bong Mining Company. The major shareholder was Wuhan Iron and Steel Corporation, an economic arm of the Chinese government. The corporation was awarded a 25-year concession agreement by the Liberian government (see Sustainable Development Institute 2014, 1).

Like other profit-seeking capitalist enterprises, China Union employed various modes of exploitation. A key one was that it paid its Liberian workers low wages (see *New Dawn* 2015, 1). Another was the recurrent reduction of the labor force. For example, in January 2017, China Union substantially reduced its workforce (Lomax 2017, 1). The characteristic argument was that the corporation needed to be made more profitable. Thus, as usual, labor had to be the "sacrificial lamb" in the interest of capital accumulation.

Angered by the greed of China Union, the workers undertook various acts of resistance, spanning from strikes to "go-slow." A major case was in May 2015, when the workers staged a "go-slow action" (see *New Dawn* 2015, 1). The workers' demands included better wages and benefits (see *New Dawn* 2015, 1). This act of labor resistance adversely affected the operations of China Union. As usual, the corporation and its handmaid, the Sirleaf regime, took various actions, including the issuance of threats and harassment to cow the workers into submission. However, the workers were undaunted in requiring that their demands be met.

The primitive accumulation of capital

The primitive accumulation of capital in Liberia's rubber and iron ore sectors was, and continues to be, driven by state managers. In the rubber sector, for example, for several years, the Firestone Plantations Company provided trucks to transport the latex from the rubber plantations of former Presidents William V. S. Tubman (1944–1971) and William R. Tolbert (1971–1980). This meant Firestone was contributing to the former presidents' accumulation of capital by covering the costs of transporting the latex from their respective plantations. The money that the two former presidents would have used to cover the cost of transportation for their latex was added to their profits. In addition, Firestone provided preferential pricing for the latex and rubber from the plantations of the two former presidents, as well as those of other prominent state managers.

Further, Firestone had several major state managers on its payroll as so-called "consultants." The truth of the matter is that these state managers were placed on Firestone's payroll and paid monthly as a quid pro quo for serving Firestone's interests through the agency of the former's official positions (a form of primitive accumulation). For example, these paid state managers, who were serving as the agents of Firestone's corporate interests, used their influence to get judges to rule in Firestone's favor in various legal cases. In the post-coup era, Firestone has adjusted its strategies for securing the services of state managers. The emergent dominant one that has been used since 1980 is the recurrent offering of bribes to various state managers to perform sundry services for Firestone.

Other corporations in the rubber and iron ore sector have used, and continue to use, bribery as the dominant strategy for securing the services of state managers. For example, since 2006, the National Legislature of Liberia has become a major epicenter for the primitive accumulation of capital through bribery and extortion. Bribery in the law-making body is so pervasive that it is referred to by legislators themselves as the "white envelope." Several major cases are instructive. Legislators were bribed to approve the concession agreements for Acerlor Mittal and the China Union Mining Company. Importantly, the Sirleaf regime had a legislative liaison who was responsible for delivering bribes from corporations channeled through the Office of the President for securing concession agreements, including in the rubber and iron ore sectors.

Conclusion

Predatory and primitive accumulation have served, and continue to serve, as the two dominant trajectories for accruing wealth for corporations and state managers in Liberia in the rubber and iron ore sectors. In the case of predatory accumulation, the peripheral capitalist Liberian state served, and continues to do so, as the handmaid for corporations to amass wealth through an assortment of exploitative modes, including dispossessing individuals and communities of their lands, paying workers low wages and cheating the Liberian government by paying minimum corporate taxes.

In terms of primitive accumulation, it is the central instrument through which state managers in the executive and legislative branches of the peripheral capitalist Liberian state enrich themselves. This is done through the use of sundry methods, including bribery and extortion, which are the payoffs for state managers using the agency of their respective offices to serve the interests of corporations in the rubber and iron ore sectors.

Finally, there has been, and continues to be, resistance to both predatory and primitive capital accumulation by workers, communities that have been adversely affected by exploitative corporate activities and other forces for social justice in the Liberian body politic. For workers, they continue to use "go-slow" and strike action as the mainstays of their resistance strategies. In the case of community groups, they continue to use protests, sit-ins and advocacy as the key methods of struggle. In addition, sections of the student movement and other civil society organizations have contributed to the resistance to capitalist pillage and plunder through public education and advocacy.

Note

1 Firestone Plantations Company was purchased by Bridgestone in 1975.

References

Advocates for Community Alternatives. 2019. "22 Liberian Indigenous Communities Accuse the Salala Rubber Corporation…of Gross Human Rights and Environmental Abuses Using World Bank Financing." June 11.

Ake, Claude. 1966. "The Political Question." In Oyeleye Oyediran (Ed.), *Governance and Development in Nigeria: Essays in Honor of Professor Billy J. Dudley*. Ibadan, Nigeria: Oyediran Consulting International.

All Africa. 2020. "Acelor Mittal." www.allafrica.com. Accessed on September 26.

Bruno, Karl. 2018. "The Government's Business? Swedish Foreign Policy and Commercial Mineral Interests in Liberia, 1955–1980." *Scandinavian Journal of History*, 48(5), 624–645.

Butty, James. 2007. "Striking Firestone Workers Accuse Liberian Government of Force and Intimidation." *Voice of America*, December 13.

Cenpetel, Henry. 2015. *Environmental and Social Due Diligence Assessment, Final Report*. Grand Bassa County: Liberian Agricultural Company. July.

Cudd, Ann E. 2006. *Analyzing Oppression*. Oxford: Oxford University Press.
David, Alloycious. 2019. "Villages Wait on as IFC Probes Salala Rubber's 'Land Grab.'" *Daily Observer,* July 31.
David, Magdalene. 1984. "The Love of Liberty Brought Us Here: An Analysis of the Development of the Settler State in the 19th Century Liberia." *Review of African Political Economy,* 31, 57–70.
Fatton, Robert. 1988. "Bringing the Ruling Class Back In: Class, State and Hegemony in Africa." *Comparative Politics,* 20(3), 253–264.
Flichman, Guillermo. 1990. "The State and Capital Accumulation in Argentina." In Christian Anglade and Carlos Fortin (Eds), *The State and Capital Accumulation in Latin America*. New York: Palgrave Macmillan, 1–31.
Frank, Andre Gunder. 1966. *The Development of Underdevelopment*. New York: Monthly Review Press.
Front Page Africa. 2019. "Sexual Violence and Threats Discovered at Liberian Agricultural Company." February 22.
Ghoshal, Animesh. 1982. "Multinational Investment and the Development of an Export Industry: Rubber in Liberia." *TransAfrican Journal of History,* 11, 92–111.
Graff, William. 1994. "The State in the Third World." Paper presented at the conference of the British International Studies Association. York, UK. December.
Harvey, David. 2007. *A Brief History of Neoliberalism*. Oxford: Oxford University Press.
Iskenderov, Akmed Akhmedovich. 1964. *The Workers' Movement of the Countries of Asia and Africa*. Redding, CA: CCM Information Corporation.
Kieh Jr., George Klay. 2008. *The First Liberian Civil War: The Crises of Underdevelopment*. New York: Peter Lang Publishers.
Kieh, Jr., George Klay. 2017. "'The Janus-Faced' Liberian State." *Liberian Studies Journal,* 42(1–2), 36–72.
Lomax, Selma. 2017. "China Union Closes Down Gradually – Leaves No Impact on Liberian Citizens." *Front Page Africa,* January 15.
Marx, Karl. 1887. *Capital: A Critique of Political Economy,* Vol. 1. Moscow: Progress Publishers.
Meisenhelder, Tom. 1993. "Amilcar Cabral's Theory of Class Suicide and Revolutionary Socialism." *Monthly Review,* 45(6), 40–48.
Menkor, Ishmael F. 2018. "Liberia: Arcelor Mittal Mine Workers Mine Workers Resume Strike for Better Working Conditions." *Daily Observer,* August 7.
Miliband, Ralph. 1973. "Poulantzas and the Capitalist State." *New Left Review,* 82(1), 83–92.
New Dawn. 2015. "Employees Go-Slow at China Union." May 8.
Obo, Ugunmanium Bassey, Maurice Ayodele Coker, and Jacob Iba Omenka. 2014. "The State as the Instrument of Primitive Accumulation: The Nigerian Example, 1999–2013." *Journal of Law, Policy and Globalization,* 26(1), 67–73.
Prado, Caio. 1966. *The Political Evolution of Brazil*. Sao Paulo: Editora Brasiliense.
Rizvi, Haider. 2005. "Liberia: Firestone Sued Over 'Slave Plantation.'" *One World. Net,* December 8.
Sustainable Development Institute. 2014. "Community Relations in the China Union Concession." Briefing #01. April.
Tah, Elton W. 2020. "Liberian Agricultural Company Workers Stage Go-Slow Over Company's 'Cold Shoulders' Toward Collective Bargaining Agreement." *Front Page Africa,* January 24.

Van der Kraaij, Fred. 1983. *The Open Door Policy of Liberia: An Economic History of Modern Liberia*. Bremer: The Netherlands Museum.

Walters, Jr., Robert Anthony. 2019. *Historical Dictionary of United States-African Relations*. Methuen, NJ: Scarecrow Press.

Wiakanly, S. S. 2018. "Firestone Condemns Workers' Strike Action as 'Misconduct.'" *Daily Observer,* August 12.

Ziemann, W. and Lanzenderfer, M. 1977. "The State in Peripheral Societies." *Socialist Register,* 14(3), 143–177.

4 The Congo paradox

Accumulation crisis and resilience in the Democratic Republic of the Congo

Musifiky Mwanasali

Overview

The history of the Democratic Republic of the Congo could be summed up as the failure of the state and the dominant development paradigm to take root in society by empowering local entrepreneurship to stimulate an endogenous process of capital formation.[1] From the slave trade and colonial conquests to the post-Mobutu era, the DRC – as the country is colloquially known – provided its abundant natural resources and the toil of its people for the expansion of capitalism and the prosperity of others. But the country seems to have drawn little benefits from its vast resources while the population continues to languish in misery.

How is it possible that this gigantic country of more than 2 million square kilometers at the heart of Africa, which Belgian geologist René Jules Cornet described as "un scandale géologique" – a geological wonderland – can be such a failure in raising the standard of living of its own inhabitants? Casual observers of this country marvel at how, born from a crisis – the scramble for Africa of 1884–1885 – the DRC seems to have lived in perpetual crisis, to the extent that some wonder whether it really is a crisis rather than the country's own peculiar way of being. Furthermore, in spite of its troubled political history, how had the DRC been able to safeguard its unity and territorial integrity within the old borders inherited from the Berlin Conference, while other former colonies around it split or disintegrated at the time of independence? The term "Congo paradox" captures these contradictions perfectly. It is for this reason I chose it as the main title and focus of this chapter.

The chapter is structured as follows. The first section lays out the conceptual and empirical ground for understanding the interdependence between capital and the state. The second section will consider the unfolding and deepening of the accumulation crisis since independence and its deepening throughout the regime of President Mobutu Sese Seko and his successors. The third section tentatively broaches the question whether there was a state and a mainstream economy under the troubled tenure of Mzee Laurent Désiré Kabila and his successor and son Joseph Kabila. The fourth section on resilience will focus on the informal sector and civil society organizations and show how they morphed from coping mechanisms into instruments for social change. The last section will close the chapter with some suggestions on how the DRC could tackle the problematic of capital accumulation in the country. But before going further, let us clarify the meaning of the term resilience and why the study is titled the Congo paradox.

The Congo paradox

I use the expression "the Congo paradox" to capture "the chronic inability of this resource-rich country to generate and sustain genuine economic growth and development" (Nzongola 1986, 4). Water and electricity distribution offer a good example of the magnitude of the ills facing this country.

The DRC holds over 50% of the water reserves of the entire African continent. Yet the rate of water distribution nationwide by the parastatal REGIDESO is only 14 percent, meaning that about 70 million people have no access to quality water in a country that has plenty of streams on its vast territory. Dug wells are now the main source of water, especially in rural areas, but water from wells is generally unsafe and unsuitable for human consumption. Households that do not have access to wells are forced to buy water containers daily. Ironically, the water company continues to send out monthly bills for a service it does not deliver.

Electricity supply is another example. The DRC holds a hydroelectric potential unique in Africa, that has been estimated at several hundred thousand gigawatt hours per year, and a usable power of about 100,000 megawatts. Yet only 2.6 percent – about 2566 megawatts – is now being used. Meanwhile, electricity supply nationwide is just 15 percent, which means that only 12 out of 80 million people receive electricity from the parastatal Société nationale d'électricité, SNEL. In rural areas, the total lack of electricity is a matter of life and death, particularly for women who are often preyed upon and become victims of sexual violence, especially in rebel-held areas, as they walk long distances in search for cooking firewood.[2]

There are many more examples of the magnitude of the Congo paradox. To grasp its roots, it is important to look for the most fundamental variables and contradictions in this society and assess their long-term impact on the country's political and economic dynamics. It is equally important to look seriously at how ordinary women and men interact with an economic paradigm that marginalizes them and a state that fails to empower them. If soundly managed, local initiatives and creativity can serve as a solid foundation for a broad-based and self-sustained national development. This, I suggest, is one of the most viable options for the DRC to finally resolve its endless crisis.[3]

Resilience: More than a set of coping mechanisms

In common usage, resilience refers to the ability to cope, to "keep going," in the face of hardship. In their struggle for "survival," resilient women and men develop "coping mechanisms" that help them deal with adversity. In this study, I use the term in much the same way to refer to the set of activities – coping mechanisms – that ordinary people use in their attempt to do away with a top-down economic paradigm dominated by foreign capital and the state institutions that sponsor it, and replace them with "something else": an alternative, that is more responsive to their needs. In this sense, resilience does not only allow someone to suck it up, as it were, and carry on. It also entails an element of agency that aims to transform the conditions that brought about the adversity and turn the situation around to one's own advantage.

Two sets of circumstances facilitated the strengthening of resilience in the DRC. One was the burgeoning of inventiveness – *la débrouillardise* in French – and the expansion of economic activities at the local level that aimed to deal with the intractable economic crisis (see MacGaffey 1991;Vwakyanakazi 1982).[4] Disenchanted by the failure of the dominant economic paradigm to improve their living conditions and frustrated by the unwieldy regulations imposed on them by the state, many Congolese resorted to the informal sector to realize their socio-economic aspirations. The other was the expansion of civil society, notably the revival of socio-cultural networks of solidarity and mutual assistance, particularly in urban areas, which prompted new forms of social interactions and helped their membership articulate collective expectations or grievances.[5]

Together, the informal sector and civil society organizations forged the rise of political awareness and facilitated the expression of grievances against the state and the economy. It was largely the mobilization and pressure exerted by these organizations that forced President Mobutu Sese Seko to dismantle the single-party regime in 1990, and President Joseph Kabila not to stand for a third term in 2018.

Capital accumulation and the state

Whenever one wonders how the Congolese people can afford to live on less than one United States dollar a day in such a rich country, the usual answer is to blame President Mobutu's kleptocracy or his successors' corrupt rule. The reality is not as simple as that. It is true that Mr. Mobutu and his cronies – not to mention his successors – are to be blamed for their shameless appropriation of the national wealth for private gains while leaving the country bankrupt. However, it is important to avoid the temptation of explaining the DRC's ills with single variables, no matter how relevant they may be. Personal misconduct and unwise policy choices since the mid-1970s did aggravate the crisis, but strictly speaking they did not cause it.

The roots of the unending crisis – and the people's resilience – lie in the nature of the top-down economic paradigm that had been dominant since the times of King Leopold II's Congo Free State in the 19th century, and its relation to the state and society. Over two centuries, this paradigm has bred major contradictions in the society upon which it was enforced. As the contradictions accumulated and society became more restive, the state gradually lost its ability to regulate the dominant economic paradigm and impose law and order.

I therefore consider the unending crisis in the DRC as being largely a crisis of capital accumulation (Bézy et al. 1981; Vwakyanakazi 1982; Nzongola 1986). Ever since its forced incorporation into the capitalist system, beginning with the Atlantic slave trade and all through the Leopoldian and (post-)colonial eras, labor and raw materials from the DRC were critical to capital accumulation and the survival and prosperity of capitalist investments in the West. But nothing was done to empower local people, stimulate local entrepreneurship and lay the ground for a locally driven process of capital accumulation. Quite the opposite: all policies were geared towards stifling local entrepreneurship and allowing economic opportunities for the natives only as workforce for capital.

To put it simply, capital accumulation is said to occur when (i) there is a surplus resulting from a productive activity; (ii) that surplus is used for investment rather mere consumption; and (iii) the process occurs in a steady and significant manner. All three conditions, particularly the last one, should be met for capital accumulation to take place.

Bottomore (1991) prefers to use a different terminology – reproduction – instead of accumulation. For him, reproduction refers to the production of both (i) the means of production and consumption, and (ii) the setting up of conditions whereby this process continues to take place, i.e., reproduce itself. In this sense, Bottomore classifies reproduction in two types: (i) simple reproduction – sometimes referred to as primitive accumulation – when the surplus is wholly consumed by the owner of the means of production, and (ii) extended reproduction, which is the same as capital accumulation under the third condition above where the process repeats itself in an extensive way (Bottomore 1991, 469–474).[6]

The study of capital accumulation is therefore critical to the understanding of society's capacity to take care of itself. For accumulation is not solely an economic activity. To paraphrase the French sociologist Alain Touraine, it is above all a social process that is central to society's efforts to transcend itself. As a result, capital accumulation often becomes an arena of class struggle where the ruling and subordinated classes are opposed (Touraine 1977, 21).

In the struggle for capital accumulation, capital and the state often – but not always – operate in symbiosis. Just like a plant, capital requires fertile ground for its growth and prosperity. On its part, the state operates as an agent of social change by performing three essential functions: (i) resource extraction and investments in areas deemed critical to the welfare of the country and its people; (ii) regulation of social behavior through the imposition of law and order and control of the monopoly of use of force; and (iii) conduct of foreign relations. It is also the state, through the ruling elite, that defines the dominant economic paradigm (Touraine 1981, 108–109) and determines the conditions favorable to capital reproduction. In this sense, capital and the state depend on each other in particular ways for their maintenance. In general, they also tend to benefit from each other's performance.

In the case of the DRC, the interdependence between capital and the state goes a long way, starting from the times of King Leopold's Congo Free State. With the support of the American government, the Belgian king secured ownership of this vast land as a personal property. Thus began a process of accumulation based on forced native labor, the establishment of an economy wholly controlled by the Belgian royal family and the collection of rubber and ivory as the main primary commodities for the metropolitan industries (Mulambu Mvuluya 1974). Large concessions were granted to Belgian and some European companies in mining exploration and, in particular, rubber and ivory collection. King Leopold II was handsomely rewarded from the huge profits these companies made in the Congo Free State.

All this came to an end with the emergence of the Congo Reform Movement so aptly described by Nzongola (2002, 23–26). Eventually, King Leopold II was forced to cede his personal property to Belgium: the Congo Free State became the Belgian Congo in 1909, within the same borders as in 1885. But the transfer of landowners did not change the already established pattern of accumulation. Quite the opposite: it strengthened anew the symbiosis between capital and the colonial state under what came to be known as the *trinité coloniale* – colonial trinity – and led to similar abuses and popular revolts, like the famous revolt of the Bapende between May and September 1931 (Mulambu Mvuluya 1971).

The colonial trinity was made of three pillars – the three Cs: the capitalists, the colonizers and the Catholic church – whose interests were closely intertwined. The colonial administration in the metropole continued to grant vast concessions to selected capitalist ventures, giving preference to Belgian corporations. On the ground, the largely Belgian corps of administrators ensured the exploitation of the colony's labor and natural resources and did not hesitate, under the pretense of maintaining law and order, to resort to draconian measures to quell any form of resistance – laziness, it was dubbed – on the part of the natives. As for the Catholic missions, they took on the ideological task of pacifying the natives by converting them to Christianity – to save their souls from paganism – and inculcating in them the rudiments of the Judeo-Christian civilization.

The colonial trinity worked well for Belgium. It made possible the prosperity of the metropole and contributed to the launch of this small European kingdom among the most advanced industrialized countries in the world. On the ground, the colonizer expanded road and rail infrastructural projects, such as the Chemin de fer du Congo Supérieur aux Grands Lacs Africains (CFL), the Chemin de fer du Bas-Congo au Katanga (BCK), as well as airport infrastructure (for the defunct SABENA airline) in selected colonial cities for the exclusive use of European companies, Catholic missionaries and colonial administrators. Interestingly, all this infrastructure was designed in such a way that roads and rails connected the point of raw material extraction to the point of export, leaving the rest of the colony with dirt trails.

`It is ironic that Belgium attends the annual celebrations of the Allied victory in World War II even though its army surrendered to the Nazi Wehrmacht without a fight. Rather, it was the natives in the Belgian Congo who fought the Italians in the Campagne d'Abyssinie – Saio, Gambela and Assossa in today's Ethiopia. Not only had the natives fought in a war they had nothing to do with, they were compelled to contribute to the war effort – *effort de guerre* – and increase production to sustain the Allied forces' pursuit of the war and keep the metropole financial afloat during and after the war.[7] It is public knowledge that the Belgian government in exile in London was fully funded and kept financially afloat thanks to the colony's war effort (Saint Moulin 1985).

None of this benefitted the colonized. In fact, the war effort generated a great deal of resentment and bitterness among the natives. Popular revolts against colonial rule in the colonial world spread in the Belgian Congo. Eventually, some political elites in the metropole began to consider measures for a relaxation of the colonial policy.

One such measure concerned the colonial education policy for the natives. Up until then, Belgium enforced a discriminatory policy based on the principle of *pas d'élite pas de problème* – no elite, no problem. Only Christian missionary schools provided a modicum of literacy and only to men who aspired to the priesthood. The change that was instituted after World War II aimed to promote an urban middle class of *évolués*, which included veterans of the Campagne d'Abyssinie. But the highest level of education was the equivalent of today's elementary certificate, and the graduates were generally employed in the subaltern categories in the colonial administration as typists ("clerks"), bookkeepers, elementary school teachers, nurse aids or agricultural monitors, depending on their aptitude.[8]

The dominant colonial paradigm was essentially paternalistic. It infantilized the colonized, excluded them from the decision-making institutions running their lives and blocked all attempts on their part at self-empowerment. The massive structural impoverishment (Illife 1987) that ensued, particularly in rural areas, and the widespread deterioration of living conditions in the cities fueled popular anger against the colonial system. Meanwhile, a new form of opposition emerged against the teachings of the predominantly white Christian missionaries and which the colonizers struggled in vain to suppress. The self-proclaimed "Prophet" Simon Kimbangu, whose life ended in a colonial prison, was among the most prominent initiators of the new resistance. Conditions were ripe for the rise of an independence movement that forced Belgium to hastily grant national sovereignty to its colony on June 30, 1960, merely four months after the beginning of the negotiations.

The state and macroeconomic crisis

Capital penetration and state intervention went hand in hand during the Leopoldian and colonial eras. The DRC's abrupt independence broke this interdependence, in that capital remained foreign – mostly Belgian – while the state was indigenized. The problematic *contentieux belgo-congolais* that arose at independence was the first sign of the rising conflict between the state and capital.

The conflict escalated in 1967 when President Mobutu ordered the nationalization of Belgian corporations and assets based in the DRC and undertook the rash of business indigenization in 1973 under the policy of Zaïrianization.

Together, these developments precipitated a massive capital flight, causing a deep hole in the DRC's mainstream economy.[9] Clobbered by the global crisis of the mid-1970s and ruined by the fiscal indiscipline that characterized President Mobutu's rule, the DRC plunged into a socio-economic abyss and a near collapse, with the catastrophic consequences that endure to this date.

Contentieux belgo-congolais

The Brussels negotiations of February 1960 – also known as the first *Table Ronde* – that resulted in Belgium's decision to grant independence to the colony were mainly focused on political issues about the administrative organization of the future independent state. They left aside crucial socio-economic issues that needed to be settled before independence, notably the fate of the colonial public debt and the future of the Belgian capital and investments in the colony (Gérard-Libois 1966; Gérard-Libois and Verhaegen 1960).

An Economic Round Table was eventually held in May 1960. Except for matters of technical cooperation and the financial aid that Belgium had promised to the upcoming independent state, the conference did not reach a conclusion on how to share the colonial public debt. Belgian delegates at the conference were of the view that the promised financial assistance should enable the new state to honor the debts it would inherit from colonization. But the Congolese side refused to commit itself on the ground that, since the Congo was still a colony, the Congolese negotiators who were present in Brussels had no constitutional mandate to commit a country that was not yet in existence.

On the other issue, the Congolese side expected Belgium, on Independence Day, to provide a detailed inventory of the colonial portfolio – *le portefeuille colonial* – detailing the nature and scope of capital investments and the assets owned by colonial enterprises in the Congo. Belgium did not reject the Congolese demand; but it never acted on it.[10]

In the first few months after independence, the new state paid off part of the outstanding colonial debt, but it stopped new payments thereafter. This was a drastic move, considering the size and importance of Belgian interests that were thus affected – nearly 95 percent of the colonial public debt – as well as the financial losses incurred by hundreds of thousands of individual Belgians who had invested in the former colony's highly profitable economy. In retaliation, Belgium decided to "temporarily" keep a hold on the management of the colonial portfolio, setting off the *contentieux belgo-congolais*.

Negotiations resumed in 1963 and culminated in the signing, two years later, of agreements on the settlement of the colonial public debt and the colonial portfolio. However, none of them provided a final resolution to the dispute between the two governments. This was where matters stood when President Mobutu took power in a coup d'état in November 1965.

President Mobutu questioned all previous agreement on the ground that they were concluded at the expense of the Congolese people. Frustrated by the lack of progress in the new rounds of talks, he decided in June 1966 to terminate the *contentieux belgo-congolais*. He also ordered the government to confiscate the assets of Belgian companies located in the DRC and the dissolution of some of them. This was the beginning of the spate of nationalization that would continue in 1967 and culminate with the policy of Zaïrianization of 30 November 1973.

Zaïrianization policy

The policy of Zaïrianization was one of the boldest attempt by President Mobutu's *parti-état* to reverse the domination effect of foreign capital in the domestic economy and replace it with a domestic capital accumulation process (Kikassa 1976a; 1976b; Korner 1991, 231).[11] The objective was to transfer to Zairian citizens the ownership of small- and medium-sized businesses hitherto owned by foreigners. The policy can be summarized in one sentence: "Today, if we made a profound analysis of our country's situation, we may say that politically we are a free nation, that culturally we are becoming free, but that economically, we are still not in control of our economy" (Mobutu 1975).

Addressing the trade imbalances between the former Zaire and its ex-metropole, President Mobutu claimed that, in the early 1970s, one-third of Belgium's trade surplus originated from Zaire. He pointed out that the Belgian economy had earned at the time approximately 2 billion Belgian francs in insurance payments for Zairian exports, and that the annual returns of Belgian total investments in Zaire – about US$100 million – were roughly US$120 million. In contrast, Belgium had invested more in Canada – over US$910 million – but earned little in comparison – only US$8 million (Mobutu 1975, 407–409). Alluding to Belgian Congo's war effort in World War II, Mobutu called the continuous transfer of the DRC's resources to Belgium as a "post-war effort" (Mobutu 1975, 424).

If President Mobutu was right that 90 percent of businesses in the mainstream economy were owned or controlled by foreigners, and if his claims on trade imbalances with Belgium were correct, then Zaïrianization made some sense. However, during its implementation and after the new owners – called *les acquéreurs* – proved their ineptitude, Zaïrianization began to show inconsistencies and the lack of serious reflection that has always plagued development planning in the DRC.

First came the problem of ownership of the new businesses: was it the foreign owner, the state or the *acquéreur*, the man or woman who had acquired it? Zaire's law suggested that Zaïrianization was a transfer of property rights to Zairian citizens, but on the condition that the business would be managed in such a manner that it would contribute to the nation's economic growth, in other words, capital accumulation (Lukombe 1979, 19). This was not to be because most of these businesses became insolvent in just a few months after their acquisition.

Another provision required the *acquéreurs* to compensate previous owners. It stipulated that only those who could provide a receipt verifying that all debts to previous owners or to the state treasury had been paid in full would be considered full owners (Lukombe 1979, 20). Evidently, this clause was not fully implemented for the same insolvency reason. So most foreign owners lost their businesses as well as their investments in the DRC. In the end, Zaïrianization wrecked the mainstream economy, caused serious shortages in domestic markets and, more tragically, failed to promote the domestication of capital accumulation as intended by President Mobutu (if his speech was to be read literally). Rather, all that the policy achieved was to precipitate capital flight. With respect to capital accumulation, Zairianization turned out to be a mistaken change of players, not a change of the game plan.

Even if the *acquéreurs* had managed their businesses in a capable manner (as some tried), they would have still gone bankrupt because they didn't have access to credit either domestically (because of a weak banking system) or internationally. And even if President Mobutu had not made that fateful policy decision, the probability of a crisis was still inevitable: the DRC's mainstream economy was already in such trouble at the end of the 1960s that it would have hardly survived the impact of the global crisis of the 1970s.

The impact of the global crisis of the 1970s

The mainstream economy hit the bottom of its recession in 1975–1976, with a negative GDP growth of 7.4 percent. By the end of the 1980s, the macroeconomic indicators were by all measures extremely bad. Taking 1970 as the base year, the GDP averaged a negative annual growth between 1975 and 1991 (National Conference 1992, 21). With the population growth estimated at around 3 percent annually during the same period, the revenue per person was computed at US$170, down from US$430 in 1970 (National Conference 1992, 19). The downwards trend continued well into the 1990s and beyond, to the extent that Congolese people are now said to live on less than one dollar a day.

It is noteworthy that much of the macroeconomic crisis the DRC has experienced over the decades, at least since the mid-1970s, has been of a financial nature (Kabuya and Kikassa 1980, 5). For example, between 1975 and 1989, the deficit of public finances reached about US$600 million while foreign exchange reserves, which were estimated at US$220 million in 1970, were almost entirely exhausted by the end of 1980.

Moreover, the mainstream economy has always been export-oriented and heavily dependent on the mining industry, making it the main recipient of national and foreign investments. For years, Congolese policy-makers and their foreign advisers promoted an industrialization paradigm based on the development of the mining sector as the key engine of growth. They argued that revenues from mineral exports would trickle down and spur growth in other sectors. But the trickledown effects never took place. The mining sector became

> an enclave economy that absorb[ed] the lion's share of national and multilateral economic effort, but whose surplus [was] either lost through unequal exchanges and loss of value or used in particular ways at particular levels that [were] not in the interest of most of the people.
>
> (Katwala 1979, 12)

The crisis of the 1970s slowed global demand for mineral exports. Between 1971 and 1991, the total volume of exports fell by as much as 67.45 percent. In the mining sector, the decline was estimated at 32.9 percent (National Conference 1992, 21–22). The sharp fall in exports and commodity prices (notably copper, the main mineral export commodity) significantly affected foreign earnings and worsened the state's already growing current account problems.

The mainstream economy was also highly dependent on imports – oil and manufactured goods for the mining industry. The sharp increase in oil prices in the 1970s inflicted serious harm in many ways. One effect was the depletion of state's foreign reserves, as described above. The other was the reliance on international borrowing, which caused a massive increase in the external debt – about US$7 billion in 2018.[12]

Fiscal indiscipline

Public spending reflects how dominant groups in control of the state use public revenues to further their own interests, that is, "to reproduce and enlarge [their] own class base" (Campbell 1985, 268). This has been the case ever since fiscal indiscipline was introduced by President Mobutu, who used his grip over the state's finances to consolidate his rule and buy external alliances. As a result, an intractable fiscal crisis engulfed the state's finances starting from the mid-1970s and bankrupt the nation. It has not gone away.

At the end of the 1960s, the DRC's mainstream economy was considered among the strongest in Africa, with a surplus in foreign reserves of about US$220 million, sufficient to cover three years of imports (Ndele 1992, 6). The situation changed shortly after 1970 when the state engaged in a pattern of public spending characterized by huge budget deficits financed by monetization and foreign borrowing. For the year 1978 alone, public spending rose to 10.2 percent of the GDP while public revenues grew by only 5.7 percent (Kabuya and Kikassa 1980, 15).

President Mobutu's office, the many agencies and specialized institutions of the *parti-état* and the ministry of defense – all under his firm grip – consumed an excessive proportion of the annual budget, compared to the measly appropriations for critical ministries like national education, agriculture or public health. In fiscal year 1987, President Mobutu's political institutions were allocated approximately 19 million zaïres – the national currency during his regime – while the combined budget appropriations for those ministries were only about 720,000 zaïres. In other words, less than 4 percent of the budget for that year was spent on social or economic projects that would have benefitted the people.

By the middle of the 1970s, it had become clear that President Mobutu and the Mobutistes, i.e., the legion of profiteers in the MPR, were using the *parti-état* to enrich themselves with impunity. The imposition of structural adjustment programs with their package of austerity measures – popularly known as *la rigueur* – further destroyed the country's socio-economic fabric and wrecked people's livelihoods. Fed up with the unending crisis, the population denounced the corrupt nature of the state, demanded radical change – *le changement* – and ultimately forced the demise of the *parti-état*.

Rise and fall of the new breed of African leaders

The 1990s sounded the death knell of the Mobutu regime at the hands of a "New Breed of African Leaders" that was conveniently godfathered by President Bill Clinton's administration.[13] Terminally ill and consumed with the feeling of having been betrayed – "stabbed in the back," he said – President Mobutu spent the rest of his presidency between Europe for medical care and his village of Gbadolite.

Much has already been said about the West's nefarious role, with the United States in the lead, in shaping the DRC's fate with total disregard for its people's will. The first "war of liberation" in October 1996 culminated in the ousting of President Mobutu in May 1997. The campaign to overthrow President Mobutu was planned and spearheaded by the Presidents of Uganda and Rwanda with the help of Mzee Laurent Désiré Kabila and the nod of Western powers and some African countries (Ngbanda 2004). During his short tenure, Mzee Kabila undertook to rebuild the quasi-state and the bankrupt economy he inherited from his predecessor. He also had to contend with the people's mixed reaction to the foreign character of the coalition that brought him to power. Eventually, the nation rallied around him in the hope that he would usher in a new era. Overall, his efforts yielded little dividend.

More sinister was the second "war of liberation" waged again by Rwanda and Uganda against one of their own in August 1998, and whose repercussions have had a lasting effect on the DRC people (Péan 2010). Launched supposedly against Mzee Kabila's dictatorial and genocidal impulses, this phony war was at once a criminal looting enterprise and an attempt to partition the country, during which some neighboring countries became exporters of minerals they did not possess (Mwanasali 2000). The looting, along with the mafia-like shakedowns of local businessmen and women, involved Rwandan and Ugandan troops and their Congolese pawns, as well as an assortment of obscure networks of profiteers of foreign wars – Lebanese, Indian and Pakistani, for the most part – along with some Western multinationals that acquired the proceeds of the loot. Unlike the first war, this one was rejected by the Congolese population in its large majority. Thousands of innocent civilians in the Kivu provinces and elsewhere in the country were killed because they opposed the foreign occupation of their land and stood bravely for the unity and territorial integrity of their country.

There is not much to say about capital accumulation during the years of *la Kabilie.*[14] The mainstream economy and its dominant paradigm were in abyss. Having lost its legitimacy and facing growing opposition from the people, the state gave up all its sovereign functions to concentrate on its self-preservation and the protection of the political elite. These trends began with President Mobutu in the mid-1970s; they continued under Mzee Kabila and his successor and son, President Joseph Kabila (2001–2018). This is the abysmal legacy of *Mobutisme* and *Kabilie* that the current President Félix Tshisekedi is striving against.[15]

Living conditions under President Mobutu were appalling; they became intolerable under his successors, to the extent that even the most ardent Kabilistes admitted to destroying the nation's socio-economic fabric. In fact, President Kabila did not fail, because he did not try. Rather, he entrusted his duties to his relatives and scions who captured whatever was left of the state and the economy to enrich themselves shamelessly and with impunity. Like his predecessor, President Kabila lost his legitimacy and relevance, as demonstrated by the massive street protests that took place all over the country under the slogan *Kabila, Dégage*! – Kabila, Get Out!

Resilience

The post-colonial history of the DRC is remarkable in the many ways in which the people have demonstrated resilience in the face of recurrent wars and economic hardship. They lived through the secession of the Katanga province (1960–1963) and the Mulelist rebellion (1963–1965). They survived attempts by white mercenaries to occupy part of the country in the 1960s, as well as two invasions of the Katanga province in the 1970s. Nor had the phony wars of liberation of the 1990s and the widespread insecurity that reigned across their land defeated their resolve to live in a united and prosperous country. Ironically, a country that has failed its citizens in every way now owes its very existence to their patriotism.

It is from this perspective that one ought to explain resilience. The inventiveness of the informal sector was ultimately an element of resilience, so was the expansion of civil society organizations and their relentless fight, at great personal cost, for human rights and democracy. As Nzongola (2002, 3) correctly puts it,

> the independence struggle of the 1950s, the popular insurrections for a "second independence" in the 1960s, the fight against Mobutu's one-party dictatorship, and the current struggle against new forms of dictatorship and external oppression have, as a common denominator, the demand for expanded rights politically and for a better life economically.

The politicization of the informal sector

As I argued earlier in this chapter, the roots of the bottomless macroeconomic crisis – and the rise of the informal sector – lie in the contradictions that developed, starting from Independence Day, between the state and foreign capital. As these contradictions accumulated, the state gradually lost its ability to contain them and, ultimately, its own legitimacy.

Having lost control of capital and its own legitimacy, the state applied various stratagems to preserve itself by other means. One consisted in the creation of loopholes in the macroeconomic structure by either relaxing, or not seriously enforcing, various rules regulating the conduct of economic activities that were already blossoming at the grassroots level, notably in the area of savings and small credit co-operatives. As these loopholes existed and small businessmen and women in the informal sector could find areas of accommodation, the state was able to claim to care about the welfare of the general population even though it did not (Ilunga Kabongo 1984, 16–17). In pursuing this laissez-faire stratagem, President Mobutu was able, though with increasing difficulties, to mediate popular discontent and ensure a relatively peaceful social order.

This laissez-faire stratagem suggests that the relationship between capital, the state and society is not a one-way street, so to speak, but a dynamic whole. Even in the most repressive regimes, the state usually tries – or pretends – to listen to the demands and protests of the ruled classes (Therborn 1978, 220). Through his numerous intelligence services or during his public rallies, President Mobutu was aware of the people's complaints about various issues affecting their lives. Occasionally, he reacted by denouncing *les dix fléaux* – the ten plagues – that ate at the core of his regime or shuffled the cabinet to get rid of disreputable officials. As Nicos Poulantzas (1978, 190) aptly remarks,

> The capitalist state has inscribed in its very structures a flexibility which concedes a certain guarantee to the economic interests of certain dominated classes, within the limits of the system. To the extent that this guarantee is in accordance with the hegemonic domination of the dominant classes, [...] this concession is part of the state's very function.

Under President Mobutu, the state allowed the informal sector to operate as a concession in return for its subservience to the *parti-état*. However, the adoption of structural adjustment programs compelled the state to crack down on the informal sector which was now depicted as a violation of the same law that had allowed it to operate, and a drain of resources from the quasi-existent mainstream economy. *La rigueur* became so intolerable and provoked such a widespread popular rejection of the single-party state that Mobutu had no other choice but to dismantle it (see also Nzongola 2002).

The informal sector remains the mainstay of economic activities at the grassroots level. Unsurprisingly, there is still some uneasiness about giving it its due, even as it has proven its resilience and has been vital for the well-being of the people over the decades.[16]

Civil society

Civil society is an old tradition in the DRC, dating back to the colonial era when native workers who migrated to the new European towns and cities began to set up *mutualités* – mutual aid and solidarity groups – along ethnic and regional lines. Gradually, some of these groups took on a political character and evolved into political parties at independence. After independence, thanks in part to Christian missions, others grew into co-operatives, focusing on organizing agricultural production or promoting savings and credit. The trend spread over the years to the point that savings and credit co-operatives became, starting from the austerity period of the mid-1980s, a credible and popular alternative for capital mobilization and a serious competitor to commercial banks.

It was during the National Conference that civil society emerged as a serious contender to the hitherto exclusive power of the state to decide society's future.[17] President Mobutu decided to convene it as a constitutional conference, as a kind of Zairian *perestroika*, and only after the consultations he had commissioned earlier in 1990 revealed widespread popular dissatisfaction with the single-party rule. But the people wanted more: thanks to their courage and persistent demands, the forum gave itself the powers not only to examine critically the institutions of the Second Republic but also to dismantle them (see, e.g., Monsengwo 1993, 275–285).[18]

The National Conference generated great expectations among the population, especially among the youth, that its decisions would be binding upon all individuals and political institutions. However, President Mobutu and his ruling coalition saw it as a mere consultative forum with no legitimacy to make binding decisions. On several occasions, the attempt by the Mobutistes to stall the deliberations were met with strong popular resistance, as was the case with the peaceful march sponsored by the Catholic church in February 1992 for the resumption of the proceedings, which resulted in deadly confrontation with President Mobutu's security apparatus.

The National Conference also crystallized public opinion around the country's social ills. Through *le déballage* – public denunciations of state officials, detailed accounts of murders and exactions, live discussions of plunder and destruction of public infrastructures – the conference presented the population with an account and the identity of those whose actions had plunged the nation into abyss. Most of the people who took an active part in the proceedings demanded radical transformation of the state and the dominant economic paradigm. This is how the expression *le changement* – radical change – entered the DRC's rich political lexicon.

Just as with the informal sector, civil society activism was at first non-political. It became political in the late 1980s when complaints about deteriorating living conditions turned into direct attacks against the state and its incumbents. Civil society, particularly, youth-led organizations, blossomed under President Joseph Kabila, especially after he decided to postpone the elections of 2016.[19] Their activism became commonplace and was usually repressed with unheard-of violence.

Whereto from here?

Let us summarize. The chapter has tried to address the question why such a resource-rich country as the DRC has failed to improve the living conditions of its citizenry. I argued that the answer is to be found in the relation between the state and capital, and particularly their failure to stimulate an endogenous process of capital accumulation by empowering the people at the grassroots level and promoting local entrepreneurship. An endogenous process is critical not just to ensuring that accumulation occurs in an extended and sustained way, but that society is transformed for the benefit of its people.

Prior to the DRC's independence, a close interdependence existed between capital and the colonial state. While this symbiosis produced high yields for Belgian and other Western investments in the colony, it did nothing to stimulate an endogenous process of capital formation. On the contrary, all was done to stifle it, as the natives were deemed good only as workforce in the mines and the plantations of coffee, cotton or rubber. Independence brought an abrupt change, but it did not pay any significant dividend as far as the promotion of a local process of capital accumulation was concerned. Nor did policy decisions under President Mobutu and his successors, which resulted in bringing the state into disrepute and the dominant economic paradigm to its knees.

But there are still some reasons to be hopeful. The DRC is still a geological wonderland despite years of mismanagement, looting and armed conflicts. Decades of suffering and living like strangers in their own country have not undermined the determination of the Congolese people to take charge of their own destiny. On the contrary, their resilience has been further strengthened. On the other hand, there is no doubt that the path to socio-economic reconstruction and political transformation will be long and arduous, and that the climb out of the abyss caused by *Mobutisme* and *la Kabilie* will be difficult. In short, the times ahead are trying for the DRC people. What to do?

Nowadays the priority seems to be to restore the trust of foreign partners and international donors in the hope of attracting foreign capital and investments. This is commendable, and the reactions of international partners, although hesitant, are encouraging. Given the country's vast untapped resources, it is likely that foreign capital will decide to come back, at first a small drop certainly, but it eventually will.

But there are major hurdles ahead. First is the transformation of the state, its core institutions and leadership. As I have argued, the state holds a crucial role in creating favorable conditions to capital accumulation. The difficulties in this regard are enormous. People wrestled power from the Kabilistes in

2018 and elected Félix Tshisekedi as the new president. But the political parties affiliated with his predecessor still control the legislature, much of the executive and even the judiciary, not to mention the provincial institutions and the state security apparatus. And they have used their grip to either slow down or simply derail the implementation of decisions that could benefit the country. Voicing his frustration with this arrangement, President Tshisekedi has now appealed directly to the people to create a "sacred union" for the development of the country. How this will be done is an open question.

The second hurdle is that the state has the critical task of defining the dominant development paradigm. However, it appears that this issue is still in limbo. Right now, the DRC seems to be run like a series of projects, and the authorities have yet to present a coherent vision on the country's future and how they plan to accomplish it. Given the DRC's dismal record in development planning, this silence is a matter of serious concern.

If the dominant development paradigm remains top-down and dependent on foreign capital, it will be exceedingly difficult to lift the Congolese people from poverty and have them benefit from their country's bountiful resources. Under this scenario, the informal sector will continue to expand, with the possibility of increased politicization. On the other hand, if the democratization process stalls, given the growing skepticism most people harbor against the state, civil society's street protests will intensify, with the probability of increased confrontations with the state security apparatus and more bloodshed.

Furthermore, assuming that the state becomes more democratic in a way that grants the population a greater say in the management of the public good – which is what President Tshisekedi is trying to do and some Kabilistes seem to resist – but little progress is made to transform the dominant development paradigm, the informal sector will continue to expand with the political consequences that I alluded to in the preceding paragraph. And if by a magic wand the state and the development paradigm are radically transformed, considering the complete disintegration of the mainstream economy during the last four decades, any plan for the DRC's economic reconstruction would have to be built from below and take inspiration from the inventiveness and dynamism of local entrepreneurs in the informal sector.

In conclusion, it is imperative to develop a deep understanding of the DRC's political economy over time and the dynamic responses it has generated at the level of ordinary men and women, more importantly how they have constantly adjusted their lives to cope with the constraints they faced and invent new opportunities for themselves. It is for this reason that I decided to focus this chapter on the people's resilience in the face of the tug of war between the state and foreign capital in the Democratic Republic of the Congo. After all, this is how the people have lived their lives amidst the unending political and economic turmoil. It is doubtful they will accept any imposition to change their ways of life.

Notes

1 I prefer the word endogenous to indigenous for the following reason. Societies, and the communities within, have their own ways of being and doing things. An endogenous process of accumulation is grounded in those local values without necessarily being in opposition to the Western ways of 'doing' capital accumulation, as the word indigenous sometimes suggests (see, e.g., Vwakyanakazi 1982). I therefore do not find the dichotomy between 'indigenous capitalism' (see, e.g., the title in MacGaffey 1987) vs. Western capitalism appropriate because it leaves out the various linkages and complementarity that may exist between the two modes of capital accumulation (Mwanasali 1994), in spite of the socio-cultural differences of where accumulation takes place. In other words, capital accumulation is not exclusively a Western process. Nor is Westernization a sine qua non for a society to achieve capital accumulation and economic prosperity.

2 Offloading and power outage are so frequent and often for such long periods that small power generators and solar panels are now a fixture in households that can afford them. But they are quite expensive to acquire and maintain. Nor can they be a substitute for hydroelectric power to support the country's industrialization.

3 This chapter is a sketch of an ongoing work on the state and the politics of informality in the Democratic Republic of the Congo. The original analysis served as the basis for the dissertation I submitted to Northwestern University for my Ph.D. degree. The conceptual framework has slightly evolved, but the main thrust remains the same.

4 Speaking of resourcefulness, the people invented a fictitious article in an equally fictitious constitution that had given them the right to fend for themselves. This is the famous expression *Article Quinze: Débrouillez-Vous!* – Article 15: Fend for yourself! – which became the leitmotif for all the people who engage in the informal sector. In the Congolese political lexicon, "Article Quinze" is used to justify involvement in informal economic activities.

5 There is a practice in the DRC known as *équilibre régional* – regional equilibrium. It is a form of exercise in ethnic arithmetic that became a policy of sort since President Mobutu's tenure. When making appointments in public offices, the appointing authority must take regional equilibrium into account and ensure a balanced and equitable representation of all the provinces and ethnic groupings.

6 In this chapter, accumulation or capital accumulation, (capital) reproduction or extended reproduction will be used interchangeably. Capital is used as a shortcut for both the means of production and their owners or top managers, also referred to as captains of industry. Investment, on the other hand, simply means the acquisition of additional capital.

7 It is well known that the first atomic bomb was produced with the Congolese uranium.

8 This is the "intellectual elite" who took over the management of the newly independent state. At independence, the DRC had only 12 university graduates. The first university – the Catholic Université Lovanium – was created in 1954, but it enrolled exceedingly few Congolese students and made sure they dropped out before graduation. On the legacy of the colonial education, see Nzongola-Ntalaja (2002, 173–175).

9 Mainstream economy refers to the network of production and exchange of goods and services that is sponsored by the state and recognized by the DRC's foreign partners. Through their investments and policy preferences, this economy serves as

the dominant development paradigm. Its performance is quantitatively measured by the central bank and international financial institutions, and serves as a yardstick of the country's economic "progress," even though evidence shows that most people in the DRC do not depend much on it for a living.

10 In reality, Belgium refused to hand over the assets of the former colony located in Belgium (financial assets, real estate and portfolio) as long as it had to assume the payment of the debt contracted by the colony and as long as Belgians who had worked or invested in the colony had not been paid their dues or compensated for their losses.

11 The term *parti-état* was used after the merger between the single party, Mouvement populaire de la révolution (MPR), which President Mobutu created in June 1967, and the Zairian state. Throughout his tenure, the MPR held sway on the state, the economy and every aspect of social life. Its ideology was *le Mobutisme*, and the political culture centered on the cult of President Mobutu as the savior of the nation. President Mobutu's cronies were collectively referred to as the *Mobutistes.*

12 This amount is low due mainly to adverse borrowing conditions in Western financial markets and fewer (and low) disbursements in general. However, it is too large for the DRC because of the low level of government revenues, which results in a low debt-carrying capacity and the vulnerability to debt repayment (International Development Association and IMF 2019, 1). For the sake of comparison, the total budget for the 2021 fiscal year is estimated at US$6.8 billion!

13 Paul Kagame of Rwanda, Yoweri Museveni of Uganda, Meles Zenawi of Ethiopia, Isaias Afewerki of Eritrea and, to some extent, Laurent Désiré Kabila. President Clinton's new generation of African leaders did not fare well together. Kagame and Museveni turned against Laurent Désiré Kabila shortly before Meles and Isaias fought twice a bitter war. Kagame and Museveni also collided in Kisangani three times during their occupation of the DRC; their relationship is still frosty.

14 The term *Kabilie* was coined by the largest opposition party at the time, Union pour la démocratie et le progrès social (UDPS), to decry the venality of state incumbents and the perversities of the regime of President Joseph Kabila, the consequences of which had devastated the country and destroyed people's lives. President Kabila's cronies are referred to collectively as the *Kabilistes*. Both terms are always used pejoratively, but not in this chapter where they are just a shortcut for the 21 years of the rule by Kabila the father and the son (1997–2018).

15 Félix Tshisekedi won the presidential elections of December 2018 as UDPS head. He has been constrained to work with his predecessor in a tense political coalition because the alliance of political parties affiliated with his predecessor is in control of the key institutions of the state (the parliament, the government and the judiciary, as well as the security apparatuses).

16 Just to give an example, President Tshisekedi launched in August 2020 a project to support small and medium enterprises (SMEs) in the mainstream economy, which is funded to the tune of US$100 million by the World Bank. The project involves four cities, including Goma, Kinshasa, Lubumbashi and Matadi. According to government figures, the DRC counts less than 10,000 such SMEs; the others – that have never been counted – are in the informal sector. By June of this year, 31 percent of those SMEs ceased operations due to the pandemic. In fact, 50 percent of companies in the mainstream economy had lost at least 30 percent of their turnover by August 2020. That gives a total of about 980 companies that have closed, including 89 companies reported as large.

17 At that time, civil society organizations were fewer than they are nowadays, and they did not carry the clout they now have. So civil society then was another way of designating ordinary people, in opposition to political parties that were just emerging and the state. Theirs was a spontaneous movement.

18 "First Republic" refers to the period between 1960 and 1965, with President Joseph Kasavubu. The Second Republic was instituted by President Mobutu in 1965 and lasted until his ousting in 1997. Mzee Laurent Désiré Kabila ushered in the Third Republic in 1997. Since independence, the DRC has changed its names at least half a dozen times. It was called the Republic of Congo at independence, followed by the Democratic Republic of the Congo in 1964. During the time of President Mobutu, it became the Republic of Zaire, which Mzee Kabila unilaterally renamed the Democratic Republic of the Congo in May 1997. Some even suggested calling it the Republic of Congo-Zaïre or the Republic of the Lualaba (the name of the upstream part of the Congo River), but the suggestions did not fly.

19 In 2016, President Joseph Kabila was due to complete his second and final term in office, as mandated by the constitution, and was expected to retire. His decision to postpone the elections then was widely interpreted as an attempt to linger longer. A third term for President Kabila was unacceptable to most people. Young activists and other civil society organizations took to the streets across the country to force him out. Many lives were lost during the ensuing repression. The protests continued until 2018 when President Kabila finally decided not to seek a third term. The opposition won the presidential elections of December 2018 with a combined three-quarters of the votes, which shows just how poor the former President's popularity was at the time.

References

Bézy, F., Peemans, J.-P.. and Wautelet, J.-M. Eds. 1981. *Accumulation et sous-développement au Zaire. 1960–1980.* Louvain-la-Neuve: Presses Universitaires de Louvain.

Bottomore, T. 1991. *A Dictionary of Marxist Thought.* 2nd ed. Cambridge: Cambridge University Press, 469–474,

Campbell, B. 1985. "The Fiscal Crisis of the State: The Case of the Ivory Coast." In H. Bernstein and B. Campbell (Eds), *Contradictions of Accumulation in Africa.* Beverly Hills, CA: Sage Publications, 267–310.

Gérard-Libois, J. 1966. "La Liquidation du contentieux belgo-congolais et ses séquelles en 1966." *Etudes congolaises. Institut national d'études politiques*, 9(5.5).

Gérard-Libois, J. and Verhaegen, B. 1960. *Congo 1960,* Vol. 1. *Dossier du Centre de recherches et d'information sociopolitiques.* Brussels: CRISP.

Illife, J. 1987. *The African Poor.* New York: Cambridge University Press.

International Development Association and International Monetary Fund. 2019. *Ethe Democratic Republic of the Congo: Joint World-Bank-IMF Debt Sustainability Analysis.* Washington, DC: IMF.

Kabuya, K. and Kikassa, M. Eds. 1980. *The stabilisation économique et financière au Zaire de 1978 à 1980: De devaluations en cascade à la demonetisation.* Kinshasa: CEPAS.

Katwala, Gh. 1979. "Export-Led Growth: The Copper Sector." In G. Gran (Ed.), *Zaire: The Political Economy of Underdevelopment.* New York: Praeger, 122–136.

Kikassa, M. 1976a. "La stabilisation des entreprises zairianisées et radicalisées." *Zaire Afrique*, 102 (février), 89–98.

Kikassa, M. 1976b. "De la stabilisation au redressement des entreprises zairianisées et radicalisées." *Zaire Afrique*, 109 (novembre), 517–525.

Korner, P. et al. 1991. *The IMF and the Debt Crisis: A Guide to the Third World's Dilemma*. London: Zed Books.

Lukombe, Ng. 1979. *Zaïrianisation, Radicalisation, Rétrocession en République du Zaïre: Considérations juridiques*. Kinshasa: Presses Universitaires du Zaïre.

MacGaffey, J. 1987. *Entrepreneurs and Parasites: The Struggle for Indigenous Capitalism in Zaire*. New York: Cambridge University Press.

MacGaffey, J. Ed. 1991. *The Real Economy in Zaire*. Pittsburgh, PA: University of Pennsylvania Press.

Mobutu, S. S.. 1975. *EDiscours, allocutions, messages: 1965–1975*. Paris: Editions Jeune Afrique.

Monsengwo, P. 1993. "La démocratisation au Zaire et ses protagonistes." *Zaire Afrique*, 275–285.

Mulambu Mvuluya, F. 1974. *Cultures obligatoires et colonisation dans l'ex-Congo Belge*. Cahiers du CEDAF, 6–7. CEDAF.

Mulambu Mvuluya, F. 1971. *Contribution à la révolte des Bapende (mai-septembre 1931): Étude d'un movement de résistance des populations rurales congolaises à la colonisation*. Cahiers du CEDAF, 1. CEDAF.

Mwanasali, M. 2000. "The View from Below." In M. Berdal and D. Malone (Eds), *Greed and Grievance: Economic Agenda in Civil Wars*. Boulder, CO: Lynne Rienner Publishers, 137–153.

Mwanasali, M. 1994. "Accumulation, Regulation and Development: The Grassroots Economy in the Upper Zaire Region (1975–1992)." Ph.D. diss., Northwestern University, Evanston, IL.

National Conference. 1992. *Rapport des commissions*. Kinshasa: Conférence nationale souveraine.

Ndele, A. 1992. "Communication de M. Albert Ndele Bamu à la CNS." *La Référence Plus*, 66 (1 juin), 6–7.

Ngbanda, H. 2004. *Crimes organisés en Afrique centrale: Révélations sur les réseaux rwandais et occidentaux*. Paris: Editions Duboiris.

Nzongola-Ntalaja, G. 2002. *The Congo from Leopold to Kabila: A People's History*. London and New York: Zed Books Ltd.

Nzongola-Ntalaja, G. 1986. "Crisis and Change in Zaire, 1960–1985." In G. Nzongola-Ntalaja (Ed.), *The Crisis in Zaire: Myths and Realities*. Trenton, NJ: Africa World Press, 3–26.

Péan, P. 2010. *Carnages: Les guerres secrètes des grandes puissances en Afrique centrale*. Paris: Fayard.

Poulantzas, N. 1978. *Political Power and Social Classes*. London: Verso.

Saint Moulin, L. de. 1985. . "De L'effort de guerre 1940–1945 au Zaire." *Zaire Afrique*, 192, 91–106.

Therborn, G. 1978. *What does the Ruling Class do When it Rules? State Apparatuses and State Power under Feudalism, Capitalism and Socialism*. London: Schoken Books.

Touraine, A. 1977. *The Self-Production of Society*. Chicago, IL: University of Chicago Press.

Touraine, A. 1981. *The Voice and the Eye: An Analysis of Social Movements*. Cambridge: Cambridge University Press.

Vwakyanakazi, M. 1982. "African Traders in Butembo." Ph.D. diss., University of Wisconsin-Madison.

5 From unfree labor to neo-colonial extraction in Sao Tome and Principe

Andrew Ikeh Emmanuel Ewoh

Throughout its history, the Democratic Republic of Sao Tome and Principe, located in the Gulf of Guinea, has played a crucial role in the world economic system despite being the smallest Portuguese-speaking country in Africa with a population of 220,501. The twin islands were the greatest producer of sugar in the 16th century and became a major supplier of cocoa and coffee in the 19th and 20th centuries, all grown with African plantation slave labor. Although cocoa remains the major export product of the country, the decline in its production has compelled the nation's political economy to be dependent on external assistance because its exports are inadequate to cover import expenditures in a situation where government spending is the hallmark of economic growth. Oil exploration began in 2011, but it has not been discovered in commercially viable quantities, and its prospects are being affected by the global decline in oil prices.

Using a political economy framework (an understanding of how history, culture and customs impact the economic system of Sao Tome Principe, STP), the purpose of this chapter is to examine the evolution of STP from forced or unfree labor in agricultural production to the practice of cultural imperialism by both the elites and capitalists in the extractive industries, such as oil and gas, in the wealth accumulation process. While the undergirding question here is who governs in STP, the chapter is organized as follows. It begins with an historical synopsis of the evolution of STP as a country based on a plantation economy and follows by an examination of the situation in contemporary STP beginning from the 1990s. The next section discusses the politics of neo-colonial oil extraction in STP in which, through the lenses of primitive accumulation theory, the question of who governs or dominates the governance structure of the country becomes obviously apparent. In the concluding section, the chapter offers some possible, and politically palatable, sustainable public policy solutions for economic development of the twin islands nation that addresses the social equity issues in its current political economic structure.

Historical background

It is generally agreed by scholars that the twin islands of Sao Tome and Principe were uninhabited when explorers from Portugal discovered them in 1470 during their explorations of the western coast of Africa. At the outset, getting people to settle in the area was very problematic. However, Africans started arriving from the mainland and among the first group of Europeans were individuals deprived of their properties or political rights due to their crimes or religious issues, mostly Jews (Eyzaguirre 1989; Tomas et al. 2002; Pillay and Dias 2020).

From its beginning, STP was very stratified and, among the African population, social standing was based on their period of settlement. Those whose ancestors arrived between the 15th and 16th centuries were the elites, while others that arrived after World War II were contract laborers. The slaves in the islands and their descendants regained their freedom after emancipation and captioned themselves the Forros. It is pertinent to note here that some of the elites within this group (the *filhos da terra*) transitioned themselves as slave traders and planters. Nonetheless, the sugar-based economy ended in 17th century due to political uprisings that prompted many white and mulatto owners and traders to relocate to more stable productive lands in Brazil and the Caribbean. At this stage, the islands became a transit point for ships involved in the transportation of slaves between Africa and the Western Hemisphere.

When the Portuguese returned in the 18th century to re-establish authority over STP, the Forros claimed that they were the rightful owners of the land, but in the 19th century the islands became the cornerstone of Portugal's control of its territories in Africa due to pressure from other European colonial powers and their capitalist groups (Eyzaguirre 1989; Clarence-Smith 1985). Between 1858 and 1978, Eyzaguirre (1989) opined that "the Portuguese implemented a series of forceful measures that undermined the political influence of the Forros. White planters were given grants of capital, labor, and land which enabled them to take control of the islands under a new type of plantation system, the rocas" (672).

The plantation economy flourished under the "rocas" system – a labor relation that is akin to slavery – that produced cocoa and coffee. Although slavery was abolished by Portugal in 1876, its practice continued until 1897. STP became the world's largest producer of cocoa in 1908 and the crop has remained very crucial in the twin islands' agriculture. In fact, the minor economic boom triggered by cocoa production in the 19th century resulted in the importation of indentured contract laborers from other Portuguese colonies in Africa such as Angola, Cape Verde and Mozambique. The indentured contract laborers and their descendants were perceived as outsiders and were labelled the Tongas, a third group in a geographical environment segregated by ethnicities. Since the earlier settlers felt uncomfortable working in plantations following the abolition of slavery, the Forros were relegated to a powerless position from their new-found elite position for about two decades, and by 1898, the Portuguese plantation owners acquired over 90 percent of the land (Eyzaguirre 1989; Lovejoy 2012). This level of land acquisition by the planters depicts the primitive accumulation of capital advanced by Marx (1977), whereby free persons through the objectification of their labor are subjected to unfree labor, and confiscation of their land through the destruction of their self-sustaining communities, among others. The turning point in the abusive contract-labor system occurred in the 20th century from a series of organized revolts that continued until 1953 when significant number of laborers were killed in clashes with the plantation owners which is now known as the "Batepa Massacre," an important event in the colonial history; its anniversary is recognized by the Sao Tomean government on the third day of February every year.

Despite its abusive nature, the arrival of indentured contract laborers became instrumental in the transformation of the social structure of the Sao Tomean society because the laborers and their descendants emerged as the largest group in the country. It is pertinent to note here that the plantation system not only pitted the Forros against the Tongas (perceived as outsiders without rights) but it resulted in the creation of clear socio-political and cultural distinctions among the inhabitants. While the system became unsustainable under the modern free labor market, it reflected the deeply rooted cultural legacy of slavery, a problem heightened by the unpredictability of the primary commodity markets during the second half of the 20th century (Frynas et al. 2003).

According to Frynas et al. (2003), the decline of the cocoa monoculture was expedited by the beginning of independence, the flight of skilled Portuguese agro-managerial elite and the unsuccessful efforts at collectivization under state ownership and land reform measures. Nonetheless, reduction in the profitability of cocoa production started in the 1920s (Frynas and Paulo 2007; Seibert 2006; Vogt 1979). In the 1950s, a group of African laborers of STP formed the Movement for the Liberation of Sao Tome and Principe (MLSTP) with a base in Gabon. Due to the MLSTP's liberation activities in the 1960s and the entropy of a dictatorial regime in Portugal by 1974, a political agreement was reached with the organization for the transfer of sovereignty to African natives. Certainly, other problems resulting from the collapse of cocoa were exacerbated by very low commodity prices in the 1970s and the 1980s, right at the beginning of the global depression and successive restructuring of the world economy. Until the 1980s when the country went through a democratization process, the center of economic activity was the nation's plantations, but by the 1990s the center moved to the capital city of Sao Tome with keen implications for the relationship between town and country as well as the elites and society at large. Within the Sao Tome town, the major economic sectors are commercial trade and government. These sectors are largely driven by foreign aid and loans instead of export earnings. What follows is an examination of the situation in contemporary STP beginning with the 1990s.

Review of modern Sao Tome and Principe

After a short period of transitional government in the mid-1970s, STP was granted independence from Portugal on July 12, 1975, with the selection of the MLSTP's Secretary General Manuel Pinto da Costa as its first president. He created a single-party system and served as the president until 1990. In 1990,

STP became one of the African nations to embrace democratic reform and constitutional changes that led to the legalization of opposition parties, and the elections in 1991 were free, transparent and nonviolent. In the 1991 elections, Miguel Trovoada, a former exiled prime minister, was elected president as an independent candidate, and subsequently reelected in 1996 in a multiparty presidential election.

Under a multiparty system form of governance, the winner of the July 2001 presidential election was an Independent Democratic Action Party (ADI) candidate, Fradique de Menezes. In the years after the March 2002 parliamentary elections, several opposition governments were formed, leading to a week-long seizure of power by the military in July 2003 due to corruption charges and the fear that potential oil revenues might be unevenly shared by the ruling elites (Weszkalnys 2008). President de Menezes was returned to office after a negotiated intervention by other international actors; he defeated two other candidates, Patrice Emery Trovoada, the son of the former President Miguel Trovoada, and an independent candidate Nilo Guimaraes, in July 2006 for a second five-year term.

In the August 2016 presidential election, Evaristo Carvalho, a former prime minister and the vice president of the ADI, was assured victory in the run-off after his opponent, the incumbent president and independent candidate Manuel Pinto da Costa, boycotted the runoff alleging irregularities in the electoral process. It is pertinent to note here that the current President Carvalho was prime minister in both 1994 and from 2001 to 2002, respectively; and he has previously served as president of the National Assembly and defense minister. Nonetheless, more members of the ruling coalition were elected in the 2016 municipal elections. Interestingly, there is now a tradition in STP where premiers and presidents from opposition camps work cooperatively and peacefully in the governance of the country. The current political landscape shows that both top executive positions are occupied by the ADI. According to the World Bank (2020), the October 7, 2018 elections depicted STP's democracy as a model to be emulated in Central Africa. Currently, the National Assembly consists of 55 seats and 25 of those are held by the ADI, 23 by the Movement for the Liberation of Sao Tome and Principe – Social Democratic Party (MLSTP-PSD), five by the coalition of three other parties (Democratic Convergence Party, Union of Democrats for Citizenship and Development and the Force for Democratic Change Movement) and two by the Sao Tome and Principe Independent Citizen Movement.

There is a constitutional provision for an independent judiciary with relatively autonomous courts in practice, but the reality is that they can bow to political influence and corruption. There were many politically motivated appointments and dismissals of the nation's Supreme Court and Constitutional Court judges under the current ADI government in 2018 protracted to 2019. In February 2019, for example, the National Assembly inducted five new judges into the Constitutional Court to replace those initially appointed by the ADI, who were dismissed in late 2018; and weeks after the lower court returned ownership of Rosema Brewery (one of the largest companies in STP) to an Angolan businessman, the Constitutional Court reversed the judgement in favor of two local politicians and businessmen. The governing coalition, seeking more Angolan investment in STP, then quickly authorized the dismissal of three Constitutional judges that voted in favor of reinstating the company to its local owners, and approved new judges to replace them by the National Assembly in August 2019 (Freedom House 2020).

In terms of political context, STP is organized into two provinces, Sao Tome and Principe; and further divided into six districts and one autonomous region. Sao Tome, the biggest island and the capital city, is about 180 miles away from Gabon, while Principe is an autonomous region with designated administrative and political responsibilities and is located 160 miles away from the Equatorial Guinea on the West African coast (Pillay and Dias 2020). The president is elected by the people for up to two consecutive five-year terms, and the prime minister is responsible for the operations of the executive authority and is appointed by the president based on the results of legislative elections.

Regarding the social context, the World Bank (2020) report shows that about one-third of the population lives on less than the $1.90 per day international poverty line, and more than two-thirds are considered poor; urban areas and communities in the southern districts experience a higher level of poverty. On the United Nations Development Program Human Development index, STP fairs better than the Sub-Saharan African average, with significant improvement in other social indicators. The official language is Portuguese and over 60 percent of the population is younger than 25 years. Due to the Extractive Industries Transparency Initiative (EITI), STP signature bonuses now require oil firms exploring in the Joint Development Zone, established by Nigeria and STP in a bilateral treaty, to engage in some social responsibility projects, which has resulted in the building of a hospital in Principe, as well as other projects worth $3.6m (EITI 2020).

Concerning the economic context, the country constantly faces the challenges of dealing with economic instability and balancing its national budget. Another problem arises out of the shortage of human capital due to the country's small population, limiting its institutional ability to achieve the efficient production of goods and services at the level required to meet both demand of domestic and export markets. The World Bank report (2020) further indicated that the indivisibility in the production of public goods, coupled with the problem of delivering services to a sparsely populated environment, results in the high cost of these public goods as well as a high level of government expenditures. Overall, while the country's economic growth is propelled by agriculture, tourism and oil-fueled foreign direct investment, it is more highly stimulated by government expenditures through external aid and borrowing. In 2018, the gross domestic product (GDP) annual per capita growth rate was 0.74 percent and dropped to 0.48 in 2019 due to fuel and power shortages, government arrears to local contractors and the increasing government interference in the market economy, with an annual GDP inflation deflator of 4.6 percent in 2019, and an average growth rate of 4.5 percent between 2010 and 2018 (World Bank 2020). At a time when economic growth is slowing down, agriculture and fisheries have been negatively impacted by agricultural pests, fuel and power shortages, and the COVID-19 pandemic is expected to depress the economy further due to a decline in tourism.

The STP legal system belongs to the civil law tradition and is based on the country's customary laws and basic Portuguese civil law dating back to the Napoleonic Code of 1804 and codified regulations (Pillay and Dias 2020). The fundamental law of STP is enshrined in the Constitution and approved by Law 1/2003, and all other laws and regulations must adhere to its provision. The law empowers workers' rights to form and/or join unions, bargain collectively and partake in strikes – a right controlled by the government, the largest employer of labor. Although the government prohibits public employees from collective bargaining, it allows anti-union discrimination by other employers of labor as well as retaliation against strikers. It further prohibits discrimination on the bases of race, sex, religious belief, political affiliation, social origin and/or philosophical conviction. Generally, labor law enforcement in STP is very inefficient because there are no regulations governing the informal sector of the economy, and workers in the palm oil and cocoa industry are very vulnerable to abuse in labor–management relationships. While the law bans all forms of forced labor including child labor, it does not clearly ban employment discrimination based on age, color, disability, language, sexual orientation, gender identity, among others, and lacks institutional capacity to effectively enforce laws (US Department of State TIP Report 2019; US Department of State, 2016).

The next section examines the evolution of the politics of neo-colonial oil extraction in STP, focusing on the attention that it brought to the country. This underscores the inherent problems associated with Africa's role in the accumulation of capital under global marketization mechanisms created by multinational companies.

Politics of neo-colonial oil extraction in STP

Although the 1990s were characterized by new oil discoveries in Angola and Equatorial Guinea, the petro-era in STP generally started in 1997 with a controversial agreement signed by a government joint venture company (STPetro) and the Environmental Remediation Holding Company (ERHC), a small US-based firm from Houston, Texas, with no history of oil exploration. This action made oil a part of STP's political-economic identity. Subsequently, both ERHC and ExxonMobil were added to the agreement with preferential exploration rights for 25 years and revenue sharing of the profits, which exceeds the oil industry standard for such contracts. In return, ERHC offered Sao Tome $5m and the usage of its expertise in marketing services at a time when the country was not only indebted but was dependent on foreign aid for funding its budget, which drew much criticism from outside groups for not being in the best interest of the country. To give many oil blocks and preferential rights to one company without a bidding process was an aberration because it grants rights to future petroleum taxation and payments that would have been transferred to the public treasury. Frynas et al. (2003) noted that there has been no similar contract in the history of oil exploration in Africa since the end of colonialism. Despite the unprecedented nature of the contract, the deal was approved, but the seismic data revelation that there could be up to 11 million barrels of oil below the sea level around the country attracted even more attention from other regional powers, Western governments, civil society organizations and major multinational corporations (Pillay and Dias 2020; Human Rights Watch 2010).

Since the most prospective oil deposit happens to be in the northern part of Principe's offshore boundary, an area claimed by Nigeria, a border dispute ensued and after a prolonged negotiation process, both the President of Nigeria Olusegun Obasanjo and STP President Miguel Trovoada signed a 45-year bilateral investment treaty in February 2001 for a Joint Development Zone in which Nigeria retains 60 percent of the profits and STP holds 40 percent. The JDZ is governed by the Joint Development Authority (JDA) with a head office in Abuja, Nigeria, which reports to a Joint Ministerial Council (JMC). The JDA board makes all policy-related decisions with ratification by JMC without any appeal to any other authority, to separate its decision from any political interference. An alternative exploratory activity is ongoing within Sao Tome in an area known as the Exclusive Economic Zone (EEZ) managed by the National Petroleum Agency, which grants licenses on behalf of the government (Pillay and Dias 2020).

After he was elected president late in 2001, Fradique de Menezes wanted to correct his predecessor's faults and modify STP's contract with ERHC, but it was acquired by Chrome Energy consortium which belongs to Nigerian billionaire Emeka Offor, who maintained a close relationship to President Obasanjo's administration. The company's name was subsequently changed to Chrome Energy Corp and the original contract was renegotiated twice with a disproportional interest for STP due to the government's inexperience in dealing with oil-related issues and pressure from Nigerian government (Frynas et al. 2003). To achieve transparency with foreign assistance, two phases of bidding processes or auctions were deployed.

When the first round of auctions were opened in 2003 for the allocation of nine out of 25 blocks, about \$506m was auctioned in seven blocks – representing about 237 percent of the STP's gross domestic product in 2003. Subsequently, in 2004, one block was assigned to a joint venture between ExxonMobil (with its preferential rights of first refusal) and Chevron Texaco (the highest bidder), with a small involvement by the Nigerian-Norwegian Dangote Energy Equity Resources Limited inserted at the political level (Vicente 2007; Weszkalnys 2008).

In the second round of bidding, in late 2004 and early 2005 – for Block numbers 2, 3 and 4 – over two dozen small companies participated; most were linked to Nigerian companies that lacked formal experience in oil production, which triggered the STP Attorney General's unsolicited report that the bid was not transparent and, therefore, "subject to serious deficiencies and political manipulation" because it produced winning bids from unqualified companies. The report claimed that ERHC's preferential rights hindered more credible firms from participating, thereby costing STP about $60m in fees. There also were allegations that some politicians were bribed. For instance, a former president's top adviser was shown to be a stakeholder in ERHC and a firm managed by former President Menezes was shown to have received $100,000 from Chrome. Both President Menezes and Chrome Energy Corp contended that the payments were legal election campaign contributions (Pillay and Dias 2020).

Notwithstanding the Attorney General's corruption charges, Sao Tomean citizens were unhappy with the exploration results because Chevron Texaco deemed the first finds of its drill in Block 1 of the JDZ in 2006 to be commercially unviable. Furthermore, in March 2007, the Sinopec (a Chinese company) and Addax (a Canadian corporation) drilling in Blocks 2 and 4 stated that they had deployed an Indian vessel to perform drillings in 2008, which was delayed until 2009, and ExxonMobil's interests in Block 1 were acquired by Addax later in 2007. These developments somehow make the prospects of STP becoming an oil-based economy very problematic to achieve. It is hoped that both Kosmos Energy (a US-based deep-water and exploration company) and Galp Energia (a Portugal-based oil and gas company), that are pursuing seismic research in Blocks 5, 6, 11 and 12 of the EEZ, may be able to yield some dividends in terms of oil discovery. Nonetheless, the STP received a $49m share of the signature bonus for Block 1 – a substantial amount for a small country but less than what it should have received in the absence of corruption (Seibert 2006; Weszkalnys 2008; Pillay and Dias 2020).

In terms of how revenue is deployed under the Joint Development Authority financed by the Nigerian and STP governments, the budget for JDA between 2004 and 2013 was $117m, which allots $47m to STP for its 40 percent share. The budget is used for the administration of the Joint Development Zone and Nigeria has consistently paid for STP's share of the administrative costs, and STP has accumulated about $21m according to estimates from the Extractive Industries Transparency Initiative (EITI). Additionally, $60m in revenue generated for STP from signature bonuses is required to be sent to the national oil account from which 20 percent is designated for annual transfer to the STP national budget; about $10m was left in the account late in 2013 (EITI 2020).

Most analyses of oil contracts between STP and multinational companies identify major flaws due to lack of experience of human resources to manage huge projects; others point to the resource curse phenomenon suffered by many petroleum-based countries regarding economic underdevelopment, military intervention and political mismanagement (Frynas et al. 2003; Sachs and Warner 1995; Human Rights Watch 2010). Although neglected in the literature, the resource curse has affected STP throughout its history due to the high inflow of foreign aid and loans since independence. In terms of economic effects of the resource curse, a 1998 food security study show that food aid and other influences have been reducing the utilization of local commodities in the people's diet. While natives still consume locally produced fish and banana, for example, over 50 percent of food consumption has been dependent on imports, a dependency that is traceable to the country's colonial history (De Carvalho 1998). Similarly, external capital flows enabled the ruling elites to ignore their domestic constituencies, and there is no doubt as Seibert (2006) contends that "the increased inflow of external funds has extended the opportunities for rent-seeking and corrupt behavior" (233). Conversely, Frynas et al. (2003) maintain that large inflows of foreign exchange make exports of agricultural and manufacturing goods more expensive and draw resources from non-mineral sectors, thus depleting the sectoral development. The same rent-seeking conduct was obvious through political connections that were instrumental in many oil exploration agreements signed in the late 1990s and early 2000s as earlier discussed. For instance, elections through the period were influenced by petro-money because access to foreign aid not only attracted potential candidates, but petro-dollars coincided with more expensive electioneering campaign as well as the entry of new actors. As discussed previously, the government of President Fradique de Menezes was deposed in a brief abortive coup attempt in 2003 by the military due to corruption charges and the fear that potential oil revenues might not be evenly shared by the ruling elites (Weszkalnys, 2008).

Concluding remarks

The foregoing analysis shows that, although STP has all the characteristics of a stable democracy when compared to other African countries, the political superstructure is dominated by a small number of families and factions via shifting alliances and temporary political coalitions that are beneficial to all the stakeholders. The electoral system enables the competing interests to cooperatively and peacefully coexist. What is commendable is the acceptance of election results whereby losers in any election patiently wait for the next election cycle, and ruling parties tolerate their rivals due to long-standing social bonds existing among and between members of the political elite where personalities and personal connections matter, in stark contrast to what is obtainable in other African nations. The answer to the question of who governs, raised at the outset in the analysis, appears when one considers the alliances existing among the political elites in the country and the influence of political campaign contributions from business corporations on electoral successes which, in turn, translate into favorable public policies that benefit multinational corporations in both oil and other non-mineral industries.

Although the country's democracy seems sustainable, the emerging oil economy needs to protect the citizens from both the resource curse phenomenon and/or the "Dutch Disease" problem that have negatively affected other emerging oil-producing countries, especially those on the West African coast (Benjamin et al. 1989; Frynas et al. 2003; Soares de Oliveira 2007). The Gulf of Guinea, as noted in the STP risk and compliance report by Gary Youinou (2018), is becoming an epicenter for international organized crime, such as piracy in the territorial waters. To ensure full protection of its jurisdictional boundaries, STP needs to work on strengthening the foundation of good governance, maintaining law enforcement imbued with the credible rule of law and committing itself to full implementation of applicable international anti-money laundering and counter-terrorist financing standards. It also needs to engage in acquiring the institutional capacity to achieve meaningful progress in administering and complying with the requirements of the Extractive Industries Transparency Initiatives as it pertains to the adoption of best practices in international oil contracts, which require, among other things, that companies in oil exploration ventures in STP must undertake social responsibility projects in addressing social equity issues in the economic development of the nation to achieve politically palatable public policy solutions in the country.

References

Benjamin, N. C., Devarajan, S. and Weiner, R. J. 1989. "The Dutch Disease in Developing Country: Oil Reserves in Cameroon." *Journal of Development Economics*, 30(1), 71–92.

Clarence-Smith, G. 1985. *The Third Portuguese Empire, 1825–1975: A Study in Economic Imperialism*. Manchester: Manchester University Press.

De Carvalho, B. R. P. 1998. "Food Security and Hedonic Behavior: A Case Study of Sao Tome E Principe." *Food Policy*, 23(3–4), 263–275.

Extractive Industries Transparency Initiatives. 2020. "Sao Tome and Principe: The 11-Year Quest under Scrutiny." Available at https://eiti.org/news/sao-tome-11year-quest-for-oil-under-scrutiny/

Eyzaguirre, P. B. 1989. "The Independence of Sao Tome E Principe and Agrarian Reform." *Journal of Modern African Studies*, 27(4), 671–678.

Frynas, J. G. and Paulo, M. 2007. "A New Scramble for African Oil? Historical, Political, and Business Perspectives." *African Affairs*, 102(423), 229–251.

Frynas, J., Wood, G. and Soares de Oliveira, R. M. 2003. "Business and Politics in Sao Tome e Principe: From Cocoa Monoculture to Petro-State." *African Affairs*, 102(406), 51–80.

Freedom House. 2020. *Sao Tome and Principe: Overview*. Washington, DC: Freedom House.

Human Rights Watch. 2010. "An Uncertain Future: Oil Contracts and Stalled Reform in Sao Tome e Principe." Available at www.hrw.org/report/2010/08/24/uncertain-future/oil-contracts-and-stalled-reform-sao-tome-e-principe#page

Lovejoy, P. E. 2012. *Transformations in Slavery: A History of Slavery in Africa*. 3rd Ed. Cambridge: Cambridge University Press.

Marx, K. 1977. *Capital: A Critic of Political Economy*, Vol. 1. New York: Vintage

Pillay, K. and Dias, N. D. 2020. "Sao Tome and Principe: Legal System and Research." https://nyulawglobal.org/globalex/Sao_Tome_Principe1.html (Retrieved on October 28, 2020).

Sacks, J. D. and Warner, A. M. 1995. Natural Resources Abundance and Economic Growth. Development Discussion Paper, Number 517. Cambridge, MA: Harvard Institute for International Development.

Seibert, G. 2006. *Comrades, Clients, and Cousins: Colonialism, Socialism and Democratization in Sao Tome and Principe*. 2nd Ed. Leiden: Brill Academic Publishers.

Soares de Oliveira, R. 2007. *Oil and Politics in the Gulf of Guinea.* London: Hurst & Co.

Tomas, G., Seco, L., Seixas, S., Faustino, P., Lavinha, J. and Rocha, J. 2002. "The Peopling of Sao Tome (Gulf of Guinea): Origins of Slave Settlers and Admixture with the Portuguese." *Human Biology*, 74(3), 397–411.

United Nations Development Programme (UNDP). N.d. *Human Development Reports: International Development Indicators.* Available at http://hdr.undp.org/en/countries/profiles/STP

United Nations. 2020. "Sao Tome and Principe Population." November 1. Available at https://worldometers.info/world-population/sao-tome-and-principe-population/

US Department of State. 2019. "Trafficking in Persons Report." Available at www.state.gov/trafficking-in-persons-report/

US Department of State. Bureau of Democracy, Human Rights, and Labor. 2016. *Country Reports on Human Rights Practices for 2016: Sao Tome and Principe.* Available at www.state.gov/documents/organization/252931.pdf

Vicente, P. 2007. "Does Oil Corrupt? Evidence from a Natural Experiment in West Africa." Discussion Papers Series, 317, 1–31. Department of Economics, University of Oxford.

Vogt, J. 1979. *Portuguese Rule in the Gold Coast, 1469–1682.* Athens, GA: University of Georgia Press.

Weszkalnys, G. 2008. "Hope and Oil: Expectations in Sao Tome e Principe." *Review of African Political Economy*, 35(117), 473–482.

World Bank. 2020. *Sao Tome and Principe.* Washington, DC: World Bank. www.worldbank.org/en/country/saotome

Youinou, G. 2018. "Sao Tome and Principe: Risk and Compliance Report." www.knowyourcountry.info/files/Saotomeam1sep2014_2.pdf (Retrieved on October 28, 2020).

6 Russia's return to Africa

Much ado but about what?

Radoslav A. Yordanov

As this book demonstrates, Africa has always been integrated into the global economy and, despite suffering from poverty and political conflicts, the continent has long played a strategic role historically in attracting the attention of the world's most powerful nations, from the so-called Scramble for Africa in the 19th century, through the Cold War, to today's multipolar world order. Just as in the Cold War, when soft power was used as a tool to further more tangible political influence in Africa, today the economy of African states is a battleground for balancing the demands of global economic powers that are competing for access to Africa's rich resources. By looking into Russia's return to Africa, which has accelerated over the past decade, this chapter aims to demonstrate that there has been a gradual adjustment of Russia's perception of the continent from a mere political and military outpost to a potentially advantageous set of economic partnerships. However, this chapter also seeks to offer a more nuanced treatment of the resurgence of Russia–Africa relations by arguing that economic interests should not overshadow the political, military and strategic infrastructural stakes which are vital for the existence of a major international actor striving to regain its global reach that has been lost in the course of the past three decades.

This chapter will show that Russia is attempting to regain the lost strategic positions it claimed before the end of the Cold War, and to assert Moscow's overall ambition to become again a notable foreign power in Africa after abruptly abandoning its stakes there – a task that would require not only investments of capital but also of trust in times of increased international competition in the strategic Northeast Africa. During the Cold War, the Soviet Union's focus on East Africa was centered on obtaining and maintaining access to the ports of the Horn of Africa, when shifting alliances between Ethiopia and Somalia complicated its relations with the United States. At present, Russia is facing a far more challenging regional setting with Africa's economic resurgence and growing economic prospects, and the increased interests from a variety of international actors, including China, EU, US, Turkey, India and Brazil. Thus, the previous accent on the military and the political forms of engagement has shifted to the introduction of more flexible economic forms of interaction based on mutual interest. However, Africa's strategic importance, both from a military point of view as well as the potential for logistic facilities for the protection of naval trade routes, remains valid for the broader Horn of Africa region given Moscow's renewed aspirations towards the continent. As a growing player in the global economy, Moscow's motivations to regain and possibly augment its influence in Africa, lost by the self-destruction of the Soviet Union, is predicated on securing a strategic presence on the continent that might benefit Moscow's political and geostrategic objectives in a swiftly changing world order.

Interpreting the motivations for Moscow's return to Africa

The motives behind Moscow's interests in Africa closely mirror the polarizing debates on Russia's foreign policy in general. To some observers, Moscow's current foreign policy continues to be driven by economic growth for the sake of power and its global position, and not for the sake of economic growth itself (Wallander 2007, 458), while others see Russian President Vladimir Putin's gradual transition toward a market economy as an opening up of opportunities for Russian producers in international markets rather than as an attempt at obtaining outside support for domestic industries (Lo 2003, 51–55). Under Putin's presidency, Russia has been making highly publicized efforts to reclaim the once leading role of its predecessor, the Soviet Union, in global politics, at a time when various African states have grown more stable politically and have become more economically successful. This time around, however, relations are focused predominantly on economics and trade, rather than on ideology, as during the Cold War period (Olivier and Suchkov 2015, 146; Abramova and Fituni 2017). As a result, Russia's foreign policy in Africa has shifted to an opportunistic and pragmatic search for forms of mutually beneficial cooperation (Melville and Shakleina 2005, 58; Kalika 2019, 4). However, as the Russian Foreign Ministry stated in March 2007 and as the approval by Putin in February 2013 of foreign policy goals demonstrate, this mutual interest is intended to provide an opportunity for Russia "to use the African factor in such a way as to make progress in our international interests and reach our economic goals" (see Fidan and Ara 2010, 53; Arkhangelskaya and Dodd 2016, 167).

Therefore, while the economic component in Russia's resurgence as a global power is undoubtedly a significant part of its engagement with Africa, it is clear that the ultimate motivation for the Kremlin's foreign policy towards the continent is strategic, as suggested by a high-profile agreement with South Africa for the launching of the Project Condor satellite system that is designed to provide surveillance of the entire African continent (Hellyer 2015; Jordan 2015). This is also partially supported by the Director of the African Department of the Russian Foreign Ministry, Andrei Kemarsky, who explained that Moscow's interest in Africa was growing not only because of the continent's economic potential but also due to African countries' increasingly active positions on key international problems (MID 2019). The strategic justification is further strengthened by the Russian Foreign Minister, Sergey Lavrov, who claims that the continent is "consistently strengthening its positions as a major pillar of the world's polycentric architecture" (Shubin 2019). Therefore, from Moscow's position, the strengthening of cooperation with African countries helps ensure their support for Russia as a revitalized great power and thus serves its global aspirations (Kulkova 2019; Pham 2014; Melville and Shakleina 2005, 58; Bugayova and Regio 2019, 2) and increase its prestige by using "low-cost, high-profile" opportunities (Stronski 2019; Rozhdestvensky et al. 2019; Gathara 2019).

Looking for partners and economic diversification

Some observers believe that Russia, as one of the world's largest producers and exporters of oil and natural gas, does not need new supplies of energy from Africa, discounting access to fossil fuels as a plausible motivation for Moscow's renewed interest in the continent. Instead, those authors infer that Moscow's ulterior motive is guided by the imperative to improve its control over Africa's abundant energy sources in order to strengthen its own economic and political power (Volman 2009, 12; Oğultürk 2017, 130). However, this does not paint the full picture of Russia's interests in Africa's energy fields. It should be noted that new resources in Russia have to be extracted mostly in ecologically vulnerable Siberian territories, which makes the development of existing oil reserves there twice as expensive as in Angola. Accordingly, up to 90 percent of Russian investments in Africa are in the exploration and extraction of natural resources, primarily in Algeria, Angola, Nigeria and South Africa. Similarly, in recent years, Russia has shown increased interest in East and Central Africa, in Tanzania and Mozambique, in particular (Shubin 2013, 3–4), but also in Uganda, where the RT Global Resources conglomerate won a $3bn oil refinery bid (Hellyer 2015). To further strengthen this thesis, it has to be recounted that Russia also has a critical shortage of certain raw materials, including aluminum, chrome, manganese, mercury and titanium, and faces the depletion of its reserves of others, including copper, nickel, tin and zinc (Pham 2014).

The access to resources argument is also supported by fact that the prospects for the further development of the Russian economy are becoming increasingly constrained by the gradual exhaustion of the raw material export model which has hallmarked the state's economic resurgence under Putin. The combination of two shocks experienced by the Russian economy – the international financial sanctions following the annexation of the Crimean Peninsula, and falling global oil prices – reportedly brought Russia a combined loss of about $0.6 trillion between 2014 and 2017. According to the development strategy outlined by President Putin, to compensate for this, Russia would have to modernize and diversify its economy. Such ambitious strategic tasks would require not only the use of all possible reserves but also the finding of an integrated approach to cooperation with developing countries. The intensification of economic expansion into those African markets which are more open and willing to cooperate with Russia and have a significant resource and prospects for growth would thus form an integral part of the modernization and diversification of the Russian economy (Abramova and Fituni 2017, 24). Nevertheless, this seems easier said than done. So far, in the last three years, Russian involvement in Africa has been limited to unrealistically ambitious and opportunistic moves that lack a discernible coherent strategy, and which subordinated Russia's foreign policy to private interests and actors (Stronski 2019).

Changing the perception of Africa's international role

At the turn of the century, Russian commentators sought to explain the "unreasonably small" (Dolgov 2001, 85) turnover between Russia and Africa with the notion that the poorer Sub-Saharan African states were less attractive to private foreign investors and less capable of taking advantage of additional development opportunities which isolated them from the processes of economic globalization (Avtonomov and Subbotina 1999, 75). However, in policy terms, Russia's continuous absence from the continent brought about notable political disadvantages for Moscow. Addressing the Russian ambassadors to African countries in the summer of 1994, then-Russian Prime Minister Viktor Chernomyrdin emphasized the fact that the prolonged pause in the relations between Russia and Africa was harmful for Moscow's international interests (Kanet et al. 1997, 168). Stemming from this realization, the hiatus in the relations between Russia and Africa was replaced in the early 2000s by Moscow's determination to reestablish its presence in the region, spurred by concerns that China, India, Brazil and the United States especially were intensifying their involvement there to secure access to the continent's natural resources and energy reserves.

Following this, in 2006, Russian President Putin visited South Africa and Morocco, while in 2009, the then-President Dmitry Medvedev visited Angola, Egypt, Namibia and Nigeria. These high-level political visits were aimed at signaling Russia's intention to return to Africa and to place the continent higher on Moscow's international agenda (Kadomtsev 2019). As the Russian Foreign Minister Lavrov (2008) suggests, Moscow's renewed interest in Africa was invigorated by its reemergence into the global scene, economically and financially, as an active, full-fledged actor that was set to take an active role in the ongoing process of global reconfiguration. However, in its rapprochement with Africa, Moscow sought to avoid repeating or copying the Soviet experience, taking into account Russia's different economic interests and political system, and acknowledging Africa's changed status and role in the international arena, as noted by Andrei Baklanov, a prominent specialist on Russia–Africa affairs and a diplomat with direct experience in several African countries (Baklanov 2018; Abramova 2018, 2–10; Kalika 2019, 14).

In the past decade, Africa has turned into one of the world's economic drivers, with growth rates exceeding the global average. Reflecting on these changes in Africa's international standing, the Russian Prime Minister Dmitry Medvedev (2019) showed appreciation for Africa's improving business climate. Arguably, this served as a strong motivator in whetting Russia's interest in the continent that led to its engaging in a set of economically pragmatic investment activities in lucrative niche markets (Procopio 2019), not only in the mining industry but also in the telecommunications and high-tech sectors. In Southern Africa, Rosneft has won a tender in Mozambique for the exploration of gas reserves on the continental shelf, Alrosa is mining diamonds at Angola's Catoca deposit site and the Renova Group is involved in the extraction of manganese ore in South Africa. Similarly, a consortium of several Russian companies, including the Vi-Holding investment and industrial group, is seeking to develop the largest metal deposit of the Darwendale platinum group in Zimbabwe. In West Africa, UC RUSAL is developing in Guinea bauxite at Friguia and is implementing a concession for the development of the mine at Dian-Dian. RUSAL also owns an 85 percent stake in Aluminium Smelter Company of Nigeria (ALSCON), while Nordgold is mining gold in Burkina Faso and Guinea, and GPB Global Resources is exploring gold in Mali and uranium in Niger. Outside the mining sector, in the field of high technologies, most interestingly, GC Rosatom has plans for creating centers for nuclear science and technology in Zambia and Nigeria (MID 2018).

Despite this flurry of business activities, the turnover with Sub-Saharan Africa, which stood at around $5bn in 2019, or less than 1 percent of Russia's total foreign turnover in 2019 (REC 2019b), remains disproportionately small compared to the same figure reached with Northern Africa, which was almost $12bn, or nearly 6 percent of total Russian trade (REC 2019a). To overcome this imbalance, the Russian Minister of Trade and Industry Denis Manturov (2019) explained that part of Russia's economic strategy for the region south of Sahara was to develop an industrial hub there similar to the one in Egypt, concentrating on ports on the Indian and the Atlantic Oceans for which it would possess access, including such facilities in Mozambique and Namibia where these states also could gain infrastructural advantages.

In admitting the need to secure new international economic and political partners and realize Africa's investment potential, Russia followed the fashionable trend set by China, the European Union, France, India and Turkey (Devermont 2019) of hosting high-profile diplomatic forums with African leaders. In late October 2019, Russia gathered in Sochi over 6,000 participants, media representatives and delegates from all 54 African states. Speaking at the conference, Russian President Putin emphasized that the development of relations with the countries of the African continent and their regional organizations had become one of Russia's foreign policy priorities. In Putin's assessment, the African states were confidently gaining political and economic weight in the world, affirming themselves as one of the important pillars of the international multipolar system. Pragmatically, these highly political gestures and statements at the Sochi Summit aimed to help Russia to substantially expand trade with African states by promoting cooperation in energy security, diversification of energy resources, the use of renewable energy sources and the implementation of joint projects in civil nuclear energy, while continuing mutually beneficial cooperation in the oil and gas industry (Sochi Summit 2019). Amongst the event's headlines was the agreement of the Russian state development corporation VEB.RF to investment in an oil refinery in Morocco and to construct oil pipelines in Congo, which came on the backdrop of agreements in the military field amounting to about $14bn (PenzaNews 2019).

There is more to Russia's interest in Africa than economy

Assessing Russian interest in Africa today would be incomplete without factoring in the strategic logistical value played by the Horn of Africa. Historically, the Soviet Union and now Russia have recognized that their geographical location, spanning two continents and eleven time zones, places in the hands of Moscow's decision-makers immense natural resources but also a limited ability to project power through naval forces in the warm seas away from the country's primary theater of operation in the north. Thus, its navy has been traditionally tasked with the defense of the homeland, rather than being used as a vehicle for projecting power overseas. However, from the mid-1960s the navy came to serve an important, though restrained, role as a logistical instrument for amplifying Moscow's global reach, especially its ability to provide support to its Third World allies while simultaneously aiming to protect oil and fish transporting sea lanes. Therefore, despite the apparent shift to furnishing mutually beneficial economic cooperation, Russia also aims to build alliances with states possessing geostrategic locations that might be of use in a potential future conflict with other major powers. This is reflected by the pattern of Moscow's reemerging interest in Africa.

During the Cold War, the Horn of Africa was one of the Soviet Union's major entry points within the continent. From a geostrategic point of view, the importance of the Suez Canal to the Soviet Union's Cold War decision-makers was justified by its ability to shorten the naval communication lanes between the Black Sea and Pacific Oceans. In the northwest corner of the Indian Ocean, the Persian Gulf–Red Sea route was a scene of heavy maritime traffic between the oil-producing Gulf States and Western Europe, which prompted the Soviets to see their regional naval presence as a significant strategic element in their complex influence-building exercise, also supplemented by political, economic and military aid. However, none of the Soviet Union's advances in the strategically important Northeast Africa in the 1970s would have been possible without the development of the Soviet navy in the second half of the 1960s. After realizing its weaknesses during the 1962 Cuban missile crisis, the Kremlin adjusted the role of its navy. Consequently, Moscow expanded its navy's wartime mandate, allowing it to engage in "long-range" (Edmonds 1975, 42) strategic tasks, augmenting its strictly defensive regional objectives (Gorshkov 1976). Accordingly, the framework of the new naval doctrine entailed "the deployment of units of battle-ready naval forces in remote regions well in advance to employ them immediately with the onset of acts of war" (Kapitanets 2002, 210–211). This doctrinal adjustment was realized in the steady build-up of the

Kremlin's naval presence in the Indian Ocean, in which the Horn and Somalia, in particular, had a pivotal role by providing a convenient base at Berbera.

However, after the end of the Cold War, the navy's inventory, equipment and personnel declined remarkably, as Russia withdrew its over-reaching international involvement. During its economic crisis and rapprochement with the West in the 1990s, Russia dismantled its military bases in former Warsaw Pact countries in Europe as well as in Cuba, Vietnam and the Horn of Africa. However, by the year 2000, Russia appeared to be increasingly interested in asserting itself again as a significant maritime power and began to see its navy as a potent foreign policy instrument, free from the shackles of the past when Tsarist Russian and later the Soviet navy struggled against the dominance of ground forces both in terms of strategy as well as technological innovations (Gottemoeller 2004, 184; Dutton et al. 2012, 2). The introduction of the new doctrine in the year 2000 provided the Russian navy with a new, more articulate vision of ensuring Russian security, allowing it an increased contribution to the implementation of Moscow's foreign policy strategy (Brannon 2009, 134; Haas 2011, 12). Initially, these prerogatives seemed more defensive than aggressive and, as the Foreign Minister Sergei Ivanov suggested in 2004, Moscow's international ambitions sought to counter the challenges aggravated by the processes of globalization (Ivanov 2004). Similarly, concerning the navy, the new doctrine tasked the Russian fleet to pursue a course of turning the Indian Ocean "into a zone of peace, stability and good neighborliness," thus justifying the Russian naval presence there (MID 2004).

However, when Washington backed Georgia in 2008 and signed a deal with Warsaw, basing US antiballistic missiles in Poland in mid-August 2008, Russia interpreted these US moves as a growing threat, which not only prompted calls for strengthening the Russian military but also led to repeated pleas from naval officers for the revival of the country's ocean-going fleet. On Navy Day, July 27, 2008, days before the outbreak of the Georgian crisis, the Commander-in-Chief of the Russian Navy Admiral Vladimir Vysotsky spoke of a revival of Russian naval power over the next decade and declared that the navy would add six carrier battle groups to its complement of warships. Later, during the exercise Zapad in 2009, the then-Russian President Medvedev repeated the call for a revival of Russian naval power and promised new acquisitions over the next decade (Kipp 2009). This call precipitated a number of diplomatic overtures with Cuba, Venezuela and Libya, in which Moscow reportedly sought to obtain basing rights, and also secured wider access to the Syrian port of Tartus (Oldberg 2010, 44).

Just as in the Cold War, Russia's interest in the Horn of Africa is part of the rising tensions between Moscow and West and the need to secure sea routes from the Suez Canal to the Gulf of Aden. Hoping to expand its network of military bases, Russia continues to seek bases in Sudan, Eritrea and Somaliland (Bugayova et al. 2018; Fabricius 2019; McGrath 2018). Russia supposedly brokered a deal for naval basing rights in Sudan before the ouster of Sudanese President Omar al-Bashir in April 2019 (Bugayova and Regio 2019, 4). The alleged deal included the possibility of installing a logistics center for Russian warships stationed in the Red Sea on Sudanese territory (*Sudan Tribune* 2018; Sputnik 2018; Shishkov 2019). Relations with Ethiopia, however, remain challenging. In early March 2018, Russian Foreign Minister Lavrov visited Ethiopia, alongside Angola, Namibia and Mozambique. In Ethiopia, Lavrov paid less attention to relaunching trade and focused instead on the strategic importance of the Horn of Africa and Djibouti, where most of Russia's competitors, France, USA, China, Turkey, UAE and Japan, have military or logistical bases. Although Russia may see Ethiopia as a possible base from which to observe developments in the Horn of Africa, its potential influence in Ethiopia remains limited to date and the bilateral trade with Addis Ababa continues to decrease, having fallen by 50 percent between 2016 and 2017, and reaching just $80m in 2019 (Kalika 2019, 13).

Conclusion: Russia enters the "new scramble for Africa"?

Sub-Saharan Africa has turned again into an arena of contest for global power influence due not only to its strong potential for economic growth but also for its wealth of natural resources. During the last decade, however, the number of engagements with African powers increased noticeably even as US interest diminished. During this time, China's trade with Africa not only caught up with America's, but has grown 20-fold to $220bn since the year 2000 (Hohler 2018). Meanwhile, Russia has been seeking to reestablish its presence and influence in Africa which was lost after the end of the Cold War. Moscow's return to Africa is, therefore, an integral part of Russia's renewed efforts to reaffirm itself as a global player and technological power, as noted by the Russian Ambassador to South Africa Ilya Rogachev (Muresan 2019, 2). To some observers, Russia's economic "pivot to Africa" so far has been rather half-hearted (Klomegah 2015) as its efforts could be interpreted as a stopgap until Moscow finds a coherent policy for the continent. In the meantime, Russian businesses and investors are culling resources and investing in Sub-Saharan Africa on strictly commercial terms (Giles 2013, 1–2). To others, Russia has been trying to strengthen its ties and status through a gradual process to minimize potential friction with the better established international powers, including China, the United States and France (Magen et al. 2019, 4), as long as they follow relatively low-cost and low-risk strategies (Stronski 2019).

The Soviet Union's engagement in Africa during the Cold War attracted significant interest among political commentators and historians. However, as the Soviet leaders did not publicize their motives, the study of Soviet activism in Africa and in the Third World, in general, remains a bit like "palm-reading" (Rubinstein 1990, 64). Following the collapse of the Soviet Union, its successor, Russia, retreated from the African continent, scaling down its commitment to the bare minimum. Today Moscow is attempting to accelerate its relations with the "global south." However, Russia is neither the Soviet Union, nor is the global south the then-Third World. Unlike Soviet foreign policy, Russia's international conduct today is devoid of ideological constraints which guided its forerunner. For its part, Africa, as a prominent global emerging market, hosts some of the most rapidly developing economies in the world.

All this makes the deciphering of Russian intentions and African interests even more difficult than before. Indeed, Moscow cannot overlook the increasing economic significance of the African continent which holds significant potential for economic growth and development. Yet, this does not entirely depict the complex interaction between development and security in Russia's national interest vis-à-vis Africa. Russia's long absence from the continent, the introduction of powerful and ambitious international players and its lack of long-term strategic vision for its regional relations curtail its ambition to challenge the status quo and emerge once again as a leading partner to the continent. As a successor to the Soviet Union and as a Eurasian regional power with increasing global aspirations, Russia cannot overcome the superpower reflexes of its predecessor. Moscow's highly publicized business initiatives across the continent go hand-in-hand with more low-key moves of military and strategic importance. Key regions of infrastructural importance, such as Southern Africa and the Horn, remain a regional priority as suggested by tacit initiatives in the security field, which accompany the flurry of Russia's economic activities across the continent.

More than a century after the European powers carved up the African continent for their own imperial needs, and 20 years after the end of the Cold War, many commentators see Russia's Africa ambitions as part of the "new scramble for Africa" alongside China's strong inroads, as well as the increasing involvement of Brazil, India and Turkey, which have upended the order established by the US and the former colonial powers (Volman 2009; Cohen 2009; Oğultürk 2017, 136–137; *The Economist* 2019b; Gathara 2019; Bennetts and Flanagan 2019; Brennan 2019; Meyer 2019). The "new scramble" metaphor, however, has many critics who object to how it depicts Africans as passive political objects, rather than acknowledging the agency and interests of individual African states as actors in their own right (Deych and Vertashov 2018; Couch 2019; Paduano 2019; Orakçı 2020). The new battle for Africa, however, does not deploy strong-arm tactics, but rather using economic and humanitarian aid (Arkhangelskaya and Taylor 2015), which gives the continent unique new opportunities for low-interest rate loans, direct foreign investment and new infrastructure.

Thus, it appears that, as Africa needs Russia's investments, Russia needs Africa's support (Korendyasov and Vasilyev 2013), which confirms the "mutual interest" argument. As for Russian investments, they cover sectors that are at the top of many African governments' strategic agendas, such as armaments and nuclear energy, and in which Russia has a competitive advantage compared to other global players. Russia's assistance also tends to benefit the African states as it comes at relatively low cost and yields high gains by bypassing caveats or conditions that restrict the room for maneuver of many Western partners (Faleg and Secrieru 2020), allowing them also to potentially profit from Moscow's well-established expertise in extracting energy resources (Barka and Mlambo

2011, 6). Also, from the African perspective, the relationship with Moscow would ideally help them diversify their sources of foreign investment to avoid becoming overdependent on the United States, France, China, Britain or India, increasing in return their maneuverability and freedom of action in the international arena (Pham 2014; Deych and Vertashov 2018, 133). Ultimately, the increased investment choice (Comins and Yermolaev 2015) would help provide African states with the ability to drive harder bargains and avoid foreign investment as a zero-sum contest (*The Economist* 2019b) and negate the subalternization metaphor depicting the reemergence of global interest in Africa's as a "new scramble" for the continent.

References

Abramova, Irina O. 2018. "Afrikanskoe turne S. V. Lavrova: novye vyzovy i perspektivy rossijsko-afrikanskogo sotrudnichestva." *Azia i Afrika*, 5, 2–10.

Abramova, Irina and Fituni, Leonid. 2017. "Potentsial Afrikanskogo Kontinenta v Strategii Razvitiya Rossiyskoy Ekonomiki." *Mirovaya ekonomika i mezhdunarodnye otnosheniya,* 61(9), 24–36. https://doi.org/10.20542/0131-2227-2017-61-9-24-35.

Arkhangelskaya, Alexandra and Taylor, Ian. 2015. "What Africa Needs." *Russia in Global Affairs,* July 16. https://eng.globalaffairs.ru/articles/what-africa-needs/ (Accessed March 9, 2020).

Arkhangelskaya, Alexandra and Dodd, Nicole. 2016. "Guns and Poseurs: Russia Returns to Africa." In Justin van der Merwe, Ian Taylor and Alexandra Arkhangelskaya (Eds), *Emerging Powers in Africa: A New Wave in the Relationship?* London: Palgrave Macmillan, 159–175.

Avtonomov, V. S. and Subbotina, T. P. Eds. 1999. *Mir i Rossiya: Materialy dlya razmyshlenii i diskusii.* St Petersburg: Ekonomicheskaya shkola.

Baklanov, A. 2018. "Rossiya-Afrika: Srednosrochnyi plan deistvii." *Russia in Global Affairs,* October 10. www.globalaffairs.ru/articles/rossiya-afrika-srednesrochnyj-plan-dejstvij/ (Accessed March 7, 2020).

Barka, Habiba Ben and Mlambo, Kupukile. 2011. "Russia's Economic Engagement with Africa." *Africa Economic Brief,* 2(7), May 11, 1–7. www.afdb.org/fileadmin/uploads/afdb/Documents/Publications/Russia%27s_Economic_Engagement_with_Africa.pdf (Accessed April 21, 2020).

Bennetts, Marc and Flanagan, Jane. 2019. "President Putin Woos Strongmen in Scramble for Africa." *The Times*, October 5. www.thetimes.co.uk/article/president-putin-woos-strongmen-in-scramble-for-africa-kwcx0bk8r (Accessed April 20, 2020).

Brannon, Robert. 2009. *Russian Civil–Military Relations*. Farnham: Ashgate.

Brennan, David. 2019. "Russia-Africa Summit: How Putin is Challenging the U.S. and China in New Continental Race." *Newsweek*, October 22. www.newsweek.com/russia-africa-summit-vladimir-putin-challenging-u-s-china-new-continental-race-sochi-1466966 (Accessed April 20, 2020).

Bugayova, Nataliya, and Regio, Darina. 2019. *The Kremlin's Campaign in Africa: Assessment Update.* Washington, DC: Institute for the Study of War.

Bugayova, Nataliya, Ulses, Jack and Johnson, Chase. 2018. "The Kremlin's Campaign in Africa." Institute for the Study of War, October 18. http://iswresearch.blogspot.com/2018/10/the-kremlins-campaign-in-africa_18.html (Accessed April 20, 2020).

Cohen, Ariel. 2009. "Russia's New Scramble for Africa." The Heritage Foundation, July 2. www.heritage.org/europe/commentary/russias-new-scramble-africa (Accessed April 20, 2020).

Comins, Marshall and Yermolaev, Dmitry. 2015. "What you Need to Know about Russia's New Commitment to Africa." *Russia Direct*, April 28. www.russia-direct.org/ opinion/what-you-need-know-aboutrussias-renewed-commitment-africa (Accessed April 21, 2020).

Couch, E. 2019. "We Need to Change How We Talk about Russia." Wilson Center, October 25.. www.wilsoncenter.org/blog-post/we-need-to-change-how-we-talk-about-russia-africa (Accessed April 20, 2020).

Devermont, Judd. 2019. "The Art of Summitry." Center for Strategic and International Studies, September 30. https://www.csis.org/analysis/art-summitry (Accessed April 19, 2020)

Deych, T. and Vertashov, Yu. 2018. "Rossiysko-Afrikanskiye Otnosheniya v Kontekste 'Povorota' Afriki na Vostok." *Mirovaya Ekonomika i Mezhdunarodnyye Otnosheniya,* 62(10), 124–133.

Dolgov, S. I. Ed. 2001. *Vneshnyaya torgovlya Rossii na rubezhe vekov*. Moscow: Ekonomika.

Dutton, Peter, Ross, Robert S. and Tunsjø, Øystein. 2012. "Introduction." In Peter Dutton, Robert S. Ross and Øystein Tunsjø, *Twenty-First Century Seapower: Cooperation and Conflict at Sea*. London: Routledge, 1–7.

Edmonds, Robin. 1975. *Soviet Foreign Policy 1962–1973*. Oxford: Oxford University Press.

Fabricius, Peter. 2019. "From Russia with Love – or Perhaps Not?" Institute for Security Services, October 4. https://issafrica.org/iss-today/from-russia-with-love-or-perhaps-not (Accessed 20 April 2020).

Faleg, Giovanni and Secrieru, Stanislav. 2020. "Russia's Forays into Sub-Saharan Africa: Do you Want to Be my Friend, Again?" Institute for Security Issues, March 31. www.iss.europa.eu/content/russias-forays-sub-saharan-africa#_what_do_africans_want_from_russia___ (Accessed April 19, 2020).

Fidan, Hakan and Aras, Bülent. 2010. "The Return of Russia-Africa Relations." *Bilig*, 52 (Winter), 47–68.

Gathara, Patrick. 2019. "Russia has Joined the 'Scramble' for Africa." Al Jazeera, November 19. www.aljazeera.com/indepth/opinion/russia-joined-scramble-africa-19110809 0406302.html (Accessed April 20, 2020).

Giles, Keir. 2013. *Russian Interests in Sub-Saharan Africa*. Carlisle, PA: Strategic Studies Institute.

Gorshkov, Sergei. 1976. *Morskaya Moshch Gosudarstva*. Moscow: Voennizdat.

Gottemoeller, Rose. 2004. "Nuclear Weapons in Current Russian Policy." In Steven E. Miller and Dmitri Trenin (Eds), *The Russian Military: Power and Policy* . Cambridge, MA: MIT Press, 183–217.

Haas, Marcel de. 2011. "Russia's Military Doctrine Development (2000–10)." In Stephen J Blank (Ed.), *Russian Military Politics and Russia's 2010 Defense Doctrine*. Carlisle, PA: Strategic Studies Institute, 1–63.

Muresan, Arina. 2019. "The Russia-Africa Summit, 23–24 October 2019." Institute for Global Dialogue, October 1. www.africaportal.org/publications/russia-africa-summit-23-24-october-2019/ (Accessed April 21, 2020).

Ivanov, Sergei. 2004. "Russia's Geopolitical Priorities and Armed Forces." *Russia in Global Affairs*, February 17. https://eng.globalaffairs.ru/articles/russias-geopolitical-priorities-and-armed-forces/ (Accessed March 9, 2020).

Hellyer, Caroline. 2015. "Russia Returns to Africa amid Increasing Isolation," Al Jazeera, March 10. www.aljazeera.com/indepth/features/2015/03/russia-returns-africa-increasing-isolation-150305071828897.html (Accessed April 21, 2020).

Hohler, E. 2018. "The New Scramble for Africa," September 7. https://moneyweek.com/494549/the-new-scramble-for-africa (Accessed April 20, 2019).

Jordan, Will. 2015. "S Africa Spied on Russia for Satellite Project Details." Al Jazeera, February 25. www.aljazeera.com/news/2015/02/south-africa-russia-joint-satellite-project-condor-spy-cables-guardian-150225154536792.html (Accessed April 21, 2020).

Kadomtsev, Andrei. 2019. "Ukrepleniye Rossii i Kitaya v Afrike vse bol'she trevozhit Zapad (Chast' 2)." *Mezhdunarodnaya Zhizn'*, March 26, https://interaffairs.ru/news/show/22021 (Accessed March 10, 2020).

Kalika, Arnaud. 2019. "Russia's "Great Return" to Africa?" *Russie.Nei.Visions*, 114. Paris: French Institute of International Affairs. www.ifri.org/en/publications/notes-de-lifri/russieneivisions/russias-great-return-africa (Accessed April 21, 2020)

Kapitanets, I. M. 2002. *Bitva za Mirovoi okean v "kholodnoi" i budushchikh voinakh.* Moscow: Veche.

Kanet, Roger E., Kozhemiakin, Alexander V. and Birgerson, Susanne. 1997. "The Third World in Russian Foreign Policy." In Roger Kanet and Alexander Kozhemiakin (Eds), *The Foreign Policy of the Russian Federation.* Basingstoke: Macmillan, 159–192.

Kipp, Jacob W. 2009. "The Shifting Strategic Priorities of the Russian Navy." *Eurasia Daily Monitor,* 6(195). https://jamestown.org/program/the-shifting-strategic-priorities-of-the-russian-navy/ (Accessed March 10, 2020).

Klomegah, Kester Kenn. 2015. "Russia: Attempting a Bridge to Africa." *Modern Diplomacy*, November 17. https://moderndiplomacy.eu/2015/11/17/russia-attempting-a-bridge-to-africa/ (Accessed April 21, 2020).

Korendyasov, Evgeny and Vasilyev, Aleksey. 2013. "Russian-African Relations in Ten Years: A New Start." Russian International Affairs Council, June 21. http://russiancouncil.ru/en/inner/?id_4=2002#top-content (Accessed April 21, 2020).

Kulkova, Olga. 2019. "Povorot Rossii k Afrike: Kakovy Perspektivy?" *Valdai Discussion Club*, March 5. http://ru.valdaiclub.com/events/posts/articles/lukomorya-bolshe-net/?sphrase_id=38196 (Accessed April 19, 2020).

Lavrov, Sergei. 2008. "Russia and the World in the 21st Century." *Russia in Global Affairs*, August 9. https://eng.globalaffairs.ru/articles/russia-and-the-world-in-the-21st-century/ (Accessed March 8, 2020).

Lo, Bobo. 2003. *Vladimir Putin and the Evolution of Russian Foreign Policy.* London: Blackwell.

Magen, Zvi, Michlin-Shapir, Vera, Rakov, Daniel and Guzansky, Yoel. 2019. "Russia in the Middle East and Africa: A Higher Gear or Media Buzz?" *Institute for National Security Studies Insight,* 1224, November 6. www.inss.org.il/publication/russia-in-the-middle-east-and-africa-a-higher-gear-or-media-buzz/ (Accessed April 21, 2020).

Malysheva, D. B. and Rogozhin, A. A. Eds. 2012. *Aziya i Afrika v sovremennoi mirovoi politike.* Moscow: IMEMO RAN.

Manturov, Denis. 2019. "Denis Manturov: Nam vygodneye sobirat' tekhniku v Afrike, chem prosto eksportirovat'." *Minpromtorg Rossii*, October 28. http://minpromtorg.gov.ru/press-centre/news/#!denis_manturov_nam_vygodnee_sobirat_ tehniku_v_afrike_chem_prosto_eksportirovat (Accessed March 8, 2020).

McGrath, Ciaran. 2018. "Putin Flexes Muscles with Plans for New African Base – with Chilling Echoes of Suez." *Express*, April 18. www.express.co.uk/news/world/948063/russia-news-vladimir-putin-naval-base-africa-somaliland-1956-suez-crisis (Accessed April 20, 2020).

Medvedev, Dmitri. 2019. "Ekonomicheskaya konferentsiya 'Rossiya–Afrika'" Speech by Dmitry Medvedev at the opening of the 26th annual meeting of shareholders of the African Export-Import Bank. *Pravitel'stvo Rossii*, June 21. http://government.ru/news/37113/ (Accessed March 8, 2020).

Melville, Andrei and Shakleina, Tatiana. Eds. 2005. *Russian Foreign Policy in Transition: Concepts and Realities*. Budapest: Central European University.

Meyer, Henry. 2019. "Putin Enters Contest for Africa After Humbling U.S. in Mideast." Bloomberg, October 23. www.bloomberg.com/news/articles/2019-10-23/putin-enters-contest-for-africa-after-humbling-u-s-in-mideast (Accessed April 20, 2020).

MID. 2004. "Morskaya doktrina Rossiyskoy Federatsii na period do 2020 goda." *Ministerstvo innostrannykh del Rossiiskoi Federatsii*, August 18. www.mid.ru/foreign_policy/official_documents/-/asset_publisher/CptICkB6BZ29/ content/ id/462098 (Accessed March 10, 2020).

MID. 2018. [Interview with Russian Minister of Foreign Affairs Sergey V. Lavrov to *Hommes d'Afrique* magazine, Moscow]. *Ministerstvo innostrannykh del Rossiiskoi Federatsii*, March 5, 2018. www.mid.ru/foreign_policy/news/-/asset_ publisher/cKNonkJE02Bw/content/id/3106421 (Accessed March 10, 2020).

MID. 2020. "Interview of the Director of the African Department of the Ministry of Foreign Affairs of Russia A.V. Kemarsky to the RIA Novosti International News Agency." *Ministerstvo innostrannykh del Rossiiskoi Federatsii*, February 14, 2020. www.mid.ru/web/guest/maps/cf/-/asset_publisher/obfEMxF2i9RB/content/id/4042444 (Accessed March 8, 2020).

Moss, Todd J. and Resnick, Danielle. 2018. *African Development: Making Sense of the Issues and Actors*. 3rd Ed. Boulder, CO: Lynne Rienner.

Oğultürk, Mehmet Cem. 2017. "Russia's Renewed Interests in the Horn of Africa as a Traditional and Rising Power." *Rising Powers Quarterly*, 2(1), 121–143.

Oldberg, Ingmar Karl. 2010. "Aims and Means in Russian Foreign Policy." In Roger E. Kanet (Ed.), *Russian Foreign Policy in the 21st Century*. Basingstoke: Palgrave Macmillan, 30–59.

Olivier, Gerrit and Suchkov, Dmitry. 2015. "Russia is Back in Africa." *Strategic Review for Southern Africa*, 37(2) (November), 146–167.

Orakçı, Serhat. 2020. "The New Scramble for Africa, Tragedy or Farce?," IHH Humanitarian and Social Research Center, January 15. https://insamer.com/en/the-new-scramble-for-africa-tragedy-or-farce_2607.html (Accessed April 20, 2020).

Paduano, Stephen. 2019. "Putin Lost his African Great Game Before he Started." *Foreign Policy*, October 31. https://foreignpolicy.com/2019/10/31/putin-russia-africa-great-game-china-united-states/ (Accessed April 20, 2019).

PenzaNews. 2019. "Forum Rossiya – Afrika v Sochi zalozhil prochnuyu osnovu dlya dal'neyshego sotrudnichestva storon." *PenzaNews*, November 9. https://penzanews.ru/analysis/139109-2019 (Accessed March 10, 2020).

Pham, J. Peter. 2014. "Russia's Return to Africa: Two Decades After Pullback, Russia Chases Gas Resources, Minerals and UN Votes." *Atlantic Council*, March 13. http://www.atlantic council.org/publications/articles/russia-s-return-to-africa (Accessed March 10, 2020).

Procopio, Maddalena. 2019. "Why Russia is Not like China in Africa." Instituto per gli Studi di Politica Internazionale, November 15. www.ispionline.it/en/ pubblicazione/why-russia-not-china-africa-24409 (Accessed April 19, 2020).

Rozhdestvensky, Ilya, Rubin, Michael and Badanin, Roman. 2019. "Shef i povar. Chast' tret'ya. Rassledovaniye o tom, kak Rossiya vmeshivayetsya v vybory v dvadtsati stranakh." *Proekt*, April 11. www.proekt.media/investigation/prigozhin-polittekhnologi/ (Accessed April 20, 2020).

Rubinstein, Alvin Z. 1990. *Moscow's Third World Strategy*. Princeton, NJ: Princeton University Press.

Russian Export Center (REC). 2019a. [Russian Export to Northern Africa] www.exportcenter.ru/international_markets/world_map/north_africa/ (Accessed April 21, 2020).

Russian Export Center (REC). 2019b. [Russian Export to Sub Saharan Africa]. www.exportcenter .ru/international_ markets/world_map/tropical_africa/ (Accessed April 21, 2020).

Shubin, Vladimir. 2013. "Russia's Policy towards Africa." Instituto per gli Studio di Politica Internazionale, analysis 168, April. www.ispionline.it/ sites/default/files/pubblicazioni/analysis_168_2013.pdf (Accessed March 10, 2020).

Shubin, V. 2019. "Africa's Unfolding Potential for Russia," Istituto per gli Studi di Politica Internazioinale, November 15. www.ispionline.it/en/pubblicazione/africas-unfolding-potential-russia-24289 (Accessed April 19, 2020).

Shishkov, Artem. 2019. "Rossia i Sudan podpisali soglasheniye o voennom sotrudnichestve." *Polit Rossiya*, May 24, https://politros.com/144528-rossiya-i-sudan-podpisali-soglashenie-o-voennom-sotrudnichestve?utm_source=yxnews&utm_medium= desktop&utm_referrer=https%3A%2F%2Fyandex.ru%2Fnews (Accessed April 20, 2020).

Sochi Summit. 2019. "Declaration of the First Russia-Africa Summit." *Russia-Africa*, October 24. https://summitafrica.ru/en/about-summit/declaration/ (Accessed March 10, 2019).

Sputnik. 2018. "The Russian Navy Negotiates to Create a Logistics Center in Sudan." *Sputnik*, September 6. mundo.sputniknews.com/defensa/201806091079432778-rusia-sudan-como-cooperan-en-sector-militar (Accessed April 20, 2020).

Stronski, Paul. 2019. "Late to the Party: Russia's Return to Africa," October 16. https://carnegieendowment.org/2019/10/16/late-to-party-russia-s-return-to-africa-pub-80056 (Accessed April 19, 2020).

Sudan Tribune. 2018. "Russia, Sudan are Discussing Naval Supply Centre, Not Military Base: Diplomat." June 9. www.sudantribune.com/spip.php?article65611 (Accessed April 20, 2020)

The Economist. 2019a. "Africa Is Attracting Ever More Interest from Powers Elsewhere." March 7. www.economist.com/briefing/2019/03/07/africa-is-attracting-ever-more-interest-from-powers-elsewhere (Accessed April 20, 2020).

The Economist. 2019b. "The New Scramble for Africa." March 7. www.economist.com/leaders/2019/03/07/the-new-scramble-for-africa (Accessed April 20, 2020).

Volman, Daniel. 2009. *China, India, Russia and the United States: The Scramble for African Oil and the Militarization of the Continent*. Uppsala: Nordisk Afrika Instituet.

Wallander, Celleste. 2007. "Global Challenges and Russian Foreign Policy." In Robert Legvold (Ed.), *Russian Foreign Policy in the Twenty-First Century and the Shadow of the Past*. New York: Columbia University Press, 443–499.

7 Diamonds in Africa and the continuing Cold War

A case study of building a capitalist ruling class in Namibia

Allan D. Cooper

The abundance of diamonds in Africa has been one to three billion years in the making. Formed in the Earth's mantle, these carbon stones began moving to the surface of the planet in volcanic eruptions or other natural processes. Other deposits, including the Popigal crater in Russia which might be the world's largest diamond deposit, appear to be the result of meteorite strikes that produced shock waves with high temperatures and pressures that formed diamonds. Although diamonds are relatively common on Earth, they are more abundant in space. In 2011, scientists discovered a planet about 4,000 light years away that appears to be one large diamond (Planck 2011).

European settlers in Africa first discovered diamonds in 1867 inside South Africa. Diamonds were then discovered in Congo in 1906, Namibia in 1908, Tanzania in 1910, Angola in 1912, the Central African Republic in 1913, Sierra Leone in 1930, Guinea-Conakry in 1930, Liberia around 1935 and Botswana in 1967 (see Cleveland 2014, 8). Ernest Oppenheimer got an early start in the diamond rush in South Africa. He moved from his native Germany to work in a diamond brokerage in London when he was 17 years old, and five years later, in 1902, he was sent to South Africa to serve as a buyer in Kimberley, where Cecil Rhodes and Charles Rudd had formed the De Beers company. In 1927, Oppenheimer pushed Cecil Rhodes out of De Beers, and in 1929 he took complete control of the company.

Oppenheimer became among the wealthiest people in the world by employing unfree labor in the diamond mines in South Africa and neighboring Namibia, whose coastal diamond fields were taken from Germany during World War One. A migrant labor system was instituted by South African military officers to recruit Ovambo labor in northern Namibia to work the diamond fields on the southern border, seeing that neighboring Herero and Nama communities had been subjected to genocide when they rose up to overthrow German rule in 1904–1908. Wages for Ovambo workers would be deferred during the contracted service; instead, credit would be transferred to company stores back in Ovamboland so that the families of the contract workers could obtain blankets and other provisions from any surplus value obtained by the worker (see Cooper 2001, 74). The kings or chiefs of each Ovambo group would get a commission for each laborer recruited, and could tax each worker on his wages earned. Whereas the average laborer earned about 200 shillings per year working on the diamond fields, the traditional authority recruiting 100 men to join the contract labor system stood to gain about 500 shillings a year (Cooper 2001, 77). By 1926, the total value of diamonds produced in Namibia exceeded £2 million.

The independence of African states from colonial rule threatened the existing relations of foreign control over Africa's resources. Companies such as De Beers scrambled to establish relations with the new leaders of post-colonial states as well as with liberation groups seeking to end colonial rule in their territory. These efforts were influenced by the Cold War global politics dominating at the time, in which the United States and the Soviet Union sought to exploit the decolonization of Africa by major European powers. The new nationalist leaders of independent African states desired to avoid any direct ties to the government or businesses of apartheid South Africa, even though from an economic point of view a relationship with the white-minority regime was inevitable if they sought to use their diamonds as a source of income. De Beers navigated these global political changes by forming an alliance with Maurice Tempelsman, an American diamond merchant with close ties to the US Central Intelligence Agency. Tempelsman began his career pretending to be an alternative to the monopolistic De Beers Corporation, securing contracts from national leaders that wished to break away from De Beers. In 1957, Tempelsman rushed to Ghana, Africa's first Sub-Saharan state to win independence. Kwame Nkrumah had plans to sell diamonds independently of De Beers. Tempelsman set up an office in Accra and began purchasing diamonds from Ghana (Roberts 2003, 172). In 1960, when Patrice Lumumba of the Congo was exploring ways to join Nkrumah in circumventing De Beers, Tempelsman befriended Mobutu Sese Seko, Lumumba's personal security officer. Mobutu was persuaded to join in a coup that resulted in Lumumba's assassination three days before the inauguration of President John F. Kennedy (Roberts 2003: 181). The new US President immediately approved legislation allowing diamonds to be used to covertly "fund wars, coups, repression and dictatorships in Africa" (Roberts 2003: 184). US aid to Mobutu was partially channeled through Tempelsman's diamonds (Roberts 2003, 185). Between 1977 and 1979 alone, Mobutu transferred nearly $4 billion to overseas bank accounts established for himself and his family (Roberts 2003, 197). Tempelsman also worked with President Siaka Stevens of Sierra Leone to establish a diamond industry in that West African country (Roberts 2003, 202). Tempelsman became an intimate companion of Jacqueline Kennedy after the death of her second husband in 1975, and became a major donor to the Democratic Party. Tempelsman also served as Chairman of the American Jewish Congress, a lobby group with alleged close ties to the Israeli military. Israel buys half of the world's rough diamonds, and two-thirds of these end up being cut and sent to the United States (Constantine 2009). Tempelsman continues to earn enormous wealth from supplying diamonds to Tiffany and Cartier.

De Beers and the scramble for Namibia

SWAPO's socialist rhetoric notwithstanding, the Namibian governing party has always had cordial relations with global capitalists. In her 1963 analysis of Namibian politics, Ruth First identifies the early competition between SWAPO and the South West Africa National Union (SWANU) to gain legitimacy as the authentic liberation movement of Namibia. When SWANU leader Uatja Kozonguizi criticized the impotence of the United Nations while he was visiting China in 1963, SWAPO criticized him for collaborating with the Communist world. SWANU, in turn, attacked SWAPO for its close relations with the American Metal Climax Corporation which owned the Tsumeb mine in northern Namibia, claiming that the company was paying bursaries to SWAPO members abroad (First 1963, 206–207).

SWAPO's collaboration with the De Beers diamond syndicate was even more extensive. Its chief executive officer in the 1960s, Harry Oppenheimer, had always placed his patriotism in the value of money. He operated on the notion that everyone has a price, and as one of Africa's richest men, he had a personal war chest of over US$3 billion to prove his point (Boer and Sherbourne 2003, 5). He had no doubt that the leadership of SWAPO would need him as a partner to advance the material interests of an independent Namibia. Argued Oppenheimer around 1980, "We now pay about 80 million dollars a year in taxes on those diamonds and that provides the territory with most of its revenues ... Whatever government comes to power they will need this revenue to survive" (see Epstein 1982: 20). The real question for outside observers was whether SWAPO President Sam Nujoma, a client of Marxist states who sent his children to Cuba to be educated, would succumb to such capitalistic extortion. The answer did not take long. In 1984, SWAPO suggested that De Beers might be welcome in an independent Namibia if the terms were acceptable to the state (Kempton and De Preez 1997, 598). As Brian Urquhart, the United Nations Under-Secretary-General for Special Political Affairs, acknowledged prior to Namibia's independence in 1990, "I doubted if Nujoma would know a Marxist-Leninist idea if he met one in the street" (Urquhart 1991, 321).

De Beers had developed an interest in SWAPO from the founding of the liberation movement. Both Harry Oppenheimer and his son Nicky relied on Maurice Tempelsman as an intermediary between De Beers and Nujoma. Tempelsman's interest in Namibia reportedly started as far back as the 1960s when he befriended Sam Nujoma and Theo-Ben Gurirab (*The Namibian*, 9 March 2001). Tempelsman presumably introduced Sam Nujoma to Holden Roberto of the FNLA in Angola, as well as Jonas Savimbi of UNITA in Angola. These three leaders developed an alliance in the early 1960s that aimed to satisfy CIA objectives in southern Africa (Dreyer 1994, 45–50, 62–65, 86–91). Tempelsman is said to have funded SWAPO operations and paid for the private expenses of several SWAPO leaders during the liberation struggle (*The Namibian*, 8 August 1989, 1, 3). In 1978, Tempelsman allegedly sent Bill Ullman, a CIA associate, to Windhoek to scout for business and political relationships with political leaders. Ullman reportedly decided that the time was not ripe to develop these contacts, and departed the country (*The Namibian,* 8 August 1989). Ullman made several trips back to Namibia during the 1980s, when Nujoma was actively courting other multinational corporations (Frankel 1984). Ullman only set up a residence in Namibia in the months prior to UN supervised elections in 1989. During the election campaign, Tempelsman loaned Nujoma his private jet so that he could travel between the UN and other destinations to negotiate Namibian independence (Roberts 2003, 317).

With the SWAPO leadership clearly entrenched within the De Beers network, no obstacles remained among the major Western powers for the transfer of Namibian sovereignty to Sam Nujoma and SWAPO. The independence of Namibia essentially represented a hostile takeover of the white minority government of South Africa, and its migrant labor system supervised by traditional authorities, by the new nationalist elite of SWAPO. Following the formal independence of Namibia in March 1990, Tempelsman arranged a State Visit for Nujoma to the United States (Roberts 2003, 318). During this trip, on June 21, 1993, Tempelsman hosted a luncheon for President Nujoma at the Metropolitan Club in New York attended by some of America's top businesspeople. Tempelsman told the crowd that the Namibian leadership had "fulfilled and exceeded the hopes its foreign friends have had for it" (*The Namibian*, 25 June 1993, 2).

In December 1994, the Namibian government entered into a formal partnership with De Beers, and Consolidated Diamond Mines (CDM) was renamed Namdeb. Under the terms of this agreement, Namdeb assumed control of all of CDM's diamond assets in Namibia, while ownership of Namdeb was divided 50-50 between the government and DeBeers. During these negotiations Namibia was reportedly advised by Maurice Tempelsman (Kempton and Du Preez 1997, 612).

The partnership between the Namibian state and De Beers provided the SWAPO leadership with the capability to radically transform Namibia into the socialist paradise that it had promised during the liberation struggle. But something else happened instead. The Namibian people actually suffered worse economic conditions. In 2008, the Central Bureau of Statistics indicated that nearly one-third of the country's 2 million people lived on less than a dollar a day. According to this same survey, the top 20 percent of the population controlled about 79 percent of the country's total income, while the bottom one-fifth accounted for 1.4 percent (Melber 2010).

The enrichment of SWAPO's governing elite transpired through a number of state actions regulating the diamond industry, as well as special arrangements by De Beers to reward Namibian leaders for their cooperation and service. In the case of President Sam Nujoma, financial gains were transacted through business relations with his brother-in-law, Aaron Mushimba, and his youngest son, Zacharias "Zacky" Nujoma. Mushimba became associated with several business initiatives following Namibian independence, ranging from fishing to construction to banking. In 1995 the Namibian government granted him the mineral rights for the Rosh Pinah zinc mine. Mushimba also partnered with Tempelsman in North Bank Diamonds, incorporated in the Bahamas (Grobler 2002). When Mushimba died in 2014, the value of his assets exceeded $20 million (Menges 2015). His estate was the largest in Namibia's history except for that of Werner List, who died in 2002 following a career of profiting off South Africa's illegal occupation of Namibia during the apartheid years. Mushimba had partnered with List's holding company, Ohlthaver & List, Namibia's largest privately held group of companies.

In addition to Mushimba, Sam Nujoma's family wealth derived from business transactions of his youngest son, Zacky. In February 2005, Diamond Ocean Enterprises was established by Vito Roberto Palazzolo to provide expertise to Nu Diamonds, a partnership between Zacky Nujoma and Palazzolo, an alleged member of the Sicilian Mafia. About the same time, Zacky acquired two other diamond companies in Namibia, Avila Investments and Marbella Investments. Ninety percent of the shared capital in these companies was transferred to Diamond Ocean Enterprises. In 2006, Zacky established Ancash Investments which then proceeded to obtain seven uranium exclusive prospecting licenses from the Namibian government's Mines and Energy ministry (Mongudhi and Kahiurika 2016).

Sam Nujoma's oldest son, Utoni Nujoma, is also involved in the diamond industry, owning 10 percent of Namibia Diamond House since 2006. Unlike his younger brother, Utoni has made politics the focus of his career (Immanuel 2014).

Another avenue for accumulating capital wealth for the Namibian governing elite came from a secretive conglomerate known as August 26 Holdings, formed by the Ministry of Defense on August 14, 1998. Named after the day on which the SWAPO armed struggle commenced, it is an independent business enterprise that is not required to report its activities or finances to the Parliament. One of its initial enterprises was to operate a diamond mine in the Democratic Republic of Congo, provided to Namibia in exchange for its military support in 1999 to maintain President Laurent Kabila in power. The transfer of the diamond mine at Maji Munene was reportedly arranged through Maurice Tempelsman and his attorney Christian Merkling (Kahiruika and Immanuel 2018). President Nujoma ordered troops into Congo to secure this mine without consulting his cabinet or the Parliament. In 2001, then Prime Minister Hage Geingob's office confirmed that the Namibian government controlled the diamond mine in Congo, but insisted that President Nujoma did not have a personal stake in the mine (BBC News 2001). The Ministry of Mines and Energy confirmed in March 2001 that the mine in DRC was run by a front company called August 26 Congo with the assistance of "an American" (Amupadhi 2001). For its part, Zimbabwe established a similar company to manage its mines in Congo called Osleg. Robert Mugabe appointed Emmerson Mnangagwa as the chief deal broker to ensure that the Congo war was profitable. Mnangagwa assumed the presidency of Zimbabwe following a coup in 2017.

The accumulation of diamonds from Congo presented an opportunity for Namibia to derive income from diamonds independent of its contractual obligations with De Beers. Once again, Maurice Tempelsman intervened to stabilize the situation. In May 2002, Tempelsman visited President Nujoma and offered to arrange a secret payment to Namibia if it entrenched the right of DeBeers to buy all of Namibia's diamonds, not just those produced by Namdeb. Tempelsman proposed an offshore loan of $80 million to be given to De Beers which would then buy Namibia's diamonds, allowing Namibia to net $50 million from the deal. In exchange, Namibia would legally guarantee that De Beers would get exclusive rights to Namibia's diamonds (Amupadhi and Roberts 2002). De Beers put pressure on Namibia to accept this deal, threatening to reduce production at Namdeb. Tempelsman employed Aaron Mushimba to persuade his brother-in-law, President Nujoma, to accept the deal (Amupadhi 2002a). In the meantime, Tempelsman's legal associate, Chris Merkling, traveled to Namibia bimonthly throughout 2002 to "advise" the Ministry of Mines and Energy on how to resolve this conflict (Amupadhi 2002b). The government removed Jesaya Nyamu as Minister of Mines and Energy following his public support of Tempelsman's proposal, but the new Mines Minister, Dr. Nicky Iyambo, finally conceded in November 2002 to Tempelsman's request to sell all diamonds to De Beers (Amupadhi 2002c). As for the "loan" offered by Tempelsman, Namibia's Finance Minister, Nangolo Mbumba, announced that "Whatever proposal there was, we don't think we will go for it. As a country, we have enough revenue" (Amupadhi 2002d).

In November 2003, Maurice Tempelsman proposed taking over the management of NamGem, Namibia's diamond cutting and polishing factory in Okahandja. NamGem had generated disappointing performance since its establishment in 1998. The Namibian government quickly accepted the deal (Ellis 2003).

SWAPO and Lev Leviev

This series of interactions with Maurice Tempelsman to consolidate all Namibian diamonds and to establish cutting and polishing factories in the territory were not universally supported within the Namibian governing elite. In 2004, Namibian Prime Minister Theo Ben Gurirab, the highest-ranking Damara in the Ovambo-dominated government, swung his support behind the establishment of a new and larger diamond cutting and polishing factory in Windhoek proposed by Lev Leviev, the richest man in Israel, who worked on behalf of Russia which was determined to dismantle the De Beers diamond cartel. Gurirab endorsed a policy of indigenization that promised to promote Namibian participation in the diamond industry. Gurirab accepted Leviev's strategy that diamond producers should manufacture diamonds domestically through local supplies and then brand them as commodities from the country of origin, rather than letting DeBeers combine them with diamonds from different countries to be jointly marketed as a company brand. At the opening of the

Windhoek factory, Gurirab praised Leviev, saying "You have reminded us that diamonds in our country belong to our people. There has been deliberate programming, indoctrination and brainwashing," from the current arrangements with De Beers (Muller 2004). The success of Leviev's factory in Windhoek led him to open a similar one in Angola.

Gurirab's hope was to place Namibia's diamond industry with the destiny of an Uzbekistan Jewish financier who had migrated to Israel in 1971, rather than an American Jewish businessman who had long-standing relations with the US CIA. Leviev had a net worth of $1.2 billion in 2017, and in addition to his residence in Israel he possessed homes in London and Florida (Chafets 2007). His business relations are organized under the name Africa Israel Investments. He began his career working with De Beers but became frustrated with the degree of control asserted by the syndicate. He then decided around 1989 to help Russia develop a diamond industry independent of De Beers (Chafets 2007). He entered the Africa diamond market when the controversy escalated over "blood diamonds," especially those from Angola. In 1997, Leviev invested in the Catoca diamond mine, Angola's largest, in a joint venture with Alrosa – the Russian state diamond company (Chafets 2007). Leviev used his connections with Israeli intelligence to secure a drone in 2001 to track UNITA troop movements and pinpoint Jonas Savimbi's location (Moorman 2015, 98). Savimbi was killed in February 2002, thus bringing to an end the Angolan civil war. By helping to defeat UNITA, Leviev had effectively pushed De Beers out of that country. Leviev earned about $1 billion in sales each year from marketing Angolan diamonds (Boer and Sherbourne 2003: 8). In 2006, Leviev helped Sam Pa (a Chinese billionaire) to join the global network of diamond investors in Angola, becoming a director of Pa's Worldpro Development corporation that would trade Angolan diamonds along with Leviev and Ascorp (the Angolan diamond company in which Leviev controls 24.5 percent, while another 24.5 percent was controlled by Isabel dos Santos, the eldest daughter of Angolan President Jose Eduardo dos Santos). Isabel was born in Azerbaijan from the President's first wife, a Russian, that he met while studying in Azerbaijan. In the last year or so of his governing of Angola, President dos Santos gave Isabel authority to invest with Leviev in the diamond industry of Angola, as well as obtaining a 25 percent stake in Unitel, Angola's largest mobile telephone company, and she also became head of Angola's state-owned petroleum firm, Sonangol EP. When Joao Manuel Goncalves Lourenco assumed the Angolan Presidency in 2017, he fired Isabel from her position with Sonangol, and initiated prosecutions against her and her Congolese-born husband for moving the wealth of Angola into their personal bank accounts in Malta and various Caribbean tax shelters. Isabel is currently living in exile in Portugal.

Leviev used his wealth from Angola to invest in Namibia. In July 2003, Leviev established a company in Namibia, Sakawe Mining Corporation (Samicor), that assumed the assets of the Namibian Minerals Corporation (Namco) which Leviev had controlled since 2001. One of the directors of Namco was Loine Geingos, the wife of the current Namibian President,

Hage Geingob (Boer and Sherbourne 2003, 9). The director of Samicor is Kombadayedu Kapwanga, who served as the President of the Chamber of Mines of Namibia from 2015 until April 2017. He currently serves as a director on the Diamond Board of Namibia that advises the Minister of Mines and Energy on matters related to the diamond industry. With his increasing wealth, Leviev began investing in properties in New York City, including a deal worth around $300 million with Jared Kushner that was later investigated for money-laundering. Leviev also has done business with Stephen Schwarzman, CEO of Blackstone Group, who is a personal friend of US President Donald Trump and the chair of the President's Strategic and Policy Forum (Zabrisky n.d.). Leviev was a business partner of Prevezon Holdings, the Russian firm represented by Natalia Veselnitskaya that was accused of money-laundering by Sergei Magnitsky, who died in a Moscow prison under suspicious conditions. Veselnitskaya's meeting with Kushner and others from the Trump campaign in Trump Tower on June 9, 2016, presumably to discuss strategies to shelve the Magnitsky Act, constituted a major piece of evidence in the investigation into Russian collusion in the 2016 presidential election (Green 2017). Leviev describes Vladimir Putin as a "true friend" (Chafets 2007). His business ties to Namibia have now earned him the title of the world's biggest cutter and polisher of diamonds (Smith 2007).

Namibia's sightholders

The Namibian ruling elite has benefitted from the competition between Tempelsman and Leviev, with each seeking to offer a sweeter arrangement to SWAPO. Tempelsman and De Beers intensified their relationship to SWAPO by creating a subsidiary of Namdeb in 2007 called the Namibia Diamond Trading Company (NDTC). The aim of the NDTC was to supply rough diamonds at a discount to selected sightholders, primarily individuals who were affiliated in some way to SWAPO's leadership, including family members. Essentially, eleven sightholders were to receive 10 percent of Namibia's diamond output; these individuals were free to do as they wished with these raw diamonds. They could sell these diamonds back to De Beers, or they could have these diamonds cut and polished at one of Namibia's factories established for this purpose. Of course, the reality is that all of Namibia's diamonds are provided to De Beers, which combines these diamonds in London or Gaborone with other diamonds from other locations, before they are sorted and made available to sightholders. Therefore, Namibian sightholders are not necessarily given diamonds from Namibia, which is known for possessing the highest value of any diamonds on the planet (Boer and Sherbourne 2003, 2).

These 11 sightholders are part of a larger group of at least 79 companies recognized by DeBeers Global Sightholder Sales purchasers worldwide. One of the 11 sightholders for Namibia is Lazare Kaplan International, Maurice Tempelsman's diamond company based in New York City. This organization's

Namibian subsidiary is Lazare Kaplan Namibia, formed in 2003 with Aaron Mushimba. Tempelsman's son, Leon, is also a director, along with Christian Merklin, Tempelsman's attorney.

Another recognized sightholder is Crossworks Manufacturing, which is partly owned by Nu Diamond, a business controlled by Zacky Nujoma. Helmut Angula, former Minister of Works and Transports, is a third sightholder through his 45 percent stake in Dinamo Diamonds, a partnership with New York-based Julius Klein Diamond Group that directly holds the sightholder's license. Angula's daughter, Phillipine Angula, is a director in Dinamo Diamonds as well as the oil company Eco Namibia (Immanuel 2014).

A fourth sightholder is Hard Stone Processing, controlled by James Auala, SWAPO's former Chief of Intelligence and the first leader of the Namibian Defence Force. Auala also serves as the CEO of the August 26 Holding Company that operates five subsidiaries, including one that runs the previously mentioned diamond mine in Congo. Hard Stone Processing is a joint venture with Burhan Seber, a Turkish diamond wholesaler with offices in the Democratic Republic of Congo. Other directors of HSP are Colonel David Ndatipo of the People's Liberation Army of Namibia, who is a Soviet-trained intelligence officer (Immanuel 2014), and Benjamin Thobias, a senior police officer in the security ministry.

A fifth sightholder is Dr. Kalumbi Shangula, who controls Ankit Gems. Shangula also chairs SWAPO's business empire, Kalahari Holdings. Schachter & Namdar is another sightholder. This Israeli company is a partnership with Sadike Nepela, the son of Lucas Nepela who founded the Owambo People's Organization (OPO), now known as SWAPO. The seventh sightholder is Laurelton Diamonds, a partnership with Frans Ndoroma who is the CEO of the state-owned telecommunications company Telecom Namibia. Ndoroma also directs Marine Namibia, an affiliate of De Beers' Namdeb. Both Ndoroma and his father were previously employed by Consolidated Diamond Mines during the apartheid era. Another sightholder is Almod Diamonds of New York that works with Sara Shikongo of Duiker Investment 142. Ms. Shikongo is the wife of Mateus Shikongo, a member of SWAPO who served as mayor of Windhoek for 17 years. The ninth sightholder is AMC-Gemxcel Diamonds, a partnership between Belgian-owned AMC Diamonds and Dantagob Gurirab and Hanganee Gurirab, sons of Theo-Ben Gurirab, the former Prime Minister and National Assembly Speaker. This company ceased operations in October 2012 when nearly $700,000 worth of diamonds were reportedly stolen from the company. Lev Leviev was a sightholder until 2012, at which time De Beers claimed that their competitor was harboring stolen diamonds at his factory. Diacor International of Johannesburg is another sightholder engaged with the Namibian diamonds industry. Diacor's agent in Namibia is NamCot, a joint venture between Steinmetz Diamond Group and Mathew Hamutenya, a local businessman, and Mwahafa Ndilula who serves on the Board of Directors of FNB Namibia Holdings, the oldest financial services group in Namibia. The Steinmetz Group is headed by Israeli billionaire

Beny Steinmetz who has faced several accusations of bribery and money-laundering in recent years.

Namibia has reached "peak diamonds" in terms of its land resources. The future of diamond mining in Namibia now consists of production in offshore areas. Namibia has the richest marine diamond deposits in the world, estimated at 80 million carats (Immanuel 2014), and these coastal deposits are dominated by Namdeb (Tempelsman) and Samicor (Leviev). Beginning in 2005 Namibia began to produce more diamonds offshore than on land (Philander 2006). In 2017, Debmarine Namibia, a subsidiary of De Beers, launched the most advanced diamond exploration vessel, the SS *Nujoma*. Lev Leviev operates a diamond mining vessel called the *Sakawe Miner*.

In March 2015, the Namibian people elected their third President, Hage Geingob. Geingob earned his Ph.D. in 2004 from the University of Leeds, completing a dissertation on how to create a democratic Namibia that benefits previously disadvantaged groups and promotes human rights. In his dissertation, Geingob acknowledged that "A new economic class is being created without any deep transformation of the society" (Geingob 2004: 206). Geingob never mentions the role of the international diamond industry in securing independence for SWAPO, but Geingob was an ally of fellow Damara Theo-Ben Gurirab when the latter aligned with Lev Leviev to promote a domestic diamond cutting and polishing industry in 2004. Just a month before Geingob assumed the Presidency, Gurirab publicly warned that the Namibian government had failed to do enough to improve the lives of most Namibians. Gwen Lister, editor of *The Namibian* newspaper, spoke for many when she opined "Why can't he and others openly and routinely acknowledge that (their) wasteful expenditure and (negligence to deal effectively with) corruption may just be part of the reason why there's been failure to address the needs of the poor?" (Lister 2015).

Three months after assuming the Presidency, Geingob commenced negotiations for a new contract with De Beers to guarantee that up to 30 percent of diamonds produced by Namdeb would stay in Namibia for cutting and polishing. Geingob also arranged for Namdeb's managing director, Inge Zaamwani-Kamwi, to leave the company and join him as an official advisor. She faced a salary reduction of $85,000 to assume her new post, from $253,000 per year to $168,000 (Immanuel and Mongudhi 2015a). Other board members of Namdeb were removed from their positions and replaced with individuals more friendly to the President. Following these actions, Maurice Tempelsman offered President Geingob the Africa-America Institute's Lifetime Achievement and Distinguished Alumnus Award in October 2015 in New York. The AAI had funded Geingob's education starting in 1964 during the liberation struggle, along with the university studies of former Prime Ministers Theo-Ben Gurirab and Nahas Angula (Immanuel and Mongudhi 2015b). President Geingob returned to New York in September 2017 to meet with Maurice Tempelsman to discuss the potential of setting up banking arrangements that could benefit the offshore diamond industry (Hendricks 2017).

SWAPO's underdevelopment of Namibia

It is difficult to measure the success of African states in redistributing wealth within their country since the quantitative values of this wealth derive from statistics generated by the governments themselves. For instance, Namibia claims that diamonds are 10 percent of GDP, and represent 50 percent of all exports. In 2002, the Namibian government received 70 percent of Namdeb's $169 million in pre-tax profits, out of an annual production of $450 million (Boer and Sherbourne 2004, 7). But these statistics are the product of whatever Namibia and De Beers agree on what the value of these diamonds are, in the absence of any transparency about how this value is determined. Plus, the value of the bids derived by sightholders is not a public process open to scrutiny by the media, so it remains impossible to identify the economic measure of the discount/bribe being offered to these sightholders, nor the taxable income to be assigned.

What we do have are statistics of income distribution within each state, measuring the reported incomes of citizens. From this we can identify the "Gini Coefficient," a measure of wealth dispersion among a country's citizenry. A Gini coefficient of zero represents perfect equality where everyone possesses the same income. A Gini coefficient of 1 (or 100 percent) means that only one person has all the income, and everyone else has none. According to the United Nations Development Programme, Namibia measures a 61 percent, making it is one of the most income disparate states in the world (exceeded only by South Africa and Botswana whose incomes also are dominated by De Beers). South Africa, Botswana and Namibia all share democratic systems that have been free of military interference. Yet, these three countries rank the highest for economic inequalities.

The bottom line is that the ruling elite of Namibia has compromised the integrity of their government by aligning themselves with foreign corporate persons who are neither socially responsible nor ethical. This is not the bias of a liberal academic. This is the judgement of Bain Capital, a private equity firm that was established in 1984 by Republican presidential nominee Mitt Romney and his partners. The firm manages more than $75 billion of investors' capital, and provides consulting services to global businesses. In the 2000s, Bain was hired by De Beers to recommend changes to their management. Bain issued a report in spring 2012 that advised DeBeers to change from their original horizontal monopoly into a more vertical company that could select "suppliers of choice" with whom to market their diamonds. This recommendation contributed to the company's development of its sightholder program.

In its 2012 report, Bain Capital noted that "De Beers is neither socially responsible nor ethical," adding that "Although De Beers had implemented socially responsible practices, their motives are not pure and these tactics are essentially a marketing ploy" (*De Beers* 2012). Bain acknowledged that, even with the advice provided them, DeBeers "still participates in anti-competitive practices that ultimately have a negative impact on the consumer in the form of increased prices" (*De Beers* 2012). Bain observed that the business of De Beers depended upon a supply of customers that were "obsessed with having high socioeconomic statuses that they could display." In short,

> De Beers is selling a product thats purpose is to show off wealth. Diamonds do not provide any food, shelter, or have any practical purpose, yet people are willing to pay sums of money for them that would feed some of the people mining those same diamonds for the rest of their lives …
>
> (*De Beers* 2012)

Bain Capital also criticized De Beers for its anti-capitalist philosophy:

> Even after the elimination of stockpiling, we believe that the business practices of De Beers are still extremely anti-competitive, which provides no aid to society. The result of anticompetitive behavior is a product that is not as good as it could be, for higher prices than it needs to be. De Beers, using its cartel leadership position, would select its buyers based on their commitment to buy from De Beers and only De Beers, offering them non-negotiable prices …
>
> (*De Beers* 2012)

Bain condemned the labor practices that De Beers follows in its mining practices:

> The stigma of underage, underpaid workers has plagued the diamond industry for years and De Beers is no stranger to this ignominy … De Beers clearly does not care about the well being of their employees and cares even less about the Earth from which they are extracting their diamonds.
>
> (*De Beers* 2012)

The St. Antoninus Institute has branded De Beers as "the most unethical corporation in the world," arguing

> Cartels are immoral because they overcharge the buying public by artificially propping up prices … They are also against the freedom of enterprise for they force possible competitors to obey the cartel directives, often under financial or even physical threats; they are victimizing their co-producers or suppliers …
>
> De Beers propped up Apartheid and ended up with owning a multitude of corporations to the tune of 40% of all corporations listed on the Johannesburg stock exchange …
>
> (St. Antoninus Institute 2005)

Namibia's political leaders have downplayed the role they play in wealth creation in their countries. Speaking before a gala dinner hosted by De Beers in Windhoek in 2006, Namibian President Hifikepunye Pohamba told the esteemed audience that, if Africa is to develop and prosper economically, its natural resources must be exploited in a sustainable manner for the benefit of its people, many of whom are living in difficult conditions. He implored Nicky Oppenheimer and other De Beers leaders "to take into consideration the plight of our people, who are the owners by birthright of these diamonds" (Philander 2006). More than a decade later, the Namibian people remain impoverished.

When government leaders do stand up and propose actions to benefit citizens rather than the diamond merchants, they tend to quickly lose their jobs. For instance, in 2002 the Namibian Minister for Mines and Energy, Jesaya Nyamu, instructed the Cabinet to inform De Beers of the Government's intention to implement Section 59 of the Diamond Act, which allows Namibia to sell diamonds outside of the De Beers monopoly. Maurice Tempelsman immediately flew to Namibia and offered President Nujoma $80 million to pay for budgeted government programs, as noted earlier. About the same time, Nujoma announced that he intended to have SWAPO Secretary General Hifekepunye Pohamba succeeed him. Nyamu, understanding the implications of such a "business as usual" move, nominated Trade and Industry Minister Hidipo Hamutenya to be the next President. When Nyamu realized that he was about to lose his job, he acknowledged publicly that "They (international diamond dealers) are the law in Namibia" (Grobler 2002). At the next SWAPO congress, Nyamu was expelled for "disobedience." He started his own political party in 2007 that included Hidipo Hamutenya.

SWAPO leaders have used their new-found wealth to send their children to formerly exclusive white schools where the medium of instruction is English and where the standard of education is generally higher than in black schools (Tapscott 1993, 35). But one is hard-pressed to find examples of SWAPO leaders diverting some of their diamond wealth to various philanthropic endeavors. President Nujoma established the Sam Nujoma Foundation in 2005 which supports housing for pensioners in Katutura and Okaundja. The only large-scale investment in the country that derives from diamond wealth is the proposed Goreangab Waterfront project that includes an upmarket residential suburb and exclusive businesses on the outskirts of Windhoek. When the project was first proposed in 2014, it was estimated to cost about $85 million and would create nearly 3,000 temporary jobs (*New Era* 2014). By April 2017, the project had grown to $170 million, capable of creating over 4,000 jobs (Ndjoze 2017). The first occupation of residences was scheduled for May 2020. The project is being led by Samicor, controlled by Lev Leviev.

SWAPO's words and actions

Namibia has parceled out its national resources to a variety of competing foreign powers. As I explained above, diamonds have been contracted with two different billionaires: one with connections to De Beers, the USA and Israel, and another with ties to Russia, Israel and the Kushner companies. Each Namibian

President has found ways to play these two groups off each other to the benefit of the SWAPO elite. The current President, Hage Geingob, has promoted special economic deals with foreign investors from all the major global powers. For instance, he approved the sale of four farms to Russian tycoon Rashid Sardarov in October 2018. In addition to managing the state treasury, SWAPO also controls its own economic enterprises. SWAPO has a 51 percent ownership of Kalahari Holdings, which in turn controls businesses such as MultiChoice Namibia.

SWAPO has also established major economic relations with China. The uranium mine at Rossing, one of the largest uranium mines in the world, is owned primarily by China National Uranium, with a minority stake by the Government of Iran. Stina Wu of China has become a major real estate investor in Namibia during the past 20 years and owns shopping malls throughout the territory (Mongudhi et al. 2018). Her company, the Helmsman Group, provided hundreds of desks and chairs in 2018 for the Etunda Farm Primary School, established by former President Sam Nujoma (Ikela 2018).

In short, SWAPO has been an equal opportunity contractor with foreign interests, representing major world powers from every political persuasion. Its only real association with "socialism" is that it exchanges Namibian resources with business interests that originate from countries that claim to support socialist programs. With regard to Namibian foreign policy, it too has followed a pragmatic approach that avoids active involvement in overseas conflicts. With regard to the Middle East, Namibia has close relations with Kuwait (an American ally), but has advocated the establishment of an independent Palestinian state, existing side-by-side with Israel (Republic of Namibia 2004, 76). They acknowledge their historical ties to European states, but note that it is the USA that is its strong trade partner (Republic of Namibia 2004, 77). They have an interest in strengthening partnerships with India and China, and prefer the dispute over Kashmir to be resolved peacefully between India and Pakistan (Republic of Namibia 2004, 78–79). In Latin America, their strongest relations are with Brazil and Cuba.

In retrospect, SWAPO's use of socialist rhetoric during its war of liberation was a useful strategy for recruiting Namibians into its military wing, and in securing support from Communist countries. But throughout its fight against apartheid South Africa, it was closely collaborating with American business interests and intelligence services. Since independence, it has developed strong financial relations with the USA, Russia and China, as well as regional powers such as Iran, India, Brazil and Cuba. Any commitment to socialism seems to have ended on Independence Day. What is clearly evident is that many SWAPO leaders have become multimillionaires, and have captured total control over the Namibian state. De Beers has moved its major operations out of South Africa to more stable (and less politically vulnerable) Botswana, while Leviev and his Russian benefactors continue to enrich themselves off diamonds from Angola. It is Namibia that remains the central battleground for global control over the diamond industry and its mission to profit off the engagements, weddings and anniversaries of middle-class patrons that remain insecure in proving their love for their partners.

References

Amupadhi, Tangeni. 2001. "Minister Told UN of American Mine Link." *The Namibian,* 9 March.

Amupadhi, Tangeni. 2002a. "Govt Gem Move in Limbo." *The Namibian,* 21 August.

Amupadhi, Tangeni. 2002b. "Lawyer Double Dates." *The Namibian,* 2 August.

Amupadhi, Tangeni. 2002c. "Govt in Gem Shuffle." *The Namibian,* 14 November.

Amupadhi, Tangeni. 2002d. "Govt Rejects Gem Dealer's Loan Offer." *The Namibian,* 4 November.

Amupadhi, Tangeni, and Roberts, Janine F. 2002. "Govt Offered Secret Gem Deal." *The Namibian,* 26 July.

BBC News. 2001. "Namibia Reveals Congo Diamond Role." 24 February.

Boer, Martin and Sherbourne, Robin. 2003. *Getting the Most out of our Diamonds: Namibia, De Beers and the Arrival of Lev Leviev.* Windhoek (Namibia): Institute for Public Policy Research. Briefing Paper No. 20. September.

Boer, Martin and Sherbourne, Robin. 2004. *Managing Diamond Dependency: Should Namibia Risk More to Gain More?* Windhoek (Namibia): Institute for Public Policy Research. Report No. 6. April.

Catholic Institute for International Relations and the British Council of Churches. 1981. *Namibia in the 1980s.* London: CIIR and BCC.

Chafets, Zev. 2007. "The Missionary Mogul." *The New York Times Magazine,* 16 September.

Cleveland, Todd. 2014. *Stones of Contention: A History of Africa's Diamonds.* Athens, OH: Ohio University Press.

Constantine, Alex. 2009. "The CIA, Maurice Tempelsman, African Blood Diamonds, Gilead, Barrick and Mobutu, etc." aconstantineblacklist.blogspot.com/2009/05/cia-maurice. May 6. Accessed 19 February 2018.

Cooper, Allan D. 2001. *Ovambo Politics in the Twentieth Century.* Lanham, MD: University Press of America.

De Beers and the Global Diamond Industry. 2012. Available at evanlyons.weebly.com/uploads/8/7/8/6/8786677/de_beers_case_analysis.pdf. Accessed 8 June 2019.

Dobell, Lauren. 1995. "SWAPO in Office." In Colin Leys and John S. Saul (Eds), *Namibia's Liberation Struggle: The Two-Edged Sword.* London: James Currey, 171–195.

Dreyer, Ronald. 1994. *Namibia and Southern Africa: Regional Dynamics of Decolonization 1945–90.* London: Kegan Paul Internatioinal.

Ellis, Hugh. 2003. "Tempelsman's Firm Won on Merit, Says NamGem." *The Namibian,* 17 November.

Epstein, Edward Jay. 1982. *The Rise and Fall of Diamonds: The Shattering of a Brilliant Illusion.* New York: Simon & Schuster.

First, Ruth. 1963. *South West Africa.* London: Penguin Books.

Forrest, Joshua Bernard. 1998. *Namibia's Post-Apartheid Regional Institutions: The Founding Year.* Rochester, NY: University of Rochester Press.

Foundation for Democracy in Namibia (FD). 1989. *Coming of Age: Choices for Namibian Voters.* Windhoek: FD (October).

Frankel, Glenn. 1984. "SWAPO Proves Durable Foe of South Africa in Contest for Namibia." *The Washington Post,* 6 May.

Geingob, Hage Gottfried. 2004. "State Formation in Namibia: Promoting Democracy and Good Governance." Dissertation submitted to the School of Politics and International Studies. University of Leeds. March.

Green, David B. 2017. "Who is Lev Leviev, the Israeli Billionaire with Ties to Jared Kushner and Putin." *Haaretz,* 25 July.

Green, Reginald Herbold. 1981. *From Sudwestafrika to Namibia: The Political Economy of Transition.* Research Report No. 58. Uppsala: Scandinavian Institute of African Studies.

Grobler, John. 2002. "Crunch Time for De Beers Over Gem Sales." *Mail and Guardian.* 28 August.

Hendricks, George. 2017. "Geingob Meets Diamond Mogul Tempelsman." *The Namibian,* 19 September.

Ikela, Selma. 2018. "Namibia: From Kindergarten Teacher to Tycoon: The Inspirational Journey of Wu." *New Era,* 2 November.

Immanuel, Shinovene. 2014. "Diamonds are SWAPO's Best Friends." *Mail and Guardian,* 18 September.

Immanuel, Shinovene, and Mongudhi, Tileni. 2015a. "DeBeers Meets Gov'ts Diamond Demands." *The Namibian,* 23 June.

Immanuel, Shinovene, and Mongudhi, Tileni. 2015b. "Geingob's Questionable Taste." *The Namibian,* 14 December.

Kahiruika, Ndanki, and Immanuel, Shinovene. 2018. "Army's Untouchable Business Wing." *Mail and Guardian,* 21 February.

Katjavivi, Peter H. 1988. *A History of Resistance in Namibia.* London: James Currey.

Kempton, Daniel R., and Du Preez, Roni L. 1997. "Namibian–De Beers State–Firm Relations: Cooperation and Conflict." *Journal of Southern African Studies,* 23(4): 585–613.

Kiljunen, Kimmo. 1980. "Namibia: The Ideology of National Liberation," *Bulletin* (Institute of Development Studies, University of Sussex), 11(4), 65–71.

Kiljunen, Kimmo. 1981. "The Ideology of National Liberation." In Reginald Green, Marja-Lisa Kiljunen, and Kimmo Kiljunen (Eds), *Namibia: The Last Colony.* London: Longman, 183–195.

Leys, Colin, and Saul, John S. Eds. 1995. *Namibia's Liberation Struggle: The Two-Edged Sword.* London: James Currey.

Lister, Gwen. 2015. "Political Perspective." *The Namibian,* 13 February.

Maseko, Sipho S. 1995. "The Namibian Student Movement: Its Role and Effects." In Colin Leys and John S. Saul (Eds), *Namibia's Liberation Struggle: The Two-Edged Sword.* London: James Currey, 115–132.

Mbuende, Kaire. 1986. *Namibia, the Broken Shield: Anatomy of Imperialism and Revolution.* Malmo: Liber Forlag.

Melber, Henning. 2010. "Namibia: A Trust Betrayed – Again?" *Africa Files,* 12 (May-October). Available at links.org.au.

Menges, Werner. 2015. "Mushimba Estate Increases to N$238m." *The Namibian,* 10 March.

Moleah, Alfred T. 1983. *Namibia: The Struggle for Liberation.* Wilmington, DE: Disa Press.

Mongudhi, Tileni, and Kahiurika, Ndanki. 2016. "Nujoma Link in 'Panama Papers.'" *The Namibian,* 7 April.

Mongudhi, Tileni, Immanuel, Shinovene, and Pinehas, Tutaleni. 2018. "Namibia's Property 'Golden Girl.'" *The Namibian,* 23 November.

Moorman, Marissa. 2015. "Along the Edges of Comparison." In Jon Soske and Sean Jacobs (Eds), *Apartheid Israel: The Politics of an Analogy.* Chicago, IL: Haymarket Books, 95–100.

Mujller, Emma. 2004. "Namibia's PM Signals Policy Change for Diamonds." *Business Day,* 30 June.

Ndjoze, Jeremiah. 2017. "N$2 Billion Goreangab Waterfront Project Delayed Again." *New Era,* 18 April.

New Era. 2014. "City Approve N$1 Billion Goreangab Waterfront Development." 3 November.

Philander, Frederick. 2006. "Diamonds are Namibia's Best Friend." *New Era,* 30 October.

Planck, Max. 2011. "A Planet Made of Diamond." https://astronomy.com/news/2011/08/a-planet-made-of-diamond. Accessed 24 February 2020.

Republic of Namibia. 2004. *Namibia's Foreign Policy and Diplomacy Management.* Windhoek (Namibia): Ministry of Foreign Affairs. March.

Roberts, Janine. 2003. *Glitter and Greed: The Secret World of the Diamond Empire.* New York: The Disinformation Company.

St. Antoninus Institute. 2005. *South Africa's De Beers: The Most Unethical Corporation in the World.* Study Report File 6/4a. Available at www.ewtn.com. Accessed 5 March 2018.

Smith, Ben. 2007. "Meet the Mogul." *Intelligencer,* 24 October..

SWAPO of Namibia. N.d. *The Constitution and The Political Programme.* Lusaka: SWAPO Department for Publicity and Information.

SWAPO. 1980. SWAPO Policy Paper, No. 13. Lusaka: SWAPO.

SWAPO. 1981. *To be Born a Nation.* London: Zed Press.

Tapscott, Chris. 1993. "National Reconciliation, Social Equity and Class Formation in Independent Namibia." *Journal of Southern African Studies,* 19(1). March.

Thomas, Wolfgang H. 1983. "The Economy in Transition to Independence." In Robert I. Rotberg (Ed.), *Namibia: Political and Economic Prospects.* Cape Town: David Phillip Publishers, 41–91.

Totemeyer, Gerhard. 1987. "The Interim Government and its Rule: The Legitimacy Crisis." In Gerhard Totemeyer, Vezera Kandetu, and Wolfgang Werner (Eds), *Namibia in Perspective.* Windhoek: Council of Churches in Namibia, 54–68.

Urquhart, Brian. 1991. *A Life in Peace and War.* New York: W.W. Norton.

Zabrisky, Zarina. N.d. "Diamond Kings Luxury Condos, Corrupt Cops and Chinese Spies." www.zarinazabrisky.com. Accessed 23 Feburary 2018.

8 Profiting from the conflict in Mogadishu

Capital accumulation in the failed state of Somalia

Mohamed Haji Ingiriis

Introduction

One of the ways of making money from war and conflict is to profit from the securitization politics during the perpetuation of urban insecurity in the post-Cold War failed states. This began in the 1980s but proliferated in the 1990s with the "booming of the crime economy" (*Horn-Observer* 1993, 3), as politics became blended with post-war economics.[1] The marketization of war in southern Somalia today remains the main driver of the insecurity in the war-torn capital city of Mogadishu and it is so entrenched in the armed conflict that the stabilization efforts of the city are an uneasy task. The insecurity empowers local and external actors, such as the so-called "business" class and the so-called international "partners." Political entrepreneurs, political brokers and war profiteers accumulate wealth from internalized and internationalized war economies that emerged from the insecurity in Mogadishu. Put it another way, the business and politics of the city intertwine with the continuation of the insecurity due to extractive and accumulative internal and external strategies for profit-making purposes. This accumulation emboldened by war spoils the creation of surplus value through what Keen (1998) calls "economics by other means." And the energetic involvement from international agents in the security sector contributes to the contemporary state fragility in southern Somalia. Sources of war economies are of central importance to the politics and conflict of southern Somalia. Jamal's (1988a, 1988b) "unconventional economy" or his "doomed economy" in the 1980s, Mubarak's (1997) "hidden hand" in the "stateless economy of Somalia" in the 1990s and Hansen's (2007) "combat economy" in the 2000s and 2010s all share one common trait: the economization by insecurity profiteers who continue to profit from the prolongation of the conflict. Emerging politico-war entrepreneurs strive to act as a state within various mini-states where the state itself has proven weak.

While the prolonged state of insecurity in Mogadishu is so deep-rooted, the fundamental question remains: how are a few people able to generate illicit income in this volatile insecure environment? This article investigates the question of the economization of the insecurity in Mogadishu by addressing the logic of how to make a profit from the war economies in southern Somalia. The objective of the article is to explore how sources of revenue sustain the insecurity in Mogadishu, prolong the armed conflict and profit certain power holders. The article contributes to the scholarship exploring politics, conflict and security of developing countries in the context of the political economy (Barnett 2006; Staff 2017). It also adds new perspectives to the wider debates and discussions on the extent to which war economies in securitization frameworks for war-torn societies and conflict-ridden states reproduce and maintain insecurity. The first section presents the theoretical discussion and conceptual framework. The second section evaluates the origins of the Somali economy to the Cold War and outlines the effects of the state collapse on emerging informal urban economy. The third section conceptualizes the recent reconstruction activities of Mogadishu and distinguishes state development from society-driven development. The fourth section identifies strategies of the participants and features for maintaining insecurity in Mogadishu through the continuation of the armed conflict. In evaluating the architecture of insecurity and the destabilizing effects of the war economy, this section explores the profits of the war economy which, when correlated with the political conflict, reveals a close connection between insecurity and business profits.

Evidence for this study is drawn from fieldwork research conducted between May–September 2015, April–August 2016, September–October 2017 and February–June 2018 in Mogadishu, Somalia. The fieldwork research consisted of ethnographic observations, interviews and discussions with Somali government authorities, the business community, civil society and diaspora members. By using various methodologies, i.e., critical ethnographic fieldwork observations in a conflict-ridden context, the findings of the research provide new insights into the correlation of chronic insecurity and economic accumulation. In its classic sense, ethnography rests upon "being there" at the field site. However, most researchers have tended to collect their data on Somalia from neighboring Kenya, and the outcome added much to the NGO-funded gray literature on Somalia. For many years, political and economic conditions in southern Somalia made it a difficult place to gather research data. As Schlee (2013) noted several years ago: "The present situation in Somalia is enormously complex, and the security situation is not conducive to field research" (265). As a result, most of the recent research on contemporary Somalia has devoted considerable attention to specific areas in the country, such as Somaliland and Puntland, while largely neglecting other vital areas like Mogadishu which has long been considered a no-go area due to insecurity issues. Suicide attacks and explosions are frequent, and restrict extended research in war-torn Mogadishu.[2] Security conditions constrain free walking of every part of Mogadishu; for example, although I visited several times the part of the city where I was born, an area very close to the so-called "green zone" around the city center, I could rarely visit the part of the capital where I last lived. However, during my research, I went beyond the green zone to enter into the Bakara market (locally known as Bakaaraha) and small villages outside the capital city, interviewing ordinary people and observing the insecurity of their everyday lives. To quote from Rush (1992): "For any society to be understood, so must its politics; and if the politics of any society is to be understood, so must that society. Ultimately, of course, the focus of political sociology is on those aspects of societal structures and behaviour that contribute to and explain politics" (13).

Perspectives of the war economies in failed states

To profit from war and conflict is an age-old phenomenon. In Africa, political power is essentially anchored on the political economy that is largely pursued to gain material wealth to keep or grab power (Keen 1998). In the Horn of Africa, the power of politics is primarily interlinked to the logics of the market that manage material resources through "real politics" (de Waal 2015). War profiteers cannot emerge where there is no war. In any rupture, some forces see their interests preserved in the continuation of armed conflicts. Academic literature on the Somali conflict has identified various ways in which war economies contribute to armed conflicts but what is rarely discussed is how war economies feed and sustain the insecurity in the post-armed conflicts. Mukhtar (1996) identified how the "war of resources" destroyed unarmed communities in the 1990s. Cassanelli (1996; 2015) also has for many years been emphasizing the economic aspects of Somalia's armed conflict.[3] Although the emergence of war economies preceded the post-collapse state condition, resources stand more as an incentive to embark on war than to sustain and contribute to its continuation. The insecurity of Mogadishu is increasingly related to the problems of economic and political power contestation. As a security black hole, Somalia is "an exceptionally insecure state" (Hills 2014, 88) where the conflict is not only Clausewitzian (Duyvesteyn 2005) but periodically punctuated by resource accumulation. Once a state is founded on such a flimsy and fragile condition, it sends a signal that it can become a functional state only if it can attract food and fuel from international donors, as is the case of the failed state of Somalia. The politico-economic "business" between the receiver and recipient is mediated by "businessmen" who have made their wealth during the long years of the armed conflict. While it is debated whether these actors can be framed as "businessmen," as they are partly involved in politics, local people consider them part of the local business community. The complex intersection of economics and insecurity, part of the wider "economic insecurity" or "insecurity economics," is central to the continuation of the conflict in southern Somalia. Not all people, however, see the failed state situation as permanently profitable. Many people who benefit from the insecurity in Mogadishu are pushed by external actors bent on pursuing economic opportunities in a country full of "militia groups and ragged entrepreneurs who could, and would, see foreign aid only as a source of power and profit" (Harding 2016, 146). Scholarship on the security sector in southern Somalia has yet to identify invisible forms of insecurity economization from the existence of an internal and external class of war profiteers who emerged out of the armed conflict. Grosse-Kettler

(2004) discussed how external actors were involved in the war economy at the peak of the civil war in the 1990s and early 2000s. Webersik (2005) also described how "powerful individuals have vested interests in the continuation of violence in Somalia" (95). In addition to local individual actors and agencies, powerful external actors and agencies have also vested interests in the insecurity in Somalia by promoting and protecting mutual interests pursuant to the violent political marketplace. The marketization of insecurity in Somalia creates what Besteman (2017) has aptly described as "security regimes" and the "new security empire." The difficult question is how to connect and combine the present with the past to understand "when the outside is inside" (Arrieta 2017).

The existing literature on Somalia has discussed the nexus between politics and (in)security in the context of the conflict in southern Somalia. While the literature has not been silent on the political economy, the political situation of the country has been paid much more attention than the interplay between insecurity and war economy. Nur (2007) and Samatar (2007) outlined the political economy dimension of the conflict in contemporary southern Somalia. Farah (2016) has most recently explored the link between insecurity and poverty but overlooked the connection between insecurity and international aid. Crips (2000) made a detailed assessment of the political economy and insecurity in Kakuma and Dadaab (*Dhadhaab* in Somali) refugee camps in Kenya. Hansen (2007) and Marchal (2002; 2010) located the state failure and state collapse in Somalia from the political economy perspective, but little research has since been done on the profits of war economies in the conflict.

Although occupying a central role in the current efforts of creating securitization mechanisms in Mogadishu, the war economy in contemporary southern Somalia originated from the war economies of the Cold War in the 1980s and subsequently the period of collapsed states in the 1990s. The profits of protracted and prolonged insecurity in Mogadishu thus warrant detailed empirical examination from the perspective of war economies. To understand the dynamics of chronic conflict in southern Somalia, one must examine the interplay between war economies and the securitization of Mogadishu. Why has the armed conflict in southern Somalia been sustained for so long? What makes the insecurity so normalized in Mogadishu?

Inspired by the concept of the "violent political marketplace" (Anten et al. 2012, 23; de Waal 2015), in which insecurity is an element of political economy strategy, this study of the armed conflict in southern Somalia contributes to scholarship on the war economies of conflict-ridden failed states. The violent political marketplace has been applied to reveal how the fusion of power and business sustains the perpetuation of the conflicts in fragile states in Africa and elsewhere (Anten 2010, 10; de Waal 2015). The political marketplaces are characterized by shifting economic alliances and politico-military group formations. Allies and former enemies become more antagonistic over war spoils not equally shared that in turn lead to violence, like the case of South Sudan (de Waal 2015). In a comparative study of war economies in five war-torn countries, namely Afghanistan, Democratic Republic of Congo, Guatemala, Kosovo and Pakistan, the violent political marketplace plays an increasingly crucial role in determining the state of failed states (Anten et al. 2012, 4). In Afghanistan, in particular, the emerging war profiteers insist on the failed state situation of the post-Taliban period. As conflict becomes prolonged, power and business combine to become the road to exploit "bouts of political instability" (Anten et al. 2012, 21). This also plays out across conflict-ridden Africa; an immeasurably vast contraband market fueled the war economies in the Democratic Republic of Congo (Anten et al. 2012). In Mogadishu, "the hub of all criminal trafficking in Somalia" (Marchal 2010, 238) where as reported "those who feed off anarchy fuel it" (Gettleman 2007), there is intra-elite competition for patronage politics, power bargaining and war profiteering, and a complex web of competing interests.

From Cold War economy to informal economy: The beginning of the war economy

When Somalia went to war with Ethiopia in the 1970s, it was first exploited by the Soviet Union and then by the United States of America. Poor and desperate after the war in 1978, Somalia was forced to comply with the conditions required by the United States to allow international aid (Ingiriis 2016a). Although providing (in)sufficient financial and military aid to secure Somalia on the side of Washington, the United States failed to rescue the Somali state from total collapse in 1991. The state collapse in Somalia led to disaster after disaster, some stemming from local dynamics, others from regional, still others from global and sometimes a combination of all. All of these events have influenced the image and imagination of Somalia both inside and outside of it. Most Western people (including analysts and observers) came to read Somalia and Somali issues through the pigeonholes of people and places characterized by war, conflict, poverty, Black Hawk Down, piracy, Al-Shabaab, an absence of real government, so on and so forth. Despite the fact that "Somalia" is not one standardized entity, since some places are safer and more peaceful than others, the Somalia that the Western audience has in their minds still remains the same: one unstable unit. The unremitting armed conflict spawned one form of violence after another, generating massive displacement of many Somalis who fled to nearly all corners and continents of the world. However, they relatively prospered as refugees in the rather refugee-friendly environments of Australia, Europe and the United States (Hammond 2010). The resettlement of large diasporic Somali communities in the West, in places like London, Melbourne, Minneapolis, Rome, San Diego, Seattle and Toronto did not curtail the ongoing armed conflict in Somalia but on the contrary fueled the violence. The Somali diaspora communities became protectors and providers of the local beneficiaries of the civil war in Somalia. The expanding war economies allowed the empowerment of some communities like the Hawiye and the Daarood clan-groups as well as the displacement of entire communities like the Bantu/Jareer (Ingiriis 2012).

The evolution of the war economy in Somalia can be traced back to the end of the authoritarian military regime of General Mohamed Siad Barre during the late Cold War period. President Siad Barre utilized the Cold War patronage politics to consolidate his powerbase and hold onto power, while shrewdly evading the pressures of his Western patrons to improve his military regime's human rights record (Ingiriis 2016a). Although one of the poorest countries on the African continent, Somalia under Siad Barre was, after Iraq, the most armed per capita country in the Third World (Lefebvre 1991; Mansur 1995; Maren 1997; Rawson 1993). First in the 1970s and later in the 1980s, the Siad Barre regime was armed to the teeth by the Soviet Union and the United States. In both the Eastern and the Western calculations, geopolitical security considerations dictated using the Berbera seaport in northern Somalia (present-day Somaliland) and Ballidoogle airport in southern Somalia. The Cold War set the stage for what would later become a flood of unprecedented aid donations for Somalia. The Structural Adjustment Programme (SAP) initiated by the International Monetary Fund (IMF) to save the sinking economy of the Third World countries that aligned with the West contributed to emerging war economies.[4] The international aid package, as part and parcel of the emergent war economy in Somalia, has since the Siad Barre regime been a contributing factor to the Somali conflict (Jamal 1988a; 1988b; Maren 1997). The privatization of security began in the 1980s, when the military regime issued licenses to Western security companies like the US-owned Group 4 in return for international aid in the form of military equipment and training facilities (interviews with members of civil society, Mogadishu, May–September 2015, April–August 2016, September–October 2017 and February–June 2018).

Economic practitioners and keen observers documented how the international aid that poured into Somalia worsened the political, economic and social situation of the country by enriching certain political actors closer to the military leaders (Laitin and Samatar 1984; Mubarak 1997). In her ethnographic work on Somalia in the late 1980s, Simons (1995) detailed how the international aid boosted and bolstered the self-enrichment of the top military regime authorities. The "aid avalanche" (Simons 1995, 7) coming from various angles in the East and the West fostered the authoritarian state system and fattened the dictatorial military regime. One of the factors that led to the dissolution of the Somali state was how powerful individuals in the inner circle of the military regime appropriated international aid. This self-enrichment culminated in the construction of a certain neighborhood in Mogadishu known to the Somali public as *Booli Qaran* (public booty), consisting of luxury real estate and expensive mansions owned by the military regime authorities and their associates. When the Siad Barre regime was toppled in 1991, all the state structures subsequently collapsed, and whatever was built from the misappropriated international aid was destroyed. Somalia became fragmented.[5] The collapse affected all areas of the country simultaneously. In northern Somalia, a violent political marketplace that developed in the late 1980s came to an end in the late 1990s following the formal cessation of the armed conflict, as will be explained in the next section (Academy for Peace and Development 2015). In southern Somalia, those who benefitted from misappropriated aid under the military regime in the 1980s were replaced by numerous factional groups that dominated the "Mogadishu crime economy" in the 1990s (*Horn-Observer* 1993, 3).[6] These politico-economic factions carved up makeshift airports and airstrips like Ballidoogle, Dayniile, Esaleey, Jasiira and Number Konton or No. 50 as well as seaports like Ceel Macaan (Sweet Well) to service their politico-economic networks and clan-based militias.[7] This new phenomenon of the violent political marketplace through generating income from airports and seaports not only existed outside Mogadishu, but it was also extended to Baydhabo, Boosaaso and Kismaayo (interviews with civil society members, Mogadishu, May–September 2015, April–August 2016, September–October 2017 and February–June 2018).

In the early 1990s, by the time Siad Barre fled the country, Somalia had plummeted into a fratricidal violent conflict characterized by clan convulsions (Aroma 2005a, 2005b). The 2003 Human Development Report by the United Nations Development Programme (UNDP) classified the 1990s in Africa as the "decade of despair" (UNDP 2003, 40; see also Lemarchand 2011; Prunier 2009). To be sure, this was a decade of devastation in Africa: from Chad to Sudan, nearly every African country was affected by a wildfire of violence. Somalis shared with other war-torn African societies the experience of going through one armed conflict after another in the transitional but torturous moment, although the Somali case seemed less violent than other conflicts. What some observers saw as a complete collapse, followed by anarchy and chaos, only gripped some parts of the country. In the first instance, the less resourceful northern part (present-day Somaliland) that saw an increased flow of international aid experienced less violence than the more resourceful southern part of the country (present-day South-Central Somalia). The Somalis overall hardly considered the acute upheaval in the 1990s as a new phenomenon, although there was a war and heavy displacement. Living under "statelessness" and enduring suffering had become normalized throughout Somali history (Brons 2001; Bulhan 2008; Cassanelli 1982; Lewis 2002). Statelessness was generally more sustained in southern than in northern Somalia in the 1990s and 2000s. Adaptive forms and formalities of security provisions emerged (Gundel and Dharbaxo 2006), as did water and electricity suppliers, banks, small industries, the *Hawala* transfer system, internet access, radio and television stations, all without state involvement, let alone interference (Eno 2015; Lindley 2009; Hammond 2010; Powell et al. 2008).

From the mid-1970s, many expatriate Somalis in the Gulf States began to use the *Hawala* (money transfer) system to send money to their families, friends and relatives back home. The spiraling nature of the war in the 1980s made the *Hawala* system very successful across Somalia. The emergence of economically influential Somali-owned *Hawala* companies such as Al-Barakaat headed by Sheikh Ahmednur Ali Jimale, and Dahabshiil headed by Abdirashid Duale "Abdirashid Dahabshiil" filled a vacuum left behind by the absence of a state-controlled central bank. The 2005 World Bank report estimated that, together with other small companies, these firms had remitted annually $1 to $3 billion to Somalia since the 1990s and this money was funneled directly into the informal economy to improve the livelihoods of many local Somalis (World Bank 2005). Although a Somali poet equated the remittance money sent from abroad to Somalia as "blood money" (quoted in Abdi 2015, 217), the resilience of the local communities astounded the international donors. This prompted some Somalis to contend that these developments were a positive aspect of the Somali clan value of *qoys iyo qaraabo* (family and relatives), while others pointed out how the war had devastated and displaced many Somalis (interviews with civil society members, Mogadishu, May–September 2015, April–August 2016, September–October 2017 and February–June 2018).

The 1980s *dambiyada abaabulan* (organized crimes) were replaced by the 1990s *dambiyada aan abaabulneyn* (unorganized crimes) (*Xog-Ogaal* 1993). Leeson (2007), Little (2003) and Mubarak (1997) all agree that the Somali economy, especially in the southern part of Somalia, in which Mogadishu is centered, experienced a boom in the post-1991 period. There is no doubt that Somali society has retransformed itself in a way invisible to many spectators since then. Western observers have struggled to explain how Somalis survived – and even succeeded – in the prolonged violent political marketplace.[8] This has mainly been done to externalize (even Westernize) the local business community and connect it to the global market economy on paper and through tantalizing titles. Visitors in today's Mogadishu encounter – and one may find it hard to believe this – attempts by local businesses to Anglicize their operations, such as opening English-type restaurants like Posh Restaurant owned by a British-Somali female merchant and Village Restaurant established by a British-Somali male chef.[9] This condition, which combines conflict with human development, not only empirically challenges the earlier declarations that Somalia was hell on earth (Maren 1997), but counters previous assumptions that the state is a prerequisite for development (Leeson 2007; Powell et al. 2008).

Whatever improvements were made without a state were shattered by incessant international intervention. In the early 2000s, external powers returned to the scene to intervene in southern Somalia purportedly in pursuit of counterterrorism activities, producing what Hesse (2016) aptly described as "two generations" with "two interventions." In November 2001, the US administration of George W. Bush – under the banner of the "War on Terror" – responded to unverified allegations of links to Al-Qaeda by announcing the closure of Al-Barakaat and its affiliated companies. The unforeseen cessation of Al-Barakaat's operations in many countries around the world with a strong Somali diaspora reignited the hostility against the US in southern Somalia as the move reinforced the assertions by the militant groups that the US is not just the "enemy of Somalis" but also the "enemy of Allah."[10] People in Mogadishu continue to talk about Al-Barakaat longingly and still recall how the closure of the firm negatively affected their lives (field interviews, Mogadishu, August 2015; May 2016). Although the United Nations removed Al-Barakaat from the list of terrorist organizations in 2009, and by now the company has reinvented itself as Hurmuud, the suspension destroyed their former hard-won good reputation, not to mention their economic earnings. However, the project of "war on terror" in Somalia with its new security dynamics has become and proved to be a profitable business where many Somalis and non-Somalis enriched themselves.

Development as something synonymous with the state: The societal development and state development

Even before the fall of the military regime in the 1980s, the informal economy had replaced the formal economy. In 1983, the Siad Barre regime prohibited the use and selling of the *khat* or *qat*, a green leaf chewed for its stimulant effects, used by many Somalis for pleasure (Somali Democratic Republic 1983). However, "the outlawing of *qat* made its smuggling a lucrative enterprise – and one from which the army and police, especially, could profit" (Simons 1995, 55). As was the case in Tanzania, the crisis of the 1980s in Somalia exposed "the state's increasing inability to provide basic social and public services" (Tripp 1997, 4).[11] As Simons (1995) observed in late 1980s Mogadishu, "one could easily purchase the best stuff Somalia could offer within a matter of days"(12). For a while this informal economy thrived without any state interference in the 1990s; writing in the early 2000s, Little (2003, xv) identified the emergence of a "second economy" in southern Somalia – that is, the informal economy (see also Webersik 2006). As elsewhere in Africa, the informal economy has turned out to be "an integral part of modern economies" (Tripp 1997, 19). Even before the beginning of the civil war, many Somalis largely operated in the private sector to profit from the informal economy by bypassing the regime-regulated formal economy (Maho-Aves and Bechtold 1996). Due to the interconnectedness of the informal economy with the state, when the public sector became dysfunctional in the 1980s, the private sector soon operated better than the public sector. As a consequence of the authoritarian tendencies of Siad Barre's military regime, many Somalis prefer all things profitable to be informal and private from the economy. Elsewhere, Anten et al. (2012) observed that the war economy "incorporates the adaptable components of the pre-war economy, like livestock trading and fishing, and has given rise to new enterprises, most of which would be considered illicit if there were law enforcement" (13). Today, there is a plethora of reasons for why war economies are sustained in southern Somalia, but not in the northern part of the country. In the latter, the Somaliland authorities regulated the political power, suppressed the violent political marketplace and blocked the emergence of insecurity profiteers, while at the same time providing political positions for those who from time to time threaten them to profit from war. By contrast, the war economy, insecurity and corruption are closely interlinked in the violent political marketplace in southern Somalia, as no one is able to unilaterally manipulate the violent political marketplace. This is something that continually aggravates the situation and fastens the correlation between local and external forces who are doing well out of the war economies.

Despite the internal and external pressures since its inception, the World Bank lauded the private sector, in other words the informal economy in Somalia, as proof of Somali adeptness and efficiency (World Bank 2012). Mobile and telecommunications systems in Somalia, a success story in the whole Horn region, started from the rubble before becoming a vibrant infrastructure (Feldman 2007). The Somali-owned banking system, like the Salaama Bank, derived economic opportunities from the informal economy of the open-ended market of Mogadishu. Yet the continuation of the conflict disrupts the return of the formal economy. Internal and external military interventions, most critically by regional forces (Ethiopia and Kenya) and the African Union Mission in Somalia (AMISOM) versus Al-Shabaab (Hansen 2013), the militant movement seeking to capture the political scene and dictate the economic resources of the country, continue to contribute to the conflict. The war between the government in Villa Somalia and the Al-Shabaab insurgents means Mogadishu has to remain the "world's most dangerous place" (Ferguson 2013). Until 2011, Al-Shabaab partly controlled the capital city and its presence prevented the would-be external economic actors from seeking economic opportunities with their local Somali "partners." The face of Mogadishu changed upon the visit of the then Turkish Prime Minister Recep Tayyip Erdoğan and his family in August 2011. The city subsequently attracted massive development aid from Turkey that coincided with the retreat of Al-Shabaab insurgents from the Mogadishu neighborhoods, including the main Bakara market that they had controlled.[12] This opened a new chapter in the southern Somalia security situation, leading to a considerable physical reconstruction and rebuilding of the ruined urban infrastructure (*The Somalia Herald* 2014; *Tusmo Qaran* 2014; *Yenisafak* 2017).

Although still unstable, there is an air of renewal in Mogadishu. Somali diaspora returnees who largely returned for the economic boom, despite acute insecurity, have invested their financial capital in the war-torn city. Everyday engagements between diaspora returnees and the local people are often punctuated by distrust. The diasporic Somalis returning to their original homeland are sarcastically labeled as *dayuus-baro*, implying that their return resulted in immorality and indecency (Harding 2016, 244), while the locals are depicted as people who lost their minds in the war. However, diasporic returnees influence not only the economic aspects of Somalia but also have sway on Somali politics. The impression of the Somali diaspora returnees is that there are only two opportunities for one to make money: either when the country collapses or when it emerges out from that collapse (interviews with Somalia diaspora members, Mogadishu, May–September 2015, April–August 2016, September–October 2017 and February–June 2018). After 2011, many rushed to establish small and large businesses. Investors rebuilt and reopened restaurants and guesthouses such as the Liido Beach and the luxurious Hotel Makka Al-Mukaramah, once the favorite hub for US embassy staff, as a former American ambassador recorded in his autobiography (Bridges 2000). The diaspora returnees also invested in locally drawn ideas like the Mogadishu International Book Fair, a project previously successful in Hargeysa in Somaliland. All of these activities are society-driven and the public mistakenly expected the Mogadishu government to encourage similar initiatives (interviews with civil society members, Mogadishu, May–September 2015, April–August 2016, September–October 2017 and February–June 2018). It is because of this paradox that Mogadishu's renewal can be conceptualized as a societal development rather than a state development. These projects were not implemented in the name of the Somali government, although the federal government authorities have quickly enumerated all societal development as state-driven developments to reach out to more international donors through the "development dance," to use Swedlund's (2017) term. It would be a grave error, nevertheless, to associate these society-driven developments with successive internationally backed governments in Mogadishu.

Local observers of the Somali conflict concur that Mogadishu has come a long way since 2011. Walking down Mogadishu's main streets, one feels both anxiety and exhilaration. From the airport all the way down to the city center, one passes Iraq- or Afghanistan-type checkpoints with fortified military walls manned by the Somali security authorities and AMISOM forces. As of today, the state of southern Somalia in Mogadishu – in the name of the Federal Government of Somalia – is heavily dependent for its political and economic survival on the international community (mainly Western donors operating under the term "partners"), as well as the AMISOM forces for its security and military operations.[13] It is still difficult for many Somalis and non-Somalis to travel through the capital city without their own heavily armed guards. Those seeking to carry out business (whatever that means) or working for international NGOs have every reason to worry about their security. Private security guards (both Somalis and non-Somalis) protect most of those working for the international community. When foreign visitors come down to Mogadishu, they surround themselves with foreign bodyguards who operate in the city, something never seen before even at the peak of the ferocious clan-based conflicts in the 1990s (field observations, Hotel City Palace, Mogadishu, 19 August 2016; field observations, Hotel Jazeera, Mogadishu, 22 February 2018). Most of the foreign embassies in the highly walled Halane compound at the Mogadishu Aden Abdulle International Airport are also guarded by African, European or American security firms. Even if this may seem strange, the top government authorities cannot freely move about the city except on the two main Mogadishu streets – the Makka Al-Mukaramah and the seaport roads – without AMISOM forces (field observations, Mogadishu, May–September 2015, April–August 2016, September–October 2017 and February–June 2018).

The present Mogadishu is somewhat different from the previous Mogadishu in terms of security; in some aspects, security seems to be more deadly than before. The phenomenon of the war economies in the late 1970s, when government-connected dealers emerged while the military regime was still claiming a Scientific Socialist economic ideology, has slightly been altered. In the 1980s, Somalia saw a *suuqa madow* (black market), similar to what is known in Sudan, Saudi Arabia, Egypt and elsewhere as *suq al-aswad*. As it was in the 1980s, contemporary Mogadishu offers special economic opportunities for external economic actors (and their local imitators) who have links with the dysfunctional state system in place in the name of international donors, but those without economic and political power consider Mogadishu as "an open prison" or a "hell on earth" (field observations, Mogadishu, May–September 2015, April–August 2016, September–October 2017 and February–June 2018). For those who can navigate a closer clan or individual interest attachment with political power holders or what locals call *Dowladda* (the government), something of a mutual economic interest in the form of contracts or power positions can be achieved. They could certainly achieve better economic opportunities in the insecurity than in the security sector for money-making purposes. As a South Sudanese put it, the business class in southern Somalia would say "[w]e have so many rules, but none that apply [the same way] to everyone. It all just depends [on] who you know and what they can do for you" (cited in Twijnstra and Titeca 2016, 268).

The rule of security in Somalia is to grasp how to bargain through insecurity. The Somali saying *muraadka magaalo kaa gala, muraayad baa kaa xigta* (the interest you have to go to the town is negotiated through the mirror) indicates how the bureaucratic government form of the dysfunctional state is a hindrance in the eyes of the ordinary people. One of the Mogadishu interviewees of this study is a young man who stayed in the city throughout the civil war. He gave me an excellent description of the contemporary capital city: "Mogadishu is like a watermelon. In the exterior, it looks green but interior there is a red cloth beneath the blood of people dying on daily basis in the capital city" (M.T., personal communication, 23 February 2019; my rough translation from Somali). As another interviewee also pointed out, "this country has become a thief country, invested in banditry" (interview with a Somali elder in Mogadishu, 28 June 2016; my rough translation from Somali). One regime after another has failed to improve the most critical aspect of all, the security sector, partly because there are no new ideas or innovation for improving the security sector. The profitable projects of the security sector in Somalia make some ministries like the Internal Security Ministry the most lucrative of all. Almost every political actor in Mogadishu prefers to lead this ministry as it allows unaccounted money from various donors through the international aid.

Developmental state or developmental society?

Development under insecurity

The following section examines insecurity profiteering within the structures of power and other interests capable of prospering in the war economy. The armed conflict in Mogadishu and, more generally, southern Somalia, is more than an income-generating business that merely profits local economic actors, some of them former diasporic people (*Radio Dalsan* 2016a; *Shabelle News* 2016a; *Shabelle News* 2016b). The insecurity combined with the absence of a functional state feeds a spatial market that creates profitable innovative economic opportunities for both local and external politico-war entrepreneurs. Focus groups held within a sample of youth groups – whether armed or unarmed – provide unique insights into the ways the violent conflict and the organized insecurity have melded both local and external actors (focus group discussions, Afgooye and Mogadishu, May and September 2015). Some security company owners in Mogadishu freely admit that they gain wealth from the association with external actors. The persistence and prevalence of insecurity enables some actors to profit from the conflict in the capital Mogadishu, a city that has suffered for so long that insecurity became the status quo (Harding 2016, 17). The insecurity profiteers extract illicit money by attracting and diverting the international aid for their own personal, family and group interests, blurring what is legal and what is illegal. Yet, the term "illegal" is not important in Mogadishu as anyone can do illegality at will without any visible state control, even when there are laws promulgated by the successive post-2000 governments that criminalize certain behaviors that continue to occur (interviews with civil society members, Mogadishu, May–September 2015, April–August 2016, September–October 2017 and February–June 2018).

The role of external actors exacerbates the economization of the insecurity as it favors the violent political marketplace, while at the same time assisting the profits of the war economy.[14] The external assistance of the security companies in Mogadishu is not as obvious as the economic dynamics of their activities. The commonality with which the diasporic stories of externalization of security are recorded in Mogadishu seems striking. A self-styled Somali businessman returned from London after some years living there in self-imposed exile. While in London, he formed a friendship with a wealthy Saudi merchant to start a profitable business in Somalia. In Mogadishu, he formed a security company with his brothers, a rather more lucrative family company than a one-man business mission in London.[15] Together with his brothers, they bought bulletproof cars to hire to government-affiliated agencies. Following some racketeering with some senior government authorities, they began to provide their "security" services to members of governmental commissions for tens of thousands of dollars. Since security service was payable by the traditional donors, the government authorities approved this proposal without public bidding, even though there are some other security firms able to provide such services (interviews with government authorities, Mogadishu, May–September 2015, April–August 2016, September–October 2017 and February–June 2018).

Following the 2011 famine, the governmental and non-governmental aid agencies of Turkey deployed food shipments to the Mogadishu seaport. It is widely known in Somalia that food and other emergency relief aid rarely reach the poor people who desperately need them.[16] Some government officials admitted that the famine was an opportunity for them, while even a blessing for some others (Harding 2016, 205). For example, the 2011 relief aid was diverted and ended up in the pockets of the Mogadishu seaport authorities. Amidst the precarious transition in 2011, some seaport authorities openly stole the Turkish food shipments and resold them on the Bakara market for self-enrichment.[17] According to the former seaport chairman, his deputy was very close to the then regime in power. After embezzling the relief aid, he sold it out of the Bakara market (field interview with S. A., Mogadishu, 9 August 2015).[18] The dirty money obtained was used to purchase a three-story hotel and lucrative houses. As the former seaport chairman opined, misappropriation of international aid within the parameters of the seaport can be possible in two transitional times: (1) the last three months of a president who lost the presidential election, and (2) the first three months of the succeeding president (field interview with S. A., Mogadishu, 9 August 2015). The former seaport chairman himself was also accused by others of looting public funds (interviews with seaport members, Mogadishu, May–June 2016). As a result, as Harding (2016) noted: "80 percent of the food aid they were supposed to be distributing in Mogadishu was actually being stolen" (208). Food diversion was also an established economization of the war in South Sudan before and after independence (Stringham and Forney 2017, 187). The foreign aid in general and famine relief in particular has made millionaires out of some politico-war entrepreneurs in Mogadishu.

The interrelations between local groups and external donors

Profiting from food aid is not a new phenomenon in Somalia, and is known even by the international donors that assist in its undertakings. In the 1980s, less than one-fourth of the food aid donated to Somalia reached the intended recipients (Askin 1987, 38). The food aid was sold at one-sixth of market value to profiteers linked to the military regime who then resold it for a profit. The scandal over food aid diversion reached US courts of law when USAID complained about transaction payment fraud within the military regime in Somalia (Leigh 1986). As was the case in the 1980s, the current profiteers of the violent political marketplace are connected one way or another to the successive governments in Mogadishu. As much as the profits of insecurity have produced politico-economic privileges for local actors, it continues to produce profit-driven war entrepreneurship. The insecurity profiteers act not only as brokers between the government and the international aid agencies, they also mediate between the government and the Somali public. In cases of *qashqashaad* (extortion) about economic opportunities and business prospects of the powerless people, the insecurity profiteers use their connections with the top leadership to facilitate business deals for both local and external actors. The monopolization of political positions and economic opportunities holds Mogadishu in the grip of insecurity profiteers, leading to complaints from many people who feel that the patronage politics and war economies obstruct access to legitimate economic opportunities (interviews with civil society members, Mogadishu, May–September 2015, April–August 2016, September–October 2017 and February–June 2018). The insecurity profiteers established independent security companies and hired young militias (mostly former Al-Shabaab members) as security guards (field observations, Mogadishu, April–August 2016).[19] Many people claim these companies providing "security beyond state" (Abrahamsen and Williams 2011) are agents of instability who use mortar shells every couple of weeks to frighten the Mogadishu public in the name of the Al-Shabaab insurgency, which still has an unseen presence in the capital (field interviews, Mogadishu, May–September 2015, April–August 2016). These acts confirm the observation of external actors that the security situation in the capital city is unreliable.

Members of the international aid agencies hire bodyguards from external security companies for their protection. Aside from the Somali-owned security companies, the non-Somali-owned security companies based in Halane, the highly walled airport compound where most non-Somalis live, also provide such services but they cannot operate freely in the town due to the insecurity (field observations, Mogadishu, May–September 2015, April–August 2016). The Mogadishu government exerts no control over the foreign security companies, despite issuing official registration certificates for cash payment. If one is to believe a statement released in July 2017 by a fact-finding mission led by several government ministers, including the then Minister of Information, the Halane-based foreign companies, 157 in total, are unregistered with the government (*Radio Dalsan* 2017). With no government oversight, these companies are unable to fully operate outside the perimeters of the ministries, but they continue to sign security contracts with international NGOs. This patron–client relationship, perhaps vital for their work, allows them to avoid reporting their operations and activities to the government. While Reno (2017) berates local security firms rather than external security firms, he also identifies elsewhere the failures of the overall "politics of security assistance" in Somalia (Reno 2018). In the eyes of the Somalis, the existence of external security assisters and the presence of non-Somali security firms may lead to a state of long-term insecurity in the country. As such, the non-Somali security firms came under increasing suspicion that they are in Somalia to prolong the conflict for their profit. Sensing another Afghanistan or Iraq, some local Somalis point out that these companies do not work in countries going through active war but in countries struggling to pull themselves out from the ruins of armed conflict (interviews with business community members, Mogadishu, May–September 2015, April–August 2016, September–October 2017 and February–June 2018). Some of the foreign security companies operating in the Halane, i.e. Bancroft, Blackwater and Seracen, famous for their work in Afghanistan, Iraq and other conflict-ridden countries, secured security deals in Somalia through informal local networks (interviews, Obulutsa 2017). Some of these security companies are contracted by international donors.

Conclusion

Somalia, the "ultra-dysfunctional state" (Leeson 2014, 170) with widespread "severe insecurity" (Reno 2017, 159), the only paradigmatically dysfunctional state yet one of the most resilient societies on the African continent (Maxwell and Majid 2016), is both a success and a surprise, depending on the angle from which one seeks to scrutinize it. Yet, the contemporary political reality in southern Somalia stands in sharp contrast to the expectations by the international community. Somalis and external actors tend to interpret the developments occurring in Mogadishu in two contrasting ways. In the minds of the many Somalis living outside of Somalia, the current state of securitization of Mogadishu is not much better than the stateless southern Somalia of the 1990s. To the international community, Somalia is "rising," a term aimed at attracting traditional donors to pour more money into Somalia (Shortland et al. 2013).[20] The main objective of the "rising" discourse is to encourage the Somali diaspora to return home to dissuade further emigration to Europe (Ingiriis 2016b). It is important to understand why some development has flourished on the societal level but floundered on the state level in southern Somalia. It is also important to understand why development has not been possible at the state level but is possible at the societal level in southern Somalia. Today, a modern state's capacity is measured by its ability to provide social services to its citizens, secure its borders and engage in the world reciprocally. These measurements, absent in southern Somalia, contribute to its continued status as a failed state. However, this does not mean Somalis are a failed society, even if the absence of state development sustains the violent political marketplace, increases economic and political contestation through illicit methods, exacerbates insecurity and undermines attempts to reinstate one single unitary state for Somalia. The twofold conceptualization of developments – state-driven and society-driven – reveals the economically motivated insecurity and resource competition from the approach of the war economy. Distinguishing the societal development from the state development leaves out the third type of development: the international NGOs-driven development, which – even though inextricably interlinked to the state development – is outside the scope of this article but warrants further research.

The protraction of insecurity in Mogadishu led to the emergence of war profiteers whose performances in contemporary politics conform to the development expectations of the international donors, a continuation of war economy by other means, which is to say the commercialization of the insecurity in the capital by groups within groups. In the late 1990s, the international donors held high expectations of Somalia achieving a "countrywide stability" (UNDP 1998, iv), but they later realized that their imagination of complete societal failure needed to be revised. The international donors, indeed, acknowledged two decades ago that the continuation of the Somali conflict and the political instability "will only lead to continuing impoverishment of the many to the benefit of the few" (UNDP 1998, iv). Several social scientists have challenged the poverty of war economies. In his influential argument "doing well out of war," Collier (1999) powerfully contended that economic profits are "central to understanding why civil wars get going" (1). One important implication of this observation is that, rather than perceiving armed conflict as a "stupid" act, one sees that war is not necessarily a bad thing, for some anyway (Cramer 2006). Future research should consider the other sides of the armed conflicts and insecurity in Somalia. Reflecting on the past dictatorial and destructive policies by the military regime, some scholars have observed that southern Somalia did better on some fronts without a state (Leeson 2007; Powell et al. 2008). The evidence provided in this study is indicative of how the entrenchment of the war economy and insecurity is a barrier to any effort at restoring security in Mogadishu. To create a security environment in Mogadishu will be much more difficult than at any other place in southern Somalia unless the security environment produces more profits than insecurity for war profiteers. Well before the Somali state collapsed, Mogadishu was a battlefield or political stadium for personality-driven patronage political networks of profit-making business through the perpetuation of war. The constant attempts in Mogadishu to build a victory peace, the so-called "republican peace" (Barnett 2006) adds a further complicated layer to an already protracted political conflict. The external involvement does not identify the political path to building peace in Mogadishu and eliminating the war economy. The short period in which southern Somalia saw a relative peace, in the summer of 2006, was when the Union of Islamic Courts (UIC) provided governance structures that gained support from the business community (Ahmad 2009; 2015), while the political factions were doing their usual job of servicing the international community. The path-dependent patterns of international aid politics cemented the war profiteering patronage.

What causes and maintains insecurity in Mogadishu is the perpetuation of profits of the war economies. The local insecurity profiteers cannot be isolated from their external counterparts. The insecurity profiteers act as intermediaries and economic providers not only to external actors but also to whoever is in power in the Villa Somalia and Halane. The Mogadishu government's involvement in the business of private security companies leads to institutionalized insecurity where the conflict has become a permanent feature in Somali politics (Ingiriis 2016b). It would be very difficult to solve the insecurity without understanding the invisible element of the war economy of Mogadishu. Until there is progress in finding responsible political leaders, the violent political marketplace will determine the course of political power competition. Moreover, the insecurity situation can be improved by advancing reconciliation efforts through conflict resolution mechanisms, such as combining peacebuilding approaches. Without specific clarifications, the UNDP Somalia made somewhat similar proposals nearly two decades ago (UNDP 2001, 62). The impunity of those who perpetuate the conflict in southern Somalia – the agents of instability – enables them to freely travel outside of Somalia. This should be carefully embargoed by the international community. To allow poor people to afford market commodities and to help the small businesses trade in peaceful ways, international aid authorities need to rethink their approach to doing business with known war profiteers of the war economy. Appreciating the interplay of all these critical factors is key to understanding why the insecurity in Mogadishu remains difficult to resolve. The role of neighboring countries in sustaining the war economy also warrants further research study.[21]

Notes

1 As Ehrhart and Petretto (2014, 187) pointed out: "Those Somalis who have been involved have mostly either been proponents of the violent conflict devastating the country or representatives of the diaspora that was able to establish a sound financial base and a close-knit support network internationally".

2 On the second week of my stay in Mogadishu at the end of April 2016, a suicide attack on the Mogadishu traffic police headquarters woke me up from sleep. Altogether I witnessed more than seven suicide bomb attacks between 2015 and 2018. However, non-Somalis are more prone to danger than to Somalis. As Harding (2016, 17) noted: "Visiting Mogadishu, particularly as a foreigner, is a risky, expensive, and, above all, logistically complicated process. Who guards you – a particular clan, foreign peacekeepers, the UN, or private security contractors?"

3 For the ambivalent roles of the private sector during the 1990s, see Cassanelli (2015, 42).

4 With self-reflexivity, Chabal noted elsewhere in Africa, "we outsiders could do worse than listen to Africans when they press us to think more carefully about the implications of our political interpretations for the well-being of the continent: supporting dictators or justifying structural adjustment all have immediate consequences for the lives of ordinary men and women" (1996, 32).

5 For how the Cold War exacerbated their precarious situations, see Besteman (2016, 42).

6 Little (2003), who provided the most detailed political economy of this period, discusses and describes less about the post-1991 economy than pre-1991. However, the 1991 public uprising against the Siad Barre regime constitutes a course-changing watershed in the Somali political conflicts.

7 I used to fly to some of these airports: Dayniile (October 2002, August 2003 and October 2003), Esaleey (December 2001), Jasiira (December 2001) and Number *Konton* or No. 50 (November 2001 and July 2002).

8 Western observers tend to refer to each other to authenticate their assumptions. For instance, no single Somali author has ever been invited to contribute to the UN Somalia human development reports.

9 In Hargeysa, Renders (2012, 7) came across a Chinese restaurant called *Ming Sing*.

10 The antagonism that emerged out from influence and control between Islam and the West did not start with the collapse of the Cold War, but it was something that has been simmering since the World War I and before (Mamdani 2004; Said 1981).

11 As Tripp (1997, 4) argued, on the whole African continent: "The growth of the informal economy is probably one of the most important developments in Africa in the 1980s."

12 The Turkish aid has decreased after allegations of corruption against the Somali government authorities (*Hürriyet Daily News* 2014). For a critical assessment of the Turkish role in Somalia, see also International Crisis Group (2012).

13 According to the IMF (2017): "The Somali economy is sustained by donors' grants, remittances, and foreign direct investment mostly by the Somali diaspora. Since 2013, the donor community has given over $4.5 billion in humanitarian and developmental grants, which is essential in contributing to finance Somalia's trade deficit of nearly 55 percent of GDP (average during 2013–16)."

14 Anten et al. (2012, 23) observed elsewhere in a similar setting that "access to formal institutional power provides important opportunities to draw on sovereign rents, such as aid money, and must be defended against competitors by force if necessary. At the same time, a certain level of lawlessness and lack of territorial control enhances the chances of accessing natural and other illegal resources."

15 Kinsey et al. (2009) and Staff (2017) offer detailed studies on the emergence and impact of the security companies in Somalia.

16 As Maxwell and Majid (2016, 45) highlighted: "The diversion of aid has long been a part of the war economy in Somalia."

17 Most recently, the Turkish news agency published this news item: "Somali aid workers said Monday Turkey's government had delivered over 8,500 tons of food – including sugar, wheat and oil – to relieve drought-hit areas of the country. Mohamed Yaqub, a local worker for the al-Manhal aid group, which is a partner of the Turkish Red Crescent, said the aid would be distributed in areas such as the Sol, Nugal, Bari Awdal and Banadir regions of northern Somalia. Turkey also delivered at least 11,100 tons of food to the capital Mogadishu, where thousands of displaced people are living. The Turkish mission in Somalia tweeted on Monday that food aid would go to people living in the capital, Somaliland and Puntland. A ship carrying thousands of tons of humanitarian aid for the East African country arrived in Somalia last week from the southern Turkish port city of Mersin. This came after the United Nations said last month more than five million people – 40 percent of the country's population – did not have enough to eat" (*Anadolu Agency* 2016).

18 The UN Monitoring Group report of 2010 also noted an exponential level of food aid diversion. This report does not substantially differ from the recent UN Monitoring Group reports. See, e.g., UN Monitoring Group 2016.

19 For a detailed study on Al-Shabaab, see Hansen (2007). Numerous other groups profiting from the war such as businessmen hired armed youths to provide protection to foreign international aid agencies.

20 By "traditional donors" is meant Western donors, whether state or non-state NGOs. The "non-traditional donors" implies non-Western donors, whether state or non-state NGOs.

21 For an overview, see Kamwende (2014).

References

Abdi, Cawo. 2015. *Elusive Jannah: The Somali Diaspora and a Borderless Muslim Identity*. Minneapolis, MN: University of Minnesota Press.

Abrahamsen, Rita, and Williams, Michael C. 2011. *Security beyond the State: Private Security in International Politics*. Cambridge: Cambridge University Press.

Academy for Peace and Development. 2015. *Pillars of Peace*. Hargeysa: Interpeace.

Ahmad, Aisha. 2009. "Taliban and the Islamic Courts Union: How they Changed the Game in Afghanistan and Somalia?" *Policy Perspectives,* 6(2), 55–72.

Ahmad, Aisha. 2015. "The Security Bazaar: Business Interests and Islamist Power in Civil .War Somalia." *International Security,* 39(3), 89–117.

Anadolu Agency. 2016. "Turkey Sends Tons of Food Aid to Somalia." 10 October.

Anten, Louise. 2010. *Strengthening Governance in a Post-Conflict District of the Democratic Republic of Congo: A Study of Ituri.* The Hague: Netherlands Institute of International Relations.

Anten, Louise, Ivan Briscoe and Marco Mezzera. 2012. "The Political Economy of State-building in Situations of Fragility and Conflict: From Analysis to Strategy." A synthesis paper based on studied of Afghanistan, Democratic Republic of Congo, Guatemala, Kosovo and Pakistan, January.

Arrieta, Itziar Ruiz-Giménez. 2017. "When the Outside is Inside: International Features of the Somali 'Civil' War." In Aleksi Ylönen and Jan Záhořík (Eds), *The Horn of Africa since the 1960s: Local and International Politics Intertwined.* Abingdon: Routledge, 123–144.

Aroma, Cabdulqaadir. 2005a. *Sababihii Burburka Soomaaliya: Yaa Iska Leh Eedda Qaranjabka?* 2nd Ed. Kuala Lumpur: Percetakan Zafar.

Aroma, Cabdulqaadir. 2005b. *Tiirka Colaadda: Maxay ka Curteen Colaadaha Sokeeye?* 2nd Ed. Kuala Lumpur: Percetakan Zafar.

Askin, Steve. 1987. "Food Aid Diversion." *MERIP Middle East Report,* 145, The Struggle for Food (March–April): 38–39.

Barnett, Michael. 2006. "Building a Republican Peace: Stabilizing States After War." *International Security,* 30(4), 87–112.

Besteman, Catherine. 2016. *Making Refuge: Somali Bantu Refugees and Lewiston, Maine.* Durham, NC: Duke University Press.

Besteman, Catherine. 2017. "Experimenting in Somalia: The New Security Empire." *Anthropological Theory*, 17(3), 404–420.

Bridges, Peter. 2000. *Safirka: An American Envoy.* Kent, OH: Kent State University Press.

Brons, Maria. 2001. *Society, Security and Sovereignty and the State in Somalia: From Statelessness to Statelessness.* Utrecht: International Books.

Bulhan, Hussein A. 2008. *Politics of Cain: One Hundred Years of Crises in Somali Politics and Society*. Bethesda, MD: Tayosan International Publishing.

Cassanelli, Lee V. 1982. *The Shaping of Somali Society: Reconstructing the History of a Pastoral People, 1600–1900.* Philadelphia, PA: University of Pennsylvania Press.

Cassanelli, Lee V. 1996. "Explaining the Somali Crisis." In Catherine Besteman and Lee V. Cassanelli (Eds), *The Struggle for Land in Southern Somalia: The War behind the War.* Boulder, CO: Westview Press, 13–26.

Cassanelli, Lee V. 2015. *Hosts and Guests: A Historical Reinterpretation of Land Conflicts in Southern and Central Somalia.* Nairobi: Rift Valley Institute (RVI).

Chabal, Patrick. 1996. "The African Crisis: Context and Interpretation." In Terence Ranger and Richard Werbner (Eds), *Postcolonial Identities in Africa.* London: Zed Press, 31–53.

Clapham, Christopher. 1996. *Africa and the International System.* Cambridge: Cambridge University Press.

Clapham, Christopher. 2016. *Horn of Africa: State Formation and Decay.* London: Hurst.

Collier, Paul. 1999. "Doing Well Out of War." Paper prepared for Conference on Economic Agendas in Civil Wars, London.

Cramer, Christopher. 2006. *Civil War is Not a Stupid Thing: Accounting for Violence in Developing Countries*. London: Hurst.

Crips, Jeff. 2000. "A State of Insecurity: The Political Economy of Violence in Kenya's Refugee Camps." *African Affairs,* 99(397), 601–632.

de Waal, Alex. 2015. *The Real Politics of the Horn of Africa: Money, War and the Business of Power*. Cambridge: Polity.

Duyvesteyn, Isabelle. 2005. *Clausewitz and African Wars: Politics and Strategy in Liberia and Somalia*. London: Frank Cass.

Ehrhart, Hans-Georg and Petretto, Kerstin. 2014. "Stabilizing Somalia: Can the EU's Comprehensive Approach Work." *European Security,* 23(2), 179–194.

Eno, Mohamed A. 2015. "The Revival of Higher Education in Somalia: Prospects and Challenges." *Journal of Somali Studies,* 2(1–2), 9–45.

Farah, A. Osman. 2016. "The Justice of Improving Security and Confronting Poverty: The Role of Transnational NGOs and Communities in Somalia." *Northeast African Studies,* 16(2), 97–128.

Feldman, Bob. 2007. "Somalia: Amidst the Rubble, a Vibrant Telecommunications Infrastructure." *Review of African Political Economy,* 34(113), 565–572.

Fergusson, James. 2013. *The World's Most Dangerous Place: Inside the Outlaw State of Somalia*. London: Bantam Press.

Foreign Policy. 2016. "Allegations of Abuse, Corruption Cloud Election in Somalia." 20 September.

Fukuyama, Francis. 1989. "The End of History?" *The National Interest,* 16 (Summer), 3–18.

Gettleman, Jeffrey. 2007. "In Somalia, Those Who Feed off Anarchy Fuel it." *The New York Times*, 25 April.

Grosse-Kettler, Sabrina. 2004. *External Actors in Stateless Somalia: A War Economy and its Promoters*. Paper 39. Bonn: Bonn International Center for Conversion (BICC).

Gundel, Joakim and Dharbaxo, Ahmed A. Omar. 2006. *The Predicament of the 'Oday': The Role of Traditional Structures in Security, Rights, Law and Development in Somalia*. Nairobi: Danish Refugee Council/Novib-Oxfam.

Hammond, Laura. 2010. "Obliged to Give: Remittances and the Maintenance of Transitional Networks Between Somalis at Home and Abroad." *Bildhaan,* 10, 125–151.

Hansen, Stig Jarle. 2007. *Civil War Economies, the Hunt for the Profit, and the Incentives for Peace*. AE Working Paper No. 1. Bath, UK: Department of Economics and International Development, University of Bath.

Harding, Andrew. 2016. *The Mayor of Mogadishu: A Story of Chaos and Redemption in the Ruins of Somalia*. London: Hurst.

Hesse, B. J. 2016. "Two Generations, Two Interventions in One of the World's Most-Failed States: The United States, Kenya and Ethiopia in Somalia." *Journal of Asian and African Studies,* 51(5), 573–593.

Hills, Alice. 2014. "Somalia Works: Police Development as State Building." *African Affairs,* 113(946), 88–107.

Horn-Observer (Mogadishu). 1993. "The Crime Economy." 3 and 5.

Hürriyet Daily News. 2014. "Turkey Cuts Somalia Aid amid Corruption Claims." 15 February.

IMF (International Monetary Fund). 2017. "IMF Country Focus: Six Things to Know About Somalia's Economy." 11 April.

International Crisis Group. 2012. *Assessing Turkey's Role in Somalia*. Brussels: International Crisis Group.

Ingiriis, Mohamed Haji. 2012 . "Redefining Somaliness through the Bantu-Jareer Community: The Absent Somalis in the Somali Socio-Political Landscape." In Marisa Fois and Alesandro Pess (Eds), *Politics and Minorities in Africa*. Milan: Centro di Studi Africani in Sardegna, 71–99.

Ingiriis, Mohamed Haji. 2015. "Politics as a Profitable Business: Patronage, Patrimony, Predation and Primordial Power in Contemporary Somalia." *Journal of Somali Studies,* 2(1–3), 67–97.

Ingiriis, Mohamed Haji. 2016a. *The Suicidal State in Somalia: The Rise and Fall of the Siad Barre Regime, 1969–1991*. Lanham, MD: University Press of America.

Ingiriis, Mohamed Haji. 2016b. "How Somalia Works: Mimicry and the Making of Mohamed Siad Barre's Regime in Mogadishu." *Africa Today,* 63(1), 57–83.

Jamal, Vali. 1988a. "Somalia: Understanding an Unconventional Economy." *Development and Change,* 19(2), 203–265.

Jamal, Vali. 1988b. "Somalia: Survival in a 'Doomed' Economy." *International Labour Review,* 127(6), 783–812.

Kamwende, Nicholas Ireri. 2014. "Somalia's War Economy and Insecurity Implications in Kenya." Research project submitted in partial fulfilment of the requirement of the degree of Master of Arts in International Studies of the Institute of Diplomacy and International Studies, University of Nairobi.

Keen, David. 1998. *The Economic Functions of Violence in Civil Wars*. Adelphi Paper, 320. London: Oxford University Press for the International Institute for Strategic Studies.

Kinsey, Christopher Paul, Hansen, Stig Jarle and Franklin, George. 2009. "The Impact of Private Security Companies on Somalia's Governance Networks." *Cambridge Review of International Affairs,* 22(1), 147–161.

Laitin, David D., and Samatar, Said S. 1984. "Somalia and the World Economy." *Review of African Political Economy,* 30, 58–72.

Laitin, David D., and Samatar, Said S. 1987. *Somalia: Nation in Search of a State*. London: Gower.

Leeson, Peter T. 2007. "Better off Stateless: Somalia Before and After Government Collapse." *Journal of Comparative Economics,* 35(4), 689–710.

Leeson, Peter T. 2014. *Anarchy Unbound: Why Self-Governance Works Better than you Think*. Cambridge: Cambridge University Press.

Lefebvre, Jeffrey A. 1991. *Arms for the Horn: U.S. Security Policy in Ethiopia and Somalia, 1953–1991*. Pittsburgh, PA: University of Pittsburgh Press.

Leigh, Monroe. 1986. "Transamerican Steamship Corp. v. Somali Democratic Republic. 767 F.2d 998." *American Journal of International Law,* 80(2), 357–359.

Lemarchand, René. 2011. *The Dynamics of Violence in Central Africa*. Philadelphia., PA: University of Pennsylvania Press.

Lewis, I. M. 2002. *A Modern History of the Somali: Nation and State in the Horn of Africa*. 4th Ed. Athens, OH: Ohio University Press.

Lindley, A. 2009. "The Early Morning Phonecall: Remittances from a Refugee Diaspora Perspective." Centre on Migration, Policy and Society, Working Paper no. 47. Oxford: Oxford University Press.

Linke, Andrew, and Raleigh, Clionardh. 2011. "State and Stateless Violence in Somalia." *African Geographical Review,* 30(1), 48–62.

Little, Peter D. 2003. *Somalia: Economy without State*. Oxford: James Currey.

Maho-Aves, A., and Bechtold, K. H. 1996. "Informal [E]conomic [S]ector Substitute for State-Hood? Somalia's Relin[q]uishment [sic] of [I]nternational Relations." Paper presented at the 6th International Congress of Somali Studies, Berlin, December.

Mamdani, Mahmood. 2004. *Good Muslim, Bad Muslim: America, the Cold War, and the Roots of Terror*. New York: Pantheon.

Mansur, Abdalla Omar. 1995. "Contrary to a Nation: The Cancer of the Somali State." In Ali Jimale Ahmed (Ed.), *The Invention of Somalia*. Lawrenceville, NJ: Red Sea Press, 107–109.

Marchal, Roland. 2002. *Survey of Mogadishu's Economy*. Nairobi: European Commission.

Marchal, Roland. 2010. "Monetary Illegalism and Civil War: The Case of Somalia." In Jean-Louis Briquet and Gilles Favarel-Garrrigues (Eds), *Organized Crimes and States: The Hidden Faces of Politics*. New York: Palgrave Macmillan, 146–221.

Maren, Michael. 1997. *The Road to Hell: The Ravaging Effects of Foreign Aid and International Charity*. New York: Free Press.

Maxwell, Daniel. 2012. "Those with Guns Never Go Hungry: The Instrumental Manipulation of Food Assistance in Conflict." In Antonio Donini (Ed.), *The Golden Fleece: Manipulation and Independence in Humanitarian Action*. Sterling: Kumarian Press, 197–218.

Maxwell, Daniel, and Majid, Nisar. 2016. *Famine in Somalia: Competing Imperatives Collecting Failures, 2011–2012*. New York: Oxford University Press.

Mubarak, Jamil A. 1997. "The 'Hidden Hand' behind the Resilience of the Stateless Economy of Somalia." *World Development,* 25(12), 2027–2041.

Mukhtar, Mohamed H. 1996. "War of Resources: The Plight of the [A]gropastoral Society of Somalia." Paper presented at the 6th International Congress of Somali Studies, Berlin, December.

Mwangi, Oscar Gakuo. 2016. "Jubaland: Somalia's New Security Dilemma and State-Building Efforts." *Africa Review,* 8(2), 129–132.

Nur, Yusuf Ahmed. 2007. "Reviving the Somali Economy: Business Regulation and Development Opportunities Associated with Globalization." *Bildhaan,* 7, 169–189.

Obulutsa, George. 2017. "'Blackwater Founder' FSG Signs Security Deal with Somali Region." Reuters, 22 June.

Powell, Benjamin, Ford, Ryan, and Nowrasteh, Alex. 2008. "Somalia After State Collapse: Chaos or Improvement?" *Journal of Economic Behaviour and Organisation,* 67(3–4), 657–670.

Prunier, Gérard. 2009. *Africa's World War: Congo, the Rwandan Genocide, and the Making of a Continental Catastrophe*. London: Hurst.

Radio Dalsan. 2016a. "Former Government Says Corruption Replaced Gun in Politics." 6 October.

Radio Dalsan. 2016b. "Somali Presidential Candidate Decries Corruption in Upper House Elections." 16 October.

Radio Dalsan. 2017. "Xalane Waa Qeyb Ka Mid Ah Muqdisho, Wasiiro Soo Arkay 150 Shirkadood Oo Sharcidaro Ku Degan Xalane." 6 July.

Rawson, David. 1993. *The Somali State and Foreign Aid*. Washington, DC: UDS Foreign Service Institute.

Renders, Marleen. 2012. *Consider Somaliland: State-Building with Traditional Elders and Institutions*. Leiden: Brill.

Reno, William. 2017. "Failed, Weak or Fake State? The Role of Private Security in Somalia." In Paul Higate and Mats Utas (Eds), *Private Security in Africa: From the Global Assemblage to the Everyday*. London: Zed Books, 32–51.

Reno, William– 2018. "The Politics of Security Assistance in the Horn of Africa." *Defence Studies,* 18(4), 498–513.
Rush, Michael. 1992. *Politics and Society: An Introduction to Political Sociology.* Hertfordshire: Harvester Wheatsheaf.
Said, Edward. 1981. *Covering Islam: How the Media and the Experts Determine How we See the Rest of the World.* New York: Routledge.
Samatar, Abdi Ismail. 2007. "Somalia's Post-Conflict Economy: A Political Economy Approach." *Bildhaan,* 7, 126–168.
Schlee, Günther. 2013. "Customary Law and the Joys of Statelessness: Idealised Traditions versus Somali Realities." *Journal of Eastern African Studies,* 7(2), 258–271.
Shabelle News. 2016a. "Government Officials Accused of Failing Mogadishu Security." 25 October.
Shabelle News. 2016b. "Presidential Candidate Says Govt Failed Security." 25 October.
Shortland, Anja, Christopoulou, Katerina, and Makatsoris, Charalampos. 2013. "War and Famine, Peace and Light? The Economic Dynamics of Conflict in Somalia, 1993–2009." *Journal of Peace Research,* 50(5), 545–561.
Simons, Anna. 1995. *Networks of Dissolution: Somalia Undone.* Boulder, CO: Westview Press.
Somali Democratic Republic, 1983. *Why Kat was Prohibited in Somalia.* Mogadishu: Ministry of Information and National Guidance.
Staff, Helge. 2017. "The Emergence of Private Security Governance: Assessing Facilitating Conditions in the Case of Somali Piracy." *Global Change, Peace and Security,* 29(1), 21–37.
Stringham, Noel, and Forney, Jonathan. 2017. "It Takes a Village to Raise a Militia: Local Politics, the Nuer White Army, and South Sudan's Civil Wars." *Journal of Modern African Studies,* 55(2), 177–199.
Swedlund, Haley J. 2017. *The Development Dance: How Donors and Recipients Negotiate the Delivery of Foreign Aid.* Ithaca, NY: Cornell University Press.
The Somalia Herald. 2014. "Editorial: Somalia Deserves Stability." November–December, 6.
Tripp, Aili Mari. 1997. *Changing the Rules: The Politics of Liberalization and the Urban Informal Economy in Tanzania.* Berkeley, CA: University of California Press.
Tusmo Qaran. 2014. "Somalis Grateful for Turkey's Engagement." *The Somalia Herald,* November, 1–15, 6.
Twijnstra, Rens, and Titeca, Kristof. 2016. "Everything Changes to Remain in the Same? State and Tax Reform in South Sudan." *Journal of Modern African Studies,* 54(2), 263–292.
UNDP. 1998. *Somalia Human Development Report 1998.* London: UNDP.
UNDP. 2001. *Human Development Report: 2001 Somalia.* Nairobi: UNDP.
UNDP. 2003. *Millennium Development Goals: A Compact among Nations to End Human Poverty.* Oxford: Oxford University Press.
UN Monitoring Group. 2010. *Report of the Monitoring Group on Somalia Pursuant to Security Council Resolution 1853 (2008).* March 10. UN Security Council (S/2010/91). New York: UN.
UN Monitoring Group. 2016. *Report of the Monitoring Group on Somalia and Eritrea pursuant to Security Council resolution 2244 (2015): Somalia,* UN doc.S/2016/919, 31 October. New York: UN.

Webersik, Christian. 2005. "Fighting for the Plenty: The Banana Trade in Southern Somalia." *Oxford Development Studies,* 33(1), 81–97.

Webersik, Christian– 2006. "Mogadishu: An Economy without a State." *Third World Quarterly,* 27(8), 1463–1480.

World Bank. 2005. *Conflict in Somalia: Drivers and Dynamics.* Washington, DC: World Bank.

World Bank. 2012. *Doing Business in Hargeisa 2012.* Washington, DC: World Bank.

Xog-Ogaal. 1993. "The Scandal of Somali Gate". 'FADEEXADII SOOMAALI GATE', Sabti 23 Okt., Sanadka 2-aad, 6–7.

Yenisafak. 2017. "Somalia's Economy Thrives with Turkey's Support." 2 January.

9 Benefitting a few

Oil rents in South Sudan

Brian Adeba

Introduction

Two years after independence, South Sudan was plunged into a civil war, with rival factions in the ruling party in a violent contest for control of the state in December 2013. According to an inquiry by the African Union (AU), multiple issues – key among them weak institutions that failed to robustly mitigate political disputes between elites – sparked the war (African Union 2015, 102). The AU observed that widespread corruption by high-level officials fed the animosity that ignited the conflict (African Union 2015, 127). The power struggle centered on control of the country's oil revenues (African Union 2015, 286). The AU noted that oil had become "a tool of harm," that was "determined by patronage and allegiance" to the ruling party and individuals who control power in the political system (African Union 2015, 286–287).

Three factors are critical to understanding the centrality of oil in the South Sudanese economy: 1) the role of external actors with interests in the oil resource; 2) the role of oil in the birth of South Sudan; and 3) the relationship of elites to the oil resource.

In 2004, when a peace deal that ended the Sudanese civil war (1983–2005) was nearing completion, the United Nations Security Council deemed South Sudan a threat to international peace and security and authorized a peacekeeping mission to support the peace process. Force generation has always been a challenge for the Security Council. But when the resolution authorizing a peacekeeping mission passed in the Council, the number of countries willing to contribute troops for the mission was exceedingly large, with requests being described as "oversubscribed." This enthusiasm to send peacekeepers was undoubtably buoyed by the country's oil resource (Thomas 2015, 82). China, a permanent member of the Security Council and a proponent of the doctrine of non-interference in the internal affairs of other states, realigned its position when the possibility of South Sudan's secession became obvious by supporting the resolution. This support was spurred on by the fact that the state-owned China National Petroleum Company owned a major stake in Sudan's oilfields and the majority of them were located in South Sudan (Madut 2020, 96–97).

In the political marketplace, oil revenues enabled ruling elites to consolidate authority and establish a modicum of political stability that allowed the birth of South Sudan. Oil proceeds enabled elites to outbid competitors – notably the Sudanese state – in the purchase of the loyalty of militia groups allied to Khartoum. These groups threatened to derail the referendum and the secessionist ambitions of southern elites in the Sudan People's Liberation Movement/Army (SPLM/A) (Connall 2014, 67). Their subsequent absorption into the political-military structures of the south neutralized their potency. Most importantly, the oil wealth was instrumental in enabling the creation of basic government structures that gave credibility to the process of building a new state in the eyes of the public and the international community.

Finally, it is important to contextualize the relationship of political elites to the oil wealth within the precincts of the governance structure that emerged at independence in 2011. Elites established a government that was as extractive in nature as it was unstable. The extractive nature of the government meant that oil revenues, which constituted 98 percent of total government revenue, were systematically looted, rendering service delivery redundant. Every social development indicator registered at abysmal levels. Oil production then stood at 220,000 barrels per day. This peak in production also coincided with a time when crude prices were high; averaging more than $100 per barrel for Brent crude (US Energy Information Administration 2011). Starting from 2005, elites amassed a budget surplus from a huge gross domestic product heavily weighted on oil resources. Estimated by the World Bank at $15 billion, this GDP surpassed that of neighboring Uganda. From 2006, this surplus continued to be higher than that of neighboring countries that were more developed and had higher populations (Thomas 2015, 82–83). The oil bonanza enabled political elites to design large budgets and at the same time, these budgets increased opportunities for rent capture. By the middle of 2012, an estimated $4 billion had been siphoned from the treasury (Smith 2012).

This chapter argues that political elites and their international accomplices used oil rents in a predatory manner that contributed to political instability in South Sudan. The chapter builds on works documenting predatory accumulation strategies in South Sudan, tracing this malfeasance from the pre-independence era to independence in 2011.

The literature of predation in South Sudan: An appraisal

Coming fast on the heels of independence, the failure of governance and the violence in its wake spawned a body of literature that attempted to understand its dynamics. Not surprisingly, the discourse tended to analyze various dimensions of predation in the political system before and after the country's independence with a particular focus on the connections between resource capture and state implosion.

Pinaud (2014) suggests that wartime predation enabled senior SPLA commanders to strengthen their social and economic conditions, leading to the creation of a dominant class – a "military aristocracy" – that built new social contracts and patron–client ties that transformed captured resources into "gifts" to subordinates (194). Thus, a new class – a lower stratum – of indebted intermediaries was created. After the war, nepotistic and clientelist networks deployed by the elites continued to reinforce their control on the lower stratum, thus preserving the status quo (Pinaud 2014, 196). Pinaud cautions that the system is neither stable nor static because it is prone to political, economic and ethnic tensions. Ultimately, these tensions compromise the capacity for long-term survival of the state because of its proclivity to provoke class and ethnic conflicts (Pinaud 2014, 210).

Taking a slightly different approach, de Waal (2014) emphasizes that predatory practices inherited from rump state Sudan are instrumental in the origins of war in South Sudan. He argues that Sudan was long governed on a neopatrimonial basis in which elites used political office to advance personal and factional interests (348). South Sudanese elites replicated many of the governance features of the Sudanese state in periphery regions, notably, monetized and militarized tribalism. Nevertheless, it is within the successor state that we should understand the context and consequences of neopatrimonialism. Here, de Waal (2014) asserts that the death of John Garang, the charismatic leader of the SPLM/A, elevated secessionist ambitions. Distrustful of Khartoum's ability to honor the self-determination stipulation in the peace deal, Garang's successor, Salva Kiir, increased spending on the military to outbid Khartoum's rental of the southern proxy militia, and he indulged the appetite of the SPLM/A fractious leaders for self-enrichment (348). South Sudanese leaders then reproduced Sudan's neopatrimonial governance style in "exaggerated form," marked by four distinct characteristics. First, it is kleptocratic and its leaders are preoccupied with the theft of resources. Second, its militarized nature means leaders utilize force or the threat of force as tools for bargaining. Third, governance transactions are monetized. Fourth (and perhaps most importantly), it is dynamic and "turbulent," meaning patron–client relations are constantly being renegotiated (de Waal 2014, 348–349). On the war, de Waal (2014) notes that "untrammelled greed, combined with the reckless decision to shut down national oil production, meant that by 2013 the South Sudanese government simply could not afford the loyalty payments to keep the system running, and it fell apart" (348).

According to de Simone (2018), the SPLA's ability to transform external resources "into assets for power accumulation and state capture" is critical to understanding the war (396). She traces this primitive accumulation from the start of the Sudanese civil war, particularly when the SPLA established a civil administrative structure in the territory it controlled, and later when South Sudan became independent in 2011 (de Simone 2018, 398–404). South Sudanese elites, she, contends, displayed a remarkable proclivity for coining donor-friendly buzzwords such as democracy, decentralization, good governance and service delivery that attracted considerable support from donors (de Simone 2018, 399). The support, in the form of humanitarian relief and capacity-building projects, enabled elites to legitimize control. After independence, elites captured state institutions, cementing control on oil revenues and foreign aid. However, the consequence of this extraversion was the birth of a dysfunctional state-building process that was not accountable (de Simone 2018, 400).

While the prevailing literature expands knowledge on the links between governance and violent conflict in South Sudan, it has inherent weaknesses. It assumes that elite corruption started with the birth of the SPLA in 1983 or the creation of Sudan in 1956. The concept of the modern state in Sudan (and by extension South Sudan) is a colonial construct rooted in predation. From the Turkiyyah to the post-colonial Sudanese state, the governments that have ruled South Sudan premised their reign on extraction and exploitation of human and natural resources (Rolandsen and Daly 2016, 12–16). The post-colonial state in Africa is an archetype of the colonial state in both political and economic orientation. African elites replicated the colonizer's governance model, incorporating traits like despotism, hegemony and predation. The literature assumes colonialism to have no bearing on the governance systems in Sudan and its successor state. The South Sudanese scholar Majak D'Agoôt (2013) argues that some of South Sudan's challenges, which he terms "traps of vulnerability," are rooted in its colonial past (2).

By focusing on the second and third layers of elite predation, namely the war economy (1983–2005) and oil-driven corruption after independence, the literature does not analyze the accumulation strategies of elites during the era of regional autonomy (1972–1982) and their impact on the actions of the SPLM elites. From 1955, southerners waged a secessionist war until the signing of the Addis Ababa Agreement in 1972. Under the terms of the pact, southerners subordinated their secessionist demands and accepted regional autonomy in the south.[1] For a decade, the south had its own president and parliament. Many of the elites of the regional government formed the vanguard of the SPLA.[2]

Lastly, the literature does not account for the role of international facilitators that enable predation to flourish in independent South Sudan. It assumes that elites in the SPLM are the sole agents involved in nefarious activity. In reality, the siphoning of oil rents involves many actors, including oil conglomerations, financial institutions and middlemen, working in tandem with elites.

Background to oil production

The American energy giant, Chevron, discovered oil in Sudan in 1973. On November 23, 1974, Chevron signed an exploration agreement with Sudan, setting the stage for drilling in the Muglad basin and near Bentiu in southern Sudan. Drilling operations near Muglad in northern Sudan proved fruitful and the first signs of oil were realized in May 1978 (Patey 2014, 14). Nevertheless, Chevron officials suspected much more oil lay below the ground in Bentiu and in fact a significant amount of oil was discovered north of Bentiu in April 1980

(Patey 2014, 16). At the time, it was estimated at 10 billion barrels (Johnson 2016, 45).

In 1973, the Arab oil embargo increased the pressure on oil producers to find new wells outside the Organization of Petroleum Exporting Countries (OPEC) (Patey 2014, 19–20). The high oil prices generated by the embargo meant that Sudan was spending three times more on oil imports than it did prior to the embargo. To offset the high cost, officials deemed it necessary to build a refinery. Chevron proposed a small refinery with a capacity of 5,000 barrels per day north of Bentiu. This proposal was unacceptable to Sudanese officials, who preferred a larger refinery in Kosti in northern Sudan with a capacity of 25,000 barrels per day (Patey 2014, 21–22).

The discovery of oil deepened the cleavages between southern and northern elites. Upon their exit in 1956, British colonialists hastily cobbled together two different parts of the country into one, undoing years of ruling the south as a separate entity from the north (Poggo 2009, 33). Economically and politically backward compared to their northern counterparts, southern elites were apprehensive of their place in a new country without safeguards for their cultural and political rights (Ruay 1994, 54). Historical grievances, including slavery, at the hands of the Muslim and Arab northerners, bred a healthy strain of antagonism toward northerners in general. Furthermore, racial and religious disparities accentuated the divide between both regions. African, Christian and missionary-educated, southern elites had little in common with their northern counterparts, who envisaged a country based on an Arab-Islamic identity.[3] Following independence, a series of political slights prompted southern elites to embrace the concept of self-determination for the south (see Sudan African National Union 1963, 1).[4] Starting from 1963, an active insurgency pursued this objective. But in 1972 southern insurgents shelved their secessionist ambitions in favor of regional autonomy in the south (Johnson 2013, 142). Although the peace agreement culminated in the allocation of political power to southern elites, it did not accord them economic power (Malwal 2015, 115). The regional government, in the words of one of its ministers, survived on "handouts from Khartoum" (Malwal 2015, 115).

Nevertheless, tensions between north and south persisted. The proposal to build a refinery in northern Sudan inflamed passions in the south. The move was preceded by attempts to redraw borders in 1980 that would demarcate Bentiu as part of the north (LeRiche and Arnold 2012, 68). The interior minister, Ahmed Abdelrahman, ruled that Bentiu and Hufrat al Nihas (a region suspected to have copper) were part of the north, despite the delineation of borders in January 1956 to the contrary. The resulting uproar in the south culminated in a judicial review, headed by chief justice Khalaf Allah al Rasheed. Basing his judgment on the strength of the borders as they stood in 1956 and as encapsulated in the Addis Ababa Agreement, the chief justice ruled that both regions belonged to the south (Khalid 2010, 147). Although it succeeded in stopping Bentiu from being annexed to the north, the southern regional government was forced to concede to a refinery in the north in return (LeRiche and Arnold 2012, 69). President Nimeri proceeded to carve "Unity" province from the oilfields, removing them altogether from southern jurisdiction (Ali and Matthews 1999, 209). Nimeri was also reluctant to announce the location of oil in the south, choosing only to say that oil had been discovered "in the Southern parts of Western Sudan," and that it would be piped to Port Sudan (Patey 2014, 34). Furthermore, the regional government in the south was not consulted on the concessions granted to Chevron (Johnson 2016, 45).

Chevron acceded to northern elites' demands to build a refinery in Kosti. However, the advent of the Islamic Revolution in Iran caused a spike in global oil prices. Chevron, realizing that it stood to make more money with the high prices (and following the discovery of more oil reserves in southern Sudan), quickly readjusted its position in favor of a pipeline from Bentiu to Port Sudan on the Red Sea coast (Patey 2014, 21). This move was disconcerting to oil minister Sherif al Tuhami, who was a strong proponent for a refinery, but he could do little to sway calculations in his favor when President Jaffar Nimeri, who had been lobbied by Chevron, overrode him on the matter (Patey 2014, 22). Subsequently, in January 1983, the government announced plans to construct the pipeline and opened bids for the project (Laki 2014, 241).

Meanwhile, southern Sudanese of various political hues viewed Chevron as a complicit actor in the attempts to deny them benefits from the oil resource. In 1978, the regional assembly issued a resolution critical of Chevron (Patey 2014, 40). Angry students held demonstrations across the south. By the early 1980s, the political situation deteriorated as northern elites enacted restrictive policies on the south. In June 1983, Nimeri exploited internal divisions among southern elites by dividing the south into three separate administrative regions: Bahr El Ghazel, Equatoria and Upper Nile (Beshir 1975, 159). This was a direct contravention of the Addis Ababa Agreement.[5] Adding insult to injury, Nimeri imposed Islamic Sharia in the south in September 1983, sparking mass demonstrations. This move was considered to be the final nail on the Addis Ababa Agreement (Ali and Matthews 1999, 209). Mansour Khalid, one of the government's negotiators of the agreement, observed that Nimeri did not have a genuine commitment to the deal. Nimeri viewed himself as above the law, noting that the "agreement is myself and Joseph Lagu, (the head of the Anyanya) and we want it that way" (see Khalid 1985, 239).

To weaken the agreement and stall future rebellion in the south, Nimeri wanted to transfer former Anyanya fighters, now absorbed into the Sudanese army, to northern Sudan. In May 1983, former Anyanya fighters in battalion 105 in the town of Bor, mutinied to protest moves to transfer them north (LeRiche and Arnold 2012, 62). This mutiny, however, was not just a protest by disgruntled southern soldiers; it was a coordinated plan to start a new rebellion. The Bor mutineers fled to the Ethiopian border to form the nucleus of the Sudan People's Liberation Army (SPLA).

The birth of the SPLA was preceded by the formation of the low-key Anyanya II movement. Starting from 1975, some Anyanya fighters, who were unhappy with the Addis Ababa Agreement, refused to be absorbed into the Sudanese army (Johnson 2016, 60–61). As separatists, the political objective of the Anyanya II groups sharply contrasted with that of the SPLA; the latter, despite its southern roots, disowned secession in favor of a transformation of the political system in the whole of Sudan (Thomas 2015, 111). Nevertheless, despite their divergent political objectives, both groups opposed the exploitation of the oil resource (including the proposed construction of the Jongolei canal in the Sudd region in the south) in the absence of an amicable political environment.

In January 1984, the SPLA Jamus battalion led by Lt. Col. Kerbino Kwanyin Bol attacked Sobat Mouth (canal), putting a stop to the construction of the Jongolei canal to date (Hutchinson 1996, 353). In February 1984, Anyanya II fighters led by Bol Nyawan, and deputized by Paulino Matip, attacked a Chevron field base at Robokona, killing seven workers (Patey 2014, 38). After the attack, Chevron determined that the Sudanese government, despite its assurances, was not capable of providing the security needed to scale up oil production in Bentiu, and decided to pull out of the country altogether (Patey 2014, 21–55). This action halted oil production for a decade.

By all accounts, southern Sudan was (and still is) one of the most backward places on earth. Its natural habitat of thick forests, inaccessible water ways and tropical diseases shielded it for decades from foreign invaders. But starting from the 1830s when the Turks first set foot in the region, its resources – timber, ostrich feathers, gold and slaves – have long served to enrich interests far beyond its borders (D'Agoot 2013, 3). Chevron's discovery of oil prompted an influx of various entrepreneurs trying to cash in on the oil bonanza, with businessmen from Chase Manhattan bank and Ford Motors descending on Khartoum to lay claim to their stake in the anticipated dividends from the oil. Sudan's struggling economy was expected to be transformed to "unimaginable heights," and Khartoum was envisaged to become the "Paris of the Arab World," rather than Dubai or Abu Dhabi (Patey 2014, 12). This influx was an iteration of an established pattern of foreigners exploiting the region's resources at the expense of its people, who are often excluded from the decision-making on their own resources. This exclusion is visible in the deliberate sidelining of the regional government in the oil negotiations with Chevron. In addition to the influx of foreign business actors, the ruling elites in the north assumed a colonial mentality toward southern Sudan, viewing the region and its resources as theirs for the taking and giving no agency to its people. For instance, a refinery in Bentiu would have transformed the area by creating job opportunities, improving its infrastructure and boosting social services (Laki 2014, 241). The Sudanese intellectual, Mansour Khalid, noted that energy minister Tuhami, who played a key role in excluding the regional government, "was not only insensitive to the anxieties of southerners, he was disdainful of all things southern" (Khalid 2010, 146).

Resumption of oil production

After the Robokona attack, the SPLA emerged as the dominant rebel group in the south, thanks to considerable materiel support from the Derge regime in neighboring Ethiopia (LeRiche and Arnold 2012, 71). Its area of control expanded, including in the Western Upper Nile region where the oilfields were located. Meanwhile, after 25 years in power, Nimeri was overthrown in a popular uprising in April 1985. But it was not until June 1989, when an Islamist-inspired military coup overthrew the democratically elected government of Prime Minister Sadiq Al Mahdi, that oil production was restarted.

Unlike in the 1980s when Chevron was the sole company in the oil sector, production in the 1990s involved diverse players from Canada, Europe and Asia. The entry of these companies was a function of the process by which Chevron sold off its concession in Sudan and the restrictions imposed by a deterioration in relations between the regime and the US.

Following the Robokona attack, Chevron was reluctant to get involved in Sudan again due to the escalating war. Extricating the oil concession from Chevron became a key objective of the junta (Sidahmed 2016, 5). Chevron, however, was only willing to sell its concession to a private company, and not the regime, in order to claim a tax rebate (Sidahmed 2016, 5). To overcome this hurdle, the regime identified an Islamist businessman, Mohamed Abdallah Garelnabi, who owned the company Concorp International, to purchase the concession on its behalf (Sidahmed 2016, 5). Although Chevron had spent $1 billion in exploration activities in the Sudan, it sold its concession to Concorp International for $23 million, which was considered a throwaway price in the industry (Human Rights Watch 2003, 121). The inadvertent consequence of this sale was the perception that the concession was a high-risk endeavor. This dissuaded the big names in the global oil industry from entering the Sudanese oil market. So, when Concorp International sold off exploration and production blocks, it was only able to attract small-time players in the industry (Human Rights Watch 2003, 123).

One of the companies to enter the untested Sudanese oil sector was Arakis from Canada, with its partner State Petroleum, which acquired the coveted Blocks 1, 2 and 4 in Unity and Heglig in December 1992 (Patey 2014, 59). Illustrating how this purchase was going to dramatically improve the company's fortunes, its CEO James Terrence Alexander called it "the opportunity of a life-time" that would transform Arakis from a small to a mid-sized company (Human Rights Watch 2003, 121). By July 1993, Arakis gained full control of the concession when it bought out State Petroleum, ostensibly to focus on raising the estimated $750 million to $1 billion required to finance the Sudan project (Human Rights Watch 2003, 123). But the company still struggled to raise capital. An announcement in 1995 that a potential financier, Arab Group International (AGI), was likely to invest $750 million, caused some excitement that increased Arakis' stock but it was short-lived: AGI did not come through on the funding (Patey 2014, 61). In August 1993, the

US listed Sudan as a state sponsor of terrorism (Molotsky 1993). The CEO, Alexander, pegged the company's challenges in finding suitable partners to a hostile US policy toward Sudan. The main issue, however, appeared to be the perception created by Chevron's withdrawal from Sudan which indicated a high-risk potential in Sudan's oilfields. Key financiers of the Chevron effort, such as the World Bank and US commercial banks, were reluctant to fund the relatively small Arakis in a project in which a giant like Chevron had failed Patey 2014, 61).

But there was still some progress. In June 1996, Arakis succeeded where Chevron failed. It opened eight wells, including a small refinery in the town of El-Obeid. Crude from oilfields in southern Sudan was shipped by trucks to this refinery (Patey 2014, 62).

This achievement, however, did not resolve Arakis' financial hurdles. Still obligated by the terms of its contract with the Sudanese government to develop the oilfields or lose a portion of its concession, Arakis changed tack and began looking for venture partners. The successful shipping of crude to the refinery signaled the potential of proven oil reserves as well as assurances that the Sudanese government was capable of providing the security necessary for drilling in the middle of a civil war. This prospect was enticing to would-be partners in the oil sector. One potential partner, Occidental, from the US, was a favorite candidate among a coterie of companies from France, China, Malaysia, Japan, Netherlands and Sweden because Sudanese officials were keen on gaining access to US technology. But in the middle of negotiations with Occidental, the US announced $20 million in non-lethal military aid to Ethiopia, Eritrea and Uganda, all key allies of the SPLA. This move infuriated the Sudanese government, which terminated talks with Occidental, effectively severing it from any deal (Patey 2014, 62–64).

The end result of the endeavor to find partners was the cobbling together of a consortium called the Greater Nile Petroleum Operating Company (GNPOC) consisting of companies from China, Malaysia and Sudan (Human Rights Watch 2003, 124). The companies in the consortium consisted of the following:

- The China National Petroleum Corporation, 40 percent of shares.
- Petronas Carigali Overseas, from Malaysia, 30 percent of shares.
- Arakis, from Canada, 25 percent of shares.
- Sudapet, state-owned Sudanese company, 5 percent of shares.

By 1998, Arakis, still facing financial hurdles, was forced to sell its shares in GNPOC to the Canadian company Talisman Energy Inc. (Johnson 2016, 162). Unlike Arakis, Talisman was a big player in the international oil industry and was considered Canada's flagship oil company with a portfolio of projects in Canada, the North Sea and Indonesia. The company moved quickly to construct a 1,500 km pipeline and by 1999, it succeeded in linking the Unity oilfields to Port Sudan.

In August 1999, for the first time, crude pumped from the Unity oilfields arrived in Port Sudan for shipping aboard a tanker bound for Singapore (Patey 2014, 66–67).

The regime utilized a divide and conquer strategy to neutralize insurgent activity around the oilfields. In August 1991, John Garang's heavy hand in managing the SPLA precipitated an ideological split. Shortly afterwards, the splinter faction, whose troops were predominant in the oil areas, ceded control to the Sudanese army. A peace deal with the regime in 1997 saw the new faction becoming part of the Sudanese government, as well as the cooptation of the Anyanya II, paving the path for production activities (Human Rights Watch 2003, 120–121).

The atrocities in the oilfields attracted wide publicity among activists in Canada, the US and Europe. Prior to Talisman's entry, church groups in Canada launched a spirited campaign against the company, arguing that it gave legitimacy to a regime that was guilty of human rights abuses and imposing an extreme form of Islam on Sudanese citizens (Patey 2014, 67). Many organizations involved in the campaign wrote investigative reports that argued that oil was fueling war in southern Sudan. This forced Talisman's stock price to fall. In the US, Christian right-wing organizations, Jewish groups and the Congressional Black Caucus joined the increasing chorus of activists opposed to Talisman. The US groups championed sanctions on Sudan and called for companies on the US financial markets to be delisted if they had investments in Sudan (Patey 2014, 71). The growing pressure forced investors to unload Talisman shares on the New York Stock Exchange. But the straw that broke the camel's back for Talisman was the threat of capital market restrictions in the then proposed Sudan Peace Act that compelled the company to search for buyers for its Sudan assets. Although Talisman reassessed its intentions after capital market restrictions were purged from the final draft of the act in July 2001, it nevertheless decided to forge ahead with selling its Sudan assets to the Indian company ONGC Videsh (OVL) on October 30, 2002 (Patey 2014, 72). Talisman was not the only casualty of activism. Lundin and OMV, a Swedish and Austrian company, respectively, that had acquired Block 5A, were forced to abandon their assets due to the activist campaigns in Europe in 2003 shortly after Talisman's exit (Patey 2014, 75).

The post-Chevron oil exploration mirrors the first phase with respect to the influx of companies from around the world but with distinct differences; the endeavor was larger in scope, more capital intensive and involved diverse players. Violence was instrumental to its success in the middle of a civil war. Whereas Chevron was a well-resourced and formidable international oil company in the 1980s, the second phase of oil exploration was not attractive to the risk-averse large global oil companies. Instead, smaller companies forged ahead with investing in Sudan's oilfields. Although smaller, these companies were able to surmount the challenges in Sudan by forming consortiums that enabled them to amass the capital required to advance their objectives.

The post-Chevron oil exploration process accentuated the deprivation of South Sudanese communities of the oil dividend on several fronts. By bureaucratic fiat, northern elites ensured that the inputs for oil production were strategically located in the north, including pipelines and refineries. In total, three refineries, in Khartoum, El-Obeid and Port Sudan, exist in northern Sudan. The 994-mile Greater Nile Oil Pipeline, with a capacity to carry 450,000 b/d, was built to connect the oilfields of Western Upper Nile to the Bashayir terminal in Port Sudan at a cost of $1.2 billion. Another pipeline, 870 miles long, and with a capacity of 500,000 b/d, was constructed by the Petrodar Operating Company Ltd at a cost of $1.2 billion to connect oilfields in Northern Upper Nile to the Bashayir terminal. Two other shorter pipelines, 110 miles long, link the Tharjath and Malá oilfields in Western Upper Nile to the El-Fula oilfields, which then connect to another 460-mile-long pipeline to the refinery in Khartoum (D'Agoot 2009, 123–124).

The international oil companies reaped huge profits but ploughed back a negligible amount of money into communities in the oil areas. Talisman, for instance, netted CAN$296 million from selling its assets to OVL. Prior to the sale, its net income was increasing at a steady pace. In 2000, it stood at $184 million. In 2001 and 2002, the company earned (CAN)$210 and $310 million, respectively (Patey 2014, 72). Talisman's concessions in southern Sudan represented an international growth vehicle for the company. The growth trajectory continued when OVL took over its assets. In 2004, OVL's profit was £262 million (sterling). This upward trend was repeated in 2005 when it earned £377 million (Patey 2014, 72).

Independence and the advent of kleptocracy

The exit of the European and North American companies opened the path for the Asian oil companies to take full control of Sudan's oil sector without pressure from Western human rights activists. Two factors are instrumental in enabling this outcome. First, as state-owned firms, the Asian oil companies were not susceptible to human rights campaigns (Madut 2020, 95). Second, a long ceasefire between the government and the SPLA that culminated in the Comprehensive Peace Agreement in 2005 weakened the potency of human rights crusaders. Independence in 2011 saw the new country gain possession of 75 percent of the oilfields in what was formerly the Republic of Sudan.

Emerging from a politico-military system with a democratic deficit, SPLM elites quickly installed a kleptocratic government that was deeply dependent on oil rents in 2011. Its distinct markers were egregious corruption and patronage along ethnic, regional and political lines. Central to this system of extraction was the maximization of rents by elites. Achieving this end entailed the hijacking of governance institutions to serve elite interests. Thus, systems for checks and balances were deliberately stymied. Institutions of governance, revenue collection and public expenditure were rendered ineffective in the following ways. First, these institutions were deprived of the funding necessary to execute their mandates. In many countries, the annual reports of the auditor general offer insight into how government officials spend public monies, including recommendations to plug sources of leakage. In South Sudan's case, the National Audit Chamber could not release reports in a timely manner because of personnel and funding shortfalls. Thus, the chamber faced a serious backlog. The few reports of the chamber that are public are for the years 2005, 2006, 2007 and 2008. All were produced on a multi-year delay. For instance, the audit for 2005 was unveiled in May 2011, the 2006 audit in June 2011 and the 2008 audit in June 2012 (Adeba 2016, 13). All these reports are for the pre-independent autonomous government and showcased egregious corruption by elites. For example, the 2008 audit unmasked the corruption in the central bank thus:

> In 2012, the auditor general was unable to provide an opinion on the financial statements of the Bank of South Sudan (central bank). Instead, the auditor general provided a disclaimer, which suggests he either lacked the right information on which to base an opinion or he received inaccurate or incomplete information.
>
> (Adeba 2016, 13)

The government, not too impressed with the reports, stopped their public release. To date, there are no audit reports of independent South Sudan, which is a direct contravention of the South Sudan constitution (Prendergast et al. 2020, 5).

Second, mandates to entrench accountability are undermined through the legal system. The anti-corruption commission, for instance, has not prosecuted anyone since its establishment. Its prosecutorial ability is hamstrung by two incompatible pieces of legislation. On one hand, the constitution grants the commission the right to investigate and prosecute corrupt officials. On the other hand, the act governing its day-to-day operations does not grant the commission prosecutorial powers. Drafted in 2009 before South Sudan's independence, the act is outdated. To the present time, officials have not reconciled the differences in the two pieces of legislation, although a draft bill was presented in 2014 (Adeba 2016, 15).

Third, elites ensure that institutions for checks and balances are headed by appointees whose role is to stymie the fight against graft. For example, the Public Accounts Committee in the legislature is an important institution for enforcing accountability in public spending. Nevertheless, the appointment of the head of the committee is determined by the president, although the nomination is by peers in the legislature (Adeba 2016, 16). The position comes with perks such as an office, a stipend and a luxury vehicle. Expedience rather than merit determines who gets appointed as chair of the committee. The normal practice in other countries is to appoint a legislator from the opposition as chair to ensure independence. In the South Sudan legislature, the opposite occurs;

the head of the committee is usually from the ruling party. This patronage compromises the independence of the committee chair.

The stymieing of institutions of accountability is complemented by lack of transparency in handling oil revenues by authorities. From extraction to export, the business of oil is opaque. In its 2019 Article IV consultations with government officials, the IMF observed that "non-transparent oil advances, oil-backed loans, and off-budget transactions are undermining fiscal discipline and budgetary integrity, which have led to high corruption vulnerabilities" (International Monetary Fund 2019). This is manifested in a couple of ways: through the revenue remittance process and also via the allocation of oil advances. The former is manifested in the shortchanging of oil revenue remittances to the central bank. Officials have created parallel accounts, often abroad, to which a portion of the oil remittances are deposited. The 2018 peace agreement, noting this anomaly, included an article that compels officials to close "any petroleum revenue accounts other than those approved by law within three months of the start of the Transition" (Intergovernmental Authority on Development 2018). Oil advance sales are conducted without the appropriate accountability measures, such as transparent procurement mechanisms. There is no discussion in the media or in parliament about these sales. For instance, in July 2020, leaked documents on social media from the Ministry of Finance purport to show the government in an "irrevocable allocation of twenty-five [25] crude oil cargoes" to an oil lifter starting from 2019 to 2023 to finance a $400 million term-loan facility from the African Export-Import Bank (Afreximbank). Dated October 10, 2019, the letter, signed by finance minister Salvatore Garang Mabiordit, and addressed to the minister of petroleum, allocates 600,000 barrels for each consignment (Republic of South Sudan 2019).

Notable in the siphoning of oil rents is the role of international actors who have raked in profits from dealings with South Sudanese officials. Nearly every illicit transaction in the sector involves an international corporation, bank, foreign government or middlemen abroad. These international partners, ranging from "Chinese-Malaysian oil giants and British tycoons to networks of traders from Ethiopia, Eritrea, Kenya and Uganda – have accumulated billions of dollars" (The Sentry 2019). Using middlemen, elites use oil rents to buy mansions and live luxurious lifestyles in neighboring countries such as Kenya, Uganda and Ethiopia (The Sentry 2020).

Instability is a unique characteristic of kleptocratic governance in South Sudan and has implications for the use of oil rents. The Washington-based investigative group, The Enough Project/The Sentry, identifies this system as a "violent kleptocracy" (Menkhaus and Prendergast 2016). The regime faces multiple internal threats from insurgents, elites within the system and pro-democracy agitators (Adeba 2020, 1). This means that it is in constant negotiation mode to purchase loyalty and neutralize threats. Oil rents play a critical role in this political marketplace; they are used to create positions for political accommodation and minimal power-sharing arrangements with competitors.

These arrangements do not often address the root cause of conflict. In July 2016, for instance, a split in the ranks of the main armed opposition, led by former Vice President Riek Machar, resulted in the installation of one of his top lieutenants, Taban Deng, as First Vice President (Butty 2016). The coup against Machar culminated in his exile. In the meantime, Deng, lacking the support of the armed opposition's rank and file, remained a figurehead in the capital, while his erstwhile colleagues expanded the war theater to new areas. As the conflict metastasized, the economy tanked and claims of genocide surfaced, attracting sanctions on the government (Dwyer, 2016). It was not until September 2018 that a new peace deal was negotiated and installed Machar as First Vice President in a bloated power-sharing government with five vice presidents from different opposition groups (Maasho 2018). Nevertheless, the agreement was not acceptable to some parties. At the same time, it caused divisions between those who supported the agreement and those opposed to it. The government accommodated the splinter factions, underscoring the piecemeal nature of the agreement. Thus, peace remains elusive as the hold-out groups elevate their price for accommodation and continue to wage war against the government.[6]

Insurgents too use the oil wealth to increase their bargaining power with the government. In the early days of the war, insurgents shut down oil production in Bentiu to leverage their position. Rebel soldiers also plotted to take over the Paloch oilfields in Upper Nile to deny the regime revenue to buy arms (Davison 2014). At the time, Machar observed that taking control of the Paloch oilfields would compel President Kiir to "talk," underscoring the bargaining power to be harnessed from controlling the oilfields (see Davison 2014).

Conclusion

Deriving legitimacy from the liberation war, elites in the ruling SPLM could count on an unchallenged supremacy in the political marketplace. Oil rents facilitated the building of the state and its legitimacy, but the absence of credible political competitors meant that elites wielded total control on spending without accountability. Sustaining control over oil rents diminished the need for strong governance institutions and SPLM elites deliberately stymied accountability mechanisms.

Oil rents are as critical to the survival of the kleptocracy in South Sudan as they are in fueling war. Oil allows officials across political divides to consolidate authority, strengthen bargaining positions and neutralize threats. Yet the purchase of loyalty, without addressing the root causes of conflict, perpetuates a never-ending cycle of war. The control of rents sustains the patronage system but alienates social groups and fosters dissent. When the government is unable to purchase loyalty, it utilizes violence to deter or eliminate threats. The use of violence by the government and dissatisfied social groups to negotiate power illustrates the instability of the political marketplace, rendering South Sudan a fragile country.

The September 2018 peace deal recognizes the role of oil rents in the civil war. It outlines a series of measures to strengthen accountability in the oil sector. Yet its only dividend is the silence of the guns. Officials have shown little inclination to prioritize institutional reform. It is possible to imagine a different future in the utilization of oil rents to benefit the larger population rather than a few elites and their international enablers. However, this possibility is contingent on the political will necessary to implement the good governance measures stipulated in the agreement.

Notes

1 Had secession been a successful outcome, a new border would have divided the south from the north. Alluding to the fact that Sudan's territorial integrity remained intact, President Nimeri remarked that the deal "did not provide new structure to the Sudan by altering international boundaries nor to divide its people in lines of racial, cultural or religious creed" (see Poggo 2009, 189).
2 For instance, Joseph Oduho, Martin Majier, Simon Mori and Justin Yaac, were ministers in the regional government.
3 For an explanation of northern elites' view of the type of country Sudan should be, see Heather Sharkey (1999, 533–539).
4 An editorial in this first edition of the publication stated that its aim was "to declare to the people of Southern Sudan, the African world and the world at large that this monthly paper is dedicated to self-determination for the Southern Sudanese." The editorial argued that the union of the northern and southern parts of Sudan was a forced one and not based on a "voluntary link," invoking the fact that the "consent" of the governed in Southern Sudan was not sought to establish the sovereign state known as Sudan.
5 Chapter II, Article 4. The article states, "The Provinces of Bahr El Ghazal, Equatoria and Upper Nile as defined in Article 3. (iii) shall constitute a self-governing Region within the Democratic Republic of the Sudan and be known as the Southern Region."
6 For example, the National Salvation Front rejected the peace agreement arguing that it does not go far enough in addressing the root causes of conflict in the country.

References

Adeba, Brian. 2016. "A Hope from Within? Countering the Intentional Destruction of Governance and Transparency in South Sudan." *The Enough Project* (July). https://enoughproject.org/files/report_AHopeFromWithin_Adeba_Enough_July 2016.pdf

Adeba, Brian. 2020. "Oversight Mechanisms, Regime Security, and Intelligence Service Autonomy in South Sudan." *Intelligence and National Security* (April 26). www.tandfonline.com/doi/full/10.1080/02684527.2020.1756624

African Union. 2015. *Final Report of the African Union Commission of Inquiry on South Sudan*. Addis Ababa: African Union, October. http://www.peaceau.org/uploads/auciss.final.report.pdf

Akol, Lam. 2003. *SPLM/SPLA: The Nassir Declaration*. Lincoln: iUniverse.

Ali, Taiseir M. and Matthews, Robert O. 1999. "Civil War and Failed Peace Efforts in Sudan." In Taisier M. Ali and Robert O. Matthews (Eds), *Civil Wars in Africa: Roots and Resolution*. Montreal and Kingston: Montreal University Press, 193–220.

Beshir, Mohamed Omer. 1975. *The Southern Sudan: From Conflict to Peace*. London: C. Hurst & Co.

Butty, James. 2016. "South Sudan to Swear in New First Vice President." *Voice of America* (July 26). www.voanews.com/africa/south-sudan-swear-new-first-vice-president

Copnall, James. 2014. *A Poisonous Thorn in our Hearts: Sudan and South Sudan's Bitter and Incomplete Divorce*. London: Hurst & Co.

D'Agoôt, Majak. 2009. "Energy Politics and the South Sudan Referendum: Anatomy of a Resource Curse." *Middle East Policy*, 16(4) (Winter), 118–130.

D'Agoôt, Majak. 2013. "Coping with Traps of Vulnerability: A Review of Post-Colonial Issues on the Independence of South Sudan." *Defence and Security Analysis*, 29(2) (April 30). www.tandfonline.com/doi/abs/10.1080/14751798.2013.787791

Davision, William. 2014. "South Sudan's Rebel Leader Machar Vows to Target Oil Fields." Bloomberg, March 31. www.bloomberg.com/news/articles/2014-03-30/south-sudan-s-rebel-leader-machar-vows-to-target-key-oil-fields

de Simone, Sara. 2018. "Playing the 'Fragile' State Card: The SPLM and State Extraversion in South Sudan." *Journal of Modern African Studies*, 56(3) (September), 395–420.

de Waal, Alex. 2014. "When Kleptocracy Becomes Insolvent: Brute Causes of the Civil War in South Sudan." *African Affairs*, 113(452) (July), 347–369.

Dwyer, Colin. 2016. "South Sudan on Brink of 'Rwanda-Like' Genocide, Commission Warns." National Public Radio (December 14). www.npr.org/sections/thetwo-way/2016/12/14/505555892/south-sudan-on-brink-of-rwanda-like-genocide-commission-warns

Human Rights Watch. 2003. *Sudan, Oil, and Human Rights*. Brussels: Human Rights Watch. www.iisd.org/pdf/2002/envsec_oil_violence.pdf

Hutchinson, Sharon E. 1996. *Nuer Dilemmas: Coping with Money, War and the State*. Berkeley-Los Angelos, CA: University of California Press.

Intergovernmental Authority on Development. 2018. *Revitalized Agreement on the Resolution of the Conflict in South Sudan (R-ARCSS)*. Addis Ababa: Intergovernmental Authority on Development (September 12). www.dropbox.com/s/6dn3477q3f5472d/R-ARCSS.2018-i.pdf?dl=0

International Monetary Fund. 2020. *IMF Country Report No. 19/53, Republic of South Sudan: 2019 Article IV Consultation – Press Release; Staff Report; and Statement by the Executive Director for South Sudan*. Washington, DC: IMF (June). www.imf.org/en/Publications/CR/Issues/2019/06/04/South-Sudan-2019-Article-IV-Consultation-Press-Release-Staff-Report-and-Statement-by-the-46965

Johnson, Douglas H. 2013. "New Sudan or South Sudan? The Multiple Meanings of Self-determination in Sudan's Comprehensive Peace Agreement." *Civil Wars*, 15(2). www.tandfonline.com/doi/abs/10.1080/13698249.2013.817850

Johnson, Douglas H. 2016. *The Root Causes of Sudan's Wars: Old Wars and New Wars*. Woodbridge: James Currey.

Khalid, Mansour. 1985. *Nimeiri and the Revolution of Dis-May*. London: Routledge & Kegan Paul.

Khalid, Mansour. 2010. *War and Peace in Sudan: A Tale of Two Countries*. London and New York: Routledge.

Laki, Sam L. 2014. "The Role of Oil in the Sudanese Civil War." In Souad T. Ali, Stephanie Beswick, Richard Lobban, and Jay Spaulding (Eds), *The Road to the Two Sudans.* Newcastle upon Tyne: Cambridge Scholars Publishing, p. xx.

LeRiche, Matthew, and Arnold, Matthew. 2012. *South Sudan: From Revolution to Independence.* London: Hurst & Co.

Maasho, Aaron. 2018. "South Sudan's President, Rebel Leader Sign Peace Deal." Reuters (September 12). www.reuters.com/article/us-southsudan-unrest/south-sudans-president-rebel-leader-sign-peace-deal-idUSKCN1LS2PW

Madut, Akok. 2020. "Genesis of South Sudan's Engagement with China." In Christopher Zambakari (Ed.), *Courting Africa: Asian Powers and the New Scramble for the Continent.* Phoenix, AZ: The Zambakari Advisory, 96–97. www.zambakari.org/special-issue-summer-2020.html

Malwal, Bona. 2015. *Sudan and South Sudan: From One to Two.* Basingstoke: Palgrave Macmillan.

Menkhaus, Ken and Prendergast, John. 2016. "Defining Violent Kleptocracy in East and Central Africa." *The Enough Project* (October 20). https://enoughproject.org/blog/defining-violent-kleptocracy-east-and-central-africa

Molotsky, Irvin. 1993. "U.S Expected to Place Sudan on Terrorism List." *New York Times,* August 17. www.nytimes.com/1993/08/17/nyregion/us-expected-to-place-sudan-on-terrorist-list.html.

Patey, Luke. 2014. *The New Kings of Crude: China, India, and the Global Struggle for Oil in Sudan and South Sudan.* London: C. Hurst & Co.

Pinaud, Clémence. 2014. "South Sudan: Civil War, Predation, and the Making of a Military Aristocracy." *African Affairs,* 113(451) (April), 192–211.

Poggo, Scopas. 2009. *The First Sudanese Civil War: African, Arabs, and Israelis in the Southern Sudan, 1955–1972.* New York: Palgrave Macmillan.

Prendergast, John, Mossburg, Hilary and Swamy, Megha. 2020. "Targeted Sanctions and Anti-Money Laundering Measures in Support of Peace in South Sudan." Wilson Center, April. www.wilsoncenter.org/sites/default/files/media/uploads/documents/Targeted%20Sanctions%20and%20Anti-Money%20Laundering%20Measures%20in%20Support%20of%20Peace%20in%20South%20Sudan 2.pdf.

Republic of South Sudan: Ministry of Finance and Planning. 2019. "Subject: Irrevocable Allocation of Twenty Five [25] Crude Oil Cargoes – Loading between: 2019 – 2023 (Afreximbank USD$ 400 Million Term Loan Facility)." October 10.

Rolandsen, Øystein H. and Daly, M.W. 2016. *A History of South Sudan: From Slavery to Independence.* Cambridge: Cambridge University Press.

Ruay, Deng D. Akol. 1994. *The Politics of Two Sudans: The South and the North, 1821–1969.* Uppsala: Nordiska Afrikainstitutet.

Sharkey, Heather. 1999. "A Century in Print: Arabic Journalism and Nationalism in Sudan, 1899–1999." *International Journal of Middle East Studies,* 31(4), 533–539.

Sidahmed, Alsir. 2016. *Pursuing Transparency in Sudan's Oil Industry.* Khartoum: Sudan Democracy First Group (January 20), 5. www.democracyfirstgroup.org/wp-content/uploads/2016/01/Pursuing-Transparency-in-Sudan-Oil-Industry.pdf

Smith, David. 2012. "South Sudan President Accuses Officials of Stealing $4 Billion." *The Guardian,* June 5. www.theguardian.com/world/2012/jun/05/south-sudan-president-accuses-officials-stealing

Sudan African National Union. 1963. "Editorial." *Voice of Southern Sudan,* 1(1) (April)..

The Sentry. 2019. "The Taking of South Sudan: The Tycoons, Brokers, and Multi-National Corporations Complicit in Hijacking the World's Newest State." (September). https://cdn.thesentry.org/wp-content/uploads/2019/09/TakingOfSouthSudan-Sept2019-TheSentry.pdf

The Sentry. 2020. "Making a Killing: South Sudanese Military Leaders' Wealth Explained." (May). https://cdn.thesentry.org/wp-content/uploads/2020/07/MakingAKilling_TheSentry_May2020.pdf

Thomas, Edward. 2015. *South Sudan: A Slow Liberation*. London: Zed Books.

US Energy Information Administration. 2012. *Today in Energy, 2011 Brief: Brent Crude Averages Over $100 Per Barrel in 2011*. Washington, DC: EIA (January 12). www.eia.gov/todayinenergy/detail.php?id=4550

10 Angola's transition from war to economic powerhouse

Victor Ojakorotu

Introduction

Crude oil has been one of the dominant products in the international economic system as a result of its industrial usefulness. This natural resource has given developing countries in Africa importance in relating with core actors in the international system. Unfortunately, this relevance and the sales of the crude oil product for many decades in the continent of Africa are not reflected in the development of the African people. Extant literature has identified major factors that are instrumental to underdevelopment in most African countries with oil deposits, including Angola. Ojakorotu (2015) identifies these as external intruders in Angola's internal politics that engage in primitive accumulation, and he further notes that greed on the side of the Angola's political elites has plunged the country into a sort of colossal failure (18). In other words, political crisis and bad leadership have thwarted the path of development of Angola. The Angolan civil war following independence sank the country into huge debt. In spite of this, Angola is gradually rising from the ruins of the war to becoming a force to reckon with in Africa, particularly within the Southern African region.

After the civil war ended in 2002, visible evidence on the ground showed that the country was experiencing growth; however, this has yet to be reflected in the lives of the citizens, even two decades later. The Systematic Country Diagnostic (SCD), as a development plan of Angola, aims to reduce inequality by the year 2030, but the World Bank Group (2018) notes that the continuous fluctuations of crude oil prices in the global market has distorted the pace of development in the country. This chapter reviews the extent of development in Angola after witnessing a civil war that lasted for approximately 30 years. The next section discusses in brief the nature of Angola's struggle for independence. This is followed by an account of how the country slipped into a civil war shortly after its independence. This will help us to examine the consequences of the war and analyze the current state of the Angolan economy. The reforms and transformation of Angola and its economic growth will then be analyzed. The challenges facing the country are discussed prior to the conclusion.

Angola as a war theater: The pre-independence war 1961–1975

The Portuguese style of colonial rule in Angola led to the pre-independence war in the country. Portugal had displayed unwillingness to grant independence and suppressed nationalism in the country. Given this circumstance, in 1961, Angolan nationalists mounted an armed challenge to colonial rule using guerrilla warfare tactics in the struggle for the country's independence. This was done through three liberation movements: the People's Movement for the Liberation of Angola (MPLA), the National Liberation Front of Angola (FNLA) and the National Union for the Total Independence of Angola (UNITA) formed in 1956, 1962, 1966 and led by Agostinho Neto, Holden Roberto and Jonas Savimbi, respectively (Leao 2007). The three groups approached the struggle differently in reaction to the ways colonial rule affected the region each represented. Their onslaughts against the colonial government and the coup in Portugal in 1974 culminated in ending Portuguese colonial rule in Angola. And based on the Alvor Accord, endorsed by parties to the conflict in January 1975, the country was granted independence in November 1975 (see World Peace Foundation 2015).

The post-independence civil war in Angola: 1975–2002

The pre-independence war in Angola was directed against a common enemy – the Portuguese government – and the aim was to end colonial rule, and it was fought in that direction. The post-independence war was a result of the irreconcilable differences amongst the three liberation movements at independence, which led to a power struggle over control of the government as the Portuguese colonial government did not hand over power formally before its departure. This led to the MPLA declaring itself as the government of Angola; UNITA and the FNLA constituted parallel governments, each controlling different sections of the country (see BBC News 2018). The rivalry continued and degenerated into civil war shortly after the country's independence.

The outbreak of the war could be ascribed to the way and manner the country's independence was negotiated, which influenced and shaped political life in the immediate post-independent Angola. Thus, the liberation movements preferred resorting to the use of violence and force, rather than dialogue and compromise, to reconcile their differences. In spite of their respective ethnic bases, support and differences amongst the three liberation groups – the MPLA (by the Ambundu in the urban area), the FNLA (by the people of rural Bakongo) and UNITA (by the rural people of Ovimbundu) (see Thornton, n.d), that are often touted as being responsible for the war, studies show that it was not the ethnic identity of these movements that created the conflict; rather, the conflict itself exacerbated ethnic rivalries (da Costa Cabral Andresen Guimaraes 1992; Taylor 2015).

Unlike the pre-independence war that had been localized, the post-independence war was internationalized with varied external interests participating either directly or indirectly. The global politics of the period contributed immensely to the duration of the war from 1975 to 2002. While Cuba, China and USSR supported the MPLA because of its ideological leanings, UNITA gained the support of South Africa and the United States, and the FNLA was supported by the United States as well (see Milestones 2016; Hurst 2009). This support was in the form of arms supplies, military training, food, logistics, medicine, intelligence reports, mercenaries and financial aid which fueled and sustained the war; in exchange for this assistance, external supporters procured access to resources and revenues from oil and diamonds (manifestation of resource curse) in financing the war. The death of Jonas Savimbi and the ceasefire agreement between the MPLA and the UNITA ended the war in 2002 (see Leao 2007). However, the government continued to face limited insurgency from separatist groups beyond 2002. This was ended in 2006 by the peace agreement between the government and the Front of Liberation of the State of Cabinda (FLEC).

The effects of Angolan post-independence war

The prosecuting of the war and its duration were unprecedented in the damage to the country and its citizens. What the colonial government had put in place in terms of physical infrastructure and manpower, that would have assisted in fast tracking development in post-independent Angola, was destroyed. This included much of the roads, bridges, railways, hospitals and schools. The overall death toll from the civil war totalled more than 500,000; amputees numbered about 77,000. The number displaced was over 4 million, and those who fled the country were more than 500,000. Beyond these casualties the war contributed to rising poverty, the outbreak of disease, malnutrition and the country was left with about 10 million land mines scattered throughout the country (Ziemke 2008; Hurst 2009; Heywood 2001; World Peace Foundation 2015; Gyimah 2018).

These statistics have had grave consequences for post-war Angola in several ways. Gyimah (2018, 3) points out that:

> Firstly, the loss of many educated professionals meant that once the country began rebuilding in 2002, the government relied on personal networks and foreign intervention to help fix the country. In essence, it bolstered the patronage that had already existed during the war; those connected to dos Santos quickly became wealthy as the educated, middle-class Angolans had not returned to the country yet. Secondly, the destruction of Angolan infrastructure led to a vacuum in the labour market – nearly half of the population is younger than 15 years old. This means that the country is lacking homegrown doctors, teachers, nurses, and other professionals, resulting in a self-perpetuating cycle of poverty and underdevelopment.

In view of this, despite its rich oil deposits and diamonds that influence relations with China, Russia and other countries, Angola has yet to overcome the effects of its war after nearly two decades of post-war reconstruction.

Overview of the economy of Angola

There are many natural resources in Angola, such as oil and diamonds, that have attracted foreign investors and world powers to the country. Access to natural resources in Angola and their further exploration is the main factor that defines the country's external relations. An important partner to the government of Angola is the People Republic of China (PRC) that established a long-standing relationship with the ruling MPLA in the aftermath of the post-independence war. Of particular relevance, the PRC has given education assistance in the form of scholarships; in 2006, nine Angolan students were enrolled in a program in the PRC. This was made possible through the economic cooperation and trade forum with Portugal. Countries like Cape Verde, Mozambique, Brazil, Guinea Bissau and East Timor were also part of this economic program put in place between the Portuguese and the PRC.

Historically, the PRC has had important economic ties and treaties with Angola, such as in 1984 when both countries undertook a trade agreement; both countries set up a commission that oversaw trade and the economic system in 1988. With respect to reconstruction, the Angolan government accessed a loan to the tune of US$2 billion from the Chinese government in 2004. Furthermore, Angola has outstanding debts with China that were due to be repaid in 1999 but was granted relief in 2006 by the Chinese government. In addition to this, a further loan was granted in 2007 by the Chinese government to Angola to facilitate reconstruction. The aforementioned contracts and treaties helped Angola to reestablish infrastructure in most places in Angola; in exchange, the PRC technically "secured 10,000 barrels of oil per day from Angola" (Corkin 2008, 6). In September 2007 the China Exim Bank, that served as the loan bank for Angola, asked one of its principal officers, Li Ruogu, to visit Angola and evaluate the progress of various projects. This was done to demonstrate the interest of China in Angola and to encourage transparency in the areas of project and loan management. In the course of this tour, President Eduardo dos Santos and Li Ruogu signed a new loan agreement for more massive infrastructure projects to the tune of about $2 billion.

The Angolan government has also benefitted from the PRC in terms of technical assistance for agricultural development, leading to the training of the Angolan people in multiple sectors of the economy. The extent to which the PRC has committed enormous resources towards economic development in Angola is shown in Table 10.1.

Given the involvement of Russia, Cuba and the United States of America in the pre- and post-independence war in Angola, it might have been expected that they would have also been involved in the Angola's post-civil war reconstruction. However, the foregoing analysis shows that foreign investment in

Table 10.1 PRC investment in Angola by sector (US$ millions), September 2007

S/N	*Year*	*Project*	*Sector*	*Company*	*Costs*
1.	2007	Car plant	Manufacturing undeclared	CSG Automobile	-
2.	2006	Oil Blocks	Oil and Gas (Mining)	Sinopec Sonangol International	2, 400
3.	2005	Fixed Line infrastructure	Telecommunications	ZTE	469
	Total				**2, 869**

Source: Corkin (2008).

Angola was dominated by China. This could be traced to some of the events that transpired during the independence war and immediately after it ended. The United States of America supported UNITA and the FNLA during the war; it had also had sensitive relations with Angola that led each country to tread with caution in dealing with the other. Haas (2007) observes that "while Angola's leaders respect and, at heart, want a strong relationship with the United States, there are many in Angola who – based in part on the history of U.S.–Angola relations – are suspicious of American policy" (xi). In the case of Russia, Alves, Arkhangelskaya and Shubin (2013) point out that "Immediately after President Boris Yeltsin took power the South in general, and Africa in particular, was abandoned as an important vector of Russian foreign policy in favour of the West …" (5). These scholars offer further explanations for China's dominance in Angola:

> Following the end of the civil war in 2002 Luanda's foreign policy rapidly became driven by the urge to deliver the country's much-needed reconstruction, economic growth and political stability. Drawing on the bridges built in the 1990s with developed countries, Angola looked first to them for help to kick-start the country's massive reconstruction programme. To Luanda's disappointment, these countries were somewhat reluctant to fund a resource-rich country that was assessed by many international agencies as among the most corrupt in the world. It was China, which at this stage ranked quite low in Angola's foreign policy, that offered Luanda a way out of its predicament and unexpectedly became Luanda's strategic partner for reconstruction.
>
> (Alves et al. 2013, 6)

Angola's ties with Russia, that were mainly grounded in military and economic interests dating back to the Cold War era, have recently been revisited. Presently, Angola is ranked the third leading importer of arms and ammunitions from Russia (The Conversation 2019). Furthermore, Russia's interest in Angola's diamond industry has been sustained through the De Beers's Central

Selling Organization that transformed into the Diamond Trading Company; more recently, Angola achieved a partnership with Ruis (Russia/Israel) with Lev Leviev's LLD Diamonds (Shor 2005, 205, 210). While Leviev's initiative led to the establishment of Angola's diamond marketing agency – the Angola Selling Corporation (ASCOPR) – in which he holds about a 25 percent stake in revenues from sales, it is Russia, through its mining company – Alrosa – that dominates this diamond trade by holding about 32.8 percent of Angola's Catoca Diamond Mines (Milo 2019). Since President Joao Lourenco assumed office, both countries have exchanged several visits geared toward rekindling their relationships.

Angola's transition to an economic powerhouse: Reforms and economic growth under José Eduardo dos Santos (2002–2017)

Following the death of Augustinho Neto in 1979, José Eduardo dos Santos became the President of Angola. He won the first election conducted in the country in September 1992 and the second one in August 2012 with a five-year tenure that ended in 2017 (see Gyimah 2018). During his reign, quite of number of reforms and growth initiatives were implemented, targeted at addressing the effects and challenges of the civil war as identified in the preceding sections.

Unlike most African states endowed with natural resources, the leadership of Angola leveraged its oil deposits to finance the country's reconstruction, growth and development. This set the country on the path of transitioning to an economic powerhouse from a war theater. The key driving factors responsible for the transformation have been:

1. It is a state-led initiative driven largely by state interventions in the areas of industrialization and investment promotion;
2. The instrumentality of the oil-backed loans propels government's actions;
3. The reforms and economic growth are outcomes and spill-over effects from the convergence of local elites and Chinese interests. In other words, these interests are inevitably tied to the successful implementation of the policies, programs and execution of projects;
4. The direct involvement of foreign partners in the execution of projects reduces the propensity for diversion of funds, resulting in their abandonment;
5. The centralization of policy formulation and decision-making at the top levels of government, through enacted decrees, gives the president a wide latitude of powers;
6. Diversification of the economy from oil and gas to other sectors; and
7. The infusion of local content policy in the industrialization drive of the country.

The Angolan government has invested in visible infrastructure through funds secured via loans backed with oil and from state government support programs that provide social services for both the short and long term (see Table 10.4). They include water, transportation, power supply, education and health care delivery. According to Ovadia (2018), "these projects must be understood as part of an overall effort to rebuild and develop the country, putting in place the necessary foundations for economic growth and social development" (596). Between 2002 and 2017, Angola made reasonable progress through diversification of its economy. The evidence based on its gross domestic product in the oil and other sectors shows that the country has recorded substantial level of economic growth, as shown in Table 10.2.

The global financial crisis of 2008 impacted oil prices (Gazel 2008). Since oil is Angola's major foreign exchange earner, this affected its growth, which accounts for the fluctuations between 2008 and 2015 shown in Table 10.2.

After the war, oil prices were still high; the country experienced quick recovery as a result of growth motivated by the increased sales and production of oil production. According to the IMF (2018), "Gross Domestic Product per capita climbed from US$711 in 2002 to US$4,804 in 2013 with government revenue skyrocketing in the same period. This also meant a rapid ascent for Angola within the World Bank's country classification system, from the level of low-income country to that of upper-middle-income country" (2). All of these initiatives were captured in the World Bank reports revealing that Angola had benefitted from certain reforms resulting from Presidential Decree 52/11 of 2011 on one stop for registration of property; the intervention on Law 8/11 of 2011, and Law 14/12 of 2012. These have been described as new laws on notaries and realtors. The essence of these laws was to liberalize certain areas of

Table 10.2 The growth in Angola's real gross domestic product 2002–2015 (%)

Year	*GDP Oil Growth*	*GDP Non-Oil Growth*
2002	15.5	3.1
2003	5.2	7.8
2004	10.9	9.2
2005	18.3	12.1
2006	20.7	27.6
2007	22.6	24.4
2008	13.8	15.0
2009	2.4	8.1
2010	3.4	7.6
2011	3.9	9.5
2012	5.2	5.5
2013	6.8	10.9
2014	4.8	8.2
2015	3.0	1.6

Source: Adapted from Ovadia (2018).

the market in terms of reduction of stamp duties from 0.5 percent to 0.3 percent, while tax on housing credit was reduced from 0.3 percent to 0.1 percent.

This overhauling also led to the reduction of land registry fees. These and other regulatory changes contributed to Angola's economic development (World Bank 2018; Frank 2018). Regarding land tenure, the Angolan government established land administration solely owned by the state called the EmpresaGastora de Terrenos Infra-estruturados (EGTI), on the basis of rationality and anchored in urbanization. The EGTI was expected to generate US$773million by 2020 through the sales of land in Luanda Province; also, EGTI was awarded the management of new land in Luanda as well as 20 other real estate developments in various parts of Angola (LUSA 2017; Paulo Cunha/ LUSA 2017).

Another aspect of growth is the Angola energy sector which has geometrically increased in production processes. Production increased from 830 MW in 2002 to 2,230 MW in 2014, which remains a little lower than some Southern African states like Mozambique at 2,682 MW, or Zambia with 2,452 MW, and especially South Africa with an estimated 46,963 MW. The Republic of Angola's Ministry of Energy and Water and United Nations Development Programme (2015) notes that these developments have impacted the generation capacity and production rate, with an estimated rate of 4,133 GWh as of 2008 that far exceeded that of 1999. Research institutions have projected an annual production rate of about 9,480 as of the 2014 index. (See Table 10.3.)

The indices reveal how Angola is becoming a powerhouse in Southern Africa, as it shows growth or increase in the country's power generation. When measuring the reliability of supply and transparency of tariffs index for getting electricity, the World Bank Energy Report set Angola's score at 42.63 in 2016 (World Bank 2016, 184). In 2019, Angola was ranked 156 globally as its access to electricity score increased to 54.1 (World Bank 2020).

Furthermore, through its industrialization drive anchored by the state oil company, Sonangol Industrial Investments, the country's manufacturing sector was activated, diversifying the economy from oil and gas to other sectors. Through this approach, over 17 indigenous factories producing food, beverages and building material were established (Sonangol 2012b). An important feature of Angola's industrialization policy is the infusion of the local content policy

Table 10.3 Figures on power generation between 2014 and 2017 (NDP targets)

	Year 1999–2002	*Year 2008*	*Year 2012*	*Year 2014*	*Year 2015*	*Year 2017*
Capacity installed (MW)	830**	1200	1917	2861	3561	7879
Electricity produced (GWh)	1295*	4133	7710	12618	17018	34346
Energy distributed (GWh)			6554	10725	14465	29194

Source: Pushak and Foster (2011).

Table 10.4 EximBank and state funded projects

EximBank Funded Projects		*State Funded Projects*	
Sectors	*No. of Projects*	*Ministry*	*No. of Projects*
Transport	4	Territorial Administration	7
Agriculture	4	Agriculture, Rural Development, and Fisheries	45
Social Communication	1	Social Assistance	15
Water and Energy	21	Social Communication	49
Education	60	Water and Energy	173
Public Works	9	Education	32
Telecoms & IT	5	Health	54
Fisheries	4	Transport	84
Health	23	Telecommunications and Information Technology	52
		Urbanism and Construction	342
Total	**138**	**Total**	**853**

Source: Adapted from Ovadia. (2018).

that was predicated upon the Production Sharing Agreements (PSAs) (Wolf 2017). These indigenous factories provide products and services to oil and gas companies. On the other hand, some of the international oil companies have diversified into manufacturing in partnership with Sonangol, generating further subsidiaries (Sonangol 2012a). These have generated over 6,000 jobs directly and indirectly (Faria 2012), leading to the building of local capacities (see Table 10.4).

In the light of this, Gorito (2015) argues that the country has recorded impressive economic progress. Angola has been identified as among the world's fasting growing economies, a rare feat given its civil war experience (Hanson 2008; Wiig and Kolstad 2012; World Bank 2019).

The era of Joao Lourenco

The August 23, 2017 election, in which the MPLA won the majority in the parliament, was the third in the country. This led to the election of Joao Lourenco as the country's president in September 2017 (see Gyimah 2018).

The inauguration of Lourenço as the president in 2017 ushered in new reforms towards building a strong economic base that could strengthen other sectors. The primary objective of the reforms was to initiate a better legal framework to facilitate business, free enterprise and competition.

> His ambitious agenda includes fighting corruption, eliminating nepotism, diversifying and opening up the economy, and promoting the private sector. While the new government had initially intended to continue major

> infrastructure projects, some of these were delayed or suspended as a result of budget cuts when the magnitude of the debt of over US$40 billion inherited from the previous regime became apparent.
>
> (Cain 2018, 65)

Between 2017 and 2020, Lourenco implemented some reforms for the country. On the political front, the government started with tackling corruption, which is unarguably the country's Achilles' heel. In this regard, hundreds of state-owned enterprises were slated for privatization and a new law on the government tender process was introduced. Furthermore, the heads of strategic institutions and establishments – such as Sonangol, Central Bank, Sovereign Wealth Fund – as well as the children of the immediate past president, were removed and, in some instances, charged with crimes. After the expiration of the grace period of six months given for looted funds from the state to be returned, the bank accounts traced to Isabel dos Santos, regarded as the richest woman in Africa, were frozen (Hardings 2020). In a relatively short period of time, over $5 billion of the country's looted assets was recovered (Africa Center for Strategic Studies 2020). The merger of two previous ministries, the "Ministry of Planning and Territorial Development" and the "Ministry of Economy" also became an important aspect of President Lourenço's reforms.

From the foregoing, it is clear that Angola, after 27 years of civil war, is on the path of developmental transformation in the region of Southern Africa, and Africa in general. As a report by Scheier (2014) on the China Global Television Network (CGTN), formerly known as CCTV-9 and CCTV News, attested, Angola has made tremendous progress over the past decade. The CGTN report revealed that China has been at the forefront of Angola's path to transformation and development, especially in the reconstruction and construction of roads, power and housing in exchange for the Angola's crude oil. The Angolan government has made investments in its mining industry to achieve some diversification of its economy. In view of this, during the past decade Angola has been in the spotlight for its development of sustainable energy, much of which has been in partnership with foreign powers. The Portuguese, US and the Chinese have been major partners with Angola in terms of infrastructural development. Angola, working with world powers, is achieving its 2025 strategy goal in industrialization which has been made possible through its low electricity tariff. As part of its plan towards an industrial revolution, the country needs to diversify in other areas such as the tourism sector. The matrix of industrialization is informed through the institutionalization of 160 structural projects that are classified into clusters designed within certain levels of growth comprising a 25 percent energy consumption rate (UNDP 2015).

Since these reforms have yet to fully impact the country and its citizens, they have been received with mixed reactions in some quarters, mostly on issues that center on questions of transparency, sincerity and sustainability (Fabricius 2019). Overall, irrespective of the level of economic growth and progress recorded in the 18-year post-war transformation in Angola, the country still faces crucial challenges as will be shown in the discussion that follows.

Challenges in Angola's transition to economic powerhouse

Angola has faced numerous challenges regarding the mismanagement of public funds which has slowed down the development of the country. In 2014, the price of crude oil fell which led to the failure to accomplish most of the infrastructural goals set by the government. Because of this, there was uncertainty over the next phase of the government's development program (2018–2022). The situation was worsened by the lack of prudent utilization of oil funds during the boom period, making policy-makers unable to carry out certain projects. This was rightly captured by Jensen (2018, 3), when he remarked that

> the use of public funds has lacked proper oversight; budget assumptions have been unrealistic; planning has overemphasized transportation at the expense of other areas of infrastructure; and financing has been pro-cyclical, with debt accumulating rapidly both before and after the onset of the economic crisis in 2014.

Furthermore, Pushak and Foster (2011) point out that the Africa Infrastructure Country Diagnostic (AICD) project led by World Bank in 2011, conducted a study on infrastructure development in Angola. The study found that the major challenge facing the country is paucity of infrastructure, and to address this, "a 'basic infrastructure platform' could be established by investing US$2.1 billion per year for a decade, with 70 percent of the overall amount required for capital investments and 30 per cent required for maintenance" (Pushak and Foster 2011, 12). In order to achieve this, the World Bank recommended that meeting Angola's infrastructure needs would entail spending in the region of 7 percent of GDP, compared with an average of 14.5 percent in sub-Saharan Africa as a whole. In addition to the foregoing, the AICD study warned that Angola's infrastructure investment strategy was skewed towards transportation projects. It also identified massive inefficiencies that have raised actual infrastructure spending to around US$4.3 billion per year, or around double the estimated amount needed. As pointed out, the actual spending since 2011 seems to have exceeded even these figures; according to the AICD study, Angola should have been able to satisfy its infrastructure needs both in terms of investments and maintenance, yet it could not do so.

The transformation of Angola that led to the country's economic growth has not been translated to its development. If the looted funds stashed away in foreign banks were reinvested in the country, it would contribute to improving the well-being of the people. The diversion of the country's wealth to offshore bank accounts has contributed to the widespread poverty and high level of unemployment in the country. While the poverty rate in 2020 was estimated at 41 percent (CGTN Africa 2020), the rate of unemployment in the country was 3.87 percent in 2002, but between 2011 and 2018 it fluctuated between 7.36 percent and 7.02 percent. In 2019, it stood at 6.89 percent (Macrotrends 2020). This shows that the reforms and transformation are yet to have a direct impact on the lives of Angolans.

The investments in infrastructure were not designed to redistribute wealth, or to create employment. They were a guise for personal enrichment, not a mechanism for the reduction of poverty and inequality. These investments were not only skewed, but agriculture, education and health did not receive adequate attention, especially, in the rural areas. Investing in these sectors would build capacities of young people and open up spaces for employment. In support of this framework, the interviewees quoted in Ovadia (2018) note that projects and programs executed and implemented were not targeted at the masses (591). Ovadia (2018, 593) captures this succinctly:

> More importantly, real concerns exist about how money is being spent, whether the state is getting good value for money, and whether wise investments are being made … (Q)uestions raised about schools without teachers, hospitals without staff and low-quality infrastructure projects deserve answers …

The plausible deduction from the above is that much of the investments in the country is not channelled to areas like education, capacity-building and agriculture that have the potential for multiplier effects such as job and wealth creation. As a result of this, Angola is grappling with inefficiency in the public sector and a dearth of skilled personnel in the health field, education and other sectors (Roque 2005; Gorito 2015). As the World Bank explains:

> Angola has made substantial economic and political progress since the end of the war in 2002. However, the country continues to face massive development challenges, which include reducing its dependency on oil and diversifying the economy; rebuilding its infrastructure; and improving institutional capacity, governance, public financial management systems, human development indicators, and the living conditions of the population.
>
> (World Bank 2019, 2)

Conclusion

Angola has made a commendable level of progress given the years of post-independence civil war, especially when compared with African countries that did not have similar experiences. The country has recorded appreciable level of economic growth in terms of its gross domestic product, which is primarily due to the exploitation of Angola's rich natural resources. Importantly, concerted efforts have been made to diversify the country's economic infrastructure that could further drive the country's transformation in the long run. The level of progress experienced in Angola within a relatively short period is based on the convergence of the interests of local elites and the Chinese government that were committed to the implementation of policies, programs and the execution of projects that brought about the transformation and economic growth of the country. Angola can continue its successful transition from a war theater to an economic powerhouse, if transparency, accountability, capacity-building, poverty and unemployment reduction are adequately factored into government policies going forward.

References

Africa Center for Strategic Studies. 2020. *The Challenges of Reform in Angola.* Washington, DC: Africa Center for Strategic Studies. Retrieved June 29, 2020 from https://africacenter.org/spotlight/the-challenges-of-reform-in-angola/.

Alves, A. C., Arkhangelskaya, A. and Shubin, V. 2013. *Russia and Angola: The Rebirth of a Strategic Partnership?* Occasional Paper No. 154, Global Power and Africa Programme. Johannesburg: South African Institute of International Affairs.

BBC News. 2018. "Angola Country Profile." Retrieved January 29, 2019 from www.bb.com/news/world-africa-13036732.

Cain, A. 2018. "Angola Housing Profile." *Africa Housing Finance Yearbook 2018.* www.academia.edu/38073760/Angola_Housing_Profile__Africa_Housing_Finance_Yearbook_2018 Accessed April 15, 2020.

CGTN Africa, 2020. "Angola Poverty Rate at 41%." Retrieved July 20, 2020 from https://africa. cgtn.com/2020/06/03/angola-poverty-rate-at-41/#:~:text=Angola's%20poverty%20rate% 20 stands%20at,Report%20for%20Angola%20on%20Tuesday.

Corkin. L. 2008. *AERC Scoping Exercise on China-Africa Relations: The Case of Angola.* Nairobi: African Economic Research Consortium (AERC). http://hdl.handle.net/10419/93159. Accessed April 15, 2020.

da Costa Cabral Andresen Guimaraes, F. J. 1992. "The Origins of the Angolan Civil War: International Politics and Domestic Political Conflict 1961–1976." Thesis submitted to the University of London in fulfilment of the requirements for the degree of Doctor of Philosophy in International Relations.

Fabricius, P. 2019. "Angola under Lourenco: More than Just a Promising Start?" Retrieved June 27, 2020 from www.africaportal.org/features/angola-under-louren%C3%A7o-more-just-promising-start/.

Faria, L. 2012. "Sonangol Invests Another USD 78 Million in Six New Factories in Luanda-Bengo EEZ." May 28. Retrieved from www.opais.net/pt/opais/?det=26949.

Frank, F. 2018. *Africa Report 2017/18.* https://content.knightfrank.com/research/155/documents/en/africa-repor. -201718–4576.pdf (Accessed September 2, 2018).

Gazel, R. 2008. "Angola: Perspectives on the Financial Crisis." Retrieved August 13, 2020 from https://blogs.worldbank.org/africacan/angola-perspectives-on-the-financial-crisis#.

Gorito, A. 2015. "What's the Future of Angola's Economy?" Retrieved July 13, 2020 from www.weforum.org/agenda/2015/05/whats-the-future-of-angolas-economy/.

Gyimah, A. 2018. "Flashback: The Implications of Angola's Civil War." Retrieved May 27, 2019 from www.mironline.ca/angola-civil-war-lourenco/.

Haas, R. N. 2007. "Foreword." In V. A. Mai, F. G. Wisner, W. L. Nash, and A. P. Frankel, *Toward an Angola Strategy: Prioritizing U.S.–Angola Relations.* New York: Council on Foreign Relations.

Hanson, S. 2008. "Angola's Political and Economic Development." Retrieved February 13, 2009 from www.cfr.org/backgrounder/angolas-political-and-economic-development.

Harding, A. 2020. "Angola's Joao Lourenco – the Man Taking on Isabel dos Santos." Retrieved August 11, 2020 from www.bbc.com/news/world-africa-51221737.

Heywood, L. 2011. "Angola and the Violent Years 1975–2008: Civilian Casualties." *Portuguese Studies Review*, 19(1–2, 311–332.

Hurst, R. 2009. "Angolan Civil War (1975–2002)." Retrieved April 8, 2010 from www.blackpast.org/global-african-history/angolan-civil-war-1975–2002/.

IMF. 2018. *World Economic Outlook Database*. Washington, DC: IMF. www.imf.org/external/pubs/ft/weo /2017/02/weodata/weorept.aspx?sy=2006&ey=2014&scsm=1&ssd=1&sort=country&ds=.&br=1&pr1.x=55&pr1.y=9&c=614&s=NGDP_RPCH&grp=0&a=(accessed 20 Feb. 2018).

Jensen, S. K. 2018. *Angola's Infrastructure Ambitions through Booms and Busts Policy, Governance and Reform*. Royal Institute of International Affairs, Africa Programme. London: Chatham House.

KPMG. 2015. Angola Banking Survey. London: KPMG. www.kpmg.com/PT/en/IssuesAndInsights/ Documents/bank-ao-2015-en.pdf.

Leao, A. 2007. Different *Opportunities, Different Outcomes – Civil War* and *Rebel Groups* in Angola and Mozambique. Discussion Paper 24. Bonn: German Development Institute.

LUSA. 2017. "Dívida pública angolana financia nova Empresa Gestora de Terrenos Infraestruturados." August 3. www.dn.pt/lusa/interior/divida-publica-angolana-financia-nova-empresa-gestora-de-terrenos-infraestruturados-8682554.html.

Macauhub. 2014. "Angola could Become a Mining Powerhouse in Africa." https://macauhub.com.mo/2015/04/13/angola-could-become-a-mining-powerhouse-in-africa/. Accessed May 2, 2020.

Macrotrends. 2020. "Angola Unemployment Rate 1991–2020." Retrieved July 25, 2020 from www.macrotrends.net/countries/AGO/angola/unemployment-rate#:~:text=Unemployment%20refers%20to%20the%20share,a%200.1%25%20decline%20from%202017.

Milestones. 2016. "The Angolan crisis 1974–75." Retrieved August 1, 2018 from https://history.state.gov/milestones/1969–1976/angola.

Milo, J. 2019. "Russia's Relationship with Angola in the Spotlight Again as Lavrov Visits Luanda." Retrieved August 11, 2020 from www.foreignbrief.com/daily-news/russias-relationship-with-angola-in-the-spotlight-again-as-lavrov-visits-luanda/.

Ojakorotu, V. 2015. *Curing the Affliction: From the "Oil Curse" to Sustainable Development in Africa's "Petro-States"*. Inaugural Lecture. Mafikeng Campus, South Africa: Office of the Vice-Rector (Academic) North-West University. Accessed April 3, 2019.

Ovadia, J. S. 2018. "State-Led Industrial Development, Structural Transformation and Elite-Led Plunder: Angola (2002–2013) as a Developmental State." *Development Policy Review*, 36, 587–606.

Paulo Cunha/LUSA. 2017. "'Imobiliária' do Estado angolanoquer vender 710 milhõesem terrenosem Luanda." http://observador.pt/2017/03/30/imobiliaria-do-estado-angolano-quer-vender-710-milhoes-em-terrenos-em-luanda/. Accessed August 19, 2018.

Pushak, N. and Foster, V. 2011. *Angola's Infrastructure: A Continental Perspective*. Washington, DC: World Bank. http://documents.worldbank.org/curated/en/2011/03/ 15198830/angolas-infrastructure-continental-perspective. Accessed February 9, 2018.

Republic of Angola, Ministry of Energy and Water and United Nations Development Programme. 2015. *Rapid Assessment and Gap Analysis Angola*. Luanda: Republic of

Angola, Ministry of Energy and Water. www.ao.undp.org/content/angola/en/home/library/environment_energy/publication_3/rapid-rapid-assessment-and-gap-analysis–angola-.html. Accessed February 9, 2018.

Roque, F. M. 2005. "Transformation for Post-Conflict Angola." In A. K. Fosu and P. Collier (Eds), *Post-Conflict Economies in Africa*. International Economic Association Series. London: Palgrave Macmillan.

Scheier, J. 2014. "China-Africa Ties: Angola Emerging as an African Powerhouse." African Bureau of China Global Television Network (CGTN) www.youtube.com/watch?v=Fo9K3tXwvY4. Accessed May 2, 2020.

Shor, R. 2005. "A Review of the Political and Economic Forces Shaping Today's Diamond Industry." *Gems and Gemology*, 41(3), 202–233.

Sonangol. 2012a. "SIIND Adds More Industrial Units at Viana." *Sonangol Universo*, 34, 42.

Sonangol. 2012b. "Luanda's embrace: The Bengo region. *Sonangol Universo*, 36, 22

Taylor, A. 2015. "A 27-Year Civil War, For No Reason at All." Retrieved September 11, 2020 from www.washingtonpost.com/news/worldviews/wp/2015/10/14/a-27-year-civil-war-for-no-reason-at-all/.

The Conversation. 2019. "Russia Steps up Efforts to Fill Gaps Left by America's Waning Interest in Africa." Retrieved August 11, 2020 from https://theconversation.com/russia-steps-up-efforts-to-fill-gaps-left-by-americas-waning-interest-in-africa-125945.

Thornton, J. K. n.d. "Angola." Retrieved December 8, 2017 from https://www.britannica.com/ place/ Angola/People.

UNDP. 2015. Rapid Assessment and Gap Analysis: ANGOLA. New York: UNDP. www.seforall.org/sites/ default/files/l/2015/05/Angola_RAGA.pdf. Accessed May 5, 2020.

Wiig, A. and Kolstad, I. 2012. "Opinion: Is Oil-Rich Angola a Development Success?" Retrieved October 13, 2017 from https://edition.cnn.com/2012/08/30/opinion/opinion-angola-development-elections/index.html.

Wolf, C. 2017. "Industrialization in Times of China: Domestic-Market Formation in Angola." *African Affairs*, 116, 435–461.

World Bank. 2016. Doing Business 2016. Washington, DC: World Bank, 184. www.doingbusiness.org/reports/global- reports/doing-business-2016.

World Bank. 2018. Angola: Systematic Country Diagnostic Creating Assets for the Poor. Washington, DC: World Bank. http://documents.worldbank.org/curated/en/337691552357946557/pdf/angola-scd-03072019-636877656084587895.pdf.

World Bank. 2019. "The World Bank in Angola." Retrieved January 13, 2020 from www.worldbank.org/en/country/angola/overview.

World Bank. 2020. *Doing Business, Getting Electricity*. Washington, DC: World Bank. www.doingbusiness.org/en/data/exploretopics/getting-electricity, accessed January 12, 2021.

World Peace Foundation. 2015. "Angola: Civil War." Retrieved November 17, 2016 from https:// sites.tufts.edu/atrocityendings/2015/08/07/angola-civil-war/.

Ziemke, J. 2008. "From Battles to Massacres." Paper prepared for the 3rd annual Harvard-Yale-MIT Graduate Student Conference on Order, Conflict and Violence, Yale University, April 18–19.

11 Capitalism and Africa's (infra)structural dependency

A story of spatial fixes and accumulation by dispossession

Tim Zajontz and Ian Taylor

Introduction

Infrastructure, both physical and social, has been a key facilitator for the exploitation of Africa by external actors. Slave ports and forts were the initial marker signifying the transformation of African bodies into commodities, laying the foundations for trans-regional colonial economies built upon and sustained by primitive accumulation and "racial capitalism" (see Robinson 2000). Later, as colonial rule tightened its grip, railways were central to entrenching colonial conquest and the appropriation of African lands, resources and labor (see Nkrumah 1965; Rodney 2015[1972]), as well as embedding the continent in a dependent position in the global capitalist economy. "Soft" infrastructure, most notably colonial education systems, ingrained racist ideologies, degraded exterminated indigenous cultures and values and normalized white domination (see Fanon 1967).

As Cowen (2017, n.d.) has emphasized, "[i]nfrastructures reach across time, building uneven relations of the past into the future, cementing their persistence." Since independence, new infrastructure in the form of dams, power grids, urban structures, roads and railways were seen by post-colonial elites as being integral to "modernization" and symbols of progress. This view was encouraged by the World Bank, Western donors and private corporations, which dominated Africa's infrastructure sector in the immediate post-independence era (Wethal 2019). A lack of financial and technological capacities in most African states meant that it was primarily the West (often the former colonial powers) who were providing the advice and funding for infrastructure.

According to Gibbon (1995), it was not coincidental that the World Bank's focus on infrastructure and "modernization" necessitated large exports of capital in the form of aid, loans and investment. Gibbon designates this a capital-export model, and maintains that its rise privileged Northern interests, namely, commercial lenders with surplus capital who viewed World Bank lending as providing an accommodating framework (constructing infrastructure, promoting industrialization, etc.) for the utilization of their own capital loans. Northern manufacturing interests saw in Africa a potential market for their intermediate goods, particularly when recession in the home markets lowered demand, and political strategists saw "development" as a crucial means to oppose the spread of communism. The initial post-independence infrastructure boom ended with the sovereign debt crises that unfolded in the 1970s. For two decades onwards, infrastructure development was relegated to a niche existence in development cooperation as public goods went out of fashion due to the neoliberal counter-revolution. Structural adjustment policies subsequently slashed the role of the state as a "grand developer" and entrusted the infrastructural domain to the private sector. The result was an overall decline in infrastructure maintenance and investment (Wethal 2019).

Since the 2000s, Africa has seen a renaissance of the "development-through-infrastructure" agenda. As Nugent (2018) pointedly puts it: "If economic development has become a kind of modern religion, infrastructural investment is once again its most potent fetish" (22). Whilst the composition of foreign actors in Africa's infrastructure sector has diversified, with emerging powers, most notably China, having joined the scramble for Africa's infrastructure markets, the structural ramifications under which Africa's current infrastructure boom unfolds have by and large remained unaltered. It is yet again driven by foreign capital, in alliance with African political elites and infrastructure planners who are intrigued by the politically capitalizable "hypermodern appearance" (Kimari and Ernstson 2020, 836) of new railway lines, highways and roll-on-roll-off ports as well as by promises of "infrastructure-led development" (Schindler and Kanai 2019, 1). In a recent study on Kenya's new Standard Gauge Railway, Kimari and Ernston (2020) convincingly argue that the new boom has sustained racial capitalism through a combination of "imperial remains" and "invitations."

Instead of expediting "Africa's transformation," as suggested by the Programme for Infrastructure Development in Africa (PIDA) of the African Union (AU) (PIDA, n.d.), we argue that the recent upsurge in infrastructure development has reinforced the continent's dependency on external actors and fosters patterns of accumulation by dispossession. We do so with the help of David Harvey's theory of spatio-temporal fixes and the key functions it attributes to infrastructure and debt in the global system of capital accumulation. The chapter proceeds in four stages. We first briefly recount Harvey's concepts of the spatio-temporal fix and accumulation by dispossession. In a second step, we contextualize Africa's recent infrastructure boom and situate it against the wider saga of "Africa rising." The third part of the chapter scrutinizes China's rise as the continent's new "infrastructure giant" and problematizes particularities of the "Chinese infrastructural fix" in Africa. The chapter then concludes by extrapolating some trends that we believe will become increasingly relevant in Africa's infrastructure sector and that underline the enduring function of infrastructure as "means of dispossession" (Cowen 2017).

Overaccumulation and the spatio-temporal fix

In a series of publications, most importantly *The Limits to Capital*, David Harvey (1982) developed what he calls an "exegesis and extension of Marx's political economy onto the terrain of geography" (2004a, 544; see 1982). Harvey bestows a central role on infrastructure in the temporary mitigation of capitalist crises. In this section, we recount his concepts of the spatio-temporal fix and accumulation by dispossession, as they bear explanatory power for Africa's contemporary infrastructure boom.

Capitalism and its temporary "fix"

Harvey (1982) advances the idea that capital incessantly reverts to the production, destruction and reorganization of space in order to counter its endemic vulnerability to crisis. Building on Marx's law of value and the falling rate of profit, he derives a "pervasive tendency of capitalism to produce crises of overaccumulation" (2003, 108; see 2004b; 1982, chaps. 6, 7). Harvey suggests that overaccumulation crises within a given territory can be temporarily averted by what he calls the "spatio-temporal fix" (2003, 115). The concept has a double meaning for Harvey: a literal one and a metaphorical one. The former implies that a share of the total capital is "literally fixed in and on the land for a relatively long period of time (depending on its economic and physical lifetime)" (Harvey 2003, 115). The fundamental logic and impetus of capitalism and capital is the amassing of profits: the "boundless drive for enrichment" and the "passionate chase after value" (Marx 1976 [1867], 254). It is this "dynamic of endless accumulation" and the quest for "accumulation for its own sake" (Brenner 2006, 80) that implies a constant drive to overcome spatial barriers (Harvey 2001, 243–247; Arrighi 2005, 35–36). Marx famously argues:

> [W]hile capital must on one side strive to tear down every spatial barrier to intercourse, i.e. to exchange, and conquer the whole earth for its market, it strives on the other hand to annihilate this space with time, i.e. to reduce to a minimum the time spent in motion from one place to another.
>
> (1973[1939–1941], 539)

As spatial barriers delay and diminish the realization of profits, infrastructural facilities aim at reducing the circulation time between places of production and places of consumption (Sheppard 2004, 472).[1] As Marx notes, the costs of circulation "can be reduced by improved, cheaper and more rapid transportation" (1967, vol. 2, 142)

The literal meaning of the "fix" underscores the dependence of capital accumulation on particular spatial structures which are comprised of capital embedded in the landscape, and allows for the circulation of other physically mobile capitals in search of maximum surplus (Arrighi 2005, 35; Jessop 2006, 147). Examples include transport, communication and other physical infrastructures (Harvey 2003, 115; see 2004b; Arrighi 2005). As Harvey puts it, "[f]luid movement *over* space can be achieved only by fixing certain physical infrastructure *in* space" (2003, 99; original italics). However, the incessant tendency to reduce spatial barriers by "fixing" certain capital in the landscape "unwittingly undermin[es] the monopolistic privileges attached to specific locations through the intensification of competition across geographical space" (Arrighi 2005, 36). The necessary result is overproduction and overaccumulation, i.e., capital and/or labor can no longer be invested within a particular territory at the average rate of profit or, worse, at no profit at all (Jessop 2006, 149). Commodities pile up, as they lack profitable markets, while productive capital lies idle and finance capital is deficient of investment goods (Arrighi 2005, 36; Harvey 2003, 109). This brings us to the second meaning of the spatio-temporal fix, as overaccumulated capital which cannot be reinvested profitably (enough) within a given territory, or can be absorbed through "temporal" or "spatial displacements" or a combination of the two (Harvey 2003, 109).

The metaphorical meaning stands for "a particular solution to capitalist crises through temporal deferral and geographical expansion" (Harvey 2003, 115). Harvey employs the terms "temporal displacement" and "temporal deferral" as well as "spatial displacement" and "geographical expansion" interchangeably. The concepts refer to two analytically distinct, yet empirically oftentimes intricately interrelated, "moments" of the spatio-temporal fix. First, temporal displacement ties up surplus capital in long-term, geographically "fixed," capital projects ("secondary circuit" of capital) or long-term investments in social infrastructures ("tertiary circuit"), thereby deferring its re-entry into the "primary circuit" of capital, namely, the one of immediate production and consumption (Jessop 2006, 147–148; Harvey 2003, 109–110; Castree 2009, 47). Second, spatial displacement refers to the utilization of surplus capital by extending the spatial reach of an existing system of accumulation. This implies tapping into new markets, new production capacities or new sources of commodities, including labor (Harvey 2003, 109). The two "moments" of the spatio-temporal fix are usually interdependent. Temporal deferral constitutes the production and reorganization of space that is necessary for opening up new markets for consumption (of surplus commodities) and investment (for surplus finance and productive capital).

Debt finance and accumulation by dispossession

> [T]he question perpetually hovers: what happens when, for whatever reason, the "spatial fix" is stymied and the debts incurred by temporal displacement fall due?
>
> (Harvey 2001, 338)

In *The New Imperialism*, Harvey expands his conceptual repertoire by the notion of accumulation by dispossession, which he considers a central aspect of the "new" imperialism. The concept is a terminological modernization of Marx's notion of "primitive" or "original accumulation," as Harvey argues for a "general re-evaluation of … the latter's continuous role and persistence" (2003, 144; see 2004b; Perelman 2000; Ashman and Callinicos 2006). Marx considered "primitive accumulation" an historical prerequisite for capitalist accumulation, describing it as the "process which takes away from the labourer the possession of his means of production; a process that transforms, on the one hand, the social mean of subsistence and of production into capital, on the other, the immediate producers into wage-labourers." For Marx, primitive accumulation formed the "pre-historic stage of capital," which set the conditions for capital accumulation under expanded reproduction (2013[1867], 502). As Amin explains, "[t]he characteristic feature of primitive accumulation, in contrast to normal expanded reproduction, is unequal exchange, that is, the exchange of products whose prices of production, in the Marxist sense, are unequal" (1976, 187; see Bieler and Morton 2014).

Harvey posits that the predatory practice of dispossession is not historically confined to the transition from pre-capitalist to capitalist societies but a *continual* aspect of advanced capitalisms (2003, 144; see Shivji 2017). This follows Luxemburg who suggested that the "historical career of capitalism" is characterized by an "organic link" between surplus creation by means of commodity-based exchange of equivalents between the capitalist and the wage laborer, i.e., expanded reproduction, and predatory practices that are aimed at bringing non-capitalist modes of production under the logic of capitalist accumulation, or primitive accumulation in Marx's terminology (Luxemburg 2003[1913], 433; see Shivji 2009, 34)

Accumulation by dispossession takes on many guises and Harvey describes its modus operandi as "both contingent and haphazard" (2003, 149; see 2004a). Harvey lists, amongst others, the commodification and privatization of land and related expulsions of peasant populations, the conversion of communal or public into exclusive private property rights, the restraint of access to commons or the privatization of the same and "colonial, neo-colonial, and imperial processes of appropriation of assets (including natural resources)" (2003, 145; see Levien 2018, 16). In cases of accumulation by dispossession, "resources are expropriated once and for all from a 'commons' that has been built up over many years and/or where the rate of economic exploitation of a given resource exceeds its natural rate of renewal or the absorptive capacity of the environment" (Jessop 2006, 151). Gaining access to natural resources allows for particularly "rapid surplus production" (Harvey 2006, 91).

Infrastructure boom – for whom?

With the rise of modernist development projects since the 1950s, large-scale infrastructure projects became semiotic and material instruments to secure Western economic and political interests on the continent (Nugent 2018; Wethal 2019). Newly independent African states remained largely reliant on foreign capital and technology for embarking on the purported "development-through-infrastructure" trajectory. Infrastructure financing amounted to 60 percent of development aid to Sub-Saharan Africa (SSA) by 1973, while most contracts were awarded to European, North American or Japanese firms. Due in part to this extensive infrastructure lending, SSA's debt stock grew exponentially, from $7bn in 1970 (debt-to-GDP ratio of 11 percent), to $61bn in 1980 (22 percent) and $176bn in 1990 (58 percent) (Wethal 2019, 479–80).

Africa's first post-independence infrastructure boom faded in the late 1970s after many large-scale infrastructure projects failed to yield expected spill-over effects into productive sectors and suffered from decay (Nugent 2018, 22; Wethal 2019, 480–481). The global economic decline of the 1970s and the looming Washington consensus heralded a paradigm shift within development thinking and practice. The failure of infrastructure-led development was considered an epiphenomenon of poor governance and institutional inefficiencies related to state-steered development (Berg 1981). Henceforth, infrastructure was sidelined in development policies and budgets, while efforts were concentrated on slimming African states, ensuring conducive regulatory environments for foreign investment and private-sector development (Wethal 2019, 481).

Africa's "infrastructural renaissance"

After two decades of structural adjustment, large-scale infrastructure has experienced a political renaissance in Africa since the early 2000s. Against the background of the broader "Africa rising" story about the continent's sheer limitless economic potential (see Taylor 2014; 2020a), orthodox development economists, multilateral and bilateral donors, private investors and African governments have *unisono* invoked that GDP growth requires sound economic infrastructure (Wethal 2019, 482–483; see Sachs et al. 2004; Collier 2006). According to the World Bank, a "Time for Transformation" in Africa's infrastructure has now arrived (Foster and Briceño-Garmendia 2010). Nugent aptly notes:

> When it comes to Africa, the capacity of international organizations to champion that which they previously disavowed is nothing less than remarkable. At the present time, all the principle actors – African governments, corporate investors and the international agencies themselves – are fixated upon the transformative potentialities of infrastructure, by which they mostly mean "big infrastructure".
>
> (2018, 22)

Infrastructure is portrayed as the "magic bullet" in hegemonic development discourses (Wethal 2019, 474). It is expected that "development" will emerge and Africa's underdevelopment vanish through integrating the continent into global markets by boosting intra- and inter-regional trade, raising productivity and competitiveness, lowering transaction and transport costs and, ultimately, by boosting growth. A World Bank report on the key challenges to African growth identified four areas "in which action is needed to accelerate growth": the investment climate by "reducing indirect costs to firms (which are generally infrastructure related)"; infrastructure by "mainly targeting transactions costs in the production of goods and services"; innovation by "primarily emphasizing investment in information technology and skill formation (higher education)," i.e., social infrastructure; and institutional capacity, which is equally highly dependent on social and physical infrastructures (Ndulu et al. 2007, xix–xx). The "magic bullet" has been omnipresent, whereas issues related to the structural position of Africa within the global economy are usually ignored.

Continental, regional and national development strategies were realigned accordingly, with the Africa-initiated New Partnership for Africa's Development (NEPAD) envisioning "a new division of labour in which the private sector will be the veritable engine of economic growth, while governments concentrate on the development of infrastructure and the creation of a macroeconomic environment" (African Union 2001, para. 23). More recently, the African Union's Agenda 2063 stipulates as one of its declared goals to "[c]onnect Africa with world-class infrastructure" (African Union 2015), while the Program Infrastructure Development (PIDA) for Africa (a joint initiative of the AU, NEPAD and the African Development Bank) aims at "link[ing] the major production and consumption centers, provide connectivity among the major cities, corridor modernisation, define the best hub ports, railway routes and air transport systems and open the land-locked countries to improved regional and continental trade" (African Union 2017).

Discursively, Africa's most recent infrastructure boom has perpetuated racialized representations of Africa as "not capable" of unlocking its endless economic (read capitalist) potential as a result of infrastructural backwardness (Kimari and Ernstson 2020, 831). PIDA, for instance, proclaims that

> Africa commands a powerful position on the world stage. It is seen as a land of opportunity – an emerging destination of choice for many investors and development actors as they look for high-growth markets, despite the ongoing economic turmoil and the lingering effects of the financial crisis and recession. In this rapidly changing global environment, Africa needs to seize the initiative and take advantage of these emerging conditions that will substantially boost trade, spark growth and create jobs. But right now, it is not capable of seizing the initiative or reaping the full benefits of its resources. A major problem: infrastructure. The solution: PIDA.
>
> (PIDA 2012, 1)

Interestingly, this is a theme that was enunciated by then Senegalese president, Abdoulaye Wade, when he launched his pre-NEPAD "Omega Plan" for Africa at the World Economic Forum in Davos on 30 January 2001. The Plan involved obtaining repayable treasury bonds from the North to finance what was essentially a pan-continental infrastructure scheme which, Wade readily admitted and advertised, would advantage Western contractors and businesses. As Wade asserted,

> I will show how the West will benefit. To carry out all this infrastructure work we will need foreign and European firms, which are technically

> more advanced than ours and which can build roads much faster than we could do.... So two-thirds of the resources I'm talking about would go to Western companies to carry out the work.
>
> (Quoted in Quist-Arcto 2001)

Ultimately, "modern" infrastructure is portrayed as the necessary prime mover for the continent's "rise." The "Africa rising" narrative of the past two decades is intricately interlinked with the continent's purported infrastructural "revolution," with images of new railroads, highways and dams signaling Africa's arrival in hyper-modernity. Thus in 2013, Ellen Johnson Sirleaf, then-President of Liberia, stated that "[i]n ten years [a] rapidly transforming Africa will move into the industrial age" (*New African*, May 2013: 41).

Without doubt, Africa's hard infrastructure lags behind in regional comparisons (see Table 11.1), which has hampered Africa's economic diversification and industrialization. Given that there is a correlation "between infrastructure and export diversification, and [that] the current low levels and distorted composition of exports from SSA [Sub-Saharan Africa] are partly due to poor trade infrastructure," it can be stated that the improvement in infrastructure "has per se a positive impact on SSA growth and trade capacity" (Sindzingre 2013, 44). However, as we have established at length elsewhere (see Taylor 2020a; 2015), GDP growth does not necessarily translate into structural transformation of African economies. This is particularly so when the infrastructure that is being laid down is targeted at extractive industries and/or outward-looking economic activities, developed by foreign capital. Given that unequal exchange is at the core of trade between Africa and the external world, basing the continent's developmental future on accelerating foreign trade via massive foreign-funded infrastructure projects seems rather odd. Besides, the dynamics of the incurred debt to foreign creditors no doubt will mean that a substantial portion of any capital generated by the new improved roads and ports will, in the first instance, have to go to servicing this very same debt.

(Infra)structural dependency and "financial extraction"

Africa's construction and infrastructure sectors have remained dominated by foreign firms (Wethal 2019; Mold 2012). A Deloitte study which surveyed 286 construction projects[2] that had broken ground by June 1, 2016, and were valued at $50m or above, found that only 26.6 percent of the projects were built by private domestic companies. About three-quarters of the construction projects were implemented by foreign firms, with China (22.4 percent) leading the stats, followed by Italy (6.3), France (4.9), Portugal (3.5) and South Africa (3.5) (Deloitte 2016, 10). The reasons offered for the weakness of local firms ranged from limited access to finance and credit to a lack of technical capacity and equipment – and cannot be discussed in detail here (see Wethal 2019; Burke 2007). What is obvious, however, is that the foreign dominance of the infrastructure sector has been sustained by foreign-centered value and supply chains

Table 11.1 Access to infrastructure in regional comparison

Indicator	*Africa*	*Asia*	*Europe*	*Latin America*
Transport				
Paved road density (km of paved road per 100km² of land area)	2	25	122	3
Railway lines (km)	46,380	197,610	85,986	89,002
Power				
Electricity production per capita (kWh)	572	1,930	3,355	2,116
Electricity access (% of total population)	46	88	100	97
Water supply and sanitation				
Improved water (% of total population)	69	90	99	94
Improved sanitation (% of total population)	39	61	93	82

Source: Adaption from AfDB (2018, 76), data of 2013.

with limited local links as well as by tied aid. Wethal (2019) finds that "Sub-Saharan Africa is the only region in the developing world where the dominance of domestic regional firms decreased in infrastructure projects financed by international financing institutions between 1995 and 2013" (486).

Equally, Africa remains heavily dependent on foreign finance capital and the credit industry for infrastructural endeavors. As a result, the infrastructure–aid nexus has ensured that financial capital flows back to its origins. Kwame Nkrumah's assessment, dating back to the period of the first post-independence infrastructure boom, still applies to the current boom: "Before the decline of colonialism what today is known as aid was simply foreign investment" (1965, 51). Flanked by mantra-like invocations of Africa's "infrastructure investment gap," the global aid regime shifted development finance towards infrastructure in the 2000s. Infrastructure financing tripled between 2004 and 2012 (Wethal 2019, 481). The 2005 G-8 Summit at Gleneagles established the Infrastructure Consortium for Africa (ICA) which was tasked to "encourage[s], support[s] and promote[s] increased investment in infrastructure in Africa, from both the public and private sectors" (ICA n.d.). Besides the G-8 countries, the ICA brings together the World Bank, the United Nations Economic Commission for Africa, NEPAD, the African Development Bank (AfDB), the continent's regional development banks, the AU and EU commissions, the European Investment Bank, the Islamic Development Bank and the Republic of South Africa. ICA members contribute about a fifth of Africa's total infrastructure financing (see Table 11.2). Some 70.8 percent of the funds come in the form of loans, while only 11.9 percent are grants; the remaining shares are for blended funds (6.6 percent), guarantees (4.3), equity investment (1.1) and other funding types (5.3) (ICA 2018, 33).

Table 11.2 Funding for African infrastructure by source (in $ million)

	2015	*2016*	*2017*	*2018*
ICA members*	**19,832**	**18,615**	**19,650**	**20,243**
France	2,445	2,887	2,123	1,936
Germany	1,139	1,127	838	1,608
Japan	1,768	1,941	2,361	517
US	307		292	297
South Africa	929	1,211	497	1,055
AfDB	4,166	3,956	3,364	4,538
European Investment Bank	1,414	1,250	1,852	2,225
World Bank	6,285	4,055	7,516	7,989
Other ICA members	1,379	2,188	807	78
Non-ICA members	**51,687**	**45,766**	**59,592**	**68,736**
African governments	24,000	30,700	34,345	37,525
China	20,868	6,413	19,403	25,680
India	524	1,197	704	762
South Korea	88	432	10	
Non-ICA European bilaterals	238	287	277	282
African regional development banks	419	924	541	328
Arab Coordination Group**	4,412	5,528	2,985	2,442
European Bank for Reconstruction & Development	638	105	1,327	744
New Development Bank		180		500
Other non-ICA bilaterals/ multilaterals	500			473
Private Sector	**7,400**	**2,600**	**2,320**	**11,824**
TOTAL Financing	**78,919**	**66,981**	**81,562**	**100,803**

Source: Adapted from ICA (2018, 8).

Notes: * Membership: G8 members (Canada, France, Germany, Italy, Japan, Russia, United Kingdom, USA), South Africa, the World Bank, International Finance Corporation (IFC), European Commission (EC), European Investment Bank (EIB), Islamic Development Bank (IsDB), African Development Bank (AfDB), Development Bank of Southern Africa (DBSA).
** Membership: Kuwait Fund for Arab Economic Development (KFAED), Saudi Fund for Development (SFD), Abu Dhabi Fund for Development (ADFD), Qatar Development Fund (QDF), Arab Fund for Economic and Social Development (AFESD), Islamic Development Bank (IsDB), OPEC Fund for International Development (OFID), Arab Bank for Economic Development in Africa (BADEA), Arab Gulf Program for United Nations Development Organizations (AGFUND), Arab Monetary Fund (AMF).

The Western-dominated club of traditional donors has been joined by emerging powers that have become increasingly involved in Africa's infrastructure sector (see Taylor 2014; Anthony and Ruppert 2020). As Rampa and colleagues (2012) note, "[i]t is clear that [emerging economies'] growing presence on the continent brings trade, massive investment in infrastructure and resources development. Politically it helps Africa become more assertive in the world and increases development aid and technical assistance" (248). Notwithstanding a temporary decline in the aftermath of the 2007–2008 global financial crisis, investment in Africa's infrastructure sectors has been continuously growing, not least as a result of China's rise as the continent's "infrastructure giant." According to ICA figures, infrastructure finance totalled $100.8bn in 2018, with $37.5bn thereof emanating from African government coffers. As Table 11.2 depicts, China has become by far Africa's largest bilateral infrastructure financier, contributing about a fourth of the continent's infrastructure finance in 2018 (ICA 2018, 4; see also Sun et al. 2017, 20; Edinger and Labuschagne 2019). Despite a new all-time record in infrastructure finance in 2018, the African Development Bank (AfDB) estimates Africa's infrastructure "needs" at least $130–170bn per annum and suggests a yearly infrastructure financing gap of $68–108bn (AfDB 2018, 63; World Bank 2017; see Prinsloo 2019, 2).

To fill the gap, private investments have been considered crucial to complement strained public budgets and loan-grant financing by multi- and bilateral donors. The AfDB urges "Africa … to attract private capital to accelerate the building of critical infrastructure needed to unleash its potential," cautioning that "Africa's legal, regulatory, and institutional frameworks are major constraints to attracting private capital to infrastructure" (2018, 64, 76). In 2013, the Bank launched the Africa50 Infrastructure Fund to institutionally streamline equity investment into African infrastructure (Wethal 2019, 483). As stated on its website,

> Africa50 mobilizes funds not only from African states and international financial institutions, but also from institutional investors such as pension and sovereign wealth funds, insurance companies and other private sector entities. It operates as a commercial financial institution, seeking to provide an attractive return to investors.
>
> (Africa50 n.d.)

The World Bank has actively promoted public–private partnerships to share the "burden" of infrastructure finance (Nugent 2018, 26; see World Bank 2014; Wethal 2019, 488). The strategic "outsourcing" of onerous infrastructure funding has found entry into national development plans and legislation across the continent. Zambia's PPP Act of 2009, for instance, intends

> to promote and facilitate the implementation of privately financed infrastructure projects and effective delivery of social services by enhancing transparency, fairness and long term sustainability and removing undesirable restrictions on private sector participation in the provision of social sector services and the development and operation of public infrastructure.
>
> (GRZ 2009, 79)

PPP models that involve project finance can be seen as "an accounting trick, a way round the government's own constraints on public borrowing. This remains the overwhelming attraction for governments and international institutions" (Hall 2015, 7). Yet, in his study aptly headlined *Licenced Larceny*, Hildyard (2016) shows that PPPs are a lucrative means for "financial extraction." In 2014, annual returns of toll roads in developing countries ranged between 8 and 26 percent (Hildyard 2016, 48–49). Hildyard (2016) further emphasizes that "such extraction is not just normalized but encouraged, even at the expense of some of the poorest people in the world" (32). Generally secured by an entire series of state-backed guarantees, PPPs as a governance modality have transformed infrastructure into an "asset class capable of providing yield-hungry investors with the returns that they seek" (Hildyard 2016, 31). Foreign involvement in Africa's infrastructure sector remains key to advance along the "final frontier" of global capitalism (Kimari and Ernstson 2020, 837). This becomes apparent when we look closer at the "convenient conjuncture" of Africa's incessantly invoked "infrastructure gap" and China's contemporary spatio-temporal fix.

China's rise as Africa's "infrastructure giant"

Sino-African cooperation in the infrastructure sector has been discursively framed as the new driver of economic development that yields "mutual benefits" and "win-win results." Further fostered by Africa's gradual inclusion into China's Belt and Road Initiative (BRI) (see Taylor and Zajontz 2020), Chinese state-owned enterprises (SOEs), policy banks and private corporations have become increasingly involved in the financing, construction, rehabilitation and, in some cases, operation of African ports, railways, highways, airports, pipelines, power plants and information technology networks.

"Moving out" concrete, rails and technology

China's growing investment in African infrastructure (and other sectors, of course) is largely driven by an overaccumulation crisis within the Chinese economy. China's second "going out" phase has arguably constituted one of the most significant developments in the contemporary (spatial) reorganization of global capitalism (Ayers 2013). Chinese efforts to geographically relocate overcapacities within and beyond its borders has been a reaction to mounting overaccumulation within the Chinese economy in the wake of global financial and economic crises. Slumping exports, bankruptcies, growing unemployment, social unrest and deteriorating values of foreign exchange reserves challenged China's growth model and the "performance legitimacy" of the Communist Party (Sum 2019, 530–531; see Zhang 2017; Lee 2014; Cai 2018). Sum (2019) describes how early post-crisis stimulus packages, which allowed for vast investments in real estate and infrastructure within China, resulted in "ripple bubbles" in property markets, the infrastructure and construction sectors and the finance and credit industry (531–532). Premier Li's later attempts to inject liquidity and lower public debt by issuing sovereign bonds and publicly listing SOEs, a policy that was termed "Likonomics," proved unsustainable for boosting domestic demand, as it further aggravated overcapacities and financial instability through stock market bubbles (Sum 2019, 532). Since then, under President Xi's tight control, the Chinese government has embarked on a major transformation of the Chinese accumulation system, both discursively and materially. The "New Normal" narrative promises "slower but higher quality growth" (Sum 2019, 533).

In 2013, the Chinese government launched the Belt and Road Initiative (BRI), which has been characterized as a "China-oriented infrastructural mode of growth in production, finance and security" (Sum 2019, 529; see Li 2016). This was to be achieved by moving overcapacities abroad by a combination of spatially expanding the Chinese accumulation system and "recycling" capital that lacked profitable outlets within existing capital circuits (Zhang 2017, 322; see Summers 2016). The BRI is a continuation – or rather intensification – of Beijing's *zouchuqu zhanlue* ("Go Global" strategy) whereby state entreprises are encouraged to invest overseas, set up operations in other countries and seek economic cooperation with foreign partners (Taylor and Zajontz, 2020). It is worth citing China's former Deputy Foreign Minister, He Yafei, at some length, as he aptly depicts the rationale behind China's current geo-economic strategy:

> The excess capacity has been caused by China's fundamental economic readjustments against the global economy. With the ensuing knock-on effects of the global financial crisis manifesting in the economic stagnation of advanced nations, coupled with the slowdown in China's domestic demand, industrial overcapacity, accumulated over several decades, has been brought into sharp relief ... This has resulted in a steep drop in profits, the accumulation of debt and near bankruptcy for many companies. If left unchecked, it could lead to bad loans piling up for banks, harming the ecosystem, and bankruptcy for whole sectors of industries that would, in turn, affect the transformation of the [Chinese] growth model and the improvement of people's livelihoods. It could even destabilise society. The Chinese government ... has put forward guidelines for its resolution. The most important thing is to turn the challenge into an opportunity by "moving out" this overcapacity on the basis of its development strategy abroad and foreign policy.
>
> (He 2014)

China's construction and infrastructure sectors had been particularly affected by dwindling domestic demand in the aftermath of the global economic crisis, leaving the country's gigantic state-owned construction conglomerates short of projects and suppliers with oversupplies of construction materials. According to one source, overcapacities in some industries, notably steel, iron, aluminum, glass, cement and power generation, exceeded 30 percent in the early 2010s, as returns in the domestic infrastructure market turned negative and many SOEs faced major profitability crises (Jones and Zeng 2019, 1422).

"Deferring" surplus finance capital in African infrastructure

In line with Harvey's (2003) conceptualization of the "fix," the "moving out" of overcapacities in the identified sectors has been strongly facilitated by China's financial institutions. The latter had been piling up foreign exchange reserves to more than $3 trillion, whilst the post-crisis environment continuously deprived them of secure lending opportunities within China (Jones and Zeng 2019, 1422). Hence, the Chinese move into foreign infrastructure markets is fueled by "another round of stimulus package based on loan-debt investment" – this time on a global scale (Sum 2019, 539; see Alden and Large 2019, 338). To boost demand for Chinese infrastructure firms, the Chinese government has drawn on a host of financial instruments, such as the extensive disbursement of concessional and commercial loans from state-owned banks (SOBs), sovereign guarantees and insurance schemes for both state-owned and private companies that invest abroad, as well as the promotion of equity investment in infrastructure projects (Sum 2019; Lee 2014; Alden and Jiang 2019). As former Deputy Foreign Minister He explains, China's SOBs were instructed to "smooth the transfer of overcapacity overseas." Consequently,

> [t]he China Banking Regulatory Commission has issued directives for Chinese banks to assist in addressing overcapacity in a number of ways, including by expanding green credit, supporting efficient expansion of demand, and supporting the "go out" strategy and overseas M&As [mergers and acquisitions]. Banks have been asked to provide such companies with domestic insurance and overseas credit, more credit both in renminbi and foreign exchange, trade finance and international insurance, as appropriate, thus also facilitating the export of Chinese equipment, products and services, together with Chinese standards.
>
> (He 2014)

Moreover, new financial institutions, such as the Silk Road Fund, the BRICS New Development Bank and the Asian Infrastructure Investment Bank, were established to raise further liquidity for Chinese infrastructure projects all across the world (Sum 2019). In the African context, the "moving out" policy has translated into dominant market positions of Chinese companies in the infrastructure and construction sectors, alongside a stark rise in the provision of concessional loans and credit lines to African countries. As discussed above, China has become Africa's largest infrastructure funder (see Table 11.3).

To the surprise of few, this has been warmly welcomed among neoliberal-inclined consultancies, with McKinsey reasoning that "[t]he Chinese government and Chinese firms will need to continue to invest and engage in infrastructure to fill Africa's financing gap." Africa is not only assumed to profit from the slim cost structures of China's infrastructure firms but Chinese foreign direct investment is also expected to help "eliminate extreme poverty" in Africa

(Sun et al. 2017, 63–64). McKinsey attests that Chinese firms won about half of all international Engineering-Procurement-Construction (EPC) contracts and, by value, 42 percent of World Bank tenders in Sub-Saharan Africa (see Sun, Jayaram, and Kassiri 2017, 39). The Deloitte study, referenced earlier, finds that Chinese firms built 41.9 percent of all construction projects in East Africa, 17.6 percent in Southern Africa, 50 percent in Central Africa, 17.4 percent in West Africa and 7.1 percent in North Africa (Deloitte 2016). According to *Xinhua*, which refers to government sources, Chinese companies had constructed 6,200km of railways in Africa by the end of 2017 (Xinhua 2017).

China's extensive loan financing for African infrastructure projects has attracted much public attention and academic scrutiny. The country's supposed "debt trap diplomacy" (Chellaney 2017) in relation to infrastructural loans has caused fierce public debate in Africa and beyond. All the way to the White House, it has been politically instrumentalized to discredit Chinese engagements with Africa (see Reuters 2018; *The Economist* 2019; Nyabiage 2019). There have been commendable attempts, notably by scholars at Johns Hopkins' China Africa Research Initiative (CARI), to demystify the highly politicized "debt trap" narrative by providing more reliable data on Africa's actual indebtedness to China and by pointing out that, thus far, Chinese lending has not resulted in asset seizures in Africa and that China's SOBs have proven willing to restructure debt obligations (see Brautigam 2020; Hancock 2019; Kratz et al. 2019).

While the idea of a Chinese "debt trap", which would imply an intentional attempt to ensnare the continent in debt, must be refuted, critical examination of contradictions that arise from Africa's growing indebtedness are necessary (see Carmody 2020). Africa's current debt-financed infrastructure boom has significantly contributed to the continent's external debt, which almost doubled between 2010 and 2018 (see Figure 11.1). Estimates suggest that 20 percent of Africa's external debt is owed to China (BBC 2018). For 40 low-income African countries, Chinese debt accounted for 60 percent of bilateral lending, and 17 percent of public and publicly guaranteed debt (World Bank 2018, 11). According to CARI, Chinese loan commitments to African governments amounted to $148 billion between 2000 and 2018 (Brautigam et al. 2019). However, whilst CARI certainly offers the most comprehensive data base available on Chinese loan financing in Africa, it is likely that actual amounts borrowed are even higher due to the overall opacity of Chinese loan financing. Table 11.3 shows the top five African states in terms of amounts borrowed from Chinese lenders over the past two decades. CARI data also shows that transport infrastructure has received the largest share of Chinese loan finance ($44.3 billion), followed by the power ($36.9 billion) and mining sectors ($18.5 billion) (Brautigam et al. 2019). Recently, countries like Ethiopia, Kenya and Zambia have struggled to service some of their Chinese loans for large-scale infrastructure projects, such as railways or roads (Carmody et al. forthcoming; Zajontz 2020). For China, Africa represents a welcome long-term investment outlet for surplus capital, but Africa's recent infrastructure boom has become an

Table 11.3 Amounts borrowed from Chinese lenders by selected African states, 2000–2018 (in $ million)

	Angola	*Ethiopia*	*Zambia*	*Kenya*	*Sudan*
2000	0	0	0	0	0
2001	0	1	0	6	132
2002	151	0	8	6	42
2003	11	0	0	0	1260
2004	435	0	0	0	255
2005	1043	0	0	0	355
2006	705	1900	68	46	230
2007	2186	207	40	65	1105
2008	274	0	316	57	187
2009	337	619	169	365	1891
2010	2588	555	659	263	516
2011	3832	1158	577	225	109
2012	1623	177	109	1191	19
2013	3166	5933	851	32	0
2014	2266	773	508	3730	700
2015	1367	613	699	1670	0
2016	19343	824	2177	1095	0
2017	3827	735	2218	296	15
2018	80	234	1304	0	0
Sum	43234	13729	9703	9047	6816

Source: Brautigam et al. 2019.

increasingly constraining fiscal burden for some African states and contributed to the continent's growing indebtedness.

Conclusion: Towards accumulation by dispossessing African infrastructure?

Infrastructure has long served as a means for Africa's exploitation by foreign capital. While the modes of dispossession have become less obvious and normalized in the neoliberal era, efforts to address Africa's infrastructural underdevelopment, itself a colonial legacy, have first and foremost served the capital accumulation process by the West and increasingly also by China. Chinese recent loan/debt investment in Africa's infrastructure sector resembles the long-established practices of "traditional" donors. As mentioned, 70.8 percent of infrastructure funding from ICA members is loans, whereas only 11.9 percent is grants (ICA 2018, 33). Mold (2012) rightly emphasizes that "western banks were flush with excess liquidity and not particularly concerned with the viability of projects they were funding" (244). The fact that all infrastructural loans are duly signed by African state actors has rightly shifted analytical scrutiny towards African agency in the context of Sino-African cooperation in the infrastructure sector (see Mohan and Tan-Mullins 2019; Zajontz 2020).

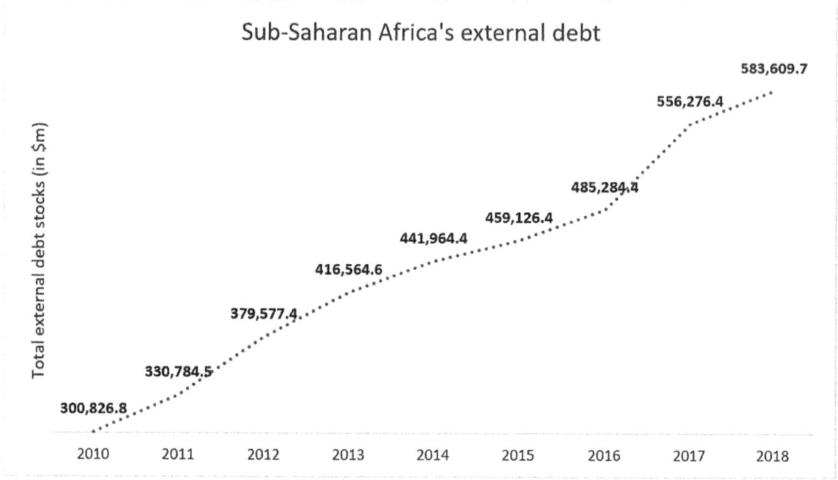

Figure 11.1 The external debt of SSA.
Source: World Bank (2020); excluding the Seychelles.

Hence, it has been argued that "[t]he resolution of the infrastructure–debt dilemma will reside in decision-making by African states in conjunction with key external partners – prominent among them, China" (Alden and Jiang 2019, 649).

In states that have incurred particularly high levels of Chinese-owned debt for infrastructure projects, the "'debt-for-equity' option" has caused growing concerns (Alden and Jiang 2019, 647). The leaking of the loan contracts between state-owned Kenya Railways and the Export-Import (Exim) Bank of China for the construction of Kenya's new SGR, for instance, revealed legal risks related to Chinese infrastructure finance. According to the Kenyan *Sunday Nation*, paragraph 5.5 of the loan agreement stipulates that "[n]either the borrower nor any of its assets is entitled to any right of immunity on the grounds of sovereignty or otherwise from arbitration, suit, execution or any other legal process with respect to its obligations under this Agreement, as the case may be in any jurisdiction." National Treasury Cabinet Secretary Henry Rotich, reportedly the very official who signed the contracts in 2014 on behalf of the Kenyan government, is cited as being "not aware" of this clause (Okoth 2019; see Taylor 2020b; Wang and Wissenbach 2019). Generally, Sum (2019), in the context of the BRI, warns against possible long-term effects of "loan-debt obligations [which] allow China to renegotiate the terms, collateralize the debt and claim assets/resources by converting debt into equity" (545).

While China has thus far proven lenient with regards to debt repayments and has allowed for debt rescheduling on an *ad hoc* basis, as in the case of Ethiopia's loans for the country's new Standard Gauge Railway (SGR) (Zajontz 2019), another form of accumulation by dispossession is well underway in Africa's infrastructure sector. The nascent shift in the governance of infrastructure from the public to the private realm is the result of the growing debt dependency of African states *vis-à-vis* both "traditional" and "emerging" infrastructure sponsors and leaves us wondering if we are witnessing the history of sovereign debt crises and resultant privatization waves of the 1980s and 1990s repeating itself (see Alden and Jiang 2019, 647–648). Alden and Jiang (2019, 648) see a chance that the start of a strategic shift on the part of Chinese companies from loan financing to equity investment might allow for a reconciliation of sustainable public budgets and continued infrastructure development in Africa:

> If equity investment, regarded by China as the future direction for financing in Africa, could gradually overtake traditional loans as one of the main financing methods, especially in the infrastructure and power sectors, this may help alleviate the dilemma posed by the combination of the need for infrastructure development and deepening debt difficulties.

Yet, the authors avoid problematizing that this implies the privatization of African roads, railways and other commons. Highly indebted states, such as Zambia, have started to commodify their trunk road network and to enter into Build-Operate-Transfer PPPs to keep up ambitious "development-through-infrastructure" agendas despite empty treasuries (Zajontz 2020). Such trends signify new forms of accumulation by dispossession with detrimental effects for those people with the smallest disposable incomes – the small-scale traders (many of them women) on their way to marketplaces or working-class commuters.

While the laying down of infrastructure in Africa has long been hailed by the West and now China as cutting the Gordian Knot of African underdevelopment, the implications of the debt incurred, and the resultant continuation of dependency, have been largely put to one side. The notion that what Africa is currently witnessing is not a kick-start to modernity, but rather accumulation by dispossession, has not been adequately discussed. Debt has in history been a device for control as well as for the pillaging of resources and the undercutting of national sovereignty. It might be averred that debt is one of the most potent tools for domination and dispossession, especially since it does not require the maintenance of an expensive empire (normatively impossible in contemporary times anyway). Once public debt reaches levels of "unsustainability" and public resources are insufficient to repay the obligation and its interest, African agency in the context of the continent's current infrastructure boom gets increasingly curtailed and creditors dictate its terms. Already, Africa is replete with rumors that Chinese-built infrastructure will be seized by Chinese companies in the case of non-payment. Although such stories appear to be without foundation, a growing narrative across the continent is that China will leverage its position in various countries, utilizing debt and infrastructure, to advance Chinese interests.

The days of Maoist solidarity are over and the irony of the People's Republic of China being accused of predatory behavior (up to and including accumulation by dispossession) in the Global South demonstrates how far Third Worldism has fallen in the age of a crisis of neoliberalism and the rise of a capitalist China.

Notes

1 Marx defines the turnover time of a given capital as the sum of its production time and its circulation time. More distant markets "eat up" profits by increasing the time lag between investment and profit realization. Hence, "any reduction in circulation time increases surplus production and enhances the accumulation process" (Harvey 2001, 244; see Marx 1967[1885], Vol. 2, 248).
2 The projects fell into the following sectors: Transport (33.6% of projects by number), real estate (22.4%), energy & power (21%), shipping & ports (8.4%), mining (2.8%), oil & Gas (4.5%), water (3.8%), healthcare (2.1%), education (0.7%), social development (0.7%) (Deloitte 2016, 6).

References

AfDB. 2018. *African Economic Outlook 2018.* Abidjan: African Development Bank. https://doi.org/10.1373/clinchem.2007.093781.

Africa50. n.d. "Financials." Accessed May 21, 2020. https://www.africa50.com/about-us/financials/.

African Union. 2001. "The New Partnership for Africa's Development: Declaration on Democracy, Political, Economic and Corporate Governance." 2001. www.un.org/en/africa/osaa/pdf/aprm-declaration.pdf.

African Union. 2015. *Agenda 2063: The Africa we Want.* Addis Ababa: African Union Commission. https://doi.org/10.1007/s40744-017-0065-3.

African Union. 2017. *Programme for Infrastructure Development in Africa (PIDA): Priority Action Plan Progress Report.* Addis Ababa: African Union.

Alden, Chris, and Jiang, Lu. 2019. "Brave New World: Debt, Industrialization and Security in China–Africa Relations." *International Affairs,* 95(3), 641–657. https://doi.org/10.1093/ia/iiz083.

Alden, Chris, and Large, Daniel. 2019. "Conclusion." In by Chris Alden and Daniel Large (Eds), *New Directions in Africa-China Studies.* Abingdon: Routledge, 329–342.

Amin, Samir. 1976. *Unequal Development: An Essay on the Social Formations of Peripheral Capitalism.* Chichester: Harvester Press.

Anthony, Ross, and Ruppert, Uta (Eds). 2020. *Reconfiguring Transregionalisation in the Global South: African-Asian Encounters.* Cham: Palgrave Macmillan.

Arrighi, Giovanni. 2005. "Hegemony Unravelling 1." *New Left Review,* 32, 23–80.

Ashman, Sam, and Callinicos, Alex. 2006. "Capital Accumulation and the State System: Assessing David Harvey's The New Imperialism." *Historical Materialism,* 14(4), 107–131.

Ayers, Alison J. 2013. "Beyond Myths, Lies and Stereotypes: The Political Economy of a 'New Scramble for Africa.'" *New Political Economy,* 18(2), 227–257. https://doi.org/10.1080/13563467.2012.678821.

BBC. 2018. "Reality Check: Is China Burdening Africa with Debt?" BBC News. 2018. www.bbc.co.uk/news/world-africa-45916060.

Berg, Elliot. 1981. *Accelerated Development in Sub-Saharan Africa: An Agenda for Action.* Washington, DC: International Bank for Reconstruction and Development/World Bank.

Bieler, Andreas, and Morton, Adam David. 2014. "Uneven and Combined Development and Unequal Exchange: The Second Wind of Neoliberal 'Free Trade'?" *Globalizations,* 11(1), 35–45.

Brautigam, Deborah. 2020. "A Critical Look at Chinese 'Debt-Trap Diplomacy': The Rise of a Meme." *Area Development and Policy,* 5(1), 1–14. https://doi.org/10.1080/23792949.2019.1689828.

Brautigam, Deborah, Hwang, Jyhjong, Link, Jordan and Acker, Kevin. 2019. *Chinese Loans to Africa Database.* Washington, DC: China Africa Research Initiative, Johns Hopkins University School of Advanced International Studies.

Brenner, Robert. 2006. "Robert Brenner What is, and What is Not, Imperialism?" *Historical Materialism,* 14(4), 79–105.

Burke, Christopher. 2007. "China's Entry into Construction Industries in Africa: Tanzania and Zambia as Case Studies." *China Report,* 43(3), 323–336. https://doi.org/10.1177/000944550704300304.

Cai, Kevin G. 2018. "The One Belt One Road and the Asian Infrastructure Investment Bank: Beijing's New Strategy of Geoeconomics and Geopolitics." *Journal of Contemporary China,* 27(114), 831–847. https://doi.org/10.1080/10670564.2018.1488101.

Carmody, Pádraig. 2020. "Dependence Not Debt-Trap Diplomacy." *Area Development and Policy,* 5(1), 23–31. https://doi.org/10.1080/23792949.2019.1702471.

Carmody, Padraig, Taylor, Ian and Zajontz, Tim. Forthcoming. "China's Spatial Fix and 'Debt Siplomacy' in Africa: Constraining Belt or Road to Development?" *Canadian Journal of African Studies.*

Castree, Noel. 2009. "The Spatio-Temporality of Capitalism." *Time and Society,* 18(1), 26–61. https://doi.org/10.1177/0961463X08099942.

Chellaney, Brahma. 2017. "China's Debt-Trap Diplomacy." Project Syndicate. January 23. www.project-syndicate.org/commentary/china-one-belt-one-road-loans-debt-by-brahma-chellaney-2017-01?barrier=accesspaylog.

Collier, Paul. 2006. "African Growth: Why a 'Big Push'?" *Journal of African Economies,* 15(suppl. 2), 188–211.

Cowen, Deborah. 2017. "Infrastructures of Empire and Resistance." www.versobooks.com/blogs/3067-infrastructures-of-empire-and-resistance.

Deloitte. 2016. *Africa's Changing Infrastructure Landscape: Africa Construction Trends Report.* Diegem: Deloitte University.

Edinger, Hannah, and Labuschagne, Jean-Pierre. 2019. "If You Want to Prosper, Consider Building Roads: China's Role in African Infrastructure and Capital Projects." *Deloitte Insights,* March 2, 2019. www2.deloitte.com/insights/us/en/industry/public-sector/china-investment-africa-infrastructure-development.html.

Fanon, Frantz. 1967. *Black Skin, White Masks.* New York: Grove Press.

Foster, Vivien, and Briceño-Garmendia, Cecilia. 2010. *Africa's Infrastructure: A Time for Transformation.* Washington, DC: International Bank for Reconstruction and Development/World Bank.

Gibbon, Peter. 1995. "Towards a Political Economy of the World Bank 1970–90." In Adebayo O. Olukoshi and Thandika Mkandawire (Eds), *Between Liberalisation and Oppression: The Politics of Structural Adjustment in Africa.* Dakar: CODESRIA, 116–155.

GRZ. 2009. *The Public-Private Partnership Act: No. 14 of 2009.* Lusaka: National Assembly of Zambia.

Hall, David. 2015. *Why Public-Private Partnerships don't Work: The Many Advantages of the Public Alternative.* Greenwich: Public Services International Research Unit.

Hancock, Tom. 2019. "China Renegotiated $50bn in Loans to Developing Countries." *Financial Times*, April 29. www.ft.com/content/0b207552-6977-11e9-80c7-60ee53 e6681d.

Harvey, David. 1982. *The Limits to Capital.* Oxford: Basil Blackwell.

Harvey, David. 2001. *Spaces of Capital: Towards a Critical Geography.* Edinburgh: Edinburgh University Press. https://doi.org/10.1016/S0962-6298(02)00091-4.

Harvey, David. 2003. *The New Imperialism.* Oxford: Oxford University Press.

Harvey, David. 2004a. "Retrospect on the Limits to Capital." *Antipode,* 36(3), 544–549. https://doi.org/papers2://publication/uuid/97396CC0-28E6-4674-9D45-0BDAA3110F4D.

Harvey, David. 2004b. "The 'New' Imperialism: Accumulation by Dispossession." *Socialist Register,* 40, 63–87. http://socialistregister.com/index.php/srv/article/view/5811/2707 /l.VJH1EXv2SK8.

Harvey, David. 2006. *Spaces of Global Capitalism: Towards a Theory of Uneven Geographical Development.* London: Verso.

He, Yafei. 2014. "China's Overcapacity Crisis Can Spur Growth through Overseas Expansion." *South China Morning Post,* January 7. www.scmp.com/comment/insight-opinion/article/1399681/chinas-overcapacity-crisis-can-spur-growth-through-overseas.

Hildyard, Nicholas. 2016. *Licenced Larceny: Infrastructure, Financial Extraction and the Global South.* Manchester: Manchester University Press.

ICA. n.d. "Vision, Mission and Activities." Abidjan: Infrastructure Consortium for Africa. Accessed May 15, 2020. www.icafrica.org/en/about-ica/vision-mission-and-activities/.

ICA. 2018. *Infrastructure Financing Trends in Africa – 2018.* Abidjan: Infrastructure Consortium for Africa.

Jessop, Bob. 2006. "Spatial Fixes, Temporal Fixes and Spatio-Temporal Fixes." In Noel Castree and Derek Gregory (Eds), *David Harvey: A Critical Reader.* Malden, MA: Blackwell Publishing, 142–166.

Jones, Lee and Zeng, Jinghan. 2019. "Understanding China's 'Belt and Road Initiative': Beyond 'Grand Strategy' to a State Transformation Analysis." *Third World Quarterly,* 40(8), 1415–1439. https://doi.org/10.1080/01436597.2018.1559046.

Kimari, Wangui and Ernstson, Henrik. 2020. "Imperial Remains and Imperial Invitations: Centering Race within the Contemporary Large-Scale Infrastructures of East Africa." *Antipode,* 52(3), 825–846. https://doi.org/10.1111/anti.12623.

Kratz, Agatha, Feng, Allen and Wright, Logan. 2019. "New Data on the 'Debt Trap' Question." Rhodium Group. April 29, 2019. https://rhg.com/research/new-data-on-the-debt-trap-question/.

Lee, Ching Kwan. 2014. "The Spectre of Global China." *New Left Review,* 89, 29–66.

Levien, Michael. 2018. *Dispossession without Development: Land Grabs in Neoliberal India.* Oxford: Oxford University Press. https://doi.org/10.1093/oso/9780190859152.001.0001.

Li, Xing. 2016. "Conceptualising the Dialectics of China's Presence in Africa." In Justin Van der Merwe, Ian Taylor and Alexandra Arkhangelskaya (Eds), *Emerging Powers in Africa: A New Wave in the Relationship?*, edited by . Basingstoke: Palgrave Macmillan, 77–106.

Luxemburg, Rosa. 2003. *The Accumulation of Capital.* London: Routledge. https://doi.org/10.4324/9780203361863.

Marx, Karl. 1967. *Capital: A Critique of Political Economy.* 3 vols. New York: International Publishers.

Marx, Karl. 1973. *Grundrisse.* New York: Random House.

Marx, Karl. 1976. *Capital: A Critique of Polical Economy,* Vol. 1. London: Pelican Books and New Left Review.

Marx, Karl. 2013. *Capital: A Critical Analysis of Capitalist Production.* Edited by Mark G. Spencer. Vol. 1. Ware: Wordsworth Editions.

Mohan, Giles and Tan-Mullins, May. 2019. "The Geopolitics of South–South Infrastructure Development: Chinese-Financed Energy Projects in the Global South." *Urban Studies,* 56(7), 1368–1385. https://doi.org/10.1177/0042098018794351.

Mold, Andrew. 2012. "Will it All End in Tears? Infrastructure Spending and African Development in Historical Perspective." *Journal of International Development,* 24(2), 237–254. https://doi.org/10.1002/jid.

Ndulu, Benno J., Chakraborti, Lopamudra, Lijane, Lebohang, Ramachandran, Vijaya and Wolgin, Jerome. 2007. *Challenges of African Growth: Opportunities, Constraints, and Strategic Directions.* Washington, DC: International Bank for Reconstruction and Development/World Bank.

Nkrumah, Kwame. 1965. *Neo-Colonialism: The Last Stage of Imperialism.* Edinburgh: Thomas Nelson & Sons.

Nugent, Paul. 2018. "Africa's Re-Enchantment with Big Infrastructure: White Elephants Dancing in Virtuous Circles?" In Jon Schubert, Ulf Engel and Macamo Elisio (Eds), *Extractive Industries and Changing State Dynamics in Africa.* Abingdon: Routledge, 22–40.

Nyabiage, Jevans. 2019. "Lender's Remorse? China Finds Africa Projects Require a Growing Wave of Debt Forgiveness." *South China Morning Post,* August 11. www.scmp.com/news/china/diplomacy/article/3022301/lenders-remorse-china-finds-africa-projects-require-growing.

Okoth, Edwin. 2019. "SGR Pact with China a Risk to Kenyan Sovereignty, Assets." *Daily Nation,* January 13. www.nation.co.ke/news/Hidden-traps-in-SGR-deal-with-China/1056-4932764-ebw46r/index.html.

Perelman, Michael. 2000. *The Invention of Capitalism: Classical Political Economy and the Secret History of Primitive Accumulation.* Durham, NC: Duke University Press.

PIDA. n.d. *Closing the Infrastructure Gap Vital for Africa's Transformation.* Abidjan: African Development Bank.

PIDA. 2012. *Programme for Infrastructure Development in Africa: Interconnecting, Integrating, and Transforming a Continent.* Abidjan: African Union Commission, United Nations Eco-Nomic Commission for Africa, African Development Bank, and New Partnership for Africa's Development. www.afdb.org/fileadmin/uploads/afdb/Documents/Project-and-Operations/PIDA note English for web 0208.pdf.

Prinsloo, Cyril. 2019. *The Pitfalls of Private Sector Investment in Infrastructure Financing.* Policy Briefing 187. Johannesburg: South African Institute of International Affairs.

Quist-Arcto, Ofeibea. 2001. *Africa: A 'Continental Strategy' For Building Africa Infrastructure Needed – Wade.* Dakar: AllAfrica. https://allafrica.com/stories/200102080307.html.

Rampa, Francesco, Bilal, Sanoussi and Sidiropoulos, Elizabeth. 2012. "Leveraging South–South Cooperation for Africa's Development." *South African Journal of International Affairs,* 19(2), 247–269. https://doi.org/10.1080/10220461.2012.709400.

Reuters. 2018. "Zambia Denies White House Claim China Taking over Power Utility." Lusaka: Reuters. December 15. www.reuters.com/article/us-zambia-economy/zambia-denies-white-house-claim-china-taking-over-power-utility-idUSKBN1OE0LD.

Robinson, Cedric J. 2000. *Black Marxism: The Making of the Black Radical Tradition.* Chapel Hill, NC: University of North Carolina Press.

Rodney, Walter. 2015. *How Europe Underdeveloped Africa.* Nairobi: East African Publishers.

Sachs, Jeffrey D., Mcarthur, John W., Schmidt-Traub, Guido, Kruk, Margaret, Bahadur, Chandrika, Faye, Michael and McCord, Gordon. 2004. "Ending Africa's Poverty Trap." *Brookings Papers on Economic Activity*, 1, 117–240. https://doi.org/10.1353/eca.2004.0018.

Schindler, Seth, and Kanai, J. Miguel. 2019. "Getting the Territory Right: Infrastructure-Led Development and the Re-Emergence of Spatial Planning Strategies." *Regional Studies,* 0(0), 1–12. https://doi.org/10.1080/00343404.2019.1661984.

Sheppard, Eric. 2004. "The Spatiality of the Limits to Capital." *Antipode,* 36(3), 470–479. https://doi.org/10.1111/j.1467-8330.2004.00426.x.

Shivji, Issa G. 2009. *Accumulation in an African Periphery: A Theoretical Framework.* Dar es Salaam: Mkuki na Nyota Publishers.

Shivji, Issa G. 2017. "The Concept of 'Working People.'" *Agrarian South: Journal of Political Economy,* 6(1), 1–13. https://doi.org/10.1177/2277976017721318.

Sindzingre, Alice N. 2013. "The Ambivalent Impact of Commodities: Structural Change or Status Quo in Sub-Saharan Africa?" *South African Journal of International Affairs,* 20(1), 23–55. https://doi.org/10.1080/10220461.2013.780327.

Sum, Ngai-Ling. 2019. "The Intertwined Geopolitics and Geoeconomics of Hopes/ Fears: China's Triple Economic Bubbles and the 'One Belt One Road' Imaginary." *Territory, Politics, Governance,* 7(4), 528–552. https://doi.org/10.1080/21622671.2018.1523746.

Summers, Tim. 2016. "China's 'New Silk Roads': Sub-National Regions and Networks of Global Political Economy." *Third World Quarterly,* 37(9), 1628–1643. https://doi.org/10.1080/01436597.2016.1153415.

Sun, Irene Yuan, Kartik Jayaram, and Omid Kassiri. 2017. *Dance of the Lions and Dragons: How Are Africa and China Engaging, and How Will the Partnership Evolve?* New York: McKinsey & Co.

Taylor, Ian. 2014. *Africa Rising? BRICS – Diversifying Dependency.* Woodbridge: James Currey.

Taylor, Ian. 2015. "Dependency Redux: Why Africa is Not Rising." *Review of African Political Economy,* 43(147), 8–25. https://doi.org/10.1080/03056244.2015.1084911.

Taylor, Ian. 2020a. "Afro-Asian Trade and the 'Africa Rising' Story." In *Reconfiguring Transregionalisation in the Global South: African-Asian Encounters.* Cham: Palgrave Macmillan, 19–40.

Taylor, Ian. 2020b. "Kenya's New Lunatic Express: The Standard Gauge Railway." *African Studies Quarterly,* 39(3–4), 29–52.

Taylor, Ian, and Zajontz, Tim. 2020. "In a Fix: Africa's Place in the Belt and Road Initiative and the Reproduction of Dependency." *South African Journal of International Affairs,* 27(3), 277–295.

The Economist. 2019. "Choices on the Continent." March 9.

Wang, Yuan and Wissenbach, Uwe. 2019. "Clientelism at Work? A Case Study of Kenyan Standard Gauge Railway Project." *Economic History of Developing Regions,* 34(3), 280–299. https://doi.org/10.1080/20780389.2019.1678026.

Wethal, Ulrikke. 2019. "Building Africa's Infrastructure: Reinstating History in Infrastructure Debates." *Forum for Development Studies,* 46(3), 473–499. https://doi.org/10.1080/08039410.2019.1616609.

World Bank. 2014. *Building Integrated Markets within the East African Community: EAC Opportunities in Private-Public Partnership Approaches to the Region's Infrastructure Needs*. Washington, DC: World Bank.

World Bank. 2017. "An Analysis of Issues Shaping Africa's Economic Future." *Africa's Pulse,* 15. https://doi.org/10.1596/978-1-4648-0468-7.

World Bank. 2018. *International Debt Statistics 2019*. Washington, DC: International Bank for Reconstruction and Development/World Bank.

World Bank. 2020. *2020: International Debt Statistics*. Washington, DC: World Bank. http://datatopics.worldbank.org/debt/ids/regionanalytical/SSA.

Xinhua. 2017. "Chinese-Built Railways Improve Transport in Africa." www.xinhuanet.com/english/2017-12/28/c_136857657.htm.

Zajontz, Tim. 2019. "'Fixing' Africa's Infrastructure: But at What Price?" *Pambazuka News*. www.pambazuka.org/economics/"fixing"-africa's-infrastructure-what-price.

Zajontz, Tim. 2020. "The Chinese Infrastructural Fix in Africa: Lessons from the Sino-Zambian 'Road Bonanza.'" *Oxford Development Studies,* online first.

Zhang, Xin. 2017. "Chinese Capitalism and the Maritime Silk Road: A World-Systems Perspective." *Geopolitics,* 22(2), 310–331. https://doi.org/10.1080/14650045.2017.1289371.

12 Wealth accumulation and the Nigerian billionaire club

The case of Aliko Dangote

Emmanuel O. Oritsejafor

Introduction

The crisis of economic development in Sub-Saharan Africa (SSA) has continued to be a preoccupation of many scholars and policy analysts. Several approaches have been advanced to address this crisis. For instance, Skocpol (1985), Brautigam (1991) and Migdal (1988) have all argued that the lack of economic development in most SSA countries is attributive to weak state capacity to meet its development objectives because these countries have not been able to effectively implement growth-driven economic policies along with the provision of good governance.

On the other hand, Ihonvbere (2013), Ake (1981) and Kieh (2018) have all approached the crisis of the state from not only the historical perspective, but in the context of its peculiarities and specificities. The inherent post-colonial contradictions of the state and class are closely examined as they relate to political and economic development. This chapter on wealth accumulation in Nigeria provides the context in which one can examine the extent to which wealth accumulation by the new generation of the Nigerian economic elite, such as Aliko Dangote, Folorunsho Alakija and Michael Adenuga, has reinforced uneven development. This chapter raises the question whether this indigenous elite serves the interest of the international capitalist class or are driven by national interests. The next section provides a background of the political economy of post-colonial Nigeria and the emergent class contradictions. The chapter addresses the question of why Nigeria has not been able to benefit from capitalist development despite the emergence of a new class of elites – who are members of the world billionaire club.

The attainment of political independence does not seem to have transformed the state because the elites that replaced the colonial administrators have failed to take steps to move the country forward politically and economically. According to Olaitan (1995), indigenous elites inherited a state that was not designed to meet the needs and wants of the people of Nigeria. Instead these leaders were content with political structures designed by the colonialists. He posits that:

> the state, given its enormous resources, was the most secured and quickest source of accumulation after independence. It meant that politics as the struggle for the control of the instruments of the state became a fierce battle. Many people became interested in the state, not because it was useful for the generality of the society, but because it could be exploited for personal and material gains.
>
> (Olaitan 1995, 129)

Capitalism as a mode of production was introduced into Nigeria through the colonial experience. As a result, Nigeria experienced the contradictory relationship between capitalists and wage laborers as well as the market-driven form of surplus extraction (Orimolade and Hyacinth 2016, 42–43). The penetration of capitalist social relations into the Nigerian society became profoundly manifested between the late 19th and early 20th centuries. The social structure of the Nigerian society has been shaped by the semi-capitalist mode of production. The political structure which is related to the state has continued to play a pivotal role in the economy. It is with this in mind that one can better understand the nature of capitalist accumulation in post-colonial Nigeria.

The nature of capitalist development in Nigeria

The nature of capitalist development in Nigeria can be traced back to long before the pre-colonial period when social political formations were dictated by migratory trends around 10,000 to 2000 BCE (Orimolade and Hyacinth 2016, 45). Social formations during this period were diverse and reflected a power structure that ranged from states with centralized power to societies with decentralized authority. However, social formations in pre-colonial Africa were established through a combination of social and geopolitical processes. This suggests that they were dictated by domestic and international trade as the basis of surplus accumulation. However, the integration of capitalist social relations in Nigeria and other African states in the 19th and 20th centuries was accentuated by uneven capitalist development (Orimolade and Hyacinth 2016, 43). For instance, economic development during the colonial period was driven by commodity trade. It entailed agricultural commodities such as cocoa, bananas, sugar, palm oil, peanuts, coffee and tea; and raw materials such as rubber, jute and other minerals (Gadzey 1992, 457). Perez (2019, 40) expounded on the nature of the colonial development in his narration of the colonial accumulation strategy in the Canary Islands:

> The islands based their productive model on the export of different raw materials concerning food (sugar, wine, bananas, tomatoes ...) or related with different industries situated of the islands (Orhilla, saltwort, Cochineal) along with the import of manufactured goods and other raw materials that met the demands of the Canarian people. This model conditioned the

> strength of the Canarian Bourgeoisie and of course the development of its industry.

Invariably, African colonial economies did not possess the major elements of a full capitalist process because of the following:

1. A self-sustaining capability for forward and backward linkage. Commodity exports in Africa did not develop a self-sustaining capability.
2. Manufacturing capabilities were centered in the metropolitan countries. Meanwhile, African states became specialized commodity suppliers.
3. There was a lack of incentives on the part of the colonialists to develop their occupied territories (Gadzey 1992, 457–460).

The nature of uneven capitalist development is further expressed in the post-colonial state, including Nigeria. While capitalism and uneven development are perpetuated though the extraction of surplus value within the process of production, this is facilitated through money which gives capital the power to exploit workers beyond its immediate territory (Gadzey 1992, 457).

The expansive nature of capitalism through wealth accumulation by members of the indigenous billionaire club draws one closer to the question: are members of this club an extension of the interests of the post-colonial elite or do they possess self-serving interests for wealth accumulation? In addition, we will examine the role of the Nigerian state in producing the crisis of uneven development. That is, the state is not extricable from the crisis of capitalist development because it reinforces the accompanying inequities. In this regard, Ashman (2009, 34) asserts:

> This is not to suggest that "politics" is extraneous to capitalist relations or that a state and coercive authority is rendered redundant: force is necessary to dispossess; to protect private property and class rule in general; to enforce contracts between the buyer and the seller of labor power; to enforce the norms of commodity exchange; to raise taxes; to set interest and exchange rates. Whilst the power of surplus extraction is not directly grounded in the coercive apparatus of the state.

Similarly, Ihonvbere (2013) postulates that the state plays a prominent role in creating a specific modality for class domination. He suggests that, "It is a modality in which the system of institutional mechanisms of class domination are differentiated and disassociated from the ruling class and appears as an objective force standing alongside society" (21). Therefore, the rise of the members of the post-Cold War indigenous elite and their continuous collaboration with the ruling elite provides a context for understanding how members of this group have contributed to the social and economic development of Nigeria. However, I argue here that the members of this group are inextricably a part of capitalist uneven development in Nigeria.

The rise of the billionaire club and primitive accumulation: A theoretical framework

The rise of the post-colonial billionaire club in Nigeria is directly linked to primitive accumulation of capital. Primitive accumulation, according to Iyayi (1986), is the capital and labor power which constitutes the starting point for the capitalist mode of production and the methods by which capital and labor power are obtained by the masses (27). It is instructive to note that the nature of capitalist penetration in the colonial period did not permit the colonialist to create and establish an indigenous *capitalist* class. Instead, a ruling indigenous *political* class was established. The dependency on the colony by the colonialist as a primary source of export resources also slowed down the process of the emergence of the indigenous capitalists (Ayayi 1986, 31). In this regard, Ayayi (1986, 31) propounded,

> Finally, the indigenous capitalist in the neo-colonial situation have to depend upon exclusively internal sources for the accumulation of monetary capital since being located in neocolonial themselves they have no colonies to loot and plunder.

At independence, although the Nigerian state was under the control of the indigenous nationalists, the Nigerian economy was primarily dominated by British multinationals. The control of the Nigerian economy by the foreign capitalist class suggests that, though Nigeria acquired political independence, the control of economic wealth was in the hands of foreign capitalists (Agbese 1990, 302). Consequently, capital accumulation in Nigeria was based on the direct exploitation of labor and the use of state power, whereby the use of state power enabled the indigenous political ruling and capitalist class to accumulate capital on a private basis (Agbese 1990, 302).

The rise of the billionaire club in post-colonial Nigeria can be traced to the relationship between the state and the evolving capitalist class. Accordingly, Beckman (1982, 37) illustrates that:

> The Nigerian state is busily promoting capitalist development. While having important roots in colonial peasant production, this development is currently fed on oil. The state plays a key role in dispensing the oil wealth, and the way it is spent generates economic activity and incomes (not for all though) in all sectors of the economy. It feeds into and transforms pre-existing social relations. It promotes capitalist accumulation and capitalist class formation.

Similarly, Akhaine (2011) suggests that the Nigerian state, because of its primary reliance on oil, is a rentier state. The rentier state, he propounded, is characterized by a "windfall wealth of unprecedented magnitude." Thus, the state collects rents from the sales of oil and other primary exports such as groundnuts and cocoa, and distributes the windfall from these exports through the state bureaucratic structures where they are at times plundered through misappropriation and other forms of corrupt practices (Akhaine 2011, 649).

However, the rise of the billionaire club that includes Aliko Dangote, the richest man in Africa, and Folorunsho Alakija, one of the richest women in Africa, must be situated in the context of the failure of the Nigerian state, military and civilian, to create a stable political environment for a cohesive capitalist development process. In this regard, Kalu (1996, 242) suggests:

> Nigerian politicians and military generals have demonstrated time and time again that rather than a unifying platform for a diversity of peoples, the state is a prize to be won for private and ethnic wealth accumulation. Thus, the problem with Nigeria is not the absence of capitalism and democracy per se … rather capitalism which is inherently anti-political freedom, especially freedom of the state to constrain capitalist methods of accumulation has found a fertile ground in Nigeria …

The Nigerian state has been an enabler of wealth accumulation under various military and civilian administrators. Most of the political leaders in Nigeria can be best described as "political merchants" because they see politics as a conduit for business deals that brings enormous profits. Therefore, Nigerian political leaders do not believe in service to the people; instead they are self-serving – they serve themselves and their economic partners (Adegbami and Uche 2016, 204).

As a result, the state, through its collaborative relationship with the economic class in Nigeria, has advanced the class struggle that gave rise to the birth of the billionaire club through bureaucratic apparatus, concession agreements and other forms of government contacts (Agbese 1990, 298). The state at times used force in asserting control and repressing the working class. This was particularly the case under various military dispensations in Nigeria whereby various Nigerian military governments in collaboration with the economic class benefitted from the award of oil contracts. Powerful interests, particularly the political and military ruling class, often ensured that the Nigerian economic elite benefited from the country's oil largesse by awarding contracts to elites that can demonstrate that they have the capacity to produce Nigerian oil content (Ovadia 2013, 258–259). The Nigerian oil content was a law that was instituted to encourage indigenous control over the production of petroleum oil. Instead, the policy has simply benefitted the indigenous economic elite and their foreign partners. This argument was readily highlighted by Beckman (1982) when he suggested that the neo-colonial character of the Nigerian state is an optical illusion. Foreign capital, he argued, continued to dominate in Nigeria as it did during the colonial period. It is just the form of domination which has changed. However, the Nigerian economic elite has become an active participant in this process (Beckman 1982, 44). Whose interests are the indigenous elites serving? Are their economic interests in oil, gas, cement, sugar and communication sectors driven by self-interest or national development?

The Nigerian billionaire club: The case of Dangote

The Nigerian billionaire club can be aptly described along the lines of what C. Wright Mills (1969) outlined in his seminal work the *Power Elite*. The power elite, according to Mills, is "composed of men and women in this case whose positions enable them to advance beyond the ordinary environments of ordinary men and women; they are positioned to make decisions having major consequences" (Mills 1969).

The nature and characteristics of the Nigerian elite are not far from those of the advanced capitalist countries of North America and Europe. The members of the billionaire club of Nigeria and the political elites have certain peculiarities consistent with those described by Mills (1969), in which he focused on the relationships and the class alliances among United States political, military and economic elites.

The members of the Nigerian billionaire club are unique because they have been able to extend their reach beyond national economic interests. They play a significant role in the international division of labor through the interplay of relations with the state and global financial institutions. The members of the Nigerian billionaire club are transnational in nature and their interests transcend national boundaries. In several instances, they have joined with international capitalist interests in the 21st century – a *scramble for Africa's* resources through primitive accumulation (*The Economist* 2019a, 19).

For example, the Dangote Group has about 9 percent equity in the Nigeria and Sao Tome and Principe Joint Oil development known as Obo-1 well, and the Nigerian government controls approximately 45 percent equity (*Offshore Magazine* 2020). The business exclusivity given to the Dangote group by the Nigerian government domestically, and in the global market, as illustrated in the case of the Obo-1 well, reflects the emerging social relationship between the Nigerian ruling class and the economic class. Bracking and Harrison (2003, 17) suggest that there are new social relations in post-colonial Africa that are shaping wealth accumulation:

> New forms of accumulation emerge within Africa, products of social relations in specific places and their articulation to broader networks of trade and production. There are complexities to the interplay between state power and private economic power, and interplay that is changing its patterns in response to both external forces and popular movements.

New forms of accumulation, which are triggered by emergent social relations, have contributed to the rise of an indigenous billionaire group in Nigeria and other parts of Africa. In the introductory chapter to this book, my co-editor and I provided a list of the members of the African Billionaire Club. Among these members are several Nigerian billionaires including Aliko Dangote, Michael Adenuga, Abdulsamad Rabiu and Folorunsho Alakiaja. Here I provide a brief examination of the background and business career of Africa's richest person, Aliko Dangote.

The case of Dangote

Alhaji Aliko Dangote was born on April 10, 1951. He is the first grandson of one of the most successful commercial magnates from Northern Nigeria, Mr. Sanusi Dantata. The Dantata commercial interest covered several parts of Nigeria in commodity trade, such as groundnuts and other agricultural products. The Dantata business framework was primarily driven by neo-patrimonial arrangements that centered around building solidarity through a clientele ascription of loyalty (Ademola and Neal 2013, 72). Wealth accumulation is often associated to a network of family interests which are accentuated by linkage to the political elites.

At the age of 20, Aliko Dangote approached his maternal grandfather Sanusi Dantata for a loan of N500,000 to import cement. As his business venture became successful, Aliko Dangote managed to repay the entire loan within three months. This was the genesis of the emergence of the Dangote Group which has positioned Aliko Dangote as the richest man in Africa with an estimated net worth of $10.3 billion (*Forbes* 2020). The accumulation of Aliko Dangote's wealth over the past four decades has been unique because he is the only African/Black billionaire who made virtually all his billions from indigenous and local manufacturing (Ademola and Neal 2013, 241). Thus, the Dangote Group is perceived as an indigenous multinational corporation. The Dangote Group is the largest employer of labor in Nigeria and one of the largest conglomerates in Africa, with business interests in Cameroon, South Africa, Rwanda, Algeria, Kenya, Uganda, Morocco and Zambia (Ademola and Neal 2013, 242).

To underscore the extent of the growth of the Dangote Group, between 1977 and 2016 the organization grew to become one of the largest indigenous multinational corporations in Nigeria that controls significant shares of the total equity capitalization of several commercial sectors in Nigeria and Africa. The Dangote Group companies, quoted on the Nigerian Stock Exchange (NSE), include Dangote Cement PLC, Dangote Sugar Refinery PLC, NASCON Allied Industries PLC and Dangote Flour Mills PLC, controlling 43 percent of NSE equity market capitalization (Akinyoade and Uche 2018, 833). Dangote Cement PLC, which is the largest company in the Dangote Group, controls about 32 percent of the total equity capitalization of the NSE. About 180 other companies control the remaining 25 percent of the total equity capitalization of the NSE (Akinyoade and Uche 2018, 833).

The metamorphosis of the Dangote Group into a major multinational organization did not take place in a vacuum. Aliko Dangote benefitted from a client relationship with present and past military and civilian governments who helped advanced his business ventures in Nigeria and Africa. For instance, Dangote Group had trade preference in 1999 under the Obasanjo administration through exclusive import rights in sugar, cement and rice (Akiyoade and Uche 2018, 834). It was also reported that the direction of the Government of Nigeria (GON) was that the Dangote Group should receive preferential treatment in nearly all areas in which they trade, including wheat, flour, cement, textiles, sugar and pasta (Akinyoade and Uche 2018, 834).

It was in the cement industry that the Dangote Group would come to have a profound influence in the political economy of Nigeria. In fact, one of Dangote's competitors in Nigeria, Ibeto Cement, accused Dangote of using his close relationship to President Obasanjo to close the Ibeto cement bagging factory (Akinyoade and Uche 2018, 834). Dangote used his close connection to the Obasanjo administration to influence the Nigerian government to adopt and sustain a Backward Integration Policy (BIP) for the cement industry in Nigeria. The BIP discouraged cement importation in favor of local production (Akinyoade and Uche 2018, 835). The Dangote Group took advantage of this preferential treatment through the import license provision granted to the company and emerged as a monopoly in the cement industry. In fact, Dangote Cement PLC was the most capitalized company in Nigeria in 2018 at a market cap of N3, 222.58 billion (Nigerian Investment Promotion Commission 2018a, 11). In addition, the Dangote Group, because of its size and economies of scale in the cement industry, received tax shelter in principle from the Nigerian Federal Revenue Service (FRS) under the Pioneer Status Incentives (PSI) for the cement industry in 2018 (Nigerian Investment Promotion Commission 2018b).

Table 12.1 shows the over 400 percent rise in the demand for cement from 2000 to 2014 – from 5.6 million metric tons to 23 million metric tons. Dangote Cement increased its cement production from 900,000 metric tons per year in 2000, when it took over the Benue to 23.2 million metric tons by 2014. At the same time, the percentage of imported cement plummeted from 59.3 percent in 2000 to 3.3 percent in 2014 (Nigerian Investment Promotion Commission 2018b). The BIP policy is primarily responsible for the rise in domestic demand for cement between 2000 and 2014. The acquired wealth from the cement industry would provide the leverage that the Dangote Group needed in the corporate expansion into the petroleum and agriculture sectors. The preferential treatment under the BIP policy in the production of cement ensured that the Group controlled 60 percent of Nigeria's cement market between 2000 and 2018 (Ademola and Neal 2013, 241).

The BIP policy would have dire economic consequences for Nigerian consumers that are not protected from high import tariffs because of rising prices for imported goods such as rice and tomatoes. Manufacturers were also adversely affected by BIP because the import tariffs contributed to high operational costs that are associated with imported spare parts and other production inputs (*The Economist* 2019b).

The rise of the Dangote Group and members of the *Billionaire Club* are inherently tied to their client relationship with military and civilian leaders. This relationship is reflective of the nature of primitive accumulation in Nigeria and elsewhere. Political and economic elites are linked by common interests of systemic accumulation of wealth through hyper-inflated contracts, and other forms of bureaucratic corrupt practices such as the award of import licenses,

Table 12.1 Cement statistics Nigeria 1986–2014

Year	*Total*	*Import (Mt)*	*Local (Mt)*	*Import %*	*Local %*
1986	4,300,000	800,000	3,500,000	18.6	81.4
1987	4,100,000	700,000	3,400,000	17.1	82.9
1988	4,088,341	688,341	3,400,000	16.8	83.2
1989	3,493,621	543,621	2,950,000	15.6	84.4
1990	3,935,595	905,595	3,030,00	23.0	77.0
1991	4,617,272	1,693,200	2,924,072	36.7	63.3
1992	4,782,857	1,985,655	2,74,97,202	41.5	58.5
1993	4,708,044	2,085,826	2,622,218	44.3	55.7
1994	3,479,794	859,886	2,61,908	24.7	75.3
1995	3,701,984	1,091,232	2,610,752	29.5	70.5
1996	3,591,298	1,060,300	2,530,998	29.5	70.5
1997	3,821,995	1,304,582	2,517,413	34.1	65.9
1998	4,198,943	1,992,588	2,206,355	47.5	52.5
1999	5,584,784	3,112,685	2,472,099	55.7	44.3
2000	5,621,640	3,336,134	2,285,506	59.3	40.7
2001	8,105,000	5,937,000	2,168,000	73.3	26.7
2002	8,112,000	6,041,000	2,071,000	74.5	25.5
2003	8,418,000	6,437,000	1,981,000	76.5	23.5
2004	8,257,000	5,20,000	2,337,000	71.7	28.3
2005	9,478,000	6,629,000	2,049,000	69.9	21.6
2006	9,972,722	6,753,000	3,219,722	67.7	32.3
2007	10,969,668	6,327,000	4,642,668	57.7	42.3
2008	13,402,880	6,977,000	6,425,880	52.1	47.9
2009	14,674,144	6,791,000	7,955,144	45.8	54.2
2010	14,600,000	5,500,000	9,100,000	37.7	62.3
2011	17,200,000	5,200,000	12,000,000	30.2	69.8
2012	18,000,000	1,800,000	16,200,000	10. 0	90.5
2013	21,3000,000	n750,000	20,550,000	3.5	96.5
2014	23,000,000	750,000	22,250,00	3.5	96.7

Source: (Akinyoade and Uche 2018, 835).

preferential trade and private access to national oil wells. It is in this context that one should closely examine the granting of 6,180 acres of swampland in a free trade zone area of the Lagos metropolis to Aliko Dangote to build a $12 billion oil refinery. The planned oil refinery is projected as the world largest refinery that will hopefully alleviate the underperforming capacity of Nigeria's refineries. Currently, Nigerian oil refineries are functioning at less than 50 percent of capacity (Edozien 2018). Nonetheless, the question that has not been addressed by the Nigerian government is why the Dangote Group was given exclusivity to build a national refinery? Why not offer the contract to build such a refinery to a consortium of indigenous manufacturers which might also include the Dangote Group?

Invariably, the access of the Nigerian billionaire club to primitive wealth accumulation has to be contextualized in the relationship between the ruling class and the economic class that includes indigenous economic elite such as

Aliko Dangote. Thus, Dangote asserts: "I am close to people in government, because I am one of the big businessmen in Nigeria. If we don't have the right people there then all the money I have is useless" (Fayemiwe and Neal 2013, 292). This relationship is accented by the nature of capitalist accumulation in post-colonial Africa. In this case, the Nigerian government, starting with the Yakubu Gowon military administration in 1972, embarked on an indigenization program that emphasized state investment and national development driven by import-substitution industrialization. Subsequently, the Muritala Mohammed and the Obasanjo administrations between 1975 and 1976 continued along the same path. State-driven capitalism would serve as the genesis of powerful business elites such as Aliko Dangote (Akinyoade and Uche 2018, 838). The nature of the relationship between the business class and the ruling class was aptly described by Akinyoade and Uche (2018, 839) as follows:

> Given that Nigerian bureaucrats and senior military personnel became some of the major beneficiaries of the indigenization policies, it can rightly be said that the adoption of the policy was a major landmark in the development of crony capitalism in Nigeria …

However, the problem with state-driven capitalist strategies such as import-substitution is that it advances class divisions and contradictions that alienate a significant segment of the population. Though the economic strategy focuses on growing local industries such as the Dangote Group, at the same time it creates very high costs for domestic manufacturing which invariably contributes to low job creation (Wengraf 2018, 52). As a result, state capitalism, as envisioned under various military and civilian governments in Nigeria between the 1970s and 2000s, has contributed to lopsided economic development that has advanced class contradictions (Wengraf 2018, 34). For instance, in Nigeria, "80 percent of the nation's oil wealth is concentrated in the hands of 1 percent of the population" (Wengraf 2018, 34). Along the same lines, the overall economic outlook of Nigeria has been mixed. The economy experienced an unprecedented boom in the early 1960s and the early 1970s. During these periods, the growth rate of GDP per capita ranged from 2 percent to 14 percent (Guseh and Oritsejafor 2019, 52–53). However, by the 1980s, the country was plunged into economic crisis, stemming largely from two broad factors: economic mismanagement and emphasis on revenues from the oil boom at the expense of agricultural production (Guseh and Oritsejafor 2019, 53). The pattern and nature of state capitalism that has led to ascendancy of the billionaire club and its members through crony capitalism and other forms of state–business relationship has not been transformative. The combined wealth of the four richest Nigerians – $22.2 billion dollars – could address and more than halve extreme poverty in Nigeria (see Aderemi 2019). Moreover, Nigeria's richest men earn approximately 8,000 times more in one day than a poor Nigerian will spend on basic needs within a year (Oxfam 2020).

Through wealth accumulation the economic elite has further entrenched their economic power through cronyism, corruption and excessive influence over government policies at the expense of poor Nigerians. For instance, it is projected that the Dangote Group will save Nigeria about $12 billion on the importation of refined oil and amass a projected revenue of $30 billion after the completion of the oil refinery in Lagos (Baker 2018). There are also cases of "backward integration" – a process in which a major company such as the Dangote group takes over its suppliers, such as the 2019 N13.2 billion ($341 million) corporate takeovers of Savannah Sugar Company Limited (SSLC) by the Dangote Sugar Refinery PLC (DSR). This corporate takeover led to the merger of the two companies as the largest sugar refinery in Sub-Saharan Africa (Daily Trust 2020). Aliko Dangote is positioned to remain one of the wealthiest men globally. The Dangote Group invested about $60 million in the cement production industry in Togo (Neshe 2019), and $650 million in a cement plant at the Mtwara region of Tanzania (Neshe 2017).

Conclusion

The rise of the billionaire club in Nigeria is directly linked to the nature of primitive accumulation. This process is reinforced by the relationship between the ruling elite and the economic class of Nigeria. This chapter suggests that the relationship between the ruling elite, either under the military or the civilian government in Nigeria, advanced class contradictions and the lopsided economy which also gave birth to the billionaire club and its staunchest member Aliko Dangote.

The rise of the billionaire club has not transformed the social and economic conditions of Nigerians. Instead, there is growing unevenness in the social and economic conditions that are reflected by the nature of class polarization in Nigeria. What has ensued in the post-colonial state, in Nigeria and elsewhere, is that new forms of social relations have deepened wealth inequalities. Accordingly, Burgis (2015, 6–7) suggests that the old empires have been replaced by hidden networks of multinationals, middlemen and African potentates. These networks further tend to fuse state and corporate power. They are also not aligned to any nation and belong, instead, to transnational elites that have flourished in the period of globalization (Burgis 2015, 6–7).

Since the beginning of Nigeria's new democracy in 1999, economic performance shows that 70 percent of Nigerians live below a poverty level of one dollar a day (Burgis 2015, 55). At the same time, economic stagnation, which was estimated at 2.8 percent in 2000, has continued to fall below the 3 percent annual rate of population growth (Burgis 2015, 55). Meanwhile, members of the billionaire club have continued to accumulate wealth through various state concession agreements and other forms of exclusive partnerships with the Nigerian state.

Therefore, wealth accumulation by members of the Nigerian billionaire club has reinforced social inequalities between those who own capital, that is, the means of production, and those who do not, but have to find a way to survive with what they can earn from their labor (Piketty 2015, 26). Moreover, giving Dangote, who is from Northern Nigeria, preferential treatment in building a refinery and selling a major national resource in the international market may very well reinforce regional and ethnic inequalities.

How can social and economic development be transformative in Nigeria under the current social relations between members of the billionaire club, the ruling class, private banks and other international interests when only a selected few benefit from such social relations? For instance, contrary to the suggestion that the Dangote refinery will transform Nigeria from a petrol import dependent country to one that exports refined oil petroleum products, the Dangote refinery is not likely to sell its petroleum products below prevailing international market prices (Business Highlights 2020). Moreover, the Dangote Group is positioned to earn revenue of approximately $30 billion annually from the Lagos refinery (Business Highlights 2020). The decision by the Nigerian government to provide the Dangote Group exclusivity in the production of refined oil reinforces a monopoly environment in the domestic oil sector. Moreover, petroleum products will remain an import; costs will consequently shift to domestic consumers because the Dangote Group will not be able to sell petroleum products competitively below the international market value.

Given the nature of wealth accumulation by the members of the Nigerian billionaire club, such as Dangote, members of this club are driven by capitalist self-interest, using present social relations to produce intense and increased capitalist accumulation. The notion that members of this class would serve the development interests of African states, such as Nigeria, Tanzania or Togo, is yet to be substantiated. Instead, the predatory nature of the capitalist accumulation that was once advanced by foreign multinationals and other capitalists has now simply been joined and in some instances replaced by the indigenous African billionaires and oligarchs in the political economy of African states.

References

Adegbami, A. and Uche, I. N. Charles 2016. "Despotic Democrats versus Good Governance: Challenges of Administration of Nigeria's Fourth Republic." *Journal of Developing Areas,* 50(4), 195–210

Adejumobi, S. and Momoh Abubakar, Eds. 1995. *The Political Economy of Nigeria Under the Military Rule: 1984–1993.* Harare, Zimbabwe: SAPES Book.

Ademola, M. and Neal, M. Mergie. 2013. *Aliko Mohammad Dangote: The Biography of the Richest Black Person in The World.* Houston, TX: Strategic Books.

Aderemi, O. 2019. "These are Members of the African Billionaires Club as Reported by Forbes 2019 Ranking." January 10. Retrieved January 9, 2021 from www.pulse.ng/bi/finance/these-are-members-of-the-african-billionaires-club-according-to-forbes-2019-ranking/qlj4zr6.

Agbese, Pita Ogaba. 1990. "The Political Economy of Militarization in Nigeria." *Africa Spectrum,* 25(3), 293–311

Akhaine. O. S. 2011. "Democracy and Development in Nigeria: The Missing Links." *Review of African Political Economy,* 38(130), 645–652.

Akinyoade, Akinyinka and Uche, Chibuke. 2018. "Development Built on Crony Capitalism? The Case of Dangote Cement." *Business History*, 60(6). https://doi.org / 10.1080/00076791.2017.1341492.

Ake, C. 1981. *The Political Economy of Africa.* Ibadan, Nigeria; Longman Publisher.

Ashman, S. 2009. "Capitalism, Uneven and Combined Development and the Trans Historic." *Cambridge Review of International Affairs,* 22(1), 29–46.

Baker, A. 2018. "What Africa's Richest Man Thinks Would Make Africa Rich." *Time,* October 24, p. 2. Retrieved March 5, 2020 from https://time.com/5432947/ aliko=dangote-richest-man-africa/

Beckman, Bjorn. 1982. "Whose State? State and Capitalist Development in Nigeria." *Review of African Political Economy,* 23, 37–51.

Bracking, S. and Harrison, G. 2003. "Africa: Imperialism Go Naked." *Monthly Review,* 55(6), 12–18.

Brautingam, D. 1991. Governance and Economy: A Review. Working Paper WPS 815. December. Washington, DC: World Bank, Policy and Review Department.

Burgis, T. 2015. *The Looting Machine: Warlords, Oligarchs, Corporations, Smugglers, and the Theft of Africa's Wealth.* New York: Public Affairs Press.

Business Highlights. 2019. "Development Economist Faults Dangote Claims on Refinery Product Sales." April 2. Retrieved on March 16, 2020 from https:// businesshilights.com.ng/development-economist-faults-dangotes-claims-on-refinery-product-sales/.

Daily Trust. 2020. "Dangote Acquires Savannah Sugar, Pays N13.2 Billion Dividends." July 10, Retrieved July 26, 2020 from www.dailytrust.com.ng/dangote-acquires-savannah-sugar-pays-n13-2bn-dividend.html.

Edozien, F. 2018. "In Nigeria, Plans for the World's Largest Refinery." *The New York Times.* October 8. Accessed February 12, 2020. https://nyti.ms/2CBY5IK

Forbes. 2020. "Aliko Dangote: Real Time Net Worth." Retrieved February 2, 2020 from www.forbes.com/profile/aliko-dangote/#22fa4c3f22fc.

Gadzey, Anthony, T. 1992. "State and Capitalist Transformation in Sub-Saharan Africa: A Development Model." *Comparative Political Studies,* 24(2), 455–487.

Guseh, J. and Oritsejafor, E. 2019. *Governance and Democracy in Africa: Regional and Continental Perspectives.* Boulder, CO: Lexington Books.

Ihnovbere, J. 2013. *The Political Economy of Crisis and Underdevelopment in Africa: Selected Works of Claude Ake.* Ota; Nigeria: Third World Publishers.

Iyayi, F. 1986. "The Primitive Accumulation of Capital in a Neo-Colony: The Nigerian Case." *Review of African Political Economy*, 35, 27–39.

Kieh, G. 2018. *Contemporary Issues in African Societies: Historical Analysis and Perspectives.* New York: Palgrave Macmillan Press.

Kalu, A. Kelechi. 1996. "Political Economy in Nigeria: The Military, Ethnic Politics and Development." *International Journal of Politics, Culture, and Society,* 10(2), 229–247.

Migdal, Joel. 1988. *Strong Societies and Weak States: State -Society Relations and State Capabilities in Third World.* Princeton, NJ: Princeton University Press.

Mills, C. W. 1969. *The Power Elite.* Boston, MA: Beacon Press.

Neshe, Mfonobong. 2017. "Africa's Richest Man Aliko Dangote Criticizes Tanzanian President over Policies." Retrieved January 9, 2021 from www..forbes.com/sites/ mfonobongnsehe/2017/10/10/africas_richest-man-aliko-dangote-criticizes-tanzanian-president-over-policies/?sh=6749b98576f3.

Neshe, Mfonobong. 2019. "Dangote Enters Togo with Fertilizers and Cement Deals." Retrieved January 9, 2021 from www..forbes.com/sites/mfonobongnsehe/2019/11/11/africas_richest-man-aliko-dangote-to-build-60-million-cement-factory-in-togo/?sh.

Nigerian Investment Promotion Commission. 2018a. "Report of Activities. Most Capitalized Companies in 2018." Retrieved March 6, 2020, from https://nipc.gov.ng/wp.content/uploads/2019/12/annual-report-2018–2019/211.pdf.

Nigerian Investment Promotion Commission. 2018b. *Report on Pioneer Status Incentice Applications Q2: 2018–April to June 30*. Abuja, Nigeria: Nigerian Investment Promotion Commission..

Offshore Magazine. 2020. "Obo-1 Well Encounters Hydrocarbons off Nigeria." Retrieved February 28, 2020 from www.offshore-mag.com/home/article/16792838/obo1-well-encounters-hydrocarbons-off-nigeria.

Olaitan, W. 1995. "The State and Economy in Nigeria: A Conceptualization." In Said Adejumobi and Momoh Abubakar (Eds), *The Political Economy of Nigeria Under the Military Rule: 1984–1993*. Harare, Zimbabwe: SAPES Book, 125–137.

Orimolade, O. S. and Hyacinth, Iwu N. 2016. "Explaining the Lineage of Capitalist Development in Nigeria." *Canadian Social Science,* 12(11), 42–50.

Ovadia, J. S. 2013. "The Making of Oil Based Indigenous Capitalism in Nigeria." *New Political Economy,* 18(2), 258–283.

Oxfam. 2020. "Wealth of the Richest Men in Nigeria could End Extreme Poverty in Country Yet 5 Million Face Hunger." Retrieved August 3, 2020 from www.oxfam.org/es/node/10536

Perez, G. S. 2019. "The Canaries to Africa: The Atlantic Strategy of 'To Be or Not to Be'." In T. Falola, R. J. Parrott and D. Sanchez-Porter (Eds), *African Islands: Leading Edge of Empire and Globalization*. Rochester, NY: University of Rochester Press, 39–44.

Piketty, T. 2015. *The Economics of Inequality*. Cambridge, MA: President and Fellows of Harvard College.

Skocpol, Theda. 1985. "Bringing the State Back in: Strategies of Analysis in Current Research." In P. B. Evans, D. Rueschmeyer and T. Skocpol (Eds), *Bring the State Back in*. London: Cambridge University Press, 3–37.

The Economist. 2019a. "The New Scramble for Africa: And How Africans could Win it." March 19, 19–22.

The Economist. 2019b. "Protection Racket: Muhammadu Buhari has Big Ambitions for Nigerian Manufacturing." , May 29, Retrieved March 6, 2020 from www.economist.com/middle-east-and-africa/2019/05/30/muhammadu-buhari-has-big-ambitions-for-nigerian-manufacturing.

Wengraf, L. 2018. *Extracting Profit*. Chicago, IL: Haymarker Books.

13 Tanzania can feed Africa

Potentials and challenges

Kitojo Kagome Wetengere

Introduction

Background information

After independence in 1961, Tanzania inherited the colonial capitalist economic system governed by the global market economy (Boesen et al. 1977). The major activities of the economy, such as industries, plantations, banks, mines and other relatively large commercial activities, continued to be operated by British colonial masters, as well as Asian and Arab business interests (Ngowi 2009: Mandalu et al. 2018). Being a capitalistic economy, it was these private owners of the major means of production and other global market forces that drove the economy (Ngowi 2009). This economy benefitted only a small segment of the population – "the haves" (Ngowi 2009).

The majority of Tanzanians, particularly those living in rural areas, did not enjoy the fruits of freedom and prosperity they had desired (Bulhan 2014). The people's expectations were not met, as they lived in more or less the same situation as before independence; they continued to labor for the same colonial masters (Ngowi 2009; Mandalu et al. 2018). The period from 1961 to 1966 was characterized by increased differentials in rural–urban development; inadequate local expertise; unutilized land and labor resources; widespread poverty; diseases and ignorance; and dependence on foreign aid and imports. Economic growth and exports stagnated (Ngowi 2009). It was during this period that the late Father of the Nation Mwalimu Nyerere named poverty, diseases and ignorance as Tanzania's greatest enemies.

In an attempt to build an economy that would benefit the majority of Tanzanians, the government adopted a policy of socialism (*ujamaa* in Kiswahili) and self-reliance as enshrined in the Arusha Declaration of 1967 (Ngowi 2009; URT 2016). It is this policy which changed Tanzania's political and economic landscape to a greater extent (Ngowi 2009). This attempt was meant to move away from over-reliance on foreign assistance in development, and from the private-sector market-led economy inherited from the colonial power; Tanzania moved to a state-owned, centrally planned and controlled economy (Ngowi 2009). However, to implement that, all the major means of production had to be nationalized and put under government control and management (URT 2016). From then onwards, emphasis was put on public ownership and the role of the private sector was sidelined (URT 2016). Private-sector entrepreneurs were looked upon as thieves, exploiters and "enemies of the state."

Ujamaa was Nyerere's model of African socialism, placing emphasis on political stability via a one-party system, rural regeneration through the creation of collective farms and economic growth through nationalization of key sectors of the economy (SAHO 2019). Whilst *ujamaa* helped to give direction to the newly independent nation and imbued Tanzanians with a greater sense of national identity, elements of the policy, particularly collectivization and state control of production, later contributed to economic problems and widespread corruption (Jonson 2000). State-owned enterprises were typically characterized by inadequate managerial and technical skills, embezzlement, capacity under-utilization, reliance on government subsidies, non-payment of taxes, over-employment and protection from imports that were monopolistic in nature (Ngowi 2009). As a result, state-owned enterprises became loss-making entities that depended on government subsidies for their survival, and most of these enterprises later collapsed (Ngowi 2009).

Another dominant feature during that period was Tanzania's involvement in supporting liberation movements throughout Africa (SAHO 2019). The late Nyerere strongly believed that Tanzania had a responsibility to assist other nations to achieve freedom from foreign and minority rule (SAHO 2019). Speaking at the Party Conference in 1967, Nyerere declared that "total African liberation and African unity are basic objectives of our Party and our Government … we shall never be really free and secure while some parts of our continent are still enslaved" (in Legum and Mmari 1995; SAHO 2019).

During the period, Tanzania offered itself as a base for those fighting for liberation, hosting the forces of many movements from South Africa, Mozambique, Angola, Zimbabwe and Namibia (Legum and Mmari 1995; Ngowi 2009). These movements benefitted from the safety and stability of the country, as well as the experience and guidance they received from those who had already achieved independence (SAHO 2019). Tanzania also welcomed and housed large numbers of refugees from struggles across Southern Africa, providing an escape for those endangered by war or colonial oppression (Ngowi 2009; SAHO 2019). This necessarily drained the already very limited resources for the country's economic development (Ngowi 2009).

From 1975 onwards, Tanzania adopted various programs as a way to transform the economy, but without much success (URT 2016). Many projects established during the period collapsed and others were forced to undertake massive employee retrenchment, thus adding to the number of unemployed in the economy. Following all this, and the persistence of the world economic (oil) crises in the mid-1980s, the government decided to move away from a state-controlled economy to a market-led economy exhibiting trade liberalization and privatization (THDR 2014; Ngowi 2009). After that shift, various reforms continued to be undertaken until 1996 when the reforms started bearing fruit.

Poverty status/situation

Prior to 1991, Tanzania was considered one of the poorest countries in the world (Morisset 2013; CIA 2013; Edwards 2016). According to the World Bank, between 1976 and 1990 Tanzania's nominal GNP per capita declined by 45 percent from US$ 180 to US$ 100 (Edwards 2016). The collapse of the Tanzanian economy between mid-1975 and 1993 represents one of the most spectacular economic collapses ever experienced in a country not affected by a major war or natural disaster (Edwards 2016).

In addition, while in 1991/1992 basic needs poverty was 39 percent and food poverty 22 percent, in the rural areas it was 40.8 percent and 23.1 percent respectively (NBS 2014). About 13.5 million Tanzanians were trapped in poverty (URT 2013; TNBS 2009). At least 4.2 million of those constituted the "extreme poor" for whom life means constantly choosing between difficult options, such as keeping the eldest child in school or pulling her/him out of class permanently to help grow more food on the family farm (Morisset 2013). The majority of those living in extreme poverty were located in the rural areas (Morisset 2013). Poverty was widespread and highest among households that lived in the rural areas depending on agriculture for their livelihood (URT 2005; TNBS 2009).

Since 1996, there has been remarkable progress in income per capita growth, GDP growth and other social indicators. For instance, in 2010 Tanzania's average per capita income stood at US$ 570, still placing it the 176th position out of 191 countries in the world (Morisset 2013). GDP growth rate between 2008 and 2010 averaged 5.6 percent (Edwards 2016). According to the United Nations' Human Development Index (HDI), Tanzania has made significant improvements when compared to both Sub-Saharan Africa and to the rest of the world (Edwards 2016). By 2010, Tanzania had surpassed the African region as a whole, and its HDI was almost 3 percent above that of Sub-Saharan Africa as a group (Edwards 2016). A study by Robinson et al. (2011), as cited by Edwards (2016), using time series techniques revealed that the "breakpoint" of Tanzania's growth process took place in 1996.

One of the big challenges that Tanzania faced, and still faces today, is to attain inclusive growth that achieves equity in society (URT 2016). Non-inclusive growth manifests itself in several aspects of life, such as increasing unemployment, high and pervasive rural poverty and increasing income inequalities in the midst of high economic growth (URT 2016). One of the core reasons for such non-inclusive growth is that the economic growth has been driven by a number of fast-growing capital-intensive sectors whose activities are predominantly located in cities or a small number of growth centers (URT 2011; Morisset 2013). A notable characteristic of the fast-growing sectors is that they have weak forward and backward linkages with the agricultural sector, which is the mainstay of more than 80 percent of the rural population (URT 2011). This explains why the benefits of economic growth have been skewed against the agriculture sector (URT 2011).

Although the number of people living in poverty appears to have declined following the economic growth since 2007, poverty is still a problem (NBS 2014; World Bank 2015). Data show that about 12 million Tanzanian people were still living below the poverty line (World Bank 2015). Also, while the poverty headcount declined by around 18 percent, the absolute number of poor people only declined by 10 percent from 13.2 million to 11.9 million from 2007 to 2011/2012, due to population growth (World Bank 2015). Likewise, the absolute number of extreme poor decreased by only 7 percent, declining from 4.5 million to 4.2 million (World Bank 2015). Further, about 10 million people in the rural population live in poverty, and 3.4 million live in extreme poverty (World Bank 2015). In addition, a large share of the population hovers around the poverty line (World Bank 2015). This suggests that an important proportion of moderately poor people are positioned to move out of poverty, but also that an important proportion of non-poor people are vulnerable to falling into poverty (World Bank 2015).

Likewise, the 2011/2012 survey revealed that there are three main factors that are related to changes in poverty and inequality (NBS 2014). First, poverty was associated with rural status, family size, education levels, wage employment and non-farm businesses, access to public infrastructure and internal migration (World Bank 2015). Second, the decline in poverty has been unevenly distributed geographically. Most of the improvement in the poverty indicators occurred in Dar es Salaam. Poverty declined by over 70 percent in Dar es Salaam but only by around 15 percent in the rural sector (World Bank 2015). Third, there has been increasing inequality between geographic domains. Inequality is increasing between urban and rural areas, as well as between Dar es Salaam and the other regions (World Bank 2015).

This chapter examines how Tanzania has evolved from a poor country that offered a philosophical blueprint to a socialist future for Africa and a supporter of African liberation movements, into an economic powerhouse that exerts great influence over Eastern, Central and Southern Africa. Tanzania, once called a sleeping giant, has transformed itself into an economic leader capable of feeding most Southern African countries. Although poverty and income inequality coexist with economic growth, the Fifth Government has shown a determination to fight it with greater strength than ever before.

Tanzania Development Vision (TDV) 2025

Responding to the above challenges, the government prepared the Tanzania Development Vision (TDV) 2025 (URT 1999). The Vision aspires to have Tanzania transformed into a middle-income and semi-industrialized nation by 2025, characterized by high-quality and sustainable livelihoods; peace, stability and unity; good governance and the rule of law; an educated and learning society; and a strong and competitive economy (URT 1999; URT 2016). These objectives not only deal with economic issues, but also social issues like education, health, electricity, safety net, water, housing, the environment and increasing involvement of the people in their own development (URT 1999). The thrust of these objectives is to attain sustainable development of the people.

The attainment of the Vision 2025 would be made possible through the transformation of the Tanzanian economy from "a weather and market dependent agricultural economy to a self-sustaining semi-industrialized economy" (URT 1999). This shift in focus was essential for the ailing industrial sector in Tanzania (URT 2016). It was anticipated that industrialization would contribute to higher economic growth, increased average per capita income and to eradicate absolute poverty (URT 2016).

Factors driving Tanzania's economic growth

During the implementation of the Vision, Tanzania has seen remarkable economic growth and strong resilience to external shocks (World Bank 2015). During 2005–2018, the economy expanded at an annualized rate of approximately 7 percent and it is expected to grow at the same rate annually for the next years (JMT 2018). Even with the interruptions of COVID-19, it is not expected that Tanzania's growth will be affected as much as that of other countries.

However impressive the average annual growth rate has been in the past decade, it has been lower than the target rate of 8–12 percent deemed necessary to eradicate absolute poverty and to realize the projected per capita nominal income of US$ 3,000 by 2025 (URT 2016). A GDP growth rate of 8 percent and above can only be achieved with a shift to higher value-added production processes than is currently the case, where production and trade in raw primary products is predominant (Figure 13.1). In other words, the production process must shift to a higher value and faster growth path to enable the Tanzania's economy to attain a middle income country (MIC) status by 2025 (Figure 13.1).

This requirement has prompted the government to emphasize four driving factors, namely: industrialization; greater openness to regional and global trade; infrastructure development; and technology and innovation (see Figure 13.1). The former three drivers are required to cause the "jump" that will shift to a higher production process that will add value to raw primary products (URT 2016). While technology and innovation are vital at all stages, they remain an important requirement to foster steady growth (URT 2016).

The four drivers and their role to "cause a jump" are hereby briefly analyzed:

- **Industrialization** is vital to enhance rapid economic growth as it generates jobs, produces goods and services for home consumption as well as for export to earn foreign currency, generates revenue to enable the government to provide necessary services, generates technology, skills and competitiveness and, finally, fosters forward linkages. The envisaged industrialization has to be based on the country's comparative advantages and on upgrading innovativeness with a view to integrate and deepen into

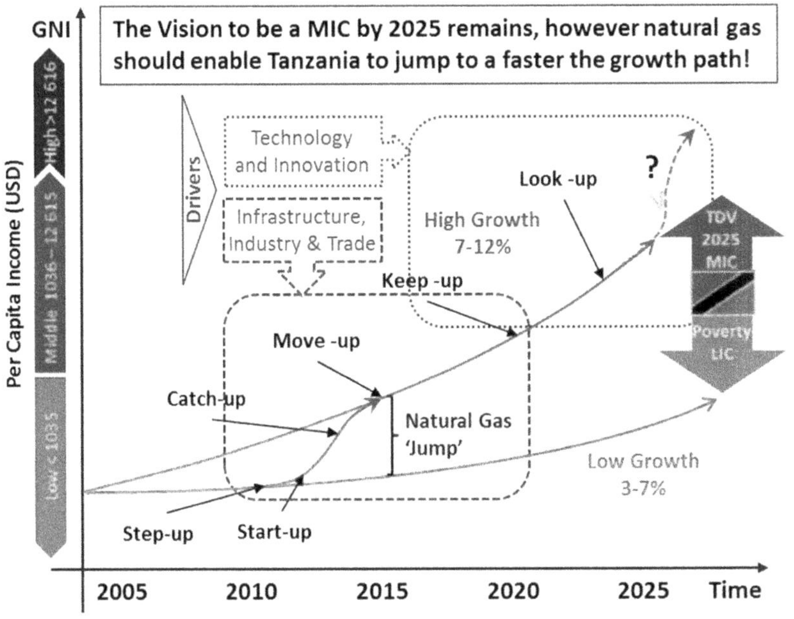

Figure 13.1 Required change in economic growth trajectory/path for MIC target.
Notes: MIC= Middle Income Country; LIC= Low Income Country.
Source: URT (2016).

regional and global value chains and pursue competitive industrialization (URT 2016).

- **International trade** opens up and widens markets for local produce and therefore enhances home production, earns revenue for the government and the highly needed foreign currency, generates jobs, enables the country to acquire goods and services not produced domestically and, finally, enhances competition by opening up products from outside.
- **Construction of infrastructure** is key to industrialization and economic growth. No country would attain industrialization and rapid economic growth without developing modern and efficient infrastructure. Infrastructure needed in Tanzania includes transport, i.e. roads, railways, air and water transport; generation of energy (hydropower, solar, gas, fuel, coal and wind); and communication and information. Modern and efficient infrastructure has a tendency to widen markets within and outside the country, to lower production costs and to enable timely delivery of people and goods, thus promoting trade, investment and tourism.
- **Modern technology and innovation** are the key drivers in improving efficiency and competition. As the late third president of Tanzania Hon. Mkapa said, "the 21st century is characterized by competition and if we are to be active participants in the global development we must among other

things embrace advanced technology" (URT 1999). Modern technology has a tendency to improve efficiency and reduce costs per unit over time, making the production process more profitable and competitive.

Another driver not mentioned in Figure 13.1 is the development of a **competent labor force** (URT 1999). Tanzania wants to be a nation with education of high quality at all levels; a nation which produces the quantity and quality of educated people sufficiently equipped with the requisite knowledge to solve society's problems, meet the challenges of development and attain competitiveness at regional and global levels (URT 1999). Despite that good intention and efforts made so far, there are still shortages in the fields of high science and technology, mining, industrial and gas exploration.

Achievements of the Tanzania Development Vision 2025

During the implementation of the Vision, commendable results have been achieved. However, the achievements would not be possible without the increase of domestic revenue collections. The Tanzanian government claims, in its Nation Budget Speech for 2020/21 Financial Year, that the annual domestic revenue collection (tax and non-tax) increased from Tshs. 11 trillion in 2014/15 to Tshs. 18.5 trillion in 2018/19. Tax revenue increased from Tshs. 9.9 trillion in 2014/15 to Tshs. 15.5 trillion in 2018/19. On a monthly basis, tax revenue collection increased from an average of Tshs. 825 billion in 2014/15 to an average of Tshs 1.5 trillion in 2018/19. Approximately 87.2 percent of funds for the implementation of major economic infrastructure (construction, transport and electricity) and social services (health, education and water) came from domestic revenue collection.

Industrialization

In the 1990s to early 2000s, the manufacturing sector growth rate averaged 8 percent (URT 2016). This rate was not enough to champion the growth of the economy of 8–12 percent as stipulated in the TDV 2025. Also, the sector contributed about 7 percent of the GDP (URT 2016). Size-wise, out of 49,247 businesses established, about 47,921 (97 percent) were small-scale, employing less than ten people (URT 2016). That means that the manufacturing sector did not have as significant an impact on employment as was expected.

A new spirit of industrialization emerged after the coming into power of the Fifth Government (October 2015–April 2020), leading to the establishment of 8,477 new industries in 26 regions of Mainland Tanzania. Out of those, 201 companies are large, 460 are medium, 3,406 are relatively small and 4,419 are very small categories. All together they have created 482,601 jobs, averaging 56 people per firm, according to public statements by the Tanzanian government.

The increase in new businesses, which coincides with the increase in production capacities, has led to increases in the supply of locally manufactured goods. For instance, installed cement production capacity has increased from 4.7 million tons in 2015 to 9.1 million tons in 2019. Further actual cement production has increased to 6.5 million tons in 2019 compared to 3.3 million tons produced in 2015. Actual demand in 2019 was 4.8 million tons, implying that cement production was sufficient to meet domestic demand and, thus, that the surplus could be exported. Generally, increases in businesses have led to availability of markets for agricultural, livestock and fisheries products, which are used as industrial raw materials as well as essential commodities for domestic and international markets.

The impact of industrialization on the disadvantaged population

Industrialization has been linked to economic growth; it plays a catalytic role in transforming the economic structure of agrarian societies and has spillover effects on the mass population (UNIDO 2012). Unfortunately, little of this has been achieved in Tanzania. Deciding whether industrialization is beneficial to the mass population or not critically depends on what kind of industrialization one is speaking about (URT 2016). Available data show that most businesses established after independence were located in only a few urban areas to serve elite consumers; they were import-dependent, capital-intensive, export-led and had weak linkages with the rest of the economy (URT 2016). That means businesses alienated the majority of poor, particularly those living in the rural areas (Wetengere 2020). So, industrialization witnessed economic growth without having significant impact on the local people (Wetengere 2020). In other words, industrialization was not organically embedded in the local economy (Wetengere 2020).

If industrialization is to have an impact on the well-being of the majority poor, it has to be comprised of businesses that are labor intensive, i.e., which employ many poor people and come with modern technology, skills, and competitiveness; they should also add value to agriculture (crops, forest, fisheries, and livestock) and produce goods and services for home consumption as well as for export to earn hard currency. Under these conditions, industrialization would generate revenue, produce equipment needed for the development of other local industries in the economy and foster forward and backward linkages (Wetengere 2020). Yet, for the industries to fulfill most of the above, they have to be located in areas where the majority poor reside. In that way, the poor will feel the spillover effects.

Such businesses play the more ambitious role of the yeast that makes the whole loaf of bread grow (Wetengere 2020). That means, since industrialization makes the national economy grow, if it is embedded in the local economy then the whole economy will grow (Wetengere 2020). And, if the local people actively participate in making the economy grow, it follows that, as the economy grows, the well-being of the local people grows as well (Wetengere 2020). This is in line with the late Father of the Nation Mwalimu Nyerere (1974) who asserted "if local people are the key participants in the growth of things like buildings, roads, airplanes, railways, irrigation schemes or production of goods and services, then such growth will have impact on their wellbeing."

Soft and hard infrastructure

Soft infrastructures: Provision of social services

Since the benefits of economic growth may not necessarily "trickle down" to the mass population, conscious efforts need to be made to reach the disadvantaged poor (Wetengere 2019). To integrate economic and human development, the government has taken deliberate actions to improve access to social services in both urban and rural areas.

HEALTH SERVICES

Health infrastructure has been enhanced through construction of 1,198 dispensaries, 487 health centers, 71 district hospitals, and regional referral hospitals for ten regions and three zonal referral hospitals; increased budget for medicines, equipment, medical equipment and reagents; and improved access to essential medicines in health facilities. Consequently, there has been a reduction in patients being referred abroad for further medical treatment by 95 percent, hence saving approximately Tshs. 20 billion in the past five years.

WATER SERVICES

The government has publicly claimed that it has improved access to clean and safe water in urban and rural areas. Access to clean and safe water has increased to 70 percent in rural and 84 percent in urban areas. Further, the government has constructed and rehabilitated 1,423 water infrastructures, of which 1,268 are in rural and 155 are in urban areas. The improved access to clean and safe water has reduced time spent in fetching water, particularly for women; this has led to greater female participation in economic activities such as farming and business. Also, accessibility to clean and safe water has reduced the outbreak of waterborne diseases, therefore reducing medical expenses and improving the health and productivity of labor force.

EDUCATION SERVICES

The government has managed to finance free basic education from primary to form four (i.e. class 12); has expanded construction and rehabilitation of learning and teaching infrastructure including classrooms, laboratories, libraries and dormitories; has increased the number of students who passed standard seven (82 percent) and form four (81 percent); has strengthened higher learning institutions and vocational training colleges; and strengthened higher education through provision of subvention to higher learning institutions and students loans. A total of Tshs. 2.20 trillion was spent for student loans during 2015 to 2020, which made it possible for more students from low-income families to acquire higher education. This effort has reduced the burden of the citizens to pay for education services, increased enrollment and improved students' performance at all levels.

Hard infrastructures: Construction, transport and energy infrastructures

The construction and rehabilitation of infrastructure projects in construction, transport and energy sectors has enabled Tanzania to have a robust and competitive economy; improve employment and income for Tanzanians; enhance efficiency in delivery and access to goods and services; and stimulate the development of towns and other sectors such as agriculture, industry, tourism and trade as well as widening the revenue base.

ROAD TRANSPORT

In the construction of roads, achievements realized in the past five years include the following. Construction of trunk, regional and districts roads of 2,624.27 km to bitumen standard was completed; construction of Mfugale flyover (Dar es Salaam), Furahisha bridge (Mwanza) and Magufuli bridge (Kilombero river) were completed; in progress are construction of 1,298.44 km of trunk roads to bitumen standard, Ubungo interchange, eight lanes Kimara to Kibaha road (19.2 km), New Selander bridge (Dar es Salaam, 1.03 km), Kigongo-Busisi bridge (Mwanza, 3.2 km), New Wami bridge (513.5 m) and Ruhuhu bridge (Ruvuma). The implementation of these projects has stimulated various economic activities; improved access to markets, schools and dispensaries; reduced transport and transaction costs; saved travel time and created employment opportunities.

PORT CONSTRUCTION

Knowing the importance of ports in economic development, efforts made to improve these services include: completion of berth numbers 1–4 and Roll on Roll off (Ro-Ro) and installation of integrated port system and inspection machines at Dar es Salaam Port; construction of 300m berth at Mtwara Port; rehabilitation of warehouse and berth numbers 1–2 at Tanga Port; completion of dredging at Tanga Port; and construction and rehabilitation of Lushamba, Ntama, Nyamirembe and Magarine berths and Mwigobero Wharf at Lake Victoria; Kagunga, Sibwesa, Kabwe, Lagosa and Kibirizi berths at Lake Tanganyika; and Ndumbi berth at Lake Nyasa. These efforts have improved services, facilitated docking of large vessels and improved revenue collection at the ports.

Other achievements include: continued building of a new ship with carrying capacity of 1,200 passengers and 400 tons of cargo in Lake Victoria and floating dock; rehabilitation of MV *Victoria* and MV *Butiama*. Likewise, the construction of one ship with carrying capacity of 200 passengers and 200 tons of cargo at Lake Nyasa has been completed; building of MV *Kigamboni,* MV *Utete*, Kigongo–Busisi, MV *Sengerema* and Nyamisati–Mafia ferries; and rehabilitation of MT *Sangara* in Lake Tanganyika.

RAILWAY TRANSPORT

In improvement of railway transport, achievements include: commencement of construction of the Standard Gauge Railway line (SGR) from Dar es Salaam to Morogoro section (300km) and Morogoro to Makutopora, Dodoma section (422km). Implementation of this project has enabled the creation of 13,177 jobs and the engagement of 640 local contractors. Other achievements include: resumption of railway cargo services from Dar es Salaam Port to Uganda; completion of rehabilitation of Dar es Salaam to Moshi railway (558.8km), which is operational; and completion of rehabilitation of Tanga to Korogwe railway (84km). Other ongoing projects include: rehabilitation of Moshi to Arusha railway (86km); and rehabilitation of Dar es Salaam to Kilosa railway (283km) and Kilosa to Isaka (in Shinyanga) railway (687).

AIR TRANSPORT

Regarding air transport, achievements include: revamping of Air Tanzania Company Limited (ATCL) with the procurement of 11 new aircraft. By April 2020, eight aircraft had been delivered and commenced operations in domestic and international routes and initial payment for the remaining three new aircraft had been made. Terminal III building at Julius Nyerere International Airport (JNIA) had been completed. The terminal has a capacity of 6 million passengers per annum. Also, three civil aviation radars have been installed in JNIA, Kilimanjaro International Airport (KIA) and Mwanza Airport; rehabilitation of KIA and Dodoma Airport have been completed; and construction and rehabilitation of various regional airports are at different stages of implementation.

ENERGY SERVICES

Regarding energy infrastructure projects, achievements include: commencement of construction of an historic project of Julius Nyerere Hydropower (2,115 MW) at Rufiji River; continuing implementation of Kinyerezi I Extension Power Plant (185 MW) and Kinyerezi II (240 MW); continuing implementation of mega power transmission projects of North West Grid Extension 400 kV (Mbeya–Sumbawanga–Mpanda–Kigoma–Nyakanazi), 220 kV (Makambako–Songea), 400 kV (Singida–Arusha–Namanga), 400 kV (Rufiji–Chalinze–Kinyerezi and Chalinze–Dodoma), 220 kV (Rusumo–Nyakanazi), 220 kV (Geita–Nyakanazi) and 220 kV (Bulyanhulu–Geita).

Also, in ensuring access to electricity in rural areas, the government has continued to implement rural electrification projects through the Rural Energy Agency (REA), whereby a total of 9,112 villages (74 percent) out of 12,268 in Mainland Tanzania were electrified by April 2020. Implementation of these projects has benefitted rural population and 11,128 institutions involved in education, health, water and religion, as well as trade services.

International trade

Tanzania continues to consolidate gains from rigorous trade reforms that began in the 1990s, resulting in a more liberalized trade regime. Restrictions on imports have been removed, except for those that are necessary for health or security reasons; export and import procedures have been simplified; and the state monopoly on the export of traditional cash crops has ended. Internal trade restrictions have also been removed, and price controls have been eliminated on most products apart from oil. Trade with non-Western economic partners, particularly China, continues to grow (MAFAP 2013).

Tanzania's exports of goods and services have shown an increase in the past few years. For instance, according to Bank of Tanzania (BOT) monthly review for January 2020, Tanzania's exports rose by 15.8 percent from US$ 8.3 billion in 2018 and to US$ 9.712 in 2019 (Lamtey 2020). An increased trend was observed until April 2020 when Tanzania was hit hard by COVID-19. This performance has been attributed to rises in service receipts and the value of non-traditional goods exports. Non-traditional goods worth $4.236 billion were exported in 2019 compared with $3.209 billion in the preceding year (Lamtey 2020). Gold exports accounted for 52.3 percent of non-traditional goods exports (Lamtey 2020).

Service earning increased from US$ 4.014 billion in 2018 to US$ 4.139 billion in 2019. Travel proceeds, mostly from tourism-related activities, accounted for 61 percent of all services (Lamtey 2020). The growth was attributed to an increase in the number of tourist arrivals, according to the BOT review (see Lamtey 2020). Manufactured goods exports grew by 24 percent to US$ 984.9 million from US$ 693 million, mainly driven by sisal yarn and twine, iron and steel products, glass and glassware, manufactured tobacco and fertilizers (Lamtey 2020). The value of traditional exports of cashew nuts, cotton and coffee rose to $829.9 million in 2019 from $772.1 million the previous year (Lamtey 2020). Although the share of foodstuffs export has been increasing over time, its share of the total exports is still meager.

Foreign private investment flows and distribution by activities

Foreign private investment is an important source of foreign exchange flows and capital, which can significantly contribute to Tanzania's economic growth (BoT 2018). Due to its importance, Tanzania has continued to implement policies aimed at improving its investment climate in order to further attract Foreign Direct Investment (FDI) inflows (BoT 2018). As a result, the stock of foreign private investment increased to US$ 15,392.9 million in 2017 from US$ 14,634.3 million in 2016 (BoT 2018). A large share of the investment inflows was FDI, to the tune of USD 13,499.5 million, accounting for 87.7 percent of the stock of foreign private investment (BoT 2018).

Despite the global decline, FDI inflows to Tanzania were 24.2 percent higher in 2017 compared with the inflows registered in 2016. The lower FDI inflows in 2016 were consistent with the general global trend and large repayment of loans and losses retained (BoT 2018). During 2017, mining and quarrying continued to be the leading activity as it accumulated a stock of FDI valued at US$ 5,419.1 million accounting for 40.1 percent, followed by manufacturing valued at US$ 1,915.9 million, information and communication valued at US$ 1,731.2 million and finance and insurance valued at US$ 1,585.2 million (Table 13.1). The mining and quarrying sector has maintained a leading role in terms of stock over the past ten consecutive years (BoT 2018).

Further, FDI inflows to the country were concentrated in three main activities namely accommodation and food services, mining and quarrying, and finance and insurance, which altogether accounted for 61.5 percent of the total inflows in 2017 (BoT 2018). Accommodation and food services became prominent in attracting FDI inflows in 2017, attributed mainly by expansion in accommodation and food service facilities following increases in tourism activities (BoT 2018).

Marxist economists, particularly those from developing countries, have long viewed foreign investments (FIs) as instruments to foster new forms of colonialism. In the same vein, objective analysis indicates that multinational corporations (MNCs) and others can and do act in ways that go against the interests of countries that receive investments. In most cases, the MNCs work for the interest of countries where they come from. Experience in Tanzania has shown that the MNCs in mining have been exploitative, leading to amendment of various mining investment laws and agreements. Also, the MNCs have been accused of evading taxes, using capital-intensive techniques, employing workers from home and investing profits in their home country. In that way, Tanzania has for so long contributed to capital accumulation in countries where the MNCs come from.

Table 13.1 Stock and flow of FDI by activity, 2013–2017 (in $ million)

S/N	*Sector*	*2013*	*2014*	*2015*	*2016*	*2017*
1	Mining and Quarrying	4,885.2	5264.9	6,650.9	6736.5	5,419.1
2	Manufacturing	1,378.4	1372.2	1,512.9	1,725.9	1,915.9
3	Information and Communication	706.7	761.9	751.7	817.1	1,731.2
4	Finance and Insurance	1,215.2	1,395.1	1,199.0	1,300.6	1,585.2
5	Wholesale and Retail Trade	452.1	472.1	541.5	559.7	802.4
6	Agriculture, Forestry & Fishing	509.2	487.5	359.1	387.8	501.4
7	Accommodation and food service	167.1	180.0	218.3	314.3	418.9

Source: BoT (2018).

But experience also shows that FIs can be very beneficial to the receiving countries. Whether the receiving countries benefit from FIs or not depend on whether the receiving states stand firm to protect their interests. In other words, where a country's interest differs with those of MNCs, it is for the investment-receiving state to be on their guard to protect their interests. The Fifth Government of Tanzania has shown vividly that, when a country stands up for its own interests, MNCs will enter into beneficial agreements and even pay compensation. Let us note that MNCs can work with anybody, be it God or the devil!

Technology and innovation development

Science, technology and innovations are key drivers to economic growth and self-reliance of any nation (URT 1996). Countries which embraced science, technology and innovations have not only attained higher economic development and broken the cycle of poverty but have also enhanced their international competitiveness (URT 1996). Realizing its importance, Tanzania has embraced it in every sector of the economy. For instance, there has been increasing application of irrigation technology, application of farm inputs, insecticides and pesticides in agriculture. Also, the application of the ICT in marketing of agriculture produce has increased. The same trend has been observed in other sectors like information and communication, manufacturing, education, fisheries, tourism, mining and in revenue collection. As a result, efficiency and productivity have increased significantly.

Development of other sectors

Agriculture development

Agriculture is the backbone of the Tanzanian economy, and achievements made in the sector includes: expansion of irrigation area from 461,326 hectares to 694,715 hectares; expansion of food crops storage capacity by National Food Reserve Agency (NFRA) and Cereals and Other Produce Board of Tanzania from 371,000 tons to 621,000 tons; expansion in major cash crops production from 796,502 tons to 1,144,631 tons; increases in the value of exports of horticulture products from USD 412 million to USD 779 million and establishment of crop insurance aiming to protect farmers from the impact of natural calamities and climate change as well as collateral for accessing loans.

Further, the embedding of agriculture with factors driving the economy to grow has had significant impact on the sector. There has been the establishment of agro-processing industries, improvement of infrastructure in rural areas, embracing modern technology in the sector, opening up of trade for agriculture produce in neighboring markets and removal of taxes and non-tax barriers. As a result, agriculture production has increased and in the past decade Tanzania has attained food self-sufficiency and surplus for export.

Livestock development

Achievements attained in the livestock sector include the increase of land reserved for grazing to 2.82 million hectares from 1.4 million hectares. This has resulted in reduction of conflicts between farmers and pastoralists. Further, the livestock sector has managed to secure loans from Tanzania Agricultural Development Bank (TADB) amounting to 22 billion shillings whereas there was no such service in the past. In addition, there has been the construction of new meat processing industries including: Tan Choice Limited, Elia Foods Oversees Limited, Binjiang Company Limited, as well as Galaxy Milk Processing Industry with a capacity to process 75,000 liters per day.

Fisheries development

Achievements in the fisheries sector include: improvement in management and control of fisheries resources; increase in the fish catch from 387,543 to 448,467 tons; increase in number of Nile Perch from 417,936 tons to 816,964 tons; increase in the value of fish exports to an average of 692 billion shillings per annum from 379 billion shillings; revamping of Tanzania Fisheries Corporation (TAFICO); elimination of illegal fishing by more than 80 percent in fresh water, and 100 percent of fishing along the coast. Furthermore, the government has continued to promote investment in aquaculture and has increased the number of fish farmers from 18,843 to 26,474.

Good governance, peace and security

Various efforts taken by the government in combatting corruption, illicit drug abuse and trafficking include: strengthening of PCCB; establishment of High Court Corruption and Economic Crimes Division and Drug Control and Enforcement Authority, resulting in notable achievements in saving public funds, prohibiting illicit traffic in narcotic drugs and psychotropic substances; establishment of sober houses; instilling discipline, integrity and accountability in various areas including public services, business and enhanced efficiency in revenue collection and public expenditure. In its Nation Budget Speech, the Tanzanian government claims that unity, peace and tranquility continue to prevail, thus allowing citizens to perform their duties peacefully. Likewise, the government has continued to maintain and strengthen the union between Mainland Tanzania and Zanzibar. In addition, the judiciary has continued to be strengthened through improving courts and court infrastructure; increasing the number of judges and other staff.

Minerals

Achievements in the mining sector include the amendment of various mining investment laws and agreements leading to the establishment of a Joint Venture Company known as Twiga Minerals Corporation Limited between the government (16 percent shares) and Barrick Gold Corporation Company (BGCC) (84 percent shares); and payment of compensation amounting to USD 100 million equivalent to Tshs. 250 billion from BGCC as initial settlement of the agreed amount of USD 300 million equivalent to Tshs. 750 billion.

Also, the amendment of mining laws has facilitated the commencement of negotiations between the government and major mining companies in order to acquire 16 percent of shares on a free carry basis. Likewise, the government established 28 markets and 25 mineral sales centers; completion of construction of four centers of excellence in Bukoba, Handeni, Bariadi and Musoma; completion of two model gold smelters in Lwamgasa and Katente; completion of a one-stop center at Mirerani; strengthening of mineral control and reduction of mineral smuggling, mainly due to construction of a 24.5 km wall around the Tanzanite mine at Mirerani; and increase in mineral revenue collection from Tshs. 196.0 billion in 2015/16 to Tshs. 470 billion shillings from July 2019 to April 2020.

Business and investment environment

The government has continued to implement the Roadmap for Improvement of Business and Investment Climate and Blueprint for Regulatory Reforms to Improve the Business Environment. This action plan is meant to ensure that the identified business and investment constraints are eliminated to attract more investment. In implementing the action plan, different measures have been taken including: abolishing 114 fees in the agriculture, livestock and fisheries sector in 2017/18, abolishing five fees that were charged by the Occupational Safety and Health Agency; removing 54 different nuisance levies and fees in various sectors in 2018/19; establishment of one stop border posts (OSBPs) between Tanzania and neighboring countries which strengthen trade; establishment of the one stop service center (OSSC) that expedite service delivery to customers; streamlining the functions of Tanzania Bureau of Standards (TBS) and Tanzania Medicines and Medical Devices Authority (TMDA) to remove duplication. Implementation of these measures has strengthened the business environment in the country.

Poverty status

Income and non-income poverty continued to decline; basic needs poverty declined from 28.2 percent in 2011/12 to 26.4 percent in 2017/18. The poverty incidence both in urban and rural areas declined to 15.8 percent and 31.3 percent, respectively from 21.7 percent and 33.3 percent. In addition, the level of poverty depth declined from 6.7 percent in 2011/12 to 6.2 percent in 2017/18 and poverty severity declined from 2.3 percent to 2.1 percent during the same period. Household monthly expenditure increased from an average of Tshs. 258,751 to Tshs. 416,927.

The decline in poverty was mainly due to efforts taken in combatting income and non-income poverty. Government efforts include: investment in supportive infrastructure in production and business activities in order to improve the economy and per capita income; management and improvement of the financial sectors; increasing availability and accessibility to primary services such as health, education, water and electricity especially in rural areas; and implementation of Productive Social Safety Nets Program through Tanzania Social Action Fund (TASAF) in order to increase income in the poor households and enable them to acquire the primary services mentioned.

Macro-economic status

The Tanzanian economy has been growing at an average of 7 percent in the past ten years. This growth has resulted in increased government revenue to finance major economic infrastructure, and to improve social services and increases in economic opportunities. The impressive GDP growth has made the country the tenth largest economy in Africa and second fastest growing in East Africa after that of Rwanda (8.6 percent). Also, the GDP per capita has increased from US$ 749.3 in 2010 to US$ 1,126 in 2019. This implies that Tanzania has attained a low middle-income country status (World Bank, 2020).

Inflation has remained stable, averaging 4.4 percent for the past five years. The stability achieved is attributed to prudent management of fiscal and monetary policies, stable oil prices and availability of food in domestic markets and in neighboring countries. It is due to this stability that the cost of living has eased, and good investment has been created. Also, by April 2020, Tanzania's foreign reserves amounted to USD 5.3 billion, sufficient to cover 6.1 months of imports of goods and services as compared to USD 4.4 billion, which was sufficient to cover 4.3 months of imports of goods and services in 2015. This was attributed to the increase in foreign investment and export of goods and services.

Emergence of business tycoons in Tanzania

Although the government has directly invested in strategic projects, the core role of the government has been to facilitate, promote and provide services. That means creating an enabling environment for inviting business and investment. By so doing, they have managed to attract business enterprises which are the main direct beneficiaries. At the same time, exports, investments and technology acquisition generate employment, contribute to higher tax revenues and help the country's socio-economic growth.

According to the Wealth Report 2020, Tanzania is topping East African Countries (EAC) in the growing list of wealthy individuals worth a million dollars (Anyanzwa 2020). The Wealth Report 2020 by the real estate consultancy firm Knight Frank shows that Tanzania is the only country in EAC to have produced a single individual controlling a net wealth of US$ 1 billion or more, with the number of ultra-high-net-worth individuals (UHNWIs) holding US$ 30 million or more worth of assets including their primary residence has risen 5 percent to 114 in 2019, from 109 in 2018 (see Anyanzwa 2020).

These business tycoons have built multibillion-dollar industries in diverse sectors, namely: agriculture, media, automotive accessories, banking, insurance, petroleum, real state, transportation, mining, energy, tourism, telecommunication, manufacturing and fast-moving consumer goods and others. Their investments in various sectors have made the country a strategic investment opportunity for global billionaires. The five richest business tycoons in the country and their estimated wealth value include: Mohamed Dewji (Tshs. 3.4 trillion), Rostam Aziz (Tshs. 2.3 trillion), Ally Awadhi (2.3 trillion), Said Bakhresa (Tshs. 1.3 trillion) and Reginald Mengi (Tshs. 1.2 trillion). Their total wealth represents 27 percent of the Tanzanians 2020/21 budget of Tshs. 34.9 trillion (Ayub 2020).

Other rich business tycoons in Tanzania include: Shehar Kanabar, Shubash Patel, Fida Hussein Rashid, Yusuf Manji, Salim Turkey, Ghalib Said Mohammed and Yogash Manek (Ayub 2020; Mbani 2020). Further, the Wealth Report 2020 shows that the number of Tanzanian high-net-worth individuals (HNWI) with $1 million or more worth of assets, including their primary residence, rose by 8 percent over the 2018–2019 period, while that of Kenya and Uganda declined during the same period (Anyanzwa 2020).

While most wealthy Africans direct their financial investments to the United Kingdom (UK), United States of America (USA), South Africa, Kenya and Australia, Tanzanian business tycoons focus their investments in Tanzania and other African countries (Anyanzwa 2020). This means the direct benefits of their investments such as employment, backward and forward linkages, tax payment, availability of goods, technology and skills accrue to the benefit of Tanzania.

All the above has made Tanzania become an economic power that provides foodstuffs and services to the neighboring countries of Uganda, South Sudan, Rwanda, Burundi, Kenya, Malawi, Democratic Republic of Congo, Mozambique and Zambia. Given the strategic position of Tanzania and its resources endowment, there are strong reasons to believe that the country will continue to sustain its economic influence throughout Africa in the years to come.

Postulations behind the upsurge of wealthy Tanzanians

One of the reasons put forward for the emergence of business tycoons in Tanzania is that the improvement of the business and investment environment has attracted more businesspeople to invest in the country. While this is true, there are other reasons that are equally likely to explain the increase in the number of wealthier Tanzanians.

Before the Fifth Government came into power in 2015, corruption thrived in all spheres of life in Tanzania (Chêne 2009; TI 2012). Scandals of corruption were commonplace and it reached a point where corruption was taken as a part of day-to-day life. Explaining the magnitude of corruption in Tanzania during that period, the Fourth President of Tanzania, Hon. Jakaya Kikwete said, "if purposive actions will not be taken to fight corruption, the ruling party will not win the 2015 election." This was said because many leaders attained leadership positions and/or became Members of Parliament (MP) through corrupt ways. Some businesspersons also aspired to political posts or to become an MP. The reason was simple; being a leader or a MP made it easier to access government resources. So, during that period, the top leaders complained about corruption, and local Tanzanians also complained, but surprisingly no action was taken against it because corrupt leaders were everywhere. All they could do was to transfer a culprit from one position to another, or ask them to resign – which was tantamount to sending them on honeymoon to eat the money siphoned through corruption.

At this period, the government lost a lot of money through corrupt ways. For instance, the Global Financial Integrity (GFI) revealed that Tanzania lost Tshs. 3 trillion each year through tax evasion by big mining companies and through export and import of goods (GFI 2014). Such a loss was equivalent to 15 percent of the 2014/15 national budget. The Controller and Auditor General (CAG) estimated that about 20 percent of the government budget was lost each year through corrupt ways (Chêne 2009). The then Director of Prevention and Combating of Corruption Bureau (PCCB) in Tanzania estimated that the amount lost was as high as 30 percent of the government budget, which was approximately 6 percent of the 2015/16 national budget. The question to ponder is, where did all this money go? Of course, the businesspeople had the lion's share. When the Fifth Government came into power many corrupt businesspeople could not withstand the wind of change and those who remained had to find other ways to survive. It is due to this that there has been mistrust between holders of power and the private sector (URT 2016). The private-sector entrepreneurs have been looked upon as thieves, exploiters and enemies of the state (URT 2016).

Similarly, there has been a tendency among businesspeople to support politicians in cash or kind during elections. Many people have questioned the purpose of such support. Was it for free? Or there was a hidden agenda? Some people have seen it as a bribe or looking for some kind of a favor once the contenders have been elected into power. Of course, once you accept the support, just like any other assistance, it is the donor not the recipient who decides its intention. That is why, during that period, most leaders were just figureheads, because it was the businessperson who put them in power that decided what should be done. It is not surprising therefore that the President of the Fifth Government His Excellence Hon. John Magufuli refused to accept any such support.

Tanzania's resource endowment, export potential and challenges

Tanzania's resource endowment related to food production and trade

Resource endowment offers great opportunities for investment, and for trade and tourism, which can lead to high growth and development if properly managed (JMT 1999; URT 2016). Tanzania is strategically located at the crossroads between Southern, Central, Eastern and Southwestern Africa. Six land-locked countries, namely Uganda, Rwanda, Burundi, Democratic

Republic of Congo (DRC), Zambia and Malawi, depend on Tanzania's harbors and other means of transport like roads, railway and waterways to transfer goods into and out of their countries (Bagenda 2003; Youging 2015). Tanzania has three harbors, namely Dar es Salaam, Tanga and Mtwara, which are gateways for international trade with countries surrounding it. The World Bank (2013b) revealed that Tanzania could benefit greatly if the harbors are managed properly.

Land is one of the most important resources of production and development of a country. Tanzania has an area of 947,300 sq. kilometers or 95,500,000 hectares. Out of the total area, 88,500,000 hectares (94 percent) are dry land and 6,000,000 hectares (6 percent) are covered by water. The area suitable for agriculture is 44,000,000 hectares (50 percent of dry land). The area under cultivation is only 14,000,000 hectares (32 percent of the total area suitable for agriculture). The land area suitable for irrigation is 29,400,000 hectares, equivalent to 67 percent of all area suitable for agriculture. However, as of 2020, only 694,715 hectares are under irrigation, which is equivalent to 2.4 percent of the total area suitable for irrigation.

Tanzania ranks tenth in the world, and second in Africa after Ethiopia, in the number of domesticated animals. It has an area of 26,000,000 hectares of land suitable for maintaining these different domesticated animals. According to URT (2017), Tanzania has 30.5 million cattle, 18.8 million goats, 5.3 million sheep, 38.2 million local chickens, 36.6 million hybrid chickens and 1.9 million pigs (URT 2017). The livestock sector employs about 50 percent of the population, which is equivalent to 4.6 million households whose income depends on livestock (URT 2017). The livestock sector plays an important role by increasing household food security, income, animal draught power, manure, foreign currency and employment opportunities while nurturing the livestock resources. This contributes to increased economic growth and government revenue.

It is evident from the above that Tanzania has enormous natural resources necessary to produce foodstuffs from agriculture, livestock as well as inland and marine fisheries.

Tanzania's export of food products in East and Southern Africa

Openness to trade in Africa, and globally, is one of the priorities of Tanzania's Development Vision 2025. It is anticipated that trade of value-added products would enable the economy to shift to a higher path of GDP growth rate of 8 percent and above.

Tanzania's exports of food products in the East African Community

Prior to the year 2000, Tanzania, which was supposed to be a major food-exporting country, struggled to meet its own food requirements (Wolter n.d.). So, instead of being a food exporter, it became a food importer (MAFAP 2013). That meant the country could not take advantage of its agri-business opportunities of being a major food exporter (Wolter n.d.). For instance, higher food prices, driven by higher costs of production and rising consumption in developing countries, provided Tanzania with ample opportunities to develop its agro-industry to tap into regional markets (FAO 2012). Surprisingly, food imports of wheat, rice and dairy products increased considerably, taking the largest share of total merchandise imports (MAFAP 2013; Wolter n.d.).

In addition, since the 1999/2000 season, the Food Self Sufficiency Ratio (SSR), which compares the volume of domestic food production against the food requirements of the country's population, has fluctuated between a low of 88 percent (2003/04) and a high of 112 percent (2006/07) (Wolter n.d.). Furthermore, significant variations in food security between different regions and districts have been experienced (FAO 2012).

However, the data and evidence available reveal that in the past eight years (2010–2018), Tanzania has emerged as a main exporter of food products within the East African Community (Table 13.2). Data show that in this period, Tanzania exported food products in the EAC ranging from 100,000 tons to 460,000 tons (Table 13.2). The value of the products ranged from US$ 10,000,000 to US$ 75,000,000.

The food products exported can be categorized in four main groups, namely: (1) sea products such as fresh or chilled fish, fish fillets and other fish meat, frozen fish, and dried, salted or smoked fish for human consumption; (2) other foodstuffs, including root crops such as potatoes, onion, garlic, ginger and nuts; (3) vegetable products including tomatoes and leguminous plants; (4) major exports include cereal crops such as wheat, maize and rice.

The main destination countries for Tanzania's food products, in order of their importance (quantity and value wise), are Kenya, Uganda, Rwanda and Burundi.

Tanzanian exports of food stuffs to Southern African Countries

Tanzania's export of food products to Southern African Countries (SADC) in terms of quantity and value is smaller compared to exports to the EAC. During the 2010–2018 period, while Tanzania foodstuffs exports ranged from 37,000 tons to 97,000 tons in a year, product value ranged from US$ 13,000,000 to US$ 75,000,000 in the period (Table 13.3). One possible reason for the difference is the distance between the exporter (Tanzania) and the importing countries, which may have made the food products uncompetitive.

The main foodstuffs exported to SADC from Tanzania include sea products such as fish, fresh or chilled; fish fillets, and other fish meat; frozen fish; dried, salted or smoked fish for human consumption and cereal crops such as wheat, maize and rice. Other food products exported in the region include root crops like potatoes, onion, garlic, ginger and nuts and vegetable products such as tomatoes and leguminous plants.

The main destination of countries for Tanzania's exports in SADC, in terms of their importance (quantity and value wise), are the Democratic Republic of Congo (DRC), South Africa, Angola, Malawi and Mauritius.

Overall, the amount of foodstuffs Tanzania exports to the EAC and SADC is small compared to its immense resource endowments (Wolter n.d.). It is clear that Tanzania has not yet realized its full economic potential. Further, while these figures represent official statistics, in reality, there are considerable amounts of foodstuffs and live animals crossing the border informally without being recorded, as there are eight countries bordering the country (FAO 2012). People from neighboring countries share various cultural and social-economic aspects and therefore trade among them is one of the common day-to-day activities. These figures should therefore be interpreted cautiously (FAO 2012).

The East African Community imports of food stuffs from the world

The East African countries have been importing considerable amounts of foodstuffs from the world (see Table 13.4). Surprisingly, most of the foodstuffs imported by the EAC from the world are exactly what they import from Tanzania.

Similar results were observed in the Southern African Development Cooperation (SADC). Countries in the region imported from the world the same foodstuffs that they import from Tanzania. Given the potential that Tanzania has to produce such goods, it is an opportunity for Tanzania to capture a larger share of that market. Tanzania needs to find out why those countries are importing these foodstuffs from distant countries instead of Tanzania.

Africa's import of foodstuffs from the world

Despite its vast agricultural potential, Africa has remained a net importer of agricultural products in the last three decades (FAO 2012). Africa lost its status as a net exporter of food and agricultural products during the early 1980s when prices of raw commodities (mainly coffee, cocoa and spices), which constituted the bulk of its agricultural export revenues, tumbled and local food production grew sluggishly (FAO 2012). Since 1980, agricultural imports have grown consistently faster than agricultural exports (FAO 2012).

Although the composition of food imports varied slightly from period to period, cereals (including rice, maize and wheat), and livestock products (dairy and meat) represented at least 50 percent of Africa's total food imports (FAO 2012). Imports of cereals and livestock products peaked at nearly 60 percent of total food imports in the early 1980s but have slightly declined thereafter (FAO 2012). The value of sugar and vegetable oil imports was about 20 percent of total imports (FAO 2012). This is an opportunity for Tanzania to provide these foodstuffs.

There is a need to determine why the EAC, SADC and Africa in general import foodstuffs from the world while food production in Tanzania has expanded and continued to attain food self-sufficiency and surplus for sale. This is not healthy for either Tanzania or the region. For Tanzania, demand for the country's foodstuffs from neighboring countries widens its market, and failure to capture that market dampens producer prices, thus negatively affecting

Table 13.2 Tanzania's export of food products to East African Community, 2010 – 2018

Year	*2010*	*2011*	*2012*	*2013*	*2014*	*2015*	*2016*	*2017*	*2018*
Quantity (tons)	135,686	122,961	384,643	162,613	468,732	91,967	116,331	98,311	330,091
Value (000 US$)	46,828	40,699	12,5015	53,724	21,0909	54,104	31,652	24,289	74,840

Source: Tanzania Trade Development Authority – TanTrade (2020).

Table 13.3 Tanzania's export of food products to Southern Africa Development Cooperation, 2010–2018

Year	*2010*	*2011*	*2012*	*2013*	*2014*	*2015*	*2016*	*2017*	*2018*
Quantity (tons)	82,985	68,403	77,142	96,332	55,237	52,964	57,961	36,035	40,408
Value (000 US$)	44,443	39,278	45,805	49,300	55,107	48,806	29,224	14,478	13,683

Source: Tanzania Trade Development Authority – TanTrade (2020).

Table 13.4 East African Community import of food products from the World, 2010–2018

Year	*2010*	*2011*	*2012*	*2013*	*2014*	*2015*	*2016*	*2017*	*2018*
Quantity (tons)	3,556,301	4,113,691	3,716,281	3,713,361	4,790,394	5,987,872	29,817,293	7,119.350	5,429,194
Value (000 US$)	1,147,719	1,683,657	1,423,418	1,451,258	1,706,380	1,639,518	1,282,777	2,117,718	1,673,401

Source: Tanzania Trade Development Authority – TanTrade (2020).

farmers' income. Also, there is enough evidence to show that when Tanzania's food products have access to external markets, farmers get more lucrative prices. For the two regions, it is beneficial to import from Tanzania because of the distance advantage, and to promote intra-country trade.

Challenges facing Tanzania to realize its export potential

If Tanzania is to take advantage of its massive agri-business opportunities to become a major food exporter, the following challenges need to be resolved.

Low productivity in agriculture

Food production remains dominated by smallholders whose productivity is among the lowest in sub-Saharan Africa (MAFAP 2013; Wolter n.d.). Smallholder farmers aim at maximizing food self-sufficiency rather than their profits, and production based on economies of scale is non-existent (Wolter n.d.). Factors which hamper the sector's productivity include overreliance on unpredictable natural precipitation, the use of manual labor in land preparation, very low usage of improved seeds and fertilizer, small farm size and low productivity of indigenous animal breeds (MAFAP 2013). Other factors affecting agricultural productivity include low public expenditure on agricultural research and development (R&D), inadequate agricultural financing and poor production techniques (MAFAP 2013; Wolter n.d.).

Poor business environment

Tanzania needs to improve its business environment. Three constraints that hinder commercial undertakings in the agricultural sector include insufficient infrastructure, which affects access to markets (roads, storage, market information system and electricity) (MAFAP 2013); lack of access to finance to buy productivity-enhancing inputs such as seeds, fertilizers, chemicals and pesticides, or intensification of technologies (MAFAP 2013); and insecure property rights as land title is unavailable in the rural areas. Also, there are many taxes and non-tax barriers such as export permits and bans.

Lack of diversification of foodstuffs

Traditional export crops such as coffee, sisal, cashew nuts and cotton are no longer as profitable to farmers, leading them to opt for foodstuff production such as cash crops (TANEXA 2012). Whilst Tanzania has high potential to produce a variety of foodstuffs, it has continued to produce and export the same foodstuffs which have been produced by their competitors (FAO 2012). There is a need to identify other foodstuffs for which Tanzania has comparative advantage and therefore increase Tanzania's exports.

Unprocessed foodstuffs

Much of the foodstuffs that are exported comprise unprocessed foodstuffs (FAO 2012). This means they export a big volume but at less value. There is a need to ensure that much of what is exported is processed to add value (FAO 2012). That means processing fruits, vegetable, meat, fish and cereals before exporting them. Recently, for instance, there have been misunderstandings between Kenya and Tanzania due to Kenya wanting to import unprocessed maize, while Tanzania wanted to export maize flour.

Internal and external barriers

The dismal performance of Tanzanian agricultural trade reflects the high levels of internal and external trade barriers despite the country's vast agricultural potential. The agricultural sector is still subject to export taxes and high local taxation; ad-hoc interventions such as tariff waivers and export bans are frequent (MAFAP 2013) and a foodstuffs export permit is required. In particular, the requirement to acquire an export permit for foodstuffs tends to increase the costs of operations, thus restraining the volume of export trade due to delays in doing business, and this contributes to corruption resulting in a loss of profit and competitiveness, all of which lead to a declining export trade (TANEXA 2012). It is argued that low agriculture production is the prime factor that underlies food export quotas/bans and/or permits (TANEXA 2012).

Low intra-country trade

Intra-country trade within the region and Africa in general is low (FAO 2012). Some countries prefer to import foodstuffs from outside the region or Africa. For instance, although Tanzania has surplus maize, Kenya imports maize from Mexico. This may be due to various reasons such as the existence of taxes and tax barriers within the region, or failure to meet quantity or quality standards, or prices may not be competitive to attract buyers within the region.

Who benefits from production and export of foodstuffs

This section deals with identifying the specific beneficiaries of exporting foodstuffs. This question is often overlooked and needs a thorough analysis.

Tanzania's economic growth has been driven by some capital-intensive sectors whose activities are predominantly located in cities and a small number of growth centers (URT 2011; Morisset 2013). These sectors together contribute approximately 60 percent of GDP growth (World Bank 2013; URT 2016; Tanzania Budget Speech 2019/20). The four sectors that expanded rapidly in the 2019–20 years include mining (17.7%), construction (14.8%), the arts and entertainment (11.2%), and transport and logistics (8.7%) (Budget Speech 2020/21 Financial Year). Other fast-growing sectors since 2005 include professional undertakings, science and vocational activities, and information and communication (Budget Speech 2019/20 Financial Year), as well as manufacturing, retail trade and the financial and tourism sectors (URT 2011; AfDB 2013). However, the main characteristics of these sectors are that they are unable to absorb a good number of job seekers – the majority of whom are less educated (URT 2011). Nor do the fast-growing sectors provide markets for the agriculture products grown inside the country, creating a weak linkage with the agricultural sector (URT 2011).

These results explain why the benefits of economic growth have been skewed against the agriculture sector (URT 2011). As mentioned previously, the agriculture sector is the mainstay of more than 80 percent of the rural population (JMT 2018) and employs 67 percent of the labor force. A notable concern is the slow growth of the agriculture sector, which has averaged 4.4 percent over the 2000–2008 period (Osberg and Bandara 2012). In 2016 it grew by 3.6 percent, and increased to 5.4 percent in 2018 (JMT 2018). This growth rate is not high enough to reduce poverty for the majority of the rural poor (Wetengere 2019). It was stated that, if poverty was to be reduced by 50 percent by 2010, the agricultural sector would have to grow at a rate of 10 percent for a period of at least five years (2006–2010). This clearly was not realized (Mashindano 2009). Further, the sector's share of GDP has also declined from 31.3 percent in 2000 to 27.2 in 2007 (Morisset 2013) but increased slightly to 28.2 percent of GDP in 2019.

Agriculture is one of the only sectors which fulfills the necessary requirements for inclusive development (to reduce poverty and inequality). First, it has wider benefits in terms of the number of people working with the sector. Second, its potential economic benefits directly improve the well-being of the poor. Third, there is a more immediate benefit in the short run resulting from agricultural productivity than other economic pursuits. Makhtar Diop, the World Bank Vice President for Africa, said that "there is global evidence showing that productivity improvements in agriculture can have a poverty impact close to 3 times that of other sectors of society" (Morisset 2013).

If agriculture is to contribute significantly to economic growth and poverty alleviation, it should play a more ambitious role as the yeast that makes the whole loaf of bread grow (Simandan 2009). That means that the agriculture sector, which employs the majority of people, should be nurtured to become one of the fast-growing sectors (10 percent and above) and the main contributor to Tanzania's economic growth. For that to happen, agriculture needs to be integrated with other factors that make the economy grow (Wetengere 2020). That means to establish businesses which incorporate the value of agriculture (crops, fisheries, and livestock) products, in other words, to industrialize agriculture (Wetengere 2020). Other factors include employing modern technology and innovation to enhance productivity in the agriculture sector; construction of modern infrastructure, i.e., transport, energy and information and communication, to connect agriculture-producing areas with the markets. Agriculture should be the main supplier of raw material for the industrial sector, and food for the urban dweller (Wetengere 2020).

This researcher's personal observations in the rural area reveal that most farmers are being highly exploited by middlemen traders. The traders purchase crops while they are still in the field at prices far below what they could have paid after harvest. The procedure typically is that the farmer and the trader enter into a formal agreement, sometimes through the village government, to purchase the crops while it is still in the field. Since most farmers have high need for cash in the period before harvest, they have no option other than selling their crops at a throw-away price. For instance, a trader makes a pre-agreement with the farmer before harvest to buy a 100 kilograms bag of paddy for Tshs. 50,000. The same bag when harvested and dehusked earns up to Tshs. 150,000. Another common practice is for a trader to agree with the farmer to purchase a mango tree when the mangos are still not ripe for sale. A trader may buy a mango tree for Tshs. 30,000–50,000, but after harvest, a trader can sell the ripe mangos in the market and earn up to Tshs. 200,000 per mango tree. This is exploitation or rather theft of a high degree.

Further, since most farmers sell their produce in raw form or unprocessed, their produce fetches a low price. For instance, three kilograms of raw cashew nuts of approximately Tshs. 9,000 produces one kilogram of processed cashew nuts, which can be sold for Tshs. 25,000 within the country. The price for the farmer's produce outside the country can be very lucrative. Also, due to a lack of information on market situation, poor transport to the market and lack of negotiation power, most farmers are forced to sell their produce in their proximity where the purchasing power is low. Price differences between the farmer's locality and distant markets can be huge.

Proponents of increasing the export of agricultural products believe doing so will increase the productivity of foodstuffs for home consumption as well. What they do not spell out is which agricultural sector should be the focus of these efforts – small-scale farmers or large farmers? Bearing in mind that increasing productivity requires a significant investment to buy inputs, it follows that most small-scale farmers lack the ability or resources to engage in the structural transformations that can generate substantial growth (Morisset 2013). In such a situation, it is unlikely that poor farmers who do not know what to eat that day will invest what little money they have to intensify agriculture. It is more likely that the larger scale farmers will possess the resources to take advantage of increasing agricultural productivity and, therefore, obtain the direct benefits that result from the increased export trade.

A simple conclusion drawn from the above analysis is that it is not the producer of agricultural crops who benefits from crop sales and export, but the sellers and the exporters of the crops. These means that, for many years, farmers have been supporting the capital accumulation and development occurring in urban areas. So, the upsurge of exports of foodstuffs does not necessarily contribute to the producers' welfare.

Conclusion and recommendations

Prior to 1991, Tanzania was considered one of the poorest countries in the world and is more remembered for its support for African liberation movements. Since 1996, a country once known as "a sleeping giant" has transformed itself into an "economic giant" that asserts great economic influence over several African countries. Given its immense resource endowment and ongoing economic transformation (hard and soft infrastructure, industrialization and technology acquisition), particularly in 2015–2020, Tanzania has acquired great potential to dominate Africa in the export of foodstuffs and other services.

If Tanzania is to achieve greater market share in Africa, the following challenges need to be addressed. First, embed agriculture with factors driving economic growth in order to increase the production of foodstuffs to meet home requirements, as well as to have surplus for exports. Second, improve the business and investment environment so as to lower the cost of production and business operation, and improve competitiveness. Third, remove barriers to foodstuff trade such as requirements for export permits and frequent export bans within and across the border. Finally, Tanzania should diversify its exports by concentrating on producing foodstuffs based on its comparative advantage.

References

African Development Bank (AfDB). 2013. "Tanzania Economic Outlook." www.afdb.org/en/countries/east-africa/tanzania/tanzania-economic-outlook/ (Retrieved on June 21, 2020).

Anyanzwa, A. 2020. "Tanzania Tops East Africa on Wealth List." *The East African News Paper*. www.theeastafrican.co.ke/tea/business/tanzania-tops-east-africa-on-wealth-list-1438606 (Retrieved on August 17, 2020).

Ayub, S. 2020. "12 Richest People in Tanzania in 2020." www.tuko.co.ke/334777-12-richest-people-tanzania-2020.html (Retrieved on August 22, 2020).

Bagenda, P. M. 2003. "Combating Money Laundering in the SADC Sub-Region: The Case of Tanzania." In C. Goredama (Ed.), *Profiling Money Laundering in Eastern and Southern Africa*. Cape Town: ISS. Available at www.iss.co.za..

Boesen. J., Madsen, B. S. and Moody, T. 1977. *Ujamaa-Socialism from Above*. Uppsala: Scandinavian Institute of African Studies.

Bulhan, H. A. 2014. "Stages of Colonialism in Africa: From Occupation of Land to Occupation of Being." *Journal of Social and Political Psychology*, 3(1), 239–256, doi: 10.5964/jspp.v3i1.143. https://jspp.psychopen.eu/article/view/143/139 (Retrieved on May 28, 2020).

Central Intellegence Agency (CIA). 2013. "Tanzania." *World Facts*. (www.theodora.com/wfbcurrent/tanzania/tanzania_economy.html (Accessed on May 29, 2020).

Chêne, M. 2009. *Overview of Corruption in Tanzania*. (U4 Expert Answers): Transparency International. www.u4.no/publications/overview-of-corruption-in-tanzania.pdf. (Accessed August 16, 2020).

The Citizen. 2016. "The Government Now Opts to Import Sugar itself." www.thecitizen.co.tz/News/Govt-now-opts-to-import-sugaritself/1840340-3179890-tdey7vz/index.html (Retrieved on October 25, 2020).

Edwards, S. 2016. *Is Tanzania a Success Story? A Long-Term Analysis.* Working Paper 17764, January. Cambridge, MA: NBER.

FAO. 2012. *Why has Africa Become a Net Food Importer? Explaining Africa Agricultural and Food Trade Deficits.* Rome: FAO.

Global Financial Integrity (GFI). 2014. *Hiding in Plain Sight: Trade Misinvoicing and the Impact of Revenue Loss in Ghana, Kenya, Mozambique, Tanzania, and Uganda: 2002–2011.* http://iff.gfintegrity.org/hiding/Hiding_In_Plain_Sight_Report-Final.pdf (Retrieved on November 4, 2020).

Jamhuri ya Muungano wa Tanzania (JMT). 1999. *Sera ya Utalii ya Taifa: Wizara ya Maliasili na Utalii.* Dar es Salaam: Kurasa 40.

Jamhuri ya Muungano wa Tanzania (JMT). 2018. *Hali ya Uchumi wa Taifa na Utekelezaji wa Bajeti ya Serikali. Taarifa ya Wizara ya Fedha na Mipango kwa Vyombo vya Habari.* December 30. Dar es Salaam: JMT.

Johnson, R.W. 2000."Nyerere: A Flawed Hero." *The National Interest*, 60, 72.

Lamtey, G. 2020. "Exports of Goods, Services Soared 15pc Last Year: Bank of Tanzania (BoT)." *The Citizen New.* www.thecitizen.co.tz/news/1840340-5453204-aefprr/index.html (Retrieved on August 15, 2020).

Legum, C. and Mmari, G., 1995. *Mwalimu: The Influence of Nyerere.* Dar es Salaam: Mkuki na Nyota.

MAFAP. 2013. *Review of Food and Agricultural Policies in the United Republic of Tanzania.* MAFAP Country Report Series. Rome: FAO.

Mandalu, M., Thakhathi, D. and Costa, H. 2018. "Investigation on Tanzania's Economic History since Independence: The Search for a Development Model." *World Journal of Social Sciences and Humanities*, 4(1), 61–68. doi: 10.12691.

Mashindano O. 2009. *Growth and Poverty Reduction in Tanzania: Why such a Mismatch?* Policy Brief Series 2009/1. Dar es Salaam: Economic and Social Research Foundation. www.esrf.or.tz/docs/growth-poverty%20.PDF (Retrieved on November 4, 2020).

Mbani, M. 2020. "435 Tanzanians Join the Billionaires' Club." www.thecitizen.co.tz/news/1840340-5484044-agb0bi/index.html (Retrieved on August 25, 2020).

Morisset, J. 2013. *Tanzania Economic Update: Raising the Game can Tanzania Eradicate Extreme Poverty?* Tanzania Economic Update, 4. Washington, DC: World Bank Group. http://documents.worldbank.org/curated/en/2013/12/18620924/tanzania-economic-update-raising-game-can-tanzania-eradicate-extreme-poverty (Accessed on June 16, 2020).

National Bureau of Statistics (NBS). 2014. *Household Budget Survey (HBS) 2011/12.* Dar es Salaam: NBS.

Ngowi, H. P. 2009. "Economic Development and Change in Tanzania since Independence: The Political Leadership Factor." *African Journal of Political Science and International Relations,* 3(4), 259–267. https://academicjournals.org/journal/AJPSIR/article-full-text-pdf/08ECB177561.

Nyerere, J. K. 1974. *Binadamu na Maendeleo.* Dar es Salaam: Oxford University Press.

Osberg, L. and Bandara, A. 2012. *Why Poverty Remains High in Tanzania: And What to Do about it?* Special Paper 12/3. Dar es Salaam: REPOA.

Pauw, K. and Thurlow, J. 2010. "Agricultural Growth, Poverty and Nutrition in Tanzania." AAAE 3rd Conference/AEASA 48th Conference, September 19–23, 2010. Capee Town: African Association of Agricultural Economists.

Simandan D. 2009. "Industrialization." In R., Kitchin and N., Thrift (Eds), *International Encyclopedia of Human Geography*. Oxford: Elsevier, vol. 5, 419–425. www.researchgate.net/publication/305725435 (Retrieved on November 5, 2019).

South African History Online (SAHO). 2019. "Tanzania and its Support of Southern African Liberation Movements." www.sahistory.org.za/article/tanzania-and-its-support-southern-african-liberation-movements (Retrieved on July 21, 2020).

TANEXA. 2012. "Problems of Official Food Export Permits to EAC and SADC. The Case of Tanzania." https://entrepreneurs.or.tz/wp-content/uploads/2016/02/Problems-of-Official-Food-Export-Permits-to-East-Africa-Community-EAC-and-Southern-Africa-Development-Community-SADC-the-case-of-Tanzania.pdf (Retrieved on August 17, 2020).

Tanzania Budget Speech. 2019/20. "Speech by the Minister for Finance and Planning, Hon. Dr. Philip I. Mpango (MP), Presenting to the National Assembly, the Estimates of Government Revenue and Expenditure, the Unuted Republic of Tanzania." June 13, 2019. www.mof.go.tz/docs/news/BUDGET%20FINAL%20JUNE%2012%20 2019%20ENGLISH.pdf (Retrieved on November 10, 2020).

Tanzania Human Development Report (THDR). 2014. *Economic Transformation for Human Development*. Dar es Salaam: Economic and Social Research Foundation.

Tanzania National Bureau of Statistics (TNBS). 2009. *Household Budget Survey (HBS) 2007*. Dar es Salaam: TNBS.

Transparency International (TI), 2012. "The Global Coalition Against Corruption. Corruption Perception Index 2012." http://cpi.transparency.org/cpi2012/results/ (Retrieved on September 4, 2020).

United Nations Industrial Development Organization (UNIDO). 2012. *Tanzania Competitiveness Report 2012*. New York: United Nations.

United Republic of Tanzania (URT). 1996. *The Tanzania National Science and Technology Policy for Tanzania*. Dar es Salaam: Ministry of Science, Technology and Higher Education.

United Republic of Tanzania (URT). 2005. National Strategy for Growth and Reduction of Poverty (NSGRP). Dar es Salaam: Vice President's Office,.

United Republic of Tanzania (URT). 2013. *Tanzania 3rd Social Action Fund: Productive Social Safety Net. Operational Manual*. Dar es Salaam: President's Office.

United Republic of Tanzania (URT). 2016. *National Five Year Development Plan (FYDP) 2016/17–2020/21. "Nurturing Industrialization for Economic Transformation and Human Development."* Dar es Salaam: Ministry of Finance and Planning, June.

United Republic of Tanzania (URT). 2017. *Tanzania Livestock Sector Analysis 2016/17–2031/32*. Dar es Salaam: Ministry of Livestock and Fisheries.

Wetengere, K., 2019. "Is Tanzania's Economic Growth Pro-Poor?" *International Journal of Advanced Economics,* 1(1), 1–17. www.fepbl.com/index.php/ijae.

Wetengere, K. 2020. "Industrialization in Tanzania: The Need for Social Inclusion." *International Journal of Advanced Economics,* 2(3), 39–51.www.fepbl.com/index.php/ijae.

Wolter, D. n.d. *Tanzania: Why a Potential Food Exporter is Still Importing Food*. Paris: OECD. www.oecd.org/dev/41302291.pdf (Retrieved on September 23, 2020).

World Bank. 2013. "Tanzania Economic Up-to-dates: Opening the Gates: How the port of Dar es Salaam can Transform Tanzania." www-wds.worldbank.org/external/default/WDSContentServer/WDSP/IB/2013/05/16/000442464_20130516111239/Rendered/PDF/777290WP0P13340onomic0Update0Report.pdf (Retrieved on August 24, 2020).

World Bank. 2015. *Tanzania Mainland Poverty Assessment*. Washington, DC: World Bank. www.worldbank.org/content/dam/Worldbank/document/Africa/Tanzania/Report/tanzania-poverty-assessment-05.2015.pdf (Retrieved on June 2, 2020).

World Bank. 2020. *World Bank Country and Lending Groups:. Country Classification*. Washington, DC: World Bank.

Youging, L. U. 2015. "Embrace Foreign Investment with Wide Open Arms." Speech by H.E. Amb. Dr. L. U., Youging – Ambassador of the People's Republic of China to the United Republic of Tanzania on the Tanzania Diaspora and SMEs Partnership Conference.

14 Conclusion

Odious debts of the African capitalist state

Allan D. Cooper and Emmanuel O. Oritsejafor

African states have been criticized for their neo-colonial tendencies, their corrupt leaders, their efforts to enrich rulers while the general population struggles to find their next meal, and in general for their diversity in showcasing "the failed state." This book reveals that these generalizations obscure the fact that African states behave much like other states in the global system, and that they produce billions of dollars in capital accumulation each year that create home-grown millionaires (and a few billionaires) while serving a world economy that craves African products such as chocolate, diamonds, petroleum, caffeinated drugs and the mineral ingredients necessary for mobile phones, computers and other products. These middle-class necessities are made affordable through systems of primitive accumulation supported by African states on behalf of foreign investors who avoid transparent oversight by stockpiling their wealth in tax havens in the Caribbean and around the world, thus depriving Africa of the surplus value being generated on the continent and sheltering potential tax revenues from governments, both large and small, that could use this treasury to aid impoverished populations, many of whom are engaged in primitive accumulation activities that created this wealth in the first place.

State structures are typically analyzed by political scientists for their adherence to democratic principles (or their opposite). The case studies that comprise this book indicate the fallacy of this methodological approach. African states have shifted from socialist leaders to capitalist ones overnight and have pursued capital accumulation for the global economy regardless of the political orientation of their leadership. As demonstrated in this book, capitalist Nigeria has helped to produce Aliko Dangote and others in the billionaire club, while socialist Angola has manufactured Isabel dos Santos to join a global elite that has billions of dollars at their disposal. At one minute, Ethiopia is a Marxist military state and neighboring Somalia is an American ally, and the next minute each has become a client of its former opponent. And then there are countries such as Namibia and Angola that have successfully played global competitors off each other, to the financial benefit of government leaders. Perhaps the best analogy to help understand this dilemma is to perceive the (African) state as a human body, similar to other humans, that by itself lacks any innate political personality. An autopsy can expose the general conditions of the state of organs within the body and can identify the likely cause of death. But the autopsy cannot tell us if the person was good or bad, a fascist or human rights activist, or whether they were racist or misogynist or a person that embraces the common humanity among the human family.

Because Africa generally is ignored by the global public, the contradictions in state analysis remain more concealed. Nowhere is this more obvious than in the discussions of Angola in this book. Portugal sustained its colony with the foreign investments of American petroleum companies such as Gulf Oil and Chevron in the Cabinda region of Angola. When the Soviet-backed MPLA assumed political control over independent Angola in 1975, these Western oil companies remained in Cabinda to support the new government which proved to be equally as loyal to these companies. When the United States supported UNITA in its terrorist activities against these companies, Angola sought the military assistance of Cuba to protect Cabinda and to preserve the financial wealth generated in that region. In summary, American oil companies made billions in profits from investing in a socialist country that secured Cuban military forces to protect these investments from attacks by a CIA-supported terrorist group. How do Americans make sense out of a situation where communist Cuba protects American financial interests from attacks from the US government? They don't. Angola is some place in Africa that is irrelevant to the world they live in. For most middle-class consumers, Africa is not an afterthought; it wasn't ever a thought at all.

At a global level, Africa continues to serve the world capitalist system as a primary source of primitive accumulation. It provided unfree labor to Mediterranean powers during Antiquity, and to rising Islamic states and European colonies in the Western Hemisphere during the Medieval era. It continued to supply unfree labor to finance European colonial enterprises after 1884 and neo-colonial investors after World War Two. The state has modified, or mutated, during each of these phases: during Antiquity the state was designed to capture territory to gain resources to enrich the political elite; during the Medieval era the state was designed to capture the souls of individuals and exercise control over individuals in addition to land; and in the modern epoch the state has served to capture labor and motivate consumers to enrich the governing elites of capitalist states. During each phase, African collaborators have enjoyed lucrative commissions by political elites for their services in securing unfree labor for primitive accumulation. The reification of Africa as a source of unfree labor has been accompanied by ideologies of racism that help to justify (mostly to foreign populations) why a significant population of humans should be subjected to inhumane conditions of exploitation. Benjamin Isaac (2006) has provided ample evidence of how the ancient world used race to pursue empire-building, while Geraldine Heng (2020) has shown how race was used to promote theocratic states in the European Middle Ages. Miriam Eliav-Feldon (2013) demonstrates how historical uses of race were adopted by modern states beginning in the eighteenth century. Such is the backdrop to explain the formation of Black Lives Matter in recent years.

From unfree labor to human rights

Scholars have debated whether capitalism requires racism, or whether primitive accumulation is sustainable in the absence of racial ideologies. Tom Brass (2013) argues that "a concept of human rights dependent for its enforcement on a benign capitalist state is going to be realized either with great difficulty or not at all" (249). He suggests that the concept of human rights is, itself, an acknowledgment that capitalism ought really to be much "nicer" than it is (269). Brass claims that capitalists no longer fear any protests from their workers "because they can draw upon what is now a global industrial reserve army of labour" (272). Both free and unfree labor are relegated to sacrificing some freedom in order to pay for the right of survival within a global capitalist system. The idea of revolution inherently poses an existential threat to any rebel. If the operation of the market depends ultimately on the intervention of the state, as proclaimed by Brass (2013, 275) and other Marxists, then the battleground for transformative change may not be in the workplace but the court houses and parliaments around the world.

In many ways, the challenges confronting Africa in the 21st century are not unlike the challenges facing Europe and Russia at the beginning of capitalism. As Stanziani (2014) notes, during the Enlightenment "some believed that economic conditions could be improved without touching the legal status quo, while others argued that only a radical overhaul of the law (suppressing serfdom, slavery, and the guilds) would ensure both social justice and economic growth" (31). African elites are continuously faced with an environment where their states were created by Europeans to facilitate export markets instead of helping Africans to maximize capital accumulation to establish national elites that could manage economic growth for their own interests and needs. Africa is the only real estate in the global economy where political boundaries are divorced from indigenous political influences. The question remains whether African state structures are capable of serving national interests, or is it the case that all state structures throughout the world are designed to serve capitalist interests?

In the meantime, the decolonization of African states has tightened the connections of Africa with global capitalist markets. African national elites serve the same function as bailiffs during Tsarist Russia's development of its capitalist economy. Bailiffs tended to be local or regional authorities that were assigned responsibility for the organization of production, taxation and the collection of economic and financial information. According to Stanziani (2014, 47–48),

> Bailiffs deployed agents among the peasants to watch them, and while bailiffs supervised such peasant agents, they were themselves viewed with great suspicion by landlords, who feared both fraud and overexploitation of peasants. To overcome this problem, landlords developed a complex system of renumeration, bonuses, and fees for the bailiffs … Bailiffs were usually corrupt individuals who appropriated a good portion of the lord's revenues

> for themselves and exploited the peasants without encouraging them. All of this resulted in losses for the lord …

The growing income inequalities generated in the global economy today remain the result of primitive accumulation. Russia and Central Asia lag behind the capital accumulation organized in the West in part because the West has always relied on the racial exploitation of Africans and members of their diaspora that utilizes more violent methods of labor exploitation. Russia and Central Asian states never established naval capacities to profit from the exploitation of Africans, so they were limited to developing slave or unfree labor from their own population (see Stanziani 2014, 64). The Nazis faced similar challenges after their African colonies were lost during World War One. China engages in such domestic exploitation today; even when China engages in infrastructure development in Africa it utilizes Chinese labor that is compensated at a fraction of the cost of African labor. In short, racial capitalism could not be fully developed in Central Europe, Russia or China and the result was the establishment of fascist and totalitarian states that forced domestic populations into work camps and gulags that left tens of millions of workers dead. In China, factories producing products for global corporations such as Sony, BlackBerry, and Nintendo, and factories assembling iPhones for Apple, cover their facilities with suicide nets to stop workers from leaping to their deaths to end their suffering from the work conditions they are forced to endure. Meanwhile, the individuals controlling these industrial operations are featured on the *Forbes* list of the richest individuals on the planet, a recognition intended to appeal to the envy of aspiring capitalists throughout the world.

When European nations could no longer rely on colonies for primitive accumulation, they integrated themselves into the European Union (EU) where they could transform East Europeans into free labor and recruit former colonial subjects to engage in primitive accumulation within the EU as migrant labor. But when these migrants sought citizenship (to become free labor), the EU balked at disrupting its racialistic order. Turkey was denied membership into the white EU. Historic national identities in Europe could not accept the challenges of allowing geography to accommodate new identities. Europe refused to become another United States. Brexit is only one consequence of this chain of events.

The USA initiated its racial integration policies in the 1950s at the same time as it pursued integration of post-colonial African states into the world economy. Both served the purposes of racial capitalism: to establish a black underclass for generating wealth for the white elite and middle class. The success of white business communities in controlling black urban mayors served as laboratories for how to control African nationalist leaders.

Capitalism relies on debt to compel forms of labor and services that are functional to capital accumulation. Domestically, instruments of debt include home mortgages, car loans, student loans, the national debt and taxation. It becomes difficult for citizens to pursue happiness without signing on to many of these forms of debt, and therefore citizens realize the acquisition of a higher wage may require the accumulation of debt to get access to the education and training that is prerequisite to the higher paying jobs they desire. It becomes a self-defeating spiral of debt and powerlessness, not unlike the system of indentured labor used in the USA in the decades following the independence from slavery.

Odious debts under international law

Africa's underdevelopment by global commercial elites and their international organizations is manifested in the continuing deprivations and hardships encountered by free and unfree labor on the continent. It matters little whether the alienated laborer resides in Nigeria where the state works to enrich Aliko Dangote and other members of the billionaire club (who reinvest some of their wealth within the country in new enterprises), or in Angola where the state served to establish Isabel dos Santos as one of the richest women in Africa, even though she lives in exile in Europe and maintains her financial wealth in tax havens in the Caribbean and beyond. Nor does it matter if the alienated labor is an African American in the USA kept in check by police forces that engage in random violence against surplus labor, or a migrant worker entering the USA who needs to fear that any organization of political demands will be met with expulsion or the abduction of the worker's children and subsequent detention of them in cages.

A central question for human rights advocates, as well as laborers throughout Africa, is whether the surplus value created by laborers in Africa, now incorporated into the economies of core capitalist powers, can be put to use in the development of economic opportunity on the continent. One potential rationale for such redistributions of wealth is the concept of "odious debts" under international law. In essence, this principle holds that legal contracts are not binding or enforceable if the result of such contracts is the oppression of the population of laborers residing within the jurisdiction of the sovereign entities that promulgated the contract, especially if the contract serves the personal enrichment of a political leader or their family members rather than public purposes. From a legal perspective, contracts are unenforceable if the end purpose of the agreement is criminal or unethical.

The doctrine of odious debt is attributed to Alexander Nahum Sack, a Russian who immigrated to the United States in 1927. Sack developed the doctrine in the aftermath of the Tinoco Arbitration where the arbitrator, US Supreme Court Chief Justice William H. Taft, ruled that the unconstitutional manner in which Federico Tinoco assumed power in Costa Rica in 1917 did not affect his authority to make legally binding laws and policies for his country. But Taft did identify a petroleum concession that was awarded by the Tinoco government to be a violation of the 1917 Constitution since it was clear that the bank covering the monetary exchange for this concession "knew that this money was to be used by the retiring president, F. Tinoco, for his personal support after he had taken refuge in a foreign country." Sack argues that unrecognized governments may have the power to form valid contracts, but he questioned whether any government can acquire debt or make contracts that are contrary to the well-being of the general population.

This principle was previously recognized under US law as early as 1885 when the US Supreme Court ruled in *Cole v. City of La Grange* that state legislatures could not issue bonds to benefit private (corporate) persons that serve no public benefit. Jeff King (2016) explains that war debts, subjugation debts, illegal occupation debts and corruption debts are all contrary to the interests of the population at hand and are therefore considered odious (57). He cites numerous examples of such debts being voided, including debts secured by rebel authorities in the Confederacy during the War for Slavery in the 1860s, as declared by the US Supreme Court in *Montgomery v. United States* (1873).

The Cuban Loans negotiations at the Paris Conference of 1898 may be the first direct application of a doctrine of odious debt in international law (see King 2016). The conference followed the Spanish-American War of 1898 and concerned loans issued by the Spanish government after 1880. The American Commissioners claimed that the debts were not contracted for the benefit of Cuba, but to enhance Spanish rule over the island:

> From no point of view can the debts above described be considered as local debts of Cuba or debts incurred for the benefit of Cuba. In no sense are they obligations properly chargeable to that island. They are debts created by the government of Spain, for its own purposes and through its own agents, in whose creation Cuba had no voice, from the moral point of view, the proposal to impose them upon Cuba is equally untenable. If, as is sometimes asserted, the struggles for Cuban independence have been carried on and supported by a minority of the people of the island, to impose upon the inhabitants as a whole the cost of suppressing the insurrections would be to punish the many for the deeds of the few. If, on the other hand, those struggles have, as the American Commissioners maintain, represented the hopes and aspirations of the body of the Cuban people, to crush the inhabitants by a burden created by Spain in the effort to oppose their independence would be even more unjust.
>
> (Quoted in King 2016, 79)

This position taken by the United States is consistent with the actions taken by that country in the immediate aftermath of securing independence from the British Crown in 1783, when it refused to assume any of the standing debt incurred by colonial authorities. Libya took a similar stance after its liberation from Italy, as did Guinea when it freed itself from France in 1958, and Congo when it separated from Belgium in 1960. Algeria, Tanzania, Eritrea, Rwanda and Burundi all assumed independence without bearing responsibility for all the debts incurred by their colonial authority. Nelson Mandela dissolved all of South Africa's debt assumed by Namibia in 1994 when he assumed the presidency of the post-apartheid state, and transferred to Namibia (a territory that had been illegally occupied by the apartheid regime) all South African state property in Namibia, including the strategic port of Walvis Bay.

In *World Duty Free Company Ltd. v. The Republic of Kenya* (2006), an arbitration claim was filed to respond to a scheme organized by Kenyan President Daniel arap Moi to operate duty-free shops at Kenyan airports in a manner that would allow the President to defraud the state of $438 million. The tribunal hearing the case concluded that "claims based on contracts of corruption or on contracts obtained by corruption cannot be upheld" (see King 2016, 121).

The principle of unjust enrichment requires that "a person who has been unjustly enriched at the expense of another is required to make restitution to the other" (see King 2016, 161). "Unjust enrichment" is valid when it is determined that "the defendant has been enriched by the receipt of a benefit that is gained at the claimant's expense in circumstances that the law deems to be unjust" (see King 2016, 161).

Efforts to regain control over the accumulation of odious debts can be seen by political elites as a violation of the concept of sovereignty that is interpreted as the monopoly of power exercised by the legal authority of a state. In other words, classic definitions of sovereignty suggest that leaders of political states have authority to govern in whatever ways they see fit, short of specific regulations adopted by the state. However, within the framework of political philosophy, "popular sovereignty" argues that the actions of the state are legitimate only if they can be justified as serving the general interests of the citizenry of the respective state. For instance, revolutionaries involved in the American Revolution argued in the 1770s that "taxation without representation" is a violation of the concept of popular sovereignty. Today, the human rights corpus developed in international law following the Holocaust has been premised on a paradigm that public policy must serve the interests of the public. The creation of odious debts by state authorities is clearly a transgression against this paradigm.

The broader question raised in this book is whether primitive accumulation within a racial capitalist framework is equally contradictory to the principles of popular sovereignty. Is it acceptable for a state to permit selected individuals to prosper disproportionately from the exploitation of labor and resources within the jurisdiction of the state? More simply, does capitalism violate the basic tenets of popular sovereignty enshrined in the international law governing human rights?

Clearly some states pursue wealth accumulation in ways that minimize the inherent abuses of free and unfree labor. States vary in their degree of hostile work conditions directed at free and unfree labor, but the outcome is always, inherently, income inequality. It would be simplistic, and historically incorrect, to argue that everyone possesses an income proportionate to their productivity. As the case studies in this book demonstrate, the accumulation of wealth in Africa is highly dependent on state structures that deliberately pick and choose who will become wealthy and who will suffer impoverishment. Wealthy individuals are wealthy because political elites privilege them with conditions of trade that permit unencumbered accumulation of capital. These same national political elites exercise power against labor in ways that mitigate against self-sufficiency and compel humans to engage in wage labor to secure the basic necessities of life. Inequality among individuals is the norm of capitalist society.

Furthermore, foreign elites also play a significant role in determining which African national elite is accorded wealth and other privileges within the global economy. Access to financial opportunities accrue from bilateral and multilateral relationships, but also from intergovernmental organizations managed by the leading state entities within the global arena. Such organizations, such as the International Monetary Fund (IMF) and the World Bank, are conduits for economic rewards directed at African political elites in exchange for "favors" met or promised that enhance the production of surplus value within international capitalist markets. Such financial exchanges can constitute commissions for national elites that have successfully participated in primitive accumulation activities on behalf of global capitalist elites, or they can represent odious debts involving IMF structural adjustment programs (SAPs) that require the national elite to develop infrastructure or new primitive accumulation strategies that permit foreign investors to extract more surplus value from the recipient of the IMF loan. In either case, much of this "foreign aid" ends up in the pockets of the national leaders whose personal wealth is divorced from the national treasury that is designed to provide for the development of the national population. The global financial elites that made the IMF loan possible are very aware of where their money is going, and are quite willing to extend similar loans to future African governments that may follow – assuming that they demonstrate a similar propensity to extract and transfer resources into the hands of this global elite. Western middle classes are told that their tax dollars are being extended to African nations in the name of foreign aid or to support the development of poor people of color; African populations are simultaneously informed that the corrupt leaders that confiscated this aid have been removed from power, but it is they that must be taxed to pay off these debts to the international community. In reality, middle-class populations inside global powers are being forced to finance the bribes benefitting African leaders that collaborate with capitalist elites that secure wealth from economic activities employing primitive accumulation against Africans. Racial capitalism breeds inequality that becomes difficult to measure at the global level.

Inequality at the national level is more complicated to measure, especially given varying degrees of cost of living standards and purchasing power parity. One of the only measures available is the Gini Index, used by the World Bank to determine, in relative terms, income inequalities within each state. Not all states provide data to the World Bank, including several that are relatively wealthy such as Saudi Arabia, Kuwait and oil-rich Equatorial Guinea. The index has been criticized as well for other shortcomings, such as the fact that it measures income inequality rather than inequality of wealth. In other words, much of the wealth of the USA is parked in offshore accounts and is not included in the statistical collection of incomes being presented to the World Bank. Consequently, inequality between the rich and the poor within the USA is much larger than the index might identify. Nevertheless, the Gini Index is perhaps the only standardized measure we have to compare one country to another in terms of income inequality.

Table 14.1 ranks countries according to the GINI Coefficient index, listing the most unequal countries at the top of the list.

Using this data, it is acknowledged that seven of the top ten states identified for income inequality are African states. The top two on the list, South Africa and Namibia, are democratic states without any history of significant political violence or electoral fraud. The same can be said for most of the countries in the top ten. Among the list as a whole, there appears to be no correlation between equality and democracy. Instead, it can be observed that most of the countries in the top 50 are countries with significant "primitive accumulation" activities within the global capitalist economy. The countries with the highest levels of equality are those that lack racial minorities that can be employed in primitive accumulation activities. These states are generally former Soviet states that historically served as unfree labor for their Russian masters.

In short, unfree labor continues to outpace free labor in the production of surplus wealth within the global economy. As this book has demonstrated, the wealth created in most of the top 50 states has been diverted into the personal bank accounts of foreigners residing among global powers who hold their wealth in tax shelters in the Caribbean and elsewhere. Clearly the global capitalist economy is dependent upon the surplus value created in Africa and other states listed in the top 50 of the Gini Index to maintain the wealth and power of the billionaires that continue to be enriched by the world economic system.

The distinguished Kenyan and scholar of international law, Makau Mutua, has argued that both the global capitalist system as well as the human rights corpus itself is inherently biased with Western norms (Mutau 2002). He questions, for instance, whether this corpus should sanction free-market capitalism (xi). Mutua reminds us that John Locke argued that the state's duty is to "protect individual rights and freedoms from invasion and to secure their more effective guarantee" (see Mutua 2002, 72). Accordingly, a government that breaches these duties becomes illegitimate.

African states were created by European capitalist powers to govern the activities of primitive accumulation that economically privileged entrepreneurs resident in the colonizing entity. The transfer of state power to African authorities did not alter the original purposes of these states to administer regulatory policies that advanced primitive accumulation for a global economy dominated by the United States and its European allies. Mutua (2002) notes that African elites remain alienated and corrupt, and are quite often devoid of a national consciousness, thus facilitating the plunder of the state and brutalization of society to maintain their personal privileges and retain power (90). He asks whether Africans should reexamine the assumptions underlying the role and purpose of the state and its organization (92). The larger question arising from

Table 14.1 GINI coefficient ranking of global states

Rank	*Country*	*Value*	*Year*
1	South Africa	63.00	2014
2	Namibia	59.10	2015
3	Suriname	57.60	1999
4	Zambia	57.10	2015
5	Central African Republic	56.20	2008
6	Lesotho	54.20	2010
7	Mozambique	54.00	2014
8	Belize	53.30	1999
8	Brazil	53.30	2017
8	Botswana	53.30	2015
11	Eswatini	51.50	2009
12	St. Lucia	51.20	2016
13	Guinea-Bissau	50.70	2010
14	Honduras	50.50	2017
15	Panama	49.90	2017
16	Colombia	49.70	2017
17	Congo	48.90	2011
18	Paraguay	48.80	2017
19	Guatemala	48.30	2014
19	Costa Rica	48.30	2017
19	Mexico	48.30	2016
22	Benin	47.80	2015
23	Cabo Verde	47.20	2007
24	Venezuela	46.90	2006
25	Seychelles	46.80	2013
26	Chile	46.60	2017
26	Cameroon	46.60	2014
28	Nicaragua	46.20	2014
29	Dominican Republic	45.70	2016
30	Jamaica	45.50	2004
31	Comoros	45.30	2013
32	Ecuador	44.70	2017
32	Malawi	44.70	2016
34	Guyana	44.60	1998
35	Philippines	44.40	2015
36	Bolivia	44.00	2017
37	Rwanda	43.70	2016
38	Ghana	43.50	2016
39	Chad	43.30	2011
39	Peru	43.30	2017
41	Zimbabwe	43.20	2011
42	Togo	43.10	2015
43	Nigeria	43.00	2009
44	Uganda	42.80	2016
45	Angola	42.70	2008
46	Madagascar	42.60	2012
47	Dem. Rep. Congo	42.10	2012
48	Turkey	41.90	2016
48	Papua New Guinea	41.90	2009

Table 14.1 (cont.)

Rank	*Country*	*Value*	*Year*
50	Djibouti	41.60	2017
51	United States	41.50	2016
51	Côte d'Ivoire	41.50	2015
53	Argentina	41.20	2017
54	Haiti	41.10	2012
55	Malaysia	41.00	2015
56	Kenya	40.80	2015
56	Turkmenistan	40.80	1998
58	Senegal	40.30	2011
58	Trinidad and Tobago	40.30	1992
60	Iran	40.00	2016
61	Sri Lanka	39.80	2016
62	Serbia	39.60	2015
63	Uruguay	39.50	2017
63	Morocco	39.50	2013
65	Tuvalu	39.10	2010
66	Israel	38.90	2016
67	Samoa	38.70	2013
68	China	38.60	2015
68	Burundi	38.60	2013
70	Mauritius	38.50	2012
71	Myanmar	38.10	2015
71	Indonesia	38.10	2017
73	El Salvador	38.00	2017
73	Gabon	38.00	2017
75	Georgia	37.90	2017
76	Tanzania	37.80	2011
77	Russia	37.70	2015
78	Vanuatu	37.60	2010
78	Tonga	37.60	2015
80	Bhutan	37.40	2017
80	Bulgaria	37.40	2014
80	Lithuania	37.40	2015
83	Solomon Islands	37.10	2013
84	Kiribati	37.00	2006
85	Fiji	36.70	2013
85	Yemen	36.70	2014
87	Thailand	36.50	2017
88	Lao PDR	36.40	2012
89	Spain	36.20	2015
90	Greece	36.00	2015
91	The Gambia	35.90	2015
91	Romania	35.90	2015
93	Australia	35.80	2014
93	Syrian Arab Republic	35.80	2004
95	India	35.70	2011
96	North Macedonia	35.60	2015
97	Portugal	35.50	2015
98	Sudan	35.40	2009

(continued)

Table 14.1 (cont.)

Rank	*Country*	*Value*	*Year*
98	Italy	35.40	2015
100	Liberia	35.30	2016
100	Uzbekistan	35.30	2003
100	Vietnam	35.30	2016
100	Burkina Faso	35.30	2014
104	Ethiopia	35.00	2015
105	Niger	34.30	2014
106	Latvia	34.20	2015
107	Canada	34.00	2013
107	Cyprus	34.00	2015
107	Sierra Leone	34.00	2011
107	Tajikistan	34.00	2015
111	Luxembourg	33.80	2015
112	Jordan	33.70	2010
112	Guinea	33.70	2012
114	Armenia	33.60	2017
115	Pakistan	33.50	2015
116	United Kingdom	33.20	2015
117	Mali	33.00	2009
117	Bosnia and Herzegovina	33.00	2011
119	Nepal	32.80	2010
119	Tunisia	32.80	2015
121	Estonia	32.70	2015
121	France	32.70	2015
123	Mauritania	32.60	2014
124	Bangladesh	32.40	2016
125	Mongolia	32.30	2016
125	Switzerland	32.30	2015
127	Japan	32.10	2008
128	Montenegro	31.90	2014
129	Ireland	31.80	2015
129	Egypt	31.80	2015
129	Poland	31.80	2015
129	Lebanon	31.80	2011
133	Germany	31.70	2015
134	Korea	31.60	2012
135	Croatia	31.10	2015
136	São Tomé and Principe	30.80	2010
137	Austria	30.50	2015
138	Hungary	30.40	2015
139	Iraq	29.50	2012
140	Malta	29.40	2015
141	Sweden	29.20	2015
142	Albania	29.00	2012
143	Timor-Leste	28.70	2014
144	Netherlands	28.20	2015
144	Denmark	28.20	2015
146	Iceland	27.80	2014
147	Belgium	27.70	2015
148	Algeria	27.60	2011

Table 14.1 (cont.)

Rank	*Country*	*Value*	*Year*
149	Norway	27.50	2015
149	Kazakhstan	27.50	2017
151	Kyrgyz Republic	27.30	2017
152	Finland	27.10	2015
153	Azerbaijan	26.60	2005
154	Slovak Republic	26.50	2015
155	Moldova	25.90	2017
155	Czech Republic	25.90	2015
157	Belarus	25.40	2017
157	Slovenia	25.40	2015
159	Ukraine	25.00	2016

Sources: World Bank, Development Research Group. Data are based on primary household survey data obtained from government statistical agencies and World Bank country departments. For more information and methodology, please see PovcalNet (www.iresearch.worldban).

the case studies in this book is the following. If Africa provides the primitive accumulation that keeps global capitalism profitable, and serves to subsidize the costs of maintaining the middle classes of global powers, then can the struggle to end the poverty created by capitalism be achieved without ending primitive accumulation activities in Africa?

The world capitalist system

The growing literature on primitive accumulation is shaped by a paradigm that views Africa as a periphery to the core economic powers of the global system. Some of the proponents of this perspective readily admit that primitive accumulation occurs even within the core economies dominating world politics. What the case studies in this book demonstrate is that the global economy is not divided by economic zones or regions, but by classes. Every region, every state, possesses its own class structure tied to the global economy. Every region has its center(s) of capital, and its own periphery. As Ayelazuno (2011) notes, the global working class is exploited in both the core capitalist countries as well as the peripheral countries (541). The real wages of these workers may appear unequal, but as a relative symbolic expression of power (see Nitzan and Bichler 2009), each of these sets of laborers are kept one paycheck away from a traumatic state of destitution that keeps them compliant to the protocols of capitalist exploitation. Workers tend to be captive to the interests of their respective immediate economic core, which itself may be beholden to a regional core subservient to a global core. As Ayayi (1986) acknowledges, the ruling class of each African state "is still subject to the overall control, direction, and domination by international capital" (38).

As we saw in the chapter on diamonds, New York issues an order for diamonds to meet the largest consumer market for that commodity, and London provides the banking services to transact the order to its subsidiaries in Johannesburg that tells Gaborone what Windhoek needs to do to compel Ovambo laborers to produce the raw diamonds from the sands and shores of Namibia. The Ovambo workers produce billions of dollars' worth of diamonds, the proceeds of which are shared proportionately with officials from each country involved in the supply chain. But the largest share of surplus capital is reserved for the investors in New York, while the Ovambo worker takes home just enough to survive until the next pay day.

Ayelazuno (2011) shares a more detailed financial accounting of the profits derived from primitive accumulation in the Ghana gold industry for 2008, where gold accounted for 40 percent of exports with a value of $2.2 billion. Ghana's government only received $116 million in taxes and royalties from this mining activity, less than 4 percent of the country's tax revenues (541). In short, Ghana generates $2.2 billion in gold production for a global economy, but only receives 5 percent of this value as compensation. Ninety-five percent of Ghana's gold production value shows up in the bank accounts of billionaires, corporate profits and GDPs of core states in the global economy whose leaders, as well as most of their citizens, consider Ghana a poor state that cannot manage to provide for the general welfare of its own people. This process is similar to the Enclosure Movement in England when small farms were taken by government officials from the 13th century to the 19th century to develop a larger wool industry that generated enormous surplus value for the elite. E. P. Thompson (1991) referred to this movement as a "case of class robbery" (237).

Ayelazuno (2011) concludes that "Unfortunately, the Ghanaian state that is supposed to protect the peasants is complicit in the violence of primitive accumulation" (546). He argues there is a paradox in understanding that the liberal state "protects the interests of capital, not its citizens" (546). Of course, the real paradox is that *every* nation-state operates under the same matrix. The birth of the modern state occurred at the same time that capitalism was articulated as a paradigm governing the application of private property; the creation of the corporate person quickly followed.

Which brings us back to the concept of odious debts. If the acts of governments that are self-serving (that is, they are not pursued for the interest of the nation as a whole) are considered odious and not legally binding upon the people of the nation, then a great many actions of the state, not just the securing of debt, are considered odious and lack legitimacy in a democratic society.

The contributors to this book have revealed how African states perform strategic and vital roles in the global accumulation of wealth that sustains the structures of power within the international system. Far from being poor or failed states, African countries (and laborers from the African diaspora) are succeeding at performing functions that are indispensable to global wealth accumulation and to maintaining the political privileges of those nations that sit atop the hierarchy of world power. Must Africans suffer to sustain the privileges of the global elite? Can capitalism operate independently of racist ideology?

Is the state capable of serving the interests of labor and not just capital? The answer to all these questions is "Maybe," but to do so requires a revolution comparable to the events that swept world history in 1776.

References

Ayayi, Festus. 1986. *Heroes*. London: Longman.
Ayayi, Festus. 1987. "The Primitive Accumulation of Capital in a Neo-Colony: The Nigerian Case." *Review of African Political Economy*, 35, 27–39.
Ayelazuno, FJasper. 2011. "Continuous Primitive Accumulation in Ghana: The Real-Life Stories of Dispossessed Peasants in Three Mining Communities." *Review of African Political Economy*, 38(130), 537–550.
Brass, Tom. 2013. *Labor Regime Change in the Twenty-First Century: Unfreedom, Capitalism and Primitive Accumulation*. Chicago, IL: Haymarket Books.
Eliav-Feldon, Miriam. 2013. *The Origins of Racism in the West*. Cambridge: Cambridge University Press.
Heng, Geraldine. 2020. *The Invention of Race in the European Middle Ages*. Cambridge: Cambridge University Press.
Isaac, Benjamin. 2006. *The Invention of Racism in Classical Antiquity*. Princeton, NJ: Princeton University Press.
King, Jeff. 2016. *The Doctrine of Odious Debt in International Law: A Restatement*. Cambridge: Cambridge University Press.
Mutua, Makau. 2002. *Human Rights: A Political and Cultural Critique*. Philadelphia, PA: University of Pennsylvania Press.
Nitzan, Jonathan and Bichler, Shimshon. 2009. *Capital as Power: A Study of Order and Creorder*. London: Routledge.
PovcalNet (www.iresearch.worldban.
Stanziani, Alessandro. 2014. *Bondage: Labor and Rights in Eurasia from the Sixteenth to the Early Twentieth Centuries*. Oxford: Berghahn Books.
Thompson, E. P. 1991. *The Making of the English Working Class*. Toronto: Penguin Books.

Index

For Product Safety Concerns and Information please contact our EU
representative GPSR@taylorandfrancis.com
Taylor & Francis Verlag GmbH, Kaufingerstraße 24, 80331 München, Germany

www.ingramcontent.com/pod-product-compliance
Ingram Content Group UK Ltd.
Pitfield, Milton Keynes, MK11 3LW, UK
UKHW020151200926
475702UK00016B/2651
9780367774196